European Film Remakes

Screen Serialities

Series editors: Claire Perkins and Constantine Verevis

Series advisory board: Kim Akass, Glen Creeber, Shane Denson, Jennifer Forrest, Jonathan Gray, Julie Grossman, Daniel Herbert, Carolyn Jess-Cooke, Frank Kelleter, Amanda Ann Klein, Kathleen Loock, Jason Mittell, Sean O'Sullivan, Barton Palmer, Alisa Perren, Dana Polan, Iain Robert Smith, Shannon Wells-Lassagne, Linda Williams

Screen Serialities provides a forum for introducing, analysing and theorising a broad spectrum of serial screen formats – including franchises, series, serials, sequels and remakes.

Over and above individual texts that happen to be serialised, the book series takes a guiding focus on seriality as an aesthetic and industrial principle that has shaped the narrative logic, socio-cultural function and economic identity of screen texts across more than a century of cinema, television and 'new' media.

Title in this series include:

Film Reboots
Edited by Daniel Herbert and Constantine Verevis

Reanimated: The Contemporary American Horror Remake
By Laura Mee

Gender and Seriality: Practices and Politics of Contemporary US Television
By Maria Sulimma

European Film Remakes
Edited by Eduard Cuelenaere, Gertjan Willems and Stijn Joye

European Film Remakes

Edited by Eduard Cuelenaere,
Gertjan Willems and Stijn Joye

EDINBURGH
University Press

Edinburgh University Press is one of the leading university presses in the UK. We publish academic books and journals in our selected subject areas across the humanities and social sciences, combining cutting-edge scholarship with high editorial and production values to produce academic works of lasting importance. For more information visit our website: edinburghuniversitypress.com

© editorial matter and organisation Eduard Cuelenaere, Gertjan Willems and Stijn Joye, 2021, 2022
© the chapters their several authors, 2021, 2022

Edinburgh University Press Ltd
The Tun – Holyrood Road
12(2f) Jackson's Entry
Edinburgh EH8 8PJ

First published in hardback by Edinburgh University Press 2021

Typeset in 11/13 Ehrhardt MT by
IDSUK (DataConnection) Ltd

A CIP record for this book is available from the British Library

ISBN 978 1 4744 6064 4 (hardback)
ISBN 978 1 4744 6065 1 (paperback)
ISBN 978 1 4744 6066 8 (webready PDF)
ISBN 978 1 4744 6067 5 (epub)

The right of Eduard Cuelenaere, Gertjan Willems and Stijn Joye to be identified as the author of this work has been asserted in accordance with the Copyright, Designs and Patents Act 1988, and the Copyright and Related Rights Regulations 2003 (SI No. 2498).

Contents

List of Figures	vii
Notes on Contributors	viii
Acknowledgements	xi
Preface *Thomas Leitch*	xii
Film Remakes in the Context of European Cinema: An Introduction *Eduard Cuelenaere, Gertjan Willems and Stijn Joye*	1

Part I: Conceptual Perspectives: Delineating and Pushing the Boundaries of Remake Studies

1. The Film Remake as Prism: Towards a Model of Systematic Textual Analysis *Eduard Cuelenaere*	19
2. The 'Secret Remake': A European Take on the Traditional Remake? *Marie Martin*	33
3. From 'Mini-Remake' to Open-Ended Coda: How to Make a 'Proper' Homage *Peter Verstraten*	45
4. Rainer Werner Fassbinder's *Berlin Alexanderplatz* (1980) as Remake? *Mario Slugan*	59
5. Remakesploitation: Exploitation Film Remakes and the Transnational *Giallo* *Iain Robert Smith*	73

Part II: Historical Perspectives: Continuity and Change

6. Re-forming *La Maternelle*: Socio-Cultural Continuity and
   the Remake   89
   Jennifer Forrest

7. Screening Transformation Processes: Post-War Remakes of
   Nazi-Era Films   103
   Stefanie Mathilde Frank

8. The Colour Remakes of Swedish Classics in the 1950s:
   Production, Promotion and Critical Reception in the Context
   of Technological Innovation   117
   Kamalika Sanyal and Eduard Cuelenaere

Part III: Contemporary Perspectives: European Film Remakes in the New Millennium

9. Remakes *à la polonaise*: From National Re-Adaptations to
   Internationally Inspired Rom-Coms   133
   Kris Van Heuckelom

10. Nostalgic Mediations of the Soviet Past in Nikolai Lebedev's
    Remake *The Crew* (2016)   149
    Boris Noordenbos and Irina Souch

11. Mistaken Identities: Millennial Remakes, Post-Socialist
    Transformation and Hungarian Popular Cinema   163
    Balázs Varga

12. Refashioning the Remake: *A Bigger Splash*   177
    Constantine Verevis

Part IV: Industrial Perspectives: Practices of Production and Circulation

13. Remake and Decline in Scottish Cinema: *Whisky Galore!*
    1949 and 2016   195
    Robert Munro and Michael Stewart

14. 'Remakable' Directors: The Contemporary Spanish Media Industry
    and Popular Discourses on Remakes and National Authorship   211
    Núria Araüna Baró

15. Remakes and Globally-Oriented European Cinema: Contemporary
    Industrial Practices and Shifting Hierarchies   225
    Christopher Meir

Index   240

Figures

Figure 5.1 Edwige Fenech looking out over the Platja de la Fragata in *The Strange Vice of Mrs. Wardh* (*Lo strano vizio della Signora Wardh*, 1971)   81

Figure 5.2 1970s European fashions and interior design reflecting a domestic cosmopolitanism in *Thirsty for Love: Sex and Murder* (*Aşka Susayanlar: Seks ve Cinayet*, 1972)   83

Figure 9.1 The priest (played by Jan Piechociński) addresses his 'son' (Karol 2) during a wedding ceremony in *Oh, Charles 2*   139

Notes on Contributors

Núria Araüna Baró is Assistant Professor of Communication Studies at the Rovira i Virgili University (Tarragona, Spain) and member of the Asterisc Communication Research Group. Her research focuses on audiovisual formats, social memory in political documentary and gender representations in film.

Eduard Cuelenaere is Postdoctoral Researcher at Ghent University (Belgium) where he is affiliated with the Department of Communication Sciences.

Jennifer Forrest is Professor of French at Texas State University, USA. Together with Leonard Koos, she is the co-editor of *Dead Ringers: The Remake in Theory and Practice* (SUNY, 2002), the editor of *The Legend Returns and Dies Harder Another Day: Essays on Film Series* (McFarland, 2008) and *Decadent Aesthetics and the Acrobat in Fin-de-Siècle France* (Routledge, 2019). Her media-related publications in journals and book chapters centre on remakes and seriality in cinema and television.

Stefanie Mathilde Frank is Academic Counsellor, film historian and media researcher at the Institute of Media Culture and Theatre at the University of Cologne, Germany. From 2015 until 2020, she was Research Associate at Humboldt University.

Stijn Joye is Associate Professor at Ghent University (Belgium) where he is affiliated with the Department of Communication Sciences.

Thomas Leitch is Professor of English at the University of Delaware, USA. His most recent books are *The Oxford Handbook of Adaptation Studies* (Oxford University Press, 2017) and *The History of American Literature on Film* (Bloomsbury, 2019).

Marie Martin is Senior Lecturer at the University of Poitiers, France. Her research focuses on hypertextuality, intermediality and film theory. She edited the issue of CINéMAS dedicated to 'Le remake: Généalogies secrètes dans l'histoire du cinéma'.

Christopher Meir is a member of the TECMERIN research group and the research team based at the Universidad de Carlos III de Madrid, Spain. He is the author of *Mass Producing European Cinema: Studiocanal and its Works* (Bloomsbury, 2019) and numerous other books and articles about the global film and television industries.

Robert Munro is Lecturer and Programme Leader in Film and Media at Queen Margaret University, UK. He has been awarded several grants to run projects in the field of film education in Scotland, and his research and teaching primarily focuses on screen adaptation, film genre, videographic film criticism, and Scottish film and culture.

Boris Noordenbos is Assistant Professor in Literary and Cultural Analysis at the University of Amsterdam, the Netherlands. He has published on post-Soviet literature and film, focusing on issues of, among others, memory, nostalgia and suspicion.

Kamalika Sanyal is Doctoral Researcher at the Institute for Media Studies of KU Leuven, Belgium. Her thesis focuses on the emergence of natural colour film in Sweden and attempts to understand the position of colour in the cinematic culture of Sweden during that transitional time-period.

Mario Slugan is Lecturer in Film Studies and Strategic Lecturer at the Institute of Humanities and Social Sciences, Queen Mary, University of London, UK. He is the author of *Montage as Perceptual Experience* (Camden House, 2017), *Noël Carroll and Film* (Bloomsbury, 2019) and *Fiction and Imagination in Early Cinema* (Bloomsbury, 2019).

Iain Robert Smith is Senior Lecturer in Film Studies at King's College London, UK. He is the author of *The Hollywood Meme: Transnational Adaptations in World Cinema* (Edinburgh University Press, 2016) and co-editor of the collections *Transnational Film Remakes* (with Constantine Verevis, Edinburgh University Press, 2017) and *Media Across Borders* (with Andrea Esser and Miguel Bernal-Merino, Routledge, 2016).

Irina Souch is Lecturer in Comparative Literature and Cultural Analysis at the University of Amsterdam, the Netherlands. She is the author of *Popular Tropes of Identity in Contemporary Russian Television and Film* (Bloomsbury, 2017) and co-editor of *Heterotopia and Globalisation in the Twenty-First Century* (Routledge, 2020).

Michael Stewart is senior lecturer in film at Queen Margaret University, UK. His key areas of interest are melodrama, genre and adaptation, and he has published articles on these topics in journals such as *Cinema Journal*, *Journal of British Cinema and Television* and *Studies in French Cinema*.

Kris Van Heuckelom is Professor of Polish Studies and Cultural Studies at KU Leuven, Belgium. He specialises in late modern Polish culture, with a particular focus on comparative and transnational perspectives, and has published several books, edited volumes and anthologies in these fields. His most recent book is *Polish Migrants in European Film 1918-2017* (Palgrave Macmillan, 2019).

Balázs Varga is Associate Professor of Film Studies at the Eötvös Loránd University, Hungary. He writes and lectures on modern and contemporary Hungarian cinema, contemporary European cinema, documentaries and the cultural history of cinema.

Constantine Verevis is Head of Film and Screen Studies at Monash University, Melbourne. With Claire Perkins, he is founding editor of *Screen Serialities* for Edinburgh University Press.

Peter Verstraten is Assistant Professor of Film and Literary Studies at Leiden University, the Netherlands. His publications include, among others, *Film Narratology* (2009), *Humour and Irony in Dutch Post-War Fiction Film* (2016) and *Dutch Post-War Fiction Film through a Lens of Psychoanalysis* (2021).

Gertjan Willems is Assistant Professor in the Departments of Literature and Communication Sciences at the University of Antwerp (Belgium) and Postdoctoral Fellow of the Research Foundation Flanders (FWO) in the Department of Communication Sciences at Ghent University (Belgium).

Acknowledgements

On 1 June 2018, we organised the symposium 'Remaking European Cinema' on the theory and practice of the film remake in a European context at Ghent University in Belgium. Earlier versions of most of the chapters in this book were presented at this symposium, and we invited other authors to contribute to it. We would like to thank all our contributors for their great work – we really appreciate the smooth collaboration and hope our paths will cross several more times in the future.

The symposium originated from the research project 'Lost in Translation? A Multi-methodological Research Project on Film Remakes between Flanders and the Netherlands', funded by the Research Foundation Flanders (FWO) to whom we express words of thanks.

In addition, we are grateful to a number of other people who have provided support in the realisation of this book. First of all, thanks to Richard Strachan from Edinburgh University Press (EUP) for his infinite support, responsiveness, and quick work. It has been a real pleasure to work with him, as well as with the other EUP staff members: Fiona Conn, Bekah Dey and freelance editor Nina Macaraig. We would also like to thank our peer reviewers for their useful and productive comments. Claire Perkins and Constantine Verevis, the series editors, deserve praise for their helpful and constructive feedback. It was Constantine who suggested that we submit a proposal to EUP's Screen Serialities book series, for which we are very grateful. Finally, we are very thankful that Katrijn Bekers was willing to conscientiously compile the index to this volume.

Eduard Cuelenaere, Gertjan Willems and Stijn Joye

Preface: Farewell, Hollywood

Thomas Leitch

Once upon a time – to begin with a phrase that must surely be engraved on the hearts of everyone who cherishes remakes – different versions of familiar stories multiplied endlessly with remarkably little attention to their governance. Virtually all of Shakespeare's plays are based on earlier sources. The surviving Athenian tragedies were almost certainly newer versions of older plays, based in turn on myths everyone in the audience would have known. Not until the rise of the novel, as Ian Watt dubbed it in the title of his influential 1957 monograph, did a literary form emerge from the proposition that entirely new stories, unsanctified by the approbation of judges of an earlier generation, might carry a positive value.

Even more than photography, lithography and the other arts associated with Walter Benjamin's age of mechanical reproduction, the rise of the cinema encouraged more critical assessments of the ancient practice of remaking. At first, these assessments took the form of evaluations by journalistic reviewers. In the 1970s and 1980s, scholars began to get in on the act, enlarging the study of remakes, from questions about which version was best to questions about how and why movie remakes sought to replicate a very particular selection of features of earlier movies, as well as how analysts might define the relations between remakes and the movies they remade. As Christopher Meir points out in his contribution to this volume, scholars approaching remakes in the years before Constantine Verevis's *Film Remakes*, the definitive work on the subject ever since its publication in 2006, focused largely on American remakes of both American and non-American films, a subject to which some of them, myself included, have returned repeatedly since then, perhaps because Hollywood has been defined largely by its voracious appetite for new material of many kinds, perhaps because the Hollywood remake seemed an apt parable of American cultural imperialism, perhaps because Hollywood remakes were simply the ones they knew best. Meir explicitly announces what every one of his fellow contributors urges implicitly: it is high time to enlarge this Hollywood-centric focus to consider remakes from around the world.

What changes when the study of what Jennifer Forrest calls remakes' characteristic 'dynamic of disavowal and invocation' shifts its focus from American remakes to European ones? This is only the most obvious of the many vital questions that the contributors to this volume raise. Other questions follow thick and fast: how do what Kathleen Loock has called diachronic remakes – those produced at a later time, allowing them to take advantage of new technological advances such as colour filmstock, as analysed by Kamalika Sanyal and Eduard Cuelenaere and termed 'cultural memory' or historical hindsight by Balázs Varga – compare to synchronic remakes – those produced shortly after the films they are remaking, in the hope of attracting new audiences that the earlier film could not hope to reach? How do monocultural film remakes – movies produced for latter-day audiences within the same national and social cultures as the films they are remaking – compare to cross-cultural remakes, in which members of one national culture presume to adapt a story from a different national culture for audiences who may have no awareness of the earlier film? How, to take the particular example explored by Robert Munro and Michael Stewart, does the changing valence of 'Scotland', 'Scottish' and 'Scottish cinema' affect the production and reception of Gillies Mackinnon's 2016 remake of *Whisky Galore!*, which is at once 'a canonical example of an Ealing Comedy, that most iconic of classic British film genres' and 'one of the best-loved "Scottish" films of all time', nearly seventy years after Alexander Mackendrick's 1949 Ealing film?

This last question in turn generates questions of its own about what Marie Martin calls the 'secret remake' – 'not a traditional remake in the sense of the commercial and legally bound practice [. . .] but rather a somewhat hidden rewriting, not necessarily noticed by its viewers or even its author', one that is 'more a product of spectatorship and interpretation than a creative practice (even though both are obviously linked somehow)'. Just how are the processes of producing and perceiving remakes linked? Must an audience be aware of a remake's status as a remake to experience it as a remake? Is it this awareness, or the producer's intentions and strategies, that defines it as a remake? If a remake is defined by its audience's double awareness of its status as the same as but different from the film it is remaking, what must that audience know about that earlier film? Is the category of remakes best restricted to films that spend their entire length replicating features of the films they remake, or should it include the kind of 'mini-remakes' that Peter Verstraten examines in Francis Ford Coppola's *The Conversation* (1974) and Valeska Grisebach's *Sehnsucht* (2006)? Are remakes typically nostalgic, as Boris Noordenbos and Irina Souch suggest, and if they are, what modes of nostalgia do they invoke? What can or must be changed in remakes to distinguish them from acts of plagiarism, and which elements must remakes preserve in order to secure their status as remakes, despite the changes they make to the films they are remaking?

The very phrase 'to secure their status as remakes' raises further questions implicit in Kris Van Heuckelom's observation that 'Hryniak's lukewarmly received *The Third* did not relieve the Polish audience's appetite for a remake'. Apart from producers, their financial backers and scholars of intertextuality, who else has an appetite for remakes and considers their status worth pursuing and securing? If, as Mario Slugan contends, 'the possibility that [Rainer Werner] Fassbinder's [1980] production [of *Berlin Alexanderplatz*] could be treated as a remake of Jutzi's is never truly contemplated' by most observers, is Fassbinder's film better described as the fulfillment of a wish for a superior remake, or a wish for an adaptation by audiences who knew nothing of Piel Jutzi's 1931 adaptation? Are some films and filmmakers, as Núria Araüna Baró suggests, simply more 'remakable' than others, and if so, on what grounds? Remakes that cross national or linguistic borders carry the potential of appealing to new audiences, but the more uncertain fate of remakes within a given culture is attested by the critical rejection of Gus Van Sant's 1998 remake of *Psycho*, the surprising commercial success of Marc Webb's 2012 reboot *The Amazing Spider-Man* and the decidedly mixed fortunes of Disney's 2019 rapid-fire release of live-action remakes of its animated features *Dumbo*, *Aladdin* and *The Lion King*. For many years, Disney deliberately staggered the video releases of its backlist to maintain a lively interest in their re-release every seven years. Have other producers or distributors sought to whet audiences' appetites for re-releases over remakes in similar ways? And how do the nature, the goals, the commercial status and the cultural assimilation of remakes change in an era of endless video archives in which past releases are not withdrawn but simply crowded out of cultural memory?

It is not the function of this brief preface, or even of the far richer and more thoughtful and extensive collection it introduces, to answer these questions. But one last pair of questions seems particularly intriguing, if only because they haunt all these chapters without ever being directly articulated by any of them. One of these questions concerns the relationship between remake studies and the (barely) more established field of adaptation studies. If intramedial remakes are to be understood, as Stefanie Mathilde Frank urges, as 'cultural phenomena of social transition', are they then the quintessential adaptations, the tip of the adaptation iceberg that does not involve transmediation, as most adaptations do, but certainly involves transculturation of some sort in time or space or both? And what do these essays, presented and consumed collectively, reveal more urgently than they do individually?

The obvious answer to this last question is of course that they provide an alternative to American-centric assumptions about the economic appropriation and cultural imperialism of the remake. But this answer is both self-evident and incomplete. Europe is not Hollywood, of course, but neither is it simply congruent with the rest of the world. If the study of European remakes broadens both the corpus and the possible methodologies of remake studies, what would happen if the field were broadened further still by scholars who followed Iain Robert Smith's call 'to supplement [the] analysis of Hollywood's transnational impact with memetic studies of the numerous cultural flows that do not centre on Hollywood'? What would happen if it extended beyond Europe to explore the cinemas of India, Turkey, Iran and other nations whose copyright laws encouraged a culture of remakes very different for both producers and consumers from the cultures regulated by the Berne Convention? Would such investigations yield a new emphasis beyond industrial dimensions and practices, or a new account of industrial practices? What place would 'the new millennial remakes' – which Constantine Verevis finds *'intermedial, transnational, post-authorial,* and *characterized by proliferation and simultaneity'* – have in such a global investigation? How much would the descriptive model of textual analysis that Eduard Cuelenaere defines as 'a continuous work-in-progress, open for interpretation, variation and uses' need to be adapted or remade to account for this still more varied corpus? The single most valuable feature of the present collection may be its invitation to interested scholars to push the field in even more adventurous directions. A culture of remakes demands nothing less.

Introduction: Film Remakes in the Context of European Cinema

Eduard Cuelenaere, Gertjan Willems and Stijn Joye

Stating that film remakes are an integral part of cinema and cinema history is stating the obvious. One of the first films ever, *Exiting the Factory* (*La Sortie de l'Usine Lumière à Lyon*, 1895), by the French engineer Louis Lumière, was even remade (at least) twice. The two versions that followed, also made by Lumière, can be discerned by, among other things, the style of clothes and the number of horses appearing in the films. Hence, the invention of the film medium itself practically coincided with the genesis of the film remake.[1] That same year, Louis Lumière also made the slapstick film *The Sprinkler Sprinkled* (*L'Arroseur Arrosé*). One year later, in 1896, the famous French filmmaker and illusionist George Méliès remade the latter into *Watering the Flowers* (*L'Arroseur*). The year 1896 also saw the production of the Société Pathé Frères' first film, titled *The Arrival of a Train* (*Arrivée d'un Train*), another remake of a Lumière film. In Pathé's version, the train arrives in a city located southeast of Paris (Vincennes), whereas the train in Lumière's version arrives in a seaside resort called La Ciotat. It was not only in France where the production of these European film remakes took place. British remakes followed as well, such as Robert William Paul's remakes of other Lumière films, or, for example, a Swedish remake by Ernest Florman of the American film *The Barbershop* (1894), produced by the Edison Manufacturing Company (Forrest 2002).

Over the past two decades, European film industries have been breathing new life into this old form of recycled filmmaking, resulting in a significant rise of European film remakes. Meir (2019: 133) has demonstrated how large European film industries and powerful pan-European studios in the early 2000s slowly started to follow Hollywood's lead by 'utilizing tried and tested generic models, [. . .] remaking older films [. . .] or readapting source material that has provided the basis for successful films'. Furthermore, as a recent study (see Cuelenaere, Joye and Willems 2019a) shows, apart from these large European industries, various culturally (and linguistically) proximate small film industries also started to remake each other's films. Next to the remake cycle in the Low Countries (Cuelenaere et al. 2019a), one could, for instance, also point towards the many Dutch-German film remakes. Examples are the Dutch *Misfit* (2017) which received a German and a Polish remake in 2019, or the German film *Joy of Fatherhood* (*Vaterfreuden*, 2014) which was remade in the Netherlands as *Made for each other* (*Voor elkaar gemaakt*, 2017).

Another example of such synchronic remaking – 'the production of remakes that takes place at roughly the same point in time as the production of the predecessors' (Loock 2019: 327) – is *Perfect Strangers* (*Perfetti sconosciuti*, 2016). This Italian comedy was included in the Guinness World Records as the most remade film in film history (Rolling Stone 2019). No less than eighteen remakes have been released (and more are coming), ranging from a French to a Spanish version, from a Chinese to a Turkish one. This case illustrates very clearly the global dimensions of contemporary remake practices.

With the above in mind, it is quite surprising that most research in the field has been restricted to Hollywood remake practices (remaking both Hollywood and foreign films) and to the question of how other film industries remake Hollywood films. Indeed, until today, due to a variety of reasons – among them Hollywood's global dominance – the association of the film remake practice with Hollywood's film industry still seems to prevail in academic literature as well as in popular discourses (see Smith and Verevis 2017). Luckily, more and more scholars in the field are making attempts to look beyond Hollywood, probing into other film industries that produce remakes, thereby showing that the remake has never been 'a peculiar American phenomenon' (Forrest 2002: 89). As the preceding paragraphs already indicated, and as the chapters in this book will clearly demonstrate, both the history and the present of European cinema provide numerous opportunities for a rich analysis of the remake from a non-Hollywood perspective.[2] Hence, focusing on the European remake practice, this book aims to expand and rethink the research field of remake studies.

As the title *European Film Remakes* shows, this volume clearly focusses on the remaking of films. In valuable attempts to better grasp the research object, many different scholars and critics have come up with a variety of specifications and categorisations of the general idea of the film remake as being a new version of a previous film (see, for instance, Horton and McDougal 1998; Leitch 1990; Forrest and Koos 2002; Verevis 2006; Zanger 2006; Loock and Verevis 2012; Verevis 2017). Although their endeavours might provide handy signposts, 'their competition is often characteri[s]ed by a normative insistence that we use the right words, as if cinematic formats existed as ideal forms that are then articulated more or less precisely by this or that film' (Kelleter and Loock 2017: 129–30). Yet, on the contrary, not only are filmic formats never ideal (in the Platonic sense), they also do not exist in canonised shapes as they are formed contingently. Indeed, 'formal boundaries are always fluid [and] cinematic remaking is a reflexive, multi-agential, and temporally shifting process, ultimately competition-based and spanning the fields of production and reception' (Kelleter and Loock 2017: 130). Therefore, by not adding another definition to the already long list, this volume instead embraces and promotes the complexity of the term, the phenomenon, the practice and its surrounding discourses. This does, however, not imply that some of its contributors do not demarcate their objects of research by providing a proper definition. Yet, it is clear that such an undertaking mainly meets analytical rather than terminological demands.

THE 'EUROPEAN' IN EUROPEAN CINEMA: ENTER THE FILM REMAKE

In the 1990s, the political, economic and cultural unification of Europe came with an increasing scholarly interest in European cinema. However, as Elsaesser (2005: 13) famously noted: 'Any book about European cinema should start with the statement that there is no such thing as European cinema, and that yes, European cinema exists, and has existed since the beginning of cinema a little more than a hundred years ago. It depends on where one places oneself, both in time and in space'. This paradoxical stance – European cinema *an sich* does not exist, especially not outside the critical field (Fowler 2002: 1); yet, it exists in different forms and contexts, depending on the perspective – lies at the heart of this volume. Consequently, a conceptualisation of Europe (and, therefore, European cinema) will always be questionable and intrinsically contingent. Therefore, in line with Elsaesser's plea, most studies on European cinema are quick to acknowledge the impossibility of providing a strict delineation of their subject (Kaklamanidou and Corbalán 2018).

Perspective is key in reflecting on European cinema. From an outsider perspective, Europe as a continent may look like an entity with diminished influence – its cinema being 'in view of its declining impact and seeming provincialism, merely a part of "world cinema"' (Elsaesser 2005: 30). From the inside, European cinema may be perceived as extremely diverse, but for many it is still united in this diversity, thereby recalling the European Union's motto. Acknowledging the discursive status of such an endeavour, however, does not imply that the adoption of a concept such as European cinema is analytically useless, provided that a clear contextualisation is given. The fact that 'European cinema has not become irrelevant' (Harrod, Liz and Timoshkina 2014: 7) is reflected not only in the recurrent use of the concept in academic, critical, popular and policy discourses, but also in terms of cinema admissions. Based on an analysis of the period between 2004 and 2014, 12 percent of cinema admissions in Europe were for non-national European films, while 21 percent of European movie-goers went to nationally produced films. This total of 33 percent may seem small in comparison to the 65 percent of US films, but in comparison to the 'rest category' of non-American and non-European films (2 percent) it becomes more significant (Jones 2017).

A recurring idea in discourses about European cinema posits that it is characterised by an artistic mindset, fuelling two binary oppositions that go hand in hand: commerce versus art and Hollywood versus European cinema. Even though these reductionist discourses have oftentimes been criticised, until today '[t]his stereotypical construction [. . .] still has currency with audiences, policy-makers, and filmmakers' (Meir 2019: 152). As Mazdon (2000) has pointed out, the film remake, known for its inherent, almost transcending hybrid status, directly disapproves of such easy binary oppositions.

Another issue that should be taken into account when studying European cinema is that the parameters and (historical) perspectives that have dominated the research field have failed to acknowledge 'the supranational implication of the term "European"' (Bergfelder 2005: 315). Consequently, the lion's share of studies has analysed European cinema through the national cinema lens. Luckily, in the past fifteen years, the transnational has been increasingly adopted in the concept of national cinema,[3] which partly responds to Bergfelder's (2005: 315–16) call to emphasise the 'issues of transnational interaction and cross-cultural reception, and reposition some areas of European film history which, until now, have often been seen as peripheral'.

Taking these considerations into account, this book employs the film remake to reflect on the conceptualisation of European cinema itself, instead of providing a clear-cut – whether geographical, socio-cultural, political, economic or even aesthetic – delineation of European cinema. Of course, we must be aware that, by its sheer existence, this volume also indirectly takes part in reshaping the meaning of European cinema – however, for the first time from the perspective of the film remake. Its title, *European Film Remakes*, does not designate the idea of a clear, overarching pan-European film industry and culture, but refers to the ever-changing diversity as well as common grounds of European cinema, thereby following Bergfelder (2005: 320) in his understanding of 'the "European" in European cinema [. . .] as an on-going process'.

EUROPEAN REMAKING PRACTICES IN THE PAST: DIACHRONIC OR SYNCHRONIC?

Although little is known about the particular history of European film remakes, Herbert (2008: 217) has argued that the flows of film remakes within Europe have generally 'conformed to much greater patterns of cultural and cinematic exchange'. Think, for instance, of how the expressionist cinema of Weimar Germany from the 1910s until the early 1930s circulated not only around the globe, but also resulted in, among others, a Czechoslovak-French remake of the German film *The Golem* (*Der Golem*, 1920), titled *The Golem: A Legend of Prague* (*Le Golem*, 1936) and released sixteen years later. Herbert (2008: 217) adds that 'despite this tendency of cycling, there are numerous "oddball" transnational film remakes [. . .] which defy trends or common patterns of exchange'.

What these cycles and seemingly singular remakes share, however, is their 'system of "trial and error" that, in some accounts, resembles the means by which genres develop over time' (Herbert 2008: 218). Hence, driven by a rather conservative commercial logic, these so-called 'oddball' remakes regularly launched cycles, ultimately seeking to bypass the financial risks of film production by employing tried-and-tested formulas. Because of the industrial nature of this logic, usually just a handful of financially unsuccessful remakes were sufficient to either stop a cycle, or incite a transformation in the strategy, leading to another distinct type of cycle (Herbert 2008).

According to Loock (2019), throughout history, remaking films in Europe was mainly transnational in nature, as well as highly commercially driven. Moreover, she argues, the synchronic type of remaking is most common in European cinema, whereas diachronic remaking, the 'production of remakes over decades-spanning period of time' (Loock 2019: 326–27), is rather rare – at least compared to Hollywood's history of remaking. However, even though until now there is no overarching study, dataset or index to confirm the opposite thesis, one can find much anecdotal proof that 1930s sound remakes of silent films from preceding decades ('talker remakes')[4] were also popular in national film industries across Europe (see, for instance, Bachmann 2013; Bock and Bergfelder 2009; Gundle 2013; Hake 2002; Wood 1986).

The different chapters in this volume equally show that there arguably is more evidence to be found proving the exact opposite of Loock's (2019) statement. Indeed, the different chapters on the remake practices in, for instance, post-war Germany (see Frank), post-socialist Russia (see Noordenbos and Souch) and Hungary (see Varga), as well as Sweden in the 1950s (see Sanyal and Cuelenaere) all seem to point out that, rather than synchronic transnational European film remakes, diachronic intra-national ones were more common. Nevertheless, in a way, Kris Van Heuckelom's chapter conversely seems to bring us back to Loock's findings, while relocating her thesis to the contemporary context. Indeed, Van Heuckelom argues that the four Polish remakes under analysis in his study 'mark a significant transition in terms of temporal and geographical scope: whereas the first two productions embody a particular form of "diachronic remaking" within a distinct Eastern Bloc context – offering contemporary variations on communist-era film classics – the two most recent projects (which take their cues, respectively, from a Dutch and an Italian screenplay) indicate that Polish film professionals are becoming increasingly active in the field of transnational (synchronic) film remaking'.

(RE-)ASSESSING EUROPEAN FILM REMAKES IN TODAY'S (GLOBALISED) CONTEXT

From the 1990s onwards, the critical discourses on remakes were marked by a specific take on, or interpretation of film remake practices. Adopting terms such as cultural assimilation and domination (often in tandem with 'Americanisation'), film remake practices were mostly seen as reflective of the existing hegemonic cultural forces and broader industrial hierarchies (Herbert 2008: 198). As Christopher Meir argues in this collection, Hollywood is generally 'seen as the stronger industry that exploits smaller industries such as those of Europe, virtually mining it for raw materials to turn into English-language remakes for international release, including in the home countries of the original films in question'. With Mazdon's 2000 seminal work on the Hollywood remake cycle of French films in the 1980s and 1990s (and how this remake cycle is exemplary of a complex process of exchange rather than a one-dimensional power relation) as one of the first studies and Smith's 2016 book on Turkish, Filipino and Indian remakes of Hollywood products as one of the more recent, these above-mentioned simplistic binaries have been questioned and critiqued, both theoretically and empirically.

In the new millennium, under the influence of broader globalising and digital developments, the industrial context of European cinema has drastically changed. Among other things, the quantity of European films produced annually has surpassed the number of 1,000. Between 2013 and 2017, on average, admissions to European films outside Europe itself amounted to 20 percent (90 million for a total of 440 admissions), mainly driven by the Chinese market – China, rather than the US, is now the largest export market for European films (Kanzler and Patrizia 2019). Furthermore, several vertically and horizontally integrated pan-European studios with large back catalogues have succeeded in producing mid- to big-budget films that perform well globally (Meir 2019).

In this renewed context, around the late 2000s, several European-based companies such as Crazy Cow in Brussels and Cinema Republic in Madrid started concentrating on the acquisition, representation and selling of remake rights of both European and non-European films, which is now deemed a viable financial strategy (Labayen and Morán 2019). Additionally, other recent research shows that smaller national European film industries that are culturally proximate started remaking each other's domestic hits (with or without the mediating role of a remake rights representative) in the 2000s in order to bypass the apparent European films' impotence of crossing its national borders (Cuelenaere et al. 2019). Lastly, during the same period, pan-European studios such as the French Studiocanal have also seen potential in remakes and became quite active in this specific segment of the industry by purchasing and selling remake rights. Even more, since Studiocanal's global reappearance in 2006, '[r]emakes and readaptations are at the heart of its creative strategies' (Meir 2019: 134).

One might wonder if the evolution and recent transnational and synchronic development of the European film remake industries might eventually mirror the success story of European television formats. While the US has been leading the international trade of TV formats, research by Esser (2016) reveals that since the 2000s European production companies quickly invested in the format business and became highly successful in it (for example, companies such as the Dutch Endemol and the British FremantleMedia). However, from 2011 onwards 'the U.S. media conglomerates, initially slow to reali[s]e the business potential of internationally formatted and locally produced content, have cemented their leadership in television entertainment by buying nearly all of the largest (available) groups' (Esser 2016: 3608). This makes one wonder how Hollywood will respond to the advancements in the European film remake industry.

ON THE 'EUROPEANNESS' AND HOLLYWOOD-LIKE STATUS OF EUROPEAN FILM REMAKES

This brings us to the elephant in the room: how does Hollywood relate to European film remakes? Although it is precisely this volume's purpose to look at the remake phenomenon beyond the context of Hollywood, in one way or another Hollywood always seems to be lurking in the background. Through the appropriation of 'Hollywoodian' narrative and stylistic elements, genre tropes, or even production, promotion and distribution strategies, many of the films that fall under the category of European remakes often show much 'cultural familiarity with Hollywood' (Higson 2018: 316) and could therefore be labelled 'like-Hollywood' films. This raises the question of the (perceived) 'Europeanness' of these European film remakes, not only in terms of their representations, but also in terms of industrial strategies, stake-holders and financial involvement.

Concerning the cultural identity or character of (both international and intranational) European film remakes, it is useful to summon Hjort's (2009) distinction between marked and unmarked transnationalism. According to Buonanno (2015), this can easily be translated into the idea of 'Europeanness'. Whereas 'marked Europeanness [. . .] is the peculiarity of those types of [. . .]

drama that convey and display discernible and often unmistakable evidence of European involvement and presence at some level of the creative and production process' (Buonanno 2015: 210), unmarked Europeanness characterises content that in spite of its clear European involvement (for example, in its conception or production) is not typified or recognised as European by its viewing audiences. As transnational film remakes are usually 'subjected to a process of indigeni[s]ation purposely aimed at re-framing and re-imagining the original concepts and scripts' (Buonanno 2015: 210) that were conceived in a specific cultural and industrial context, they could be considered as archetypical examples of unmarked Europeanness. Put simply, the possible foreignness and/or Europeanness of the source text can be overshadowed because of the domesticating frameworks at work in the remake process.

Next to the fact that a European identity is as equally constructed, contingent and imagined as whatever national or cultural identity, because of its subjection to the process of localisation or indigenisation, the remake process might equally so disguise, or indeed, bury the possible Europeanness of these intra-European remakes. Hence, 'remaking films in Europe could [. . .] be regarded as a process that prevents mediated cultural encounters in a kind of national echo chamber' (Cuelenaere 2020: 229). Glancing at the statistics of the Eurobarometer (Kantar Public Brussels and European Commission 2018), most EU citizens feel most attached to their country (93 percent), then to their city/town/village (89 percent), but only in third place to Europe (65 percent) and finally to the European Union (56 percent). In light of the preferences for a particular cultural or national identity in the new millennium, we should be wary of the cultural consequences of the national echo chambers that these European film remakes might be(come). Indeed, the rise of these localised versions of European films might contribute to national European spectators perceiving 'their' culture as mainly national, in spite of its 'global and European dimensions' (Bondebjerg et al. 2017: 4). Nevertheless, we can also ask if and how these intra-European film remakes condition the possible mediated encounters with 'other Europeans', and, therefore, help in 'build[ing], maintain[ing], or re-shap[ing] the perception of similarities and differences between diverse European societies and cultures and contributed to the formation of a sense of European belonging?' (Buonanno 2015: 209).

REMAKING FILMS TO OVERCOME STRUCTURAL LIMITATIONS IN THE EUROPEAN FILM INDUSTRY?

When studying European cinema, we must, as mentioned above, acknowledge its fragmented nature. Due to its linguistic and cultural diversity, the European film market is characterised by a dual economy, split between the almost crushing dominance of Hollywood films, on the one hand, and a smaller yet still significant market share for local or national films targeted solely at domestic audiences, on the other (Paris 2014). This dual economy illustrates how difficult it is for European films to cross their borders and be distributed within Europe (Jones 2017).[5] Whereas large film industries (such as Germany, France, the UK, Italy and Spain) can benefit from 'economies of scale and larger businesses with access to more substantial funds for production, distribution and marketing' (Higson 2018: 308), smaller European film industries (such as Belgium, the Netherlands, Hungary, Portugal, or Denmark) have to deal with low admission rates. Consequently, their production companies have difficulties in competing with the distribution and marketing budgets of both Hollywood and the bigger European film industries. Yet again this aspect of distribution brings us to Hollywood and its dominance in the global distribution market. Meir (2019: 4) asserts that the reasons for the weak distribution of European films (both in and outside Europe) are multiple, 'but suffice it to say that many stem from the persistent and fundamental separation in European cinema between production and distribution', while Hollywood studios have quickly commenced to vertically integrate. Hence, throughout the history of European film industries, most of the capital was allocated to the production of films, and to a much lesser amount to their distribution (Puttnam 1997). Therefore, one wonders whether the enduring prospect of low admission rates and limited budgets have forced these small film industries in Europe to increasingly resort to 'solutions' such as remaking films instead of trying to distribute them.

With the rise of intra-European film remakes, one could argue that, finally, audio-visual stories are able to travel in Europe, yet guised in the banal (national) familiarities that film remakes are able to offer us. On the one hand, they 'cater to tastes shaped by global [read: Hollywood] cinema' (Mueller 2019: 2); on the other hand, they capitalise on the audiences' desire for cultural proximity by localising culturally specific aspects that otherwise make it difficult for these films to travel outside their national borders. This volume, therefore, aspires to partly answer Bergfelder's (2005: 326) call for 'a transnational history of European cinema [that focuses] precisely on the strategies and practices by which filmic texts "travel" and become transformed according to the specific requirements of different cultural contexts and audiences'. This brings us to a thesis that certainly needs further investigation: should we understand the dissemination of intra-European film remakes as a possible new (successful) form of film circulation? We deliberately adopt the term 'circulation' here. Following Garofalo, Holdaway and Scaglioni (2018: 302), we deem 'circulation' more accurate than 'distribution' in this case, permitting 'a more nuanced image of the movements of media: accounting for the multitude of distribution windows for a film, but also foregrounding, vitally, the wider cultural impact of cinema'. From such a perspective, it appears that the practice of remaking films might present a novel and workable approach to bypass the European film industries' inability of crossing national borders.

THE STRUCTURE OF THE BOOK

In order to further deepen our knowledge and understanding of film remakes in the context of European cinema, we have collected fifteen essays that reflect the broad diversity of the issue at hand, in terms of both theoretical perspectives and practical manifestations.[6] To conclude this introduction, let us briefly wander through the different sections. While each section looks at the film remake from a different perspective – conceptual, historical, contemporary and industrial – as a whole they echo the central idea of the remake as a kind of prism, allowing us to address a broad variety of themes within the realm of European cinema.

Given the young and emerging nature of the field of remake studies, the first section ('Conceptual Perspectives') presents five chapters that contest, expand or rethink the notion and practice of the remake on a theoretical and methodological level. Eduard Cuelenaere introduces us to a model to systematically analyse film remakes which goes beyond the mere description of textual similarities and differences between source text and its remake. His holistic approach calls for an additional interpretative layer, hence reconciling the textual with dimensions of production and reception. Likewise, the following three chapters also call for broadening the field, not in terms of the applied methodology, but regarding its conceptual *vocabularium* and manners of classification. Marie Martin teases out the idea of a 'secret remake', which she presents as the European take on the traditional (Hollywood) remake given the new concept's departure from a European perspective on film. She hints at more latent, hidden or unconscious processes related to remaking films, experienced by authors as well as by the audience. In a similar vein, Peter Verstraten and Mario Slugan further problematise the ongoing debate on how to define the remake. Verstraten travels into the world of the homage as a way to expand and question our terminology used to get a grasp on the practice of remaking. Just like Martin, Verstraten equally puts forth the idea of hidden or latent familiarity either in remaking films, related to a director's admiration for a precursor film, or in watching remakes as a(n) (un)conscious viewer. The chapter by Mario Slugan further delves into the question of how multiple versions of the same narrative are connected to one another, ranging from book to adaptation and remake. Exploring the case of Rainer Werner Fassbinder's *Berlin Alexanderplatz* (1980), Slugan makes the call to understand the remake as a knowing intentional engagement with a proximate source text. Concluding the first section is Iain Robert Smith who previously coined the concept of the 'Hollywood meme' (Smith 2016) as a way to empirically explore the politics of cultural globalisation in processes of cinematic cultural exchange. In the present chapter, Smith supplements his US-centred conceptual model with the study of a cultural flow that does not focus on Hollywood. Consequently, the case-study of a low-budget Turkish remake of an Italian giallo invites a wider reflection on cinematic cultural exchange within and beyond Europe and simultaneously introduces us to the broader phenomenon of 'remakesploitation' – that is, unlicensed exploitation film remakes.

The next sections reflect the broad diversity of European cinema in general and of remake practices in particular – what could be called a European patchwork quilt of remakes, thereby embracing its heterogeneous nature while also acknowledging common grounds. Given the drastically changed nature of European cinema since the dawn of the new millennium, a first section ('Historical Perspectives') deals with cases dating back to the early years of film and expanding to post-war Europe and the subsequent decades. To kick off these historical inquiries into the remake practice, Jennifer Forest takes us back to the so-called Golden Age of French sound cinema (1930–60) with her analysis of *La Maternelle* – the novel, the adaptation and the remakes. By looking at this unique intertextual series, she lays bare a dynamic of disavowal and invocation in response to the changing historical conditions. The shaping force of a *zeitgeist* and its everyday evocation in society are also a leading principle in Stefanie Mathilde Frank's chapter on German post-war remakes during the Adenauer era (1949–63). Adopting a diachronic and synchronic approach, she explores the structural and economic conditions under which remakes were produced in post-war Germany, from the first years after the Nazi era until the demise of this particular remake cycle at the start of the 1960s. Concluding our historical section, Kamalika Sanyal and Eduard Cuelenaere head north to study the practice of the Swedish film industry in the 1950s to release colour remakes of film classics based on literary works. Through archival research, they demonstrate how the use of colour was employed as a promotional strategy. Additionally, they map out how these remakes were received, interpreted and labelled by critics and journalists alike, echoing the apparently timeless negative stance and disdain surrounding remaking practices.

Popular discourses surrounding the production and circulation of remakes are generally fuelled by comparative yet often superficial assessments of remake and source film. With our next section ('Contemporary Perspectives'), we wish to offer a scholarly sound counterweight to said evaluations. We do so by presenting the reader with a selection of contemporary case-studies of the European remake practice. Kris Van Heuckelom immediately sets the bar high by charting the largely unexplored territory of Polish remakes. Meticulously fleshing out textual features, critical discourses and marketing strategies, he is able to disclose the drastic development of Polish remake practices over the past two decades, unravelling the significant transition in terms of temporal and geographical scope. Similar ideas of transition and transformation are subject of the chapters by Boris Noordenbos and Irina Souch, as well as by Balázs Varga, who also introduce the notion of nostalgia into their analyses. Both chapters address the remake as an instrument to cope with the communist past of their respective countries of study, by approaching the remake as a cultural expression of nostalgia. For Noordenbos and Souch, this could be seen as indicative of a (potentially dangerous) desire to return to communist ideology or Soviet authoritarianism. The case of *The Crew* (Lebedev, 2016) allows them to question and understand the cultural 'work' of nostalgia in Russian society today. Balázs Varga takes us further with his fine-grained analysis of a series of Hungarian millennial remakes of classic interwar comedies. Following in the footsteps of the previous chapters, his contribution shows the unique potential of remakes in the shaping and discussion of the traditions of local popular cinema. Leaving a small European film industry such as Hungary behind us, the next stop on our journey through the European cinemascape are two of the largest film markets, France and Italy. Constantine Verevis looks at Luca Guadagnino's *A Bigger Splash* (2015), highlighting the film's status as a new millennial remake (Verevis 2017) in addition to discussing its features of commercial refashioning and authorial branding.

Capturing the above-mentioned drastic changes to the industrial context of European cinema since the new millennium, the final section of the book ('Industrial Perspectives') provides insights into contemporary practices of production and circulation of remakes. The chapter by Robert Munro and Michael Stewart traces the industrial, textual and critical differences and similarities between one of the best-loved Scottish films of all time, *Whisky Galore!* (Mackendrick, 1949), and its 2016 remake, hence combining two different eras of production and demonstrating the value of considering the peculiarities of a film's productional context. Focusing on an important agent in the network of film production, Núria Araüna Baró then takes the director as her vantage point to reflect on how the interpretation and production practices of remakes function in a transnational axis of power relationships where films move from one national context to another. She particularly problematises the relationship between Spanish and Hollywood cinema. The idea of going beyond the well-known binaries of Hollywood versus Europe is also central in the final chapter by Christopher Meir. He argues that the remake and remaking practices are unique tools to capture and study the extent and wide-ranging impact of the fundamental changes that the European film industry has undergone in the last two decades, bringing us full circle with the book volume's central notion of the remake as a kind of prism.

NOTES

1. One should note that the statement that the film remake's genesis coincided with the emergence of cinema itself very much depends on how one defines the term 'film remake'. Indeed, basing themselves on a different conceptualisation of the film remake, several scholars have criticised this very statement. More particularly, it is asserted that, on the one hand, in the early days of cinema, 'there was no conceptual or practical difference between the mechanical reproduction of film prints [that is, 'dupes'] and the re-photographing of similarly staged events or scenes [that is, film remakes]' (Herbert 2008: 127). On the other hand, it is argued that before 'film emerged from the veil of public domain to enter into the legal realm of the Copyright Statute' (Forrest 2002: 90), 'film remakes' that predate the specific year where film is added to copyright law should probably not be called 'remakes', as practically everyone re-used (or, arguably, pirated or stole) each other's material – which would imply that most of the films then produced were remakes. In most European countries (such as France, Belgium, Germany, or Norway), this (anticipated) legal step happened in 1910, following the signing of the Berlin Act in 1908, which revised the Berne Convention for the Protection of Literary and Artistic Works by adding cinematographic productions. Most other European countries followed over the next ten years.
2. See also the special issue of *Communications: The European Journal of Communication Research* entitled 'Current trends in remaking European screen cultures' (Cuelenaere, Joye and Willems 2019b), which takes a broader approach, including television remakes.
3. Higson (2006: 23) argues that 'it would be impossible – and certainly unwise – to ignore the concept [of national cinema] altogether'; yet, simultaneously, it does not seem useful 'to think through cultural diversity and cultural specificity in solely national terms', given that 'the contingent communities that cinema imagines are much more likely to be either local or transnational than national'.
4. These have already been studied in the context of Hollywood (Loock 2016).
5. The exceptions to this rule are: '(a) a big-budget Hollywood-style action/adventure blockbuster or animation; (b) a medium-budget middlebrow quality drama based on a best-selling book and an Oscar-winning Hollywood star attached; or (c) a low-budget MEDIA-supported art-house film made by a Palme-d'Or-winning auteur' (Jones 2020: 203). However, from a broader perspective, these exceptions clearly form a minority.
6. The book is for the most part a collection of keynotes and papers presented at the symposium *Remaking European Cinema* which the editors organised on 1 June 2018 at Ghent University, Belgium. The symposium also resulted in a special issue of *Communications: The European Journal of Communication Research*.

REFERENCES

Bachmann, Anne (2013), 'Locating Inter-Scandinavian Silent Film Culture: Connections, Contentions, Configurations', doctoral dissertation, Acta Universitatis Stockholmiensis.

Bergfelder, Tim (2005), 'National, Transnational or Supranational Cinema? Rethinking European Film Studies', *Media, Culture, Society*, 27: 3, 315–31.

Bock, Hans-Michael and Bergfelder, Tim (2009), *The Concise Cinegraph: Encyclopaedia of German Cinema*, New York: Berghahn Books.

Bondebjerg, Ib, Eva Novrup Redvall, Rasmus Helles, Signe Sophus Lai, Hendrik Søndergaard and Cecilie Astrupgaard (eds) (2017), *Transnational European Television Drama*, Basingstoke: Palgrave Macmillan.

Buonanno, Milly (2015), 'Italian TV Drama: The Multiple Forms of European Influence' in Eva Novrup Redvall, Ib Bondebjerg and Andrew Higson (eds), *European Cinema and Television: Cultural Policy and Everyday Life,* London: Palgrave MacMillan, pp. 195–213.

Cuelenaere, Eduard (2020), 'A "Double Take" on the Nation(al) in the Dutch-Flemish Monolingual Film Remake', in Michael Stewart and Robert Munro (eds), *Intercultural Screen Adaptation: British and Global Case Studies,* Edinburgh: Edinburgh University Press, pp. 222–40.

Cuelenaere, Eduard, Stijn Joye and Gertjan Willems (2019a), 'Local Flavors and Regional Markers: The Low Countries and Their Commercially Driven and Proximity-Focused Film Remake Practice', *Communications,* 44: 3, 262–81.

Cuelenaere, Eduard, Stijn Joye and Gertjan Willems (2019b), 'Current Trends in Remaking European Screen Cultures', *Communications,* 44: 3, 257–61.

Elsaesser, Thomas (2005), *European Cinema: Face to Face with Hollywood,* Amsterdam: Amsterdam University Press.

Esser, Andrea (2016), 'Challenging US Leadership in Entertainment Television? The Rise and Sale of Europe's International TV Production Groups', *International Journal of Communication,* 10, 3585–614.

Forrest, Jennifer (2002), 'The "Personal" Touch: The Original, the Remake, and the Dupe in Early Cinema', in Jennifer Forrest and Leonard R. Koos (eds), *Dead Ringers: The Remake in Theory and Practice,* New York: SUNY Press, pp. 89–126.

Forrest, Jennifer and Leonard R. Koos (2002), 'Reviewing Remakes: An Introduction', in Jennifer Forrest and Leonard R. Koos (eds), *Dead Ringers: The Remake in Theory and Practice,* New York: SUNY Press, pp. 1–36.

Fowler, Catherine (ed) (2002), *The European Cinema Reader,* Brighton: Psychology Press.

Garofalo, Damiano, Dom Holdaway and Massimo Scaglioni (2018), 'Introduction: The International Circulation of European Cinema in the Digital Era', *Comunicazioni sociali,* 3, 301–5.

Gundle, Stephen (2013), *Mussolini's Dream Factory: Film Stardom in Fascist Italy,* New York: Berghahn Books.

Hake, Sabine (2002), *German National Cinema,* New York: Routledge.

Harrod, Mary, Mariana Liz and Alissa Timoshkina (eds) (2014), *The Europeanness of European Cinema: Identity, Meaning, Globalization,* London: I. B. Tauris.

Harvey, James (2018), *On the Visual Cultures of the New Nationalisms,* Basingstoke: Palgrave Macmillan.

Herbert, Daniel (2008), 'Transnational Film Remakes: Time, Space, Identity', doctoral dissertation, University of Southern California.

Higson, Andrew (2006), 'The Limiting Imagination of National Cinema', in Elizabeth Ezra and Terry Rowden (eds), *Transnational Cinema: The Film Reader,* London: Routledge, pp. 15–25.

Higson, Andrew (2018), The Circulation of European Films within Europe', *Comunicazioni sociali,* 3, 306–23.

Hjort, Mette (2009), 'On the Plurality of Cinematic Transnationalism', in Natasa Durovicova and Kathleen Newman (eds), *World Cinemas: Transnational Perspectives,* London: Routledge, pp. 12–33.

Horton, Andrew and Stuart Y. McDougal (1998), *Play It Again, Sam: Retakes on Remakes,* Berkeley: California University Press.

Jones, Huw (2017), 'Remapping World Cinema through Audience Research', in Rob Stone, Paul Cooke, Stephanie Dennison and Alex Marlow-Mann (eds), *The Routledge Companion to World Cinema,* London: Routledge, pp. 467–81.

Jones, Huw (2020), 'Crossing Borders: Investigating the International Appeal of European Films', in Ingrid Lewis and Laura Canning (eds), *European Cinema in the 21st Century: Discourses, Directions and Genres*, Basingstoke: Palgrave Macmillan, pp.187–205.

Kaklamanidou, Betty and Ana Corbalán (2018), 'Introduction: Contested Terms, the European Union Contribution, and a Financial Crisis', in Betty Kaklamanidou and Ana Corbalán (eds), *Contemporary European Cinema: Crisis Narratives and Narratives in Crisis*, London: Routledge, pp. 1–19.

Kantar Public Brussels and European Commission (March 2018), *Standard Eurobarometer 89* (report), available at: http://ec.europa.eu/commfrontoffice/publicopinion/index.cfm/ResultDoc/download/DocumentKy/83538 (last accessed 10 August 2019).

Kanzler, Martin and Simone Patrizia (2019), 'The Circulation of European Films Outside Europe', European Audiovisual Observatory, Strasbourg, available at: https://rm.coe.int/the-circulation-of-european-films-outside-europe-key-figures-2017/168094629e (last accessed 2 August 2019).

Kelleter, Frank and Kathleen Loock (2017), 'Hollywood Remaking as Second-Order Serialization', in Frank Kelleter (ed), *Media of Serial Narrative*, Columbus: Ohio State University Press, pp. 125–47.

Labayen, Miguel Fernández and Ana Martín Morán (2019), 'Manufacturing Proximity Through Film Remakes: Remake Rights Representatives and the Case of Local-Language Comedy Remakes', *Communications*, 44: 3, 282–303.

Leitch, Thomas M. (1990), 'Twice-Told Tales: The Rhetoric of the Remake', *Literature/Film Quarterly*, 18: 3, 138–49.

Loock, Kathleen and Constantine Verevis (2012), 'Introduction: Remake/Remodel', in Kathleen Loock and Constantine Verevis (eds), *Film Remakes, Adaptations and Fan Productions*, Palgrave Macmillan, London, pp. 1–15.

Loock, Kathleen (2016), 'Sound Memories: "Talker Remakes", Paratexts, and the Cinematic Past', in Sara Pesce and Paolo Noto (eds), *The Political of Ephemeral Digital Media: Permanence and Obsolescence in Paratexts*, New York: Routledge, pp. 123–37.

Loock, Kathleen (2019), 'Remaking Winnetou, Reconfiguring German Fantasies of Indianer and the Wild West in the Post-Reunification Era', *Communications*, 44: 3, 323–41.

Mazdon, Lucy (2000), *Encore Hollywood: Remaking French Cinema*, London: British Film Institute.

Meir, Christopher (2019), *Mass Producing European Cinema: Studiocanal and Its Works*, London: Bloomsbury Publishing.

Mueller, Gabriele (2019), 'Boy 7 in Double Exposure: European Genre Cinema Between Transnational Industry Practices and National Consumption', *Studies in European Cinema*, 1–13.

Paris, Thomas (2014), *New Approaches for Greater Diversity of Cinema in Europe*, Technical report, European Commission, available at: https://ec.europa.eu/assets/eac/culture/library/studies/cinema-diversity-report_en.pdf (last accessed 1 August 2020).

Puttnam, David (1997), *The Undeclared War: The Struggle for Control of the World's Film Industry*, London: HarperCollins.

Rolling Stone (16 July 2019), '"Perfetti sconosciuti" nel Guinness dei primati: è il film con più remake della storia', *Rolling Stone*, available at: https://www.rollingstone.it/cinema/news-cinema/perfetti-sconosciuti-nel-guinness-dei-primati-e-il-film-con-piu-remake-della-storia/468955/ (last accessed 3 September 2019).

Smith, Iain Robert (2016), *The Hollywood Meme: Transnational Adaptations in World Cinema*, Edinburgh: Edinburgh University Press.

Smith, Iain Robert and Constantine Verevis (eds) (2017), 'Introduction: Transnational film Remakes', in Iain Robert Smith and Constantine Verevis (eds), *Transnational Film Remakes*, Edinburgh: Edinburgh University Press, pp. 1–18.
Verevis, Constantine (2006), *Film Remakes*, Edinburgh: Edinburgh University Press.
Verevis, Constantine (2017), 'New Millennial Remakes', in Frank Kelleter (ed), *Media of Serial Narrative*, Columbus: Ohio State University Press, pp. 148–66.
Wood, Linda (1986), *British Films, 1927–1939*, London: British Film Institute.
Zanger, Anat (2006), *Film Remakes as Ritual and Disguise: From Carmen to Ripley*, Amsterdam: Amsterdam University Press.

Part I
Conceptual Perspectives: Delineating and Pushing the Boundaries of Remake Studies

CHAPTER 1

The Film Remake as Prism: Towards a Model of Systematic Textual Analysis

Eduard Cuelenaere

INTRODUCTION

As demonstrated by the rich academic output of scholars in remake studies, the comparative assessment of two highly similar film texts 'is particularly well-suited for scholarly analysis as it is able to disentangle, locate or "defamiliari[s]e" the familiar, the banal, the unattainable and often invisible and render it more visible' (Cuelenaere, Joye and Willems 2019: 264). Remakes are generally known for showing many narrative commonalities with their source films, which, after comparison, makes the sometimes highly detailed (often latent and ideologically instructed) adjustments or adaptations more palpable. Hence, by juxtaposing film remakes with their filmic predecessors and inquiring into the localising and adapting processes of their (changed) narratives, one can obtain a unique glimpse into the workings of 'making meaning' in films. Yet, if one wishes to be as scientifically rigorous as possible, it is at least equally important to take into consideration how exactly this textual juxtaposition is carried out. In 2002, Quaresima remarked that '[t]he critical literature on the remake may seem vast, but it is made up almost entirely of descriptions, or of limited comparative analyses of paired texts, carried out according to the most diverse and unsystematic criteria' (78). Since then, I would argue, there have been little to no serious attempts at conceiving a descriptive textual model (with clear criteria) that helps in more systematically analysing film remakes.[1]

One of the leading scholars of television format studies, Moran, argued that, because of the serial principle present in all television formats, it seems appropriate to systematically analyse television formats through the method of semiotics, as it 'helps identify repetition as a recurring feature of popular fiction and entertainment, whether the form be printed stories, popular song or television program production' (Moran 2009: 11). As recent (both theoretically and empirically driven) research shows, the industrial, cultural and textual process of formatting television content is (to a certain extent) comparable to the process of remaking films (see, for example, Verevis 2017; Labayen and Morán 2019). Therefore, it might be useful to look at how scholars in format studies have been analysing these television formats textually in the past decades – of course, taking into account the commonalities and differences between both cultural artefacts and adapting the model correspondingly. As such, in order to systematise the comparative textual study of film remakes, I found that a set of descriptive textual codes helps in structuring the process of analysis (see Cuelenaere, Joye and Willems 2019 for an example of the method applied to Flemish-Dutch remakes). The underlying assumption and objective here is actually indebted to a structuralist thought where 'behavior, institutions and texts are seen as analy[s]able in terms of an underlying network of relationships, the crucial point being that the elements which constitute the network gain their meaning from the relations that hold between the elements' (Stam 2005: 18). The goal of this chapter is, therefore, to identify the mechanisms that form the basis for a text, which will eventually aid us in understanding the remake process and, in a next step, 'discover' the meanings of (and around) those texts that went through it.

At first glance, it may seem that a systematic textual organisation is incompatible with the late post-structuralist – or, indeed, Foucauldian – discursive idea that meaning is always governed by socio-culturally and historically defined discourses. Yet, as argued by Berry-Flint (2004), this (very justified) post-structuralist criticism does not necessarily imply that a more systematised approach to textual analyses (in his case, genre analysis) has become impossible or obsolete. A discursive stance 'does not disregard the importance of textual organi[s]ation; it simply sees films as sites rather than sources of meaning. Their reception is thus primarily determined socio-culturally because of the ways that social discourses organi[s]e what sense viewers make of films' aesthetic and phenomenological effects' (Berry-Flint 2004: 38). Indeed, even if one is convinced of the idea that the work of semioticians is highly myopic – in the sense that it disregards cultural specificities and adheres meaning to the text itself – it can still 'form the matrix, and provide much of the vocabulary, for approaches ranging from the linguistic, psychoanalytic, feminist and Marxist to the narratological, reception-oriented and translinguistic' (Stam 2005: x).

Put simply, the textual framework that I will clarify in the following adopts the structuralist idea that defines a text and thus a film text, as an amalgam of codes and mechanisms that together form a structure. Yet, as film remakes are generally quite clearly connected to their source (texts), one should naturally integrate an analysis of those remade texts as well – with 'source text' taken broadly, thus not only referring to 'acknowledged' source text(s). Therefore, by systematically analysing a set of films – or, in this case, tandems of source films and their remakes – through a set of clearly defined codes, and looking for specific patterns, one can get a hold of the mechanisms that transform these texts and create meaning. However – and this is where the discursive influence comes in – in a next step, one should open up the overall structure by adding human agency (both in individual and cultural forms) to the equation, thus acknowledging that cultural artefacts' meanings are always polysemic and that meaning always comes into being intertextually and discursively. Hence, 'a concern with the historical, social and cultural aspects [. . .] can at least help counter the frequent recourse to the structuralist goal of "discovering" deep structures and ahistorical essences' (Van der Heide 2002: 35). This suggests that the formal elements in texts are always simultaneously social (that is, not individually, nor collectively, but rather inter-subjectively defined) properties, inscribed in one or more cultures. Hence, given that the meanings of a film are inter-subjectively 'created' and, therefore, part of a never-ending process of interpretation, one should not only analyse the film remake textually, but also investigate its discursive nature. As argued by Verevis (2006: 101), 'textual accounts of remaking need to be placed in a contextual history, in "a sociology [of remaking] that takes into account the commercial apparatus, the audience, and the [. . . broader] culture industry"', mirroring Staiger's (2000) historical materialist approach. Consequently, the next essential phase in the analysis is to conduct production and reception research. In conclusion, the model that I will describe in the following helps in descriptively analysing film remakes. Yet, the analyst that uses it should acknowledge that merely describing the similarities and differences is insufficient. A more holistic analysis of the film remake necessitates, next to a descriptive layer, an interpretative layer calling for both production and reception analysis. Therefore, the model will demarcate the lines between textual and extra-textual elements of analysis as clearly as possible.

A DESCRIPTIVE ANALYSIS OF FILM REMAKES: FORMAL, TRANSTEXTUAL AND CULTURAL CODES

Moran (2009) stated that various scholars from many different fields have attempted to address the issue of cultural transformation by building on models of adaptation. Yet, he continues, these attempts have hitherto resulted in highly abstract or idealist versions of models, which, however useful theoretically, have perhaps been less so when applied methodically, or, indeed, practically. When investigating the remaking of television formats, one of the important analyses to be done is concerned with the process of adaptation or translation, for which Moran builds on Heylen's (1994) work in the field of translation studies. Subsequently, Moran came up with three different types of codes – namely, linguistic, intertextual and cultural codes –which range from elementary to more complex degrees of text. It is important to note that these codes should not be seen as mutually exclusive. On the contrary, they signify a multi-layered and complex process of remaking, which means that these codes interact and overlap rather than forming clearly distinct textual matters. These codes are, therefore, to be seen as a suggestive set or structuring of ideas that 'can help frame the discussion of the adaptation process relating to TV formats' (Moran 2009: 46) and, for our purposes, to the analysis of film remakes.

Before elaborating on Moran's model and adapting his way of framing the textual analysis of remaking television formats to the film remake process, it is necessary to critically reflect on his focus on the process of localisation. Indeed, one of the important underlying mechanisms that Moran seeks to locate with his framework is culturally driven and generally typified as 'localisation'. In other words, Moran built his entire model around that specific notion, indirectly assuming that the process of localising textual elements in television formats is quintessential if one wants to understand commonalities and differences found through the use of the textual codes. Applying this to transnational or cross-cultural remakes, one should, therefore, be equally wary of interpreting the found textual differences solely in terms of localisation.[2] In addition, what is often taken for granted when conducting cross-cultural analyses is that through the found differences culturally local themes or essential contextual factors are inevitably revealed (Livingstone 2003). Such an assumption overstates 'internal homogeneity while underplaying heterogeneity, ambiguity and borderline phenomena' (Livingstone 2003: 479), which can partly be solved by deliberately tracing cultural similarities as well.

Another justified critique for the localisation approach can be summarised in what is typified as the 'cultural opacity' of the scholar. In other words, the analyst who investigates film remakes may, of course, lack an adequate comprehension of a specific cultural context. Therefore, when tracing the mechanism of localisation in the analysis of film remakes, one should acknowledge a few pitfalls: first of all, there is no final or perfect way of 'correctly' interpreting a text culturally. Thinking that one can 'correctly' understand a text culturally will not result in a 'wrong' interpretation, but rather in what has been defined as projective appropriation – that is, the projection of one's own belief system and theoretical viewpoints on (film) texts from other cultures (Willemen 1994). Probably even more problematic is when an analyst 'adopts an ethnographic persona by reading texts as culturally, socially and historically authentic, thereby interpreting social behavio[u]r and even the presence of art[e]facts and particular landscapes as culturally accurate' (Van der Heide 2002: 31–32). As such, the preferred relationship between analyst and cultural object of research is labelled 'creative understanding' (Willemen 1994): a dialectical interconnection where 'the analyst is conscious of his or her own cultural location when engaging in the analysis of cultural texts [which necessarily involves] a process of "othering" oneself, but not of becoming (or attempting to become) the "other"' (Van der Heide 2002: 29).

Moreover, as I have argued earlier (see Cuelenaere, Joye and Willems 2019), the comparative analysis of film remakes itself helps when interpreting similarities and differences culturally, simply because narratives of both the source film and remake are often very similar, making the differences more explicit. Indeed, '[w]hen the border asserts itself so blatantly, there are ways of acquiring an intra-cultural interpretation (note that this is an interpretation and not an explanation) for the analyst to consider' (Van der Heide 2002: 31). This mirrors Bakhtin's notion of 'outsidedness' (1986), arguing that meaning often 'reveals' itself more clearly when it is placed in contact with other (alien) meaning(s), resulting in dialogue. Even though apples and oranges can, of course, be compared, 'there is perhaps more to be gained, because the range of variables is narrower, by comparing a ripe apple to one that is worm-eaten, or by comparing a market-ready Granny Smith to an equally saleable McIntosh or Fuji' (Wierzbicki 2015: 166). Hence, a possible solution of the above-mentioned pitfall can be found in the dynamics of the comparative film analysis itself. Of course, it is much recommended to compare the findings and results also with analyses by other analysts, 'preferably from other cultural and ideological perspectives' (Van der Heide 2002: 31). Moreover, research in the field of television formats shows that localisation processes 'might be much more limited, unintentional and more constrained than is usually argued' (Van Keulen and Krijnen 2014: 290). As such, if one wishes to understand the film remake more holistically, the textual analysis of film remakes is only one step in the right direction. Indeed, one should not only look at culturally driven (for example, employing cultural stereotypes to create recognisability) decisions in the remake process, but equally so the personally (for example, bringing homage to the source film), industrially (for example, omitting scenes because of budgetary reasons), textually (for example, genre-specific constraints) and even accidentally motivated (for example, forgetting to change specific elements while filming) choices (Cuelenaere 2020). The model, therefore, wishes to point to the importance of keeping a distance between *what* has been changed in remakes, *why* it has been altered, *how* this has been done, by *whom* it was done and, finally, *what* this all means.

Starting from the theoretical basis put forward by Moran (2009) – and clearly signalling where I modify or take distance from his model – I will now elaborate on a framework (see Table 1) that distinguishes between three different codes (formal, transtextual and cultural). This set of codes should help the analyst in more systematically studying film tandems.[3] The general idea is that they inform, structure and guide the textual analysis. As such, these codes

Table 1 The Descriptive Model

Formal code	Transtextual code	Cultural code
- *Mise-en-scène* - Cinematography - Sound - Editing - Characters - Narrative	- *Intertextual* elements (presence of an *indirect* source text in the text): quotation and allusion - *Architextual* elements (relationship between the text and a text of its kind) - *Hypertextual* markers (explicit reference to *direct* source text, or hypotext) - *Metatextual* elements (references of one text on another text) - *Intratextual* elements (reference to [the status of] the text itself) - *Paratextual* elements (textual elements that accompany the text)	- Explicit cultural references (clear and manifest) - Implicit cultural references (unclear, implied)

(and, therefore, the model) are to be seen as instruments or possible means, not an end in itself. Moreover, as mentioned above, the codes overlap in many ways; yet, in accordance with Moine (2013),[4] I claim that it is specifically at the moment of imbrication that these codes become interesting and prove to be productive. Also, it is of course perfectly possible to employ the model only partly in a comparative analysis – for instance, by focusing solely on the transtextual codes while ignoring the formal and cultural codes. Lastly, the model could equally function as a set of parameters for more quantitatively oriented analyses of film remakes.

Formal Code

The poetics of cinema arguably differs from a literary or televisual one. Yet, Moran (2009) adopts the concepts of form and style, as defined by Bordwell and Thompson (2004), when describing the 'linguistic code'. Given that Bordwell and Thompson have actually coined the umbrella term of 'film form', consisting of a formal as well as a stylistic system, I call the textual set that deals with form and style the 'formal code'. The film form signifies the overall system of relationships between the different elements or parts, consisting of both the formal and stylistic system which constantly interact (Bordwell and

Thompson 2004). Put simply, the formal system broadly consists of the narrative or non-narrative, and how these are discursively constructed. These may also include the themes of a narrative, or specific acts, as well as differences in time and space. One could also add focalisation points or the overall structure of how scenes are arranged. Equally important are the characters that are part of the (non)narrative, how they behave, their names, their histories and so on. The stylistic system, on the other hand, deals with the *mise-en-scène* (clothing, make-up, props, locations), cinematography (camera use, colour, light), sound (rhythm, silence, tonality, musical scores) and finally the editing. Simplified, the first system looks at *what* is being told on screen, and the second at *how* this is being done – yet, both these systems cannot be seen as isolated or highly distinct from each other.

Moran argues that '[a]t this level, the adaptation of a program format will involve one or more of these [. . .] codes in a relatively simple operation of omission, inclusion, substitution or permutation' (2009: 46). As we are dealing with at least two film texts and given that these naturally are put in a comparative framework, things get a bit more complicated. Indeed, describing the processes of 'omission', 'inclusion', 'substitution', or 'permutation' all depends on which film was analysed first. However, a rule of thumb here could be that one should always keep the broader aim or focus of the analysis in mind and openly communicate which approach was taken and why. For instance, it often makes sense to analyse films and their remakes in a chronological way, asking which film or script was released first, and which film(s) came after that and was, therefore, directly based on one or more of those previous texts. The danger of the latter approach, however, is that one can fall into the trap of seeing the direct source film as more original – which often results in connecting value to this status – only because it was 'first'. Yet, at the same time it should be acknowledged that, when explaining processes of, for instance, omission and inclusion, a linear chronology is always already implied – which basically justifies or normalises said approach.

Transtextual Code

The second type of translation that Moran adds to his adaptation model is the very broadly defined 'intertextual code'. In Moran's view, these intertextual elements are a lot less discrete than the previous code, as they connect 'with specific bodies of knowledge held by particular communities' (2009: 48). Consequently, this code transcends the texts themselves and looks at the broader industrial, as well as national contexts which shape these texts. Finally, Moran also sets the overarching element of genre under this code. For the sake of methodological clarity, as well as conceptual hygiene, I decided not to integrate an actual contextual analysis (such as information gathered through in-depth interviews) in the textual model. Instead of using such a broad (and, *in se*, both textually and extra-textually defined) code, I suggest to exchange the idea of intertextuality with Genette's conceptualisation of textual transcendence, which signifies 'all that sets the text in a relationship, whether obvious or concealed, with other texts' (1997: 1). There is no straightforward way to fully, or indeed ahistorically, define the film remake textually. Yet, it could be said that, in comparison to non-remakes, a film remake is more clearly defined by (its relationship with) one or more previous source texts. Indeed, 'the smallest common denominator uniting [the] attempts to come to grips with the remake seems to be their tendency to restrict the notion of remaking to intra-medial re-workings of texts' (Heinze and Krämer 2015: 10). If one wants to analyse film remakes textually, it therefore seems logical to fully consider the textual relationships that exist between a film remake and its direct and indirect source texts.

In the 1980s, Genette stated that the object of a theory of literary forms should not solely consider the text itself, but rather its so-called textual transcendence – the textual connections with other preceding and succeeding texts. Here, Genette builds on Kristeva's notion of intertextuality (1980), which states that every text is a mosaic of quotations, absorbing and transforming other texts. However, as asserted by Prince in the foreword of one of Genette's books, 'though all literary texts are hypertextual, some are more hypertextual than others, more massively and explicitly palimpsestuous' (Genette 1997: ix). This is probably the realm where the film remake belongs. There have been several scholars (for instance, Horton and McDougal 1998; Quaresima 2002; Zanger 2006; Moine 2013) who have adopted Genette's poetics intending to define the film remake and its relationship(s) with other texts. In *Film Remakes*, Verevis (2006), building on Stam's work (2005), suggested that Genette's work on transtextuality may also be helpful when analysing film remakes and comparing them to their source text(s) (see also Herbert 2008). Therefore, in the following pages I will elaborate on Genette's notion of transtextuality and zoom in on its different categories and subcategories. Hence, I will adopt his poetics and associated (sub)categories and demonstrate how these can be used to systematically compare film remakes with their source texts and thus help us build a more cohesive methodology to scrutinise remakes textually.

Genette classified five types of transtextual relationships and listed them 'more or less in the order of increasing abstraction, implication, and comprehensiveness' (1997: 1): intertextuality, paratextuality, metatextuality, architextuality and hypertextuality. These categorisations prove to be useful tools – mainly as a way of framing the (trans)textual findings – when comparing film remakes with their direct and indirect source texts. They can be adopted in at least two ways: on one hand, they guide the analyst in finding transtextual relationships between two or more texts (in a broad sense, they are quite clearly operationalised); on the other hand, they can help the analyst in better describing (that is, in a more detailed way) what happens on screen. Building on, and slightly diverging from, the application of Genette's framework by Stam (2005) and later Verevis (2006) on film analysis and film remake analysis, respectively, I will demonstrate why adding the transtextual code to the textual model is valuable.

The first type of relationship that Genette discusses is the intertextual one, which he defines in a stricter sense than generally conceived – that is, as 'a relationship of copresence between two texts or among several texts: that is to say, eidetically and typically as the actual presence of one text within another' (1997: 1–2). Yet, in the context of film remakes, I would argue that it becomes even more convenient when it is narrowed to only the presence of an indirect source text in the text. Otherwise, this category would include both the indirect (to many different source texts) and the direct (to the direct, often 'acknowledged' source text[s]) relationships, which are two distinct matters in the analysis of film remakes. In a next step, Genette concretises this type of relationship by supplying some subcategories, of which two are useful when analysing film (remakes): quotation and allusion. In the model I propose, quotation can appear as a direct insertion of one or more clips of whatever other film (except for the direct source text[s]) into the film text. An allusion could be interpreted as a more abstract form of quotation, as it 'can take the form of a verbal or visual evocation of another film' (Stam 2005: 211).

Another type of relationship between a film remake and direct or indirect source texts may be called architextual – that is, its designation as being part of one or more genres. For the remake model, it makes sense to broaden this category to those elements that link the film text to one or more texts of its kind. Examples of such elements could be both textual and paratextual (see below), such as the usage of genre-specific tropes, motifs or clichés. They may also consist of specific phrases, quotations, themes and other conventions or rules. Including this type of relationship into the model answers the need to extend the comparative analysis of film remakes with source texts to other film texts that are, for example, part of the same genre.

The third type of relationships that can be found when comparatively analysing film remakes is the hypertextual one. This is different from the others, as it presupposes a direct and explicit relationship with its source text(s), instead of an indirect and possible implicit one. Indeed, hypertextual markers point towards explicit references to the direct source text(s) (or, as Genette described it, the hypotext[s]) of the film remake. A hypertextual relationship can be established in many different ways: through dialogue, the use of specific props, the names of characters, or even direct insertions of clips of the source film.

Another kind of relationship between the film remake and other texts is a metatextual one – namely, where the film itself, or parts of it (critically) comment on another film text, or body of texts (genres, for example). Next is the so-called intratextual relationship, which signifies references to the (status of) the text itself, or 'refer[s] to the process by which films refer to themselves through mirroring, microcosmic, and mise-en-abyme structures, while auto-citation would refer to an author's self-quotation' (Stam 2005: 211). Lastly, paratextual elements are those that directly accompany the text (such as the opening and end credits, post-credit scenes and so on). Important here is that the notion of paratextuality is in fact defined in a much narrower sense, which means that I clearly steer away from Genette's signification and the general use of the word. This is, however, necessary, since this model wants to emphasise a more holistic analysis (see above) that also includes production and reception research, including, for example, the analysis of trailers, teasers, press material or even film reviews.

Cultural Code

The last code that I would like to add to the textual model is the cultural code, which consists of both explicit and implicit references to a cultural context or situation. Of course, there exists a whole range of cultural references that could be found in a film text: humour; religion; language; gender; stereotypes; nudity; sexuality; specific situations; periods; and broader political, judicial, economic and geographical circumstances. There are several reasons why this type of element requires a different code. First, categorising these references as a separate code forces scholars to not interpret every commonality or difference between source text and remake in terms of localisation (see above). Secondly, and this might seem to contradict the former, it is clear that a lot of the omissions, additions and other transformative processes in film remakes are often being done to cultural elements, which is why they deserve a separate code. Lastly, there are many different ways of altering such cultural codes, based on different underlying motives or incentives. Because of this – and for the sake of the model's overall clarity – it makes sense to integrate a distinction between the textually found codes and cultural processes of, for example, localisation or delocalisation (which give meaning to those codes and, therefore, form the interpretative layer).

This cultural code is theoretically informed by Hjort's concept of banal aboutness (2000) and the study of imagology. The latter points towards 'the study of national and cultural images as represented in textual discourse, [which] is a fruitful approach for disciplines dealing with textual change' (Van Doorslaer 2019: 56) – the approach being descriptive instead of explanatory. As such, this (sub)discipline wishes to theorise national and cultural stereotypes comparatively, concentrating 'on more constructionist models, away from essentialist definitions' (Van Doorslaer 2019: 57). Lastly, according to van Doorslaer (2019), adopting imagology as a lens also marks the importance of 'diachronic viewpoints or the centrality of change and hybridity' (62), as well as the role of the mediating 'author' or, in our case, the filmmakers. The concept of banal aboutness, however, follows Billig's notion of banal nationalism (1995), which contends that nationalism (in film, for example) should not be reduced to only the explicit or apparent references to, or indeed the reproductions of, the nation. Applied to the realm of film and slightly (yet not fully) steering away from the loaded term 'nationalism', Hjort coins the concept of banal aboutness, signalling those elements that mirror the material aspects of a specific culture which make a film 'about' that culture (2000: 99). Moreover, she creates the essential division between banal occurrences of aboutness and the type 'that is constitutive of full-blown themes of nation' (Hjort 2000: 101). What defines the difference between both instances is the degree to which the reference (taken broadly) is vital or fundamentally important to the narrative. As such, focal attention acts as the defining characteristic between films that are about a nation and films that have the nation as a central theme – which should not be conceived of as binary, but as existing on a continuum.

Explicit and implicit cultural references are found in both banal and thematised representations of the nation, which means that one or more explicit references to a specific cultural context do not necessarily make a film nationalistic in a thematic way. To operationalise these concepts more clearly, it could be said that explicit cultural references are those elements that clearly (from the analyst's perspective) refer to an extratextual cultural reality, leaving nothing implied. In every case, this makes a film 'about' a specific culture or nation and, in some cases, makes the nation the central theme of the film. Think, for example, of the use of (popular) television programmes, known magazines or newspapers, theme parks, (local) celebrities, food, art, locales and so on. In contrast, implicit cultural references are those elements that are implied but not manifestly or obviously uttered. These references are mostly found in specific representations or portrayals of, for example, sexuality, nudity, religion, sports, ethnicity, cultural habits or traditions, as well as in humour, stereotypes, clichés and the like. Imagology's focus on stereotypes might be of interest here. Throughout its existence as a discipline, it has pointed towards at least three recurring (overarching) findings: the stereotypical oppositions of North-South (for instance, in Italy, Belgium, France, or even Europe as a whole) and centre-periphery (a country's capital city versus the rest), as well as the more meta-reflexive finding that 'there are contradictory stereotypes available for more or less each country, showing the relativity of typicality' (Van Doorslaer 2019: 62). Obviously, there is no clear theoretical line that can be drawn between explicit and implicit cultural references. This suggests that they function more like conceptual frames or lenses which can help trace these cultural elements, in line with the overall goal of the proposed model: framing the discussion of the remake and systematising its analysis.

CONCLUSION

The descriptive textual model explored in the preceding paragraphs is only a first step to grasping and understanding the film remake process. Therefore, the next step is to gather and interpret the found data while looking for specific patterns. Even though interpreting textual findings often comes in an almost natural or intuitive way, one should always try to be as reflexive as possible. Weber (1949) once wrote that it 'is not the "actual" interconnections of "things" but the conceptual interconnections of problems which define the scope of the various sciences' (cited in Koshul 2005: 69). Hence, the outcome of one's analysis is always (at least partly) determined by the theoretical lenses one adopts when analysing film remakes. These lenses are indirectly accompanied by specific goals as well as assumptions about the interpretation of data. Consequently, although theories never just come into being – because 'they need a leap, a wager; a hypothesis, to get started' (Moretti 2000: 55) – a self-reflexive and iterative approach seems highly justifiable. Such an approach demands to constantly repeat the whole research process in a circular manner, instead of a linearly defined process of data selection, collection and analysis. Hence, the proposal to more systematically analyse film remakes by introducing the textual model described above does not imply that one has to strictly adhere to the latter model (in its current form). Indeed, I consider my textual model as a continuous work-in-progress, open for interpretation, variation and uses. This equally implies that, if done critically, the present model could also form the basis for a comparative descriptive analysis of other serial screen formats, both inter- and intra-medial (such as sequels, serials, franchises, series, or reboots). Aware of the fact that employing a textual model is only one measure to bring about scientific rigorousness, with this chapter I hope to (at least) convince that finding a similar language is quintessential, if one aims to forge a scientific field that is theoretically and methodologically sound, as well as empirically driven.

NOTES

1. Probably, the only exception would be Verevis' semantic/syntactic model (2006) – based on Altman's genre theory – which is useful, yet somewhat underdeveloped and not widely adopted in the context of film remakes.
2. The process of localisation is, moreover, often interpreted solely in terms of the nation. This reminds of what is known as methodological nationalism – that is, (unconsciously) holding the idea that the nation-state is the natural starting point for every explanation of data (Beck and Sznaider 2006).
3. Although I conceived the model specifically for the analysis of film remakes, the model could certainly form the basis for scrutinising other, similar forms of serialities (see the concluding paragraphs of this essay).

4. Moine actually talks about the categories proposed by Genette (which I will adopt in the transtextual code), but the assumptions and conclusions are equally applicable to the codes I propose. The original quote is the following: 'les catégories proposées par Genette se révél[e]nt beaucoup plus productives quand on les envisage non de façon cloisonnées, mais qu'on s'intéresse à leurs zones de recouvrement ou de cohabitation partielle' (Moine 2013: 41).

REFERENCES

Bakhtin, Michail (1986), *Speech Genres and Other Late Essays*, Austin, TX: University of Texas Press.
Beck, Ulrich and Natan Sznaider (2006), 'Unpacking Cosmopolitanism for the Social Sciences: A Research Agenda', *The British Journal of Sociology* 57: 1, 1–23.
Berry-Flint, Sarah (2004), 'Genre', in Toby Miller and Robert Stam (eds), *A Companion to Film Theory*, Hoboken: Blackwell Publishing, pp. 25–44.
Billig, Michael (1995), *Banal Nationalism*, Thousand Oaks: Sage.
Bohman, James (1991), *New Philosophy of Social Science: Problems of Indeterminacy*, Cambridge: Polity Press.
Bordwell, David and Kristin Thompson (2004), *Film Art: An Introduction*, New York: McGraw Hill.
Cuelenaere, Eduard (2020), 'Towards an Integrative Methodological Approach of Film Remake Studies', *Adaptations* online first.
Cuelenaere, Eduard, Stijn Joye and Gertjan Willems (2019), 'Local Flavors and Regional Markers: The Low Countries and their Commercially Driven and Proximity-Focused Film Remake Practice', *Communications* 44: 3, 262–81.
Genette, Gérard (1997), *Palimpsests: Literature in the Second Degree*, Lincoln: University of Nebraska Press.
Heinze, Rüdiger and Lucia Krämer (2015), *Remakes and Remaking: Concepts, Media, Practices*, Bielefeld: transcript Verlag.
Herbert, Daniel (2008), 'Transnational Film Remakes: Time, Space, Identity', doctoral dissertation, University of Southern California.
Heylen, Romy (1994), *Translation Poetics and the Stage: Six French Hamlets*, London: Routledge.
Hjort, Mette (2000), 'Themes of Nation', in Mette Hjort and Scott MacKenzie (eds), *Cinema and Nation*, London: Routledge, pp. 103–17.
Horton, Andrew and Stuart Y. McDougal (1998), *Play It Again, Sam: Retakes on Remakes*, Berkeley: California University Press.
Hutcheon, Linda (2006), *A Theory of Adaptation*, London: Routledge.
Koshul, Basit Bilal (2005), *The Postmodern Significance of Max Weber's Legacy: Disenchanting Disenchantment*, Berlin: Springer.
Kristeva, Julia (1980 [1977]), 'Word, Dialogue, and Novel', in Leon S. Roudiez (ed), *Desire in Language: A Semiotic Approach to Literature and Art*, New York: Columbia University Press, pp. 64–91.
Labayen, Miguel Fernández and Ana Martín Morán (2019), 'Manufacturing Proximity through Film Remakes: Remake Rights Representatives and the Case of Local-Language Comedy Remakes', *Communications* 44: 3, 282–303.
Livingstone, Sonia (2003), 'On the Challenges of Cross-National Comparative Media Research', *European Journal of Communication*, 18: 4, 477–500.
Moine, Raphaëlle (2013), *Remakes: Les films français à Hollywood*, CNRS Éditions via OpenEdition.

Moran, Albert (2009), 'When TV Formats are Translated', in Albert Moran (ed), *TV Formats Worldwide: Localizing Global Programs*, Bristol: Intellect books, pp. 41–54.
Moretti, Franco (2000), 'Conjectures on World Literature', *New Left Review* 1, 54–68.
Quaresima, Leonardo (2002), 'Loving Texts Two at a Time: The Film Remake', *Cinémas: revue d'études cinématographiques/Cinémas: Journal of Film Studies*, 12: 3, 73–84.
Staiger, Janet (2000), *Perverse Spectators: The Practices of Film Reception*, New York: New York University Press.
Stam, Robert (2005), *New Vocabularies in Film Semiotics*, London: Routledge.
Van der Heide, William (2002), *Malaysian Cinema, Asian Film: Border Crossings and National Cultures*, Amsterdam: Amsterdam University Press.
Van Doorslaer, Luc (2019), 'Embedding Imagology in Translation Studies', *Slovo.ru: The Baltic Accent* 10: 3, 56–68.
Van Keulen, Jolien and Tonny Krijnen (2014), 'The Limitations of Localization: A Cross-Cultural Comparative Study of Farmer Wants a Wife', *International Journal of Cultural Studies* 17: 3, 277–92.
Verevis, Constantine (2006), *Film Remakes*, Edinburgh: Edinburgh University Press.
Verevis, Constantine (2017), 'New Millennial Remakes', in Frank Kelleter (ed), *Media of Serial Narrative*, Columbus: Ohio State University Press, pp. 148–66.
Wierzbicki, James (2015), 'Subtle Differences: Sonic Content in "Translation" Remakes', *Journal of Adaptation in Film and Performance*, 8: 2, 155–69.
Willemen, Paul (1994), 'The National', in Paul Willemen (ed), *Looks and Frictions: Essays in Cultural Studies and Film Theory*, Bloomington: Indiana University Press, pp. 206–19.
Zanger, Anat (2006), *Film Remakes as Ritual and Disguise: From Carmen to Ripley*, Amsterdam: Amsterdam University Press.

CHAPTER 2

The 'Secret Remake': A European Take on the Traditional Remake?*

Marie Martin

WHAT IS A 'SECRET REMAKE'?

Let me begin by saying what it is not: the 'secret remake' is not a traditional remake in the sense of the commercial and legally bound practice (Moine 2007: 5–35). Rather, it is a somewhat hidden rewriting, not necessarily noticed by its viewers or even its author, since filmmaking builds not only on control and craft, but also on blind urges and unconscious processes – hence the term 'secret', even though it does not automatically entail a deliberately concealed information, as in the 'disguised remake' (Druxman 1975: 13).

So why, circa 2010, did I coin such an apparently inadequate term to label a phenomenon that was a mere hunch at the time? Finding a name, however inadequate, meant taking the few cases I had already studied to the next level of a film category, which, to my knowledge, was still unaccounted for. A name would allow for theorising the phenomenon's content and boundaries by cross-referencing, and it would also allow other scholars to relate to it with a tag that is able to conjure up all the images and shared experiences it could muster. In French, *le remake secret* is evocative of a Jamesian 'figure in the carpet' of sorts, a way of potentially discerning a film's reframing, concealing and encoding of the core of a previous film that has obviously left an impression on either the artists, or the audience, or both. This perception of a latent design reproducing itself with a twist is no different from the displaced repetition, which is precisely the trademark of unconscious processes. Rather than an 'Œdipal significance' for the director, as in Harvey Roy Greenberg's 'contested homage' (Greenberg 1991: 169), a psychic dynamic of repetition (and difference) is therefore at stake in the secret remake, for viewers and filmmakers, compelling them to try and overcome a filmic shock by re-enacting it almost beyond recognition. There lies the core of secret remaking 'as a practice' (Dusi 2012) and not a pointless desire to add another category to the many that are already existing and founded on different assumptions – that is, industrial, textual, or critical (Verevis 2006: 1–34), the former being void by definition in the case at hand and the latter two lacking consistency to unify such an unstable phenomenon.

This quick survey of the history of the expression hopefully allows me now to define what a 'secret remake' stands for and what questions its definition has prompted. Whereas intertextuality entails 'an endless process of recycling, transformation, and transmutation, with no clear point of origin' (Stam 2000: 66), a secret remake offers a new perspective on filmic hyper-textuality, namely a rewriting based on the Freudian *Traumarbeit* (dreamwork) as used by Thierry Kuntzel for film analysis in 'Le travail du film 2' (filmwork) (Kuntzel 1975: 136–89): a previous film remade by a second one which, by employing the logic of condensation, displacement and considerations of representability (*figurability*), brings to the fore its repressed traumatic quality, a distinctive feature resulting from unconscious processes (Martin 2015: 13–32). In this respect, the difference between an unofficial but obvious remake – such as an '*acknowledged, transformed remake*' (Greenberg 1991: 170) or an 'homage' (Leitch 1990: 144) – and a secret one appears clearer when comparing the many films produced in the wake of Antonioni's *Blow Up* (1966). If Argento's *Deep Red* (*Profondo Rosso*, 1975) and De Palma's *Blow Out* (1981) claim their diegetic connection by way of a name or an actor (David Hemmings, in Antonioni and Argento's movies) in order to better mark their mannerist variations in the *mise-en-scène*, Rohmer's *The Aviator's Wife* (*La Femme de l'aviateur*, 1981) and Greenaway's *The Draughtsman's Contract* (1982) are, conversely, disguised rewritings that highlight the uncanniness of their source (Martin 2007: 158–68; 2009: 133–43; 2014: 261–76). Moreover, the hypothesis that secret remakes conform to the same criteria as dreamwork is confirmed by the analysis of several pairs of films that reveal what the latent trauma at hand consists of and what exactly 'the core of a film' being rewritten is.

A continually expanding body of films can indeed be labelled 'secret remakes', and these have already been studied as such. In 2005, even though he referred to it as a *film volé* (a tribute to *The Purloined Letter* by Poe) and did not try to find other examples of such 'stolen movies' or to theorise them, the French critic Jean-François Buiré first noticed that Losey's *Monsieur Klein* (1976) was an off-the-record variation on Hitchcock's *North by Northwest* (1959) (Buiré 2005: 87–97). Both films deal with a trip across a country, either north- or eastbound, which doubles as a sentimental journey as the protagonist transforms his identity. In Hitchcock's movie, Roger Thornhill, an apparently ordinary advertising executive, reluctantly embodies a spy, Kaplan; he travels from New York to Mount Rushmore and in the process reveals himself to be talented, daring and virile. In Losey's film, Alain Delon plays a wealthy, egotistical art dealer who is mistaken for a Jewish man by the same name. Wondering about his double's as well as his own family's roots, he goes from Paris to Strasbourg and back, finally allowing himself to be deported in the Vel d'Hiv raid in an unsuccessful attempt to finally meet his *alter ego*. The similarities between the two films include narrative details – for instance, the atmosphere of dark menace around the unscrupulous American spies finds an echo in the French police scrupulously obeying the Gestapo's orders – as well as characteristic shots, such as Saul Bass' opening credits focused on the square lines of the United Nations headquarters complex in New York, or the high-angle shot showing the empty crossroads where Kaplan is eventually chased by a crop duster. The same geometrical perspective seems to guide Losey's *mise-en-scène*.

Identifying a secret remake, therefore, amounts to playing 'spot the resemblance' between two very different movies – and they must differ greatly for there to be any secrecy, relying on an effective disguise. *Monsieur Klein* approaches a tragic era with a spurious detachment; even though *North by Northwest* displays some nerve-wracking situations and a trio of fearsome villains, its mood is definitely light-hearted, characterised by the usual Hitchcockian humour that verges on the absurd. But not everyone may be sympathetic to the Kafkaesque tone of Kaplan's adventure which, as Kundera would put it, 'takes us inside, into the guts of a joke, into the *horror of the comic*, [depriving us of] the grandeur of tragedy' (Kundera 1988: 92). In his *mise-en-scène*, Losey seems to emphasise precisely the grim aspect of the Kafkaesque trap closing on Monsieur Klein, depriving it of its absurd side as he chooses to bring out the underlying World War II context of *North by Northwest*. Buiré actually points out that Hitchcock was a treatment advisor for *Memory of the Camps* and speculates on the impact that this must have had on him: for instance, the scene when Thornhill shaves in the train station bathroom and draws the notorious Hitler moustache with shaving foam can be analysed as the symptom of a denied traumatic background (*Verneinung*) which *Monsieur Klein* addresses in the foreground. This shows how prominent the disguised re-enactment of latent trauma should be in the acknowledgement of a secret remake. Many more pairs of films confirm this hypothesis, whether the trauma stems from historical violence, intimate scars, or both – such as in Truffaut's *The Green Room* (*La Chambre verte*, 1978), which secretly remakes Gance's *Paradise Lost* (*Paradis perdu*, 1940) and takes the private loss of a widower to the point of an obsessive preservation of the dead of World War I (Martin and Veray 2015: 75–95). The lasting wound that constitutes trauma can occur not only in the film story, but also in the context of viewing the film, as a crucial experience whose mark is even deeper, as it is not fully understood or processed. This is precisely the case here, since the young Truffaut watched Gance's film over and over in a Parisian theatre used as shelter during the German bombing in

World War II. I shall develop this point below, in connection with the way in which cinema projects and screens reality.

For now, let us return to the necessary dissemblance in tone and details masking the same overall script. Does the resemblance between two movies only stem from the way in which their story is told, levelling off obvious differences to better reveal their common structural pattern, in which case all scenarios somewhat look alike at a minimal level and every movie could be seen as a more or less far-fetched remake? In other words, even though the hypothesis that any film is a secret remake cannot be proven wrong, to what extent can it be backed up by actual data and not mere perceptions? This is where Lefebvre's theory of the figure comes in handy to answer the questions raised by the process of an oblique rewriting of the so-called core of a film (Lefebvre 1997). The figure cannot be located precisely in a movie, since it occurs when a film has been seen, remembered and even imagined anew, which creates another semiotic encoding, 'the (imaginary) pattern standing out from the impression-forming content of a movie' (Lefebvre 1997: 65). It results from the five processes (perceptual, cognitive, argumentative, affective and symbolic) at stake in spectatorship and, as such, is both individual and collective, private and based on objective traits and features. For instance, the figure of Hitchcock's *Psycho* (1960) is epitomised by the shower scene, which is not so much a rape as a cannibal attack. Lefebvre convincingly points out the many symbolic associations, such as the murder weapon being not just any knife, but a kitchen knife; he concludes that the sequence revolves around death as ingestion and digestion. Beyond this emblematic scene, the figure unfurls throughout the whole film in three interlaced archetypes: liquidity (from rain to money to swamp), impurity (adultery just as much as flushing the toilet) and the Great Mother, both nourishing and devouring.

The presence of these archetypes in Frears' *The Grifters* (1990) points towards a possible rewriting of *Psycho*, but would not be sufficient proof of a secret remake if, beyond the imaginary configurations of the figure, it were not for the roughly similar overall narrative, along with some crucial markers in the *mise-en-scène*. For instance, deceptive appearances and disguise are important in both films, from cross-dressing to backlit or high-angle shots: the same perverted threesome of mother, son and lover is linked by their jealousy and shady business, till death do them part. The final scene can be analysed as a disguised shower scene with many pints of crimson blood spilled when the mother, dressed as her daughter-in-law, slices her son's throat by accident with the shard of a broken drinking glass. This mere description shows how Frears redistributes *Psycho*'s shocking developments in a grotesque and outrageous way, overstating whatever remained latent in Hitchcock's film, from bodily fluids in full colour to incest by way of food-related double *entendres*.

Thus, a preliminary conclusion is that the figure according to Lefebvre provides a valuable and theoretically sound tool to delineate the core of the film that is supposedly rewritten. But, as we have already seen, it is not enough to assert a secret remake since it does not account for the concealment: for instance, *The Grifters* is not featured in the many *Psycho* rewritings studied by Lefebvre in the second part of his book, because there is no actual shower scene in it, only a metaphorical one. Yet, the redistribution of the main topics forming the figure – the disguised core – would be too flimsy a requirement and must also be reinforced by considering how the narrative clusters throughout the whole movie are systematically remade or, so to speak, tampered with, and how the filmmaker addresses or plays with the markers of the original style.

CAN IT BE DEEMED EUROPEAN?

The next step now is to determine whether the secret remake is a European phenomenon in particular; this raises at least one question: what exactly is Europeanness? On the one hand, almost every film mentioned above was directed by a European filmmaker: to Rohmer, Greenaway, Truffaut and Frears we can add, for instance, Buñuel, whose *Un Chien andalou* seems to be an oneiric rewriting of Pabst's *Secrets of a Soul* (1926), recalling and expanding the seminal figure of the phantasmal murder by razor (Martin 2012: 73–75). Or the long and more or less secret posterity of Hitchcock's *Vertigo* (1958) (Cerisuelo 2015: 119–37), from Marker's *La Jetée* (1962) to Gondry's *Eternal Sunshine of the Spotless Mind* (2004) by way of Resnais' *Je t'aime je t'aime* (1968), or, again from the latter, *Wild Grass* (*Les Herbes folles*, 2009). Dominique Païni described *Wild Grass* as 'a new cover version of Buñuel's *L'Âge d'or* (1930), which seems an apt rewording of the secret remake since the two films are so different (Païni 2009: 17). The nationality of any collective work of art remains an open question, whether it is the production, cast, writer, or director who is taken into consideration: even though Frears is English, there is no denying that *The Grifters* is an American film in every other respect and would be considered the exception proving the rule, if there were no other components at stake in a secret remake. Conversely, Losey was born in Wisconsin, but self-educated by his trips to USSR or Germany and later exiled to Great Britain during Senator McCarthy's witch-hunt. His work belongs to neither the classical Hollywood cinema nor the New Hollywood.

However, the birthplace of the directors in a mere sample, whose representativity cannot be verified, does not present compelling evidence. Instead, it is a consequence of the lack of expertise in Chinese, Japanese, Latin American, African and Indian films among the few scholars who have so far taken an interest in secret remakes. In the first edited volume devoted to the subject, for instance, Lucia Ramos Monteiro pointed out the allusive figurative similarities between Jia Zhang-ke's *Still Life* (2006) and the modern cinema of both Rossellini and Antonioni (especially *Germany Year Zero* (*Germania anno zero*, 1948) and *The Red Desert* [*Deserto Rosso*, 1964]) in light of the same concern for the iconography of ruins and the narrative of imminent catastrophe. Nevertheless, Jia has shown a definite affinity for European culture, often claiming neorealism as a major influence on his work (Ramos Monteiro 2015: 97–117). But there must be many more, still waiting for an observant eye, such as Hervé Aubron (2005: 4–13) suggesting that Weerasethakul's *Tropical Malady* (2004) is a secret rewriting of Lynch's *Mulholland Drive* (2001). This kind of *de facto* perspective is of limited use, however, when trying to establish a rigorous theory, and it is better to focus on the reasons why the secret remake apparently thrives in the European context, or, to put it differently, what Europeanness entails in terms of a cinema that resonates with the notion of the secret remake.

As far as the creation component is concerned, all secret remakes share one common point: they relate to the Deleuzian crystal-image (Deleuze 1985: 92–128). With the previous movie's trauma and features virtually present as requirements, it is no wonder that the secret remake works according to the cornerstone concept of the philosopher's second book on cinema, which is deeply rooted in European history and cinema (specifically, shell-shock from the utter destruction of Italy or Germany transforming action and reaction into mere stunned contemplation). Thus, even though Deleuze does not claim to demarcate either geographical or temporal boundaries in film history and acknowledges the cinematic modernity of some American filmmakers such as Welles and Cassavetes, his diptych has nevertheless led to an incorrect pair of assumptions: the association between the movement-image and the classical American film and, in contrast, the association between the time-image and the European modernist film. Such easy mistakes can, therefore, explain why the secret remake seems so strongly European, despite any counter-examples.

As a matter of fact, are there films in the US context which look like and by comparison shed light on secret remakes? For instance, Michael Brashinsky wrote a paper about Craven's *The Last House on the Left* (1972) as an unofficial remake of Bergman's *The Virgin Spring* (1969) (Brashinsky 1998: 162–71). Without considering it as a sample of a possible new filmic category, he actually addressed the way in which Craven disguised and never acknowledged his Bergmanian source, even claiming 'the events [. . . in the film were] true and names and locations [. . .] changed to protect those individuals still living', as if the similarities between the two films were so obvious they could only be denied by reality itself. Yet, John Carpenter never hid the fact that many of his films were only new ways of remaking over and over one of his favourite movies from his childhood, Hawks' *Rio Bravo* (1959), restaging it from the West Texan frontier to Precinct 13, or even to Mars.

Nevertheless, the best way to account for these examples is not primarily as more or less secret remakes, but rather in terms of genre (Altman 1999), which is also a way to categorise films. In the American context, these unconfessed or freely transformed remakes seem to depend on semantic changes and syntactic hybridity. In other words, their resemblances are caused by their similar structural outlines (for example, a besieged, closed space from which horror or dramatic tension rises as two rival camps fight) and their differences by the broad contrasts between genres. In Greenberg's taxonomy, they are named 'the *unacknowledged, disguised remake[s]*' and, far from any unconscious motivations or traumatic dream work, they result from industrial requirements of efficiency and economy: 'Major alterations are undertaken in time, setting, gender, or – most particularly – genre. The audience is deliberately uninformed about the switches. Disguised remaking peaked roughly from the 1930s through the early 1950s – the heyday of the studio system, when the relentless demand for new films, wedded to a perennial lack of fresh material, compelled frequent reuse of earlier screenplays' (Greenberg 1991: 170). Conversely, neither genre nor intertextuality at large in 'the endless chain of connections – both voluntary and involuntary – which characterises film remaking' (Verevis 2006: 27) is really operative in the way in which European filmmakers secretly remake masterpieces of classical or modern cinema since they (or the audience) focus on the way in which the detailed outline of an idiosyncratic plot, the symbolic network of its figure and the style of *mise-en-scène* are conjured and yet altered beyond any easy recognition. For this reason, I am not sure whether Huston's *The Unforgiven* (1960) and Howard's *The Missing* (2002) are indeed secret remakes of Ford's *The Searchers* (1956) (Mellier 2015: 33–53). Although they share a specific configuration revolving around blood ties and family secrets (taboo love and miscegenation), which both films re-enact and displace, the very fact that they all work within the framework of the Western means that they are more likely generic variations, *répliques* which in French can simultaneously describe a copy, a line of dialogue and the second tremor occurring after an earthquake.

THE SECRET REMAKE AS A CINEPHILIC AND PROJECTIVE REMAKE

Working on the assumption that the secret remake is more a product of spectatorship and interpretation rather than a creative practice (even though both are obviously linked somehow), how can the continental vibe around it be explained? If what is at stake in the secret remake is indeed a 'way of seeing' (Berger 1972), then what exactly is its connection to Europe? Since they share many striking similarities, let us start with Anat Zanger's seminal take on remakes, American and European alike, as ritual and disguise revealing the blind spots of patriarchy. I could argue that Zanger is Israeli, and that her book is published by the Amsterdam University Press, which makes her more European than American. However, as we have already seen about a film's nationality, especially in an age of global research when visual studies are dominant across the academic world, these factual details do not add up to a general reason why, on a theoretical level, the secret remake would appear European. As a matter of fact, the mere differences between Zanger's conception of remakes and the idea of secret ones could point towards some specificity dating back to an indisputably European critical tradition.

If official remakes display their source from the start on a referential level, then conversely what Zanger calls 'latent versions' are only discernible on a textual level – hence her use of mythemes to encapsulate the narrative of famous feminine characters, such as Carmen or Joan of Arc, and track and interpret their many avatars 'recurring [. . .], either manifestly or implicitly [. . . but] differently each time' (Zanger 2007: 72). Joan is thus characterised by three mythemes – the voices, the dress and the trial – which are 'the components that appear again and again and that, in retrospect, disclose the "contours" of the meta-version' (Zanger 2007: 107), for instance, in Fincher's *Alien III* (1992) or Von Trier's *Breaking the Waves* (1996). Reflecting on 'the elements necessary to insure that the version – even in disguise – will be recognized as such, that is, as a version' (Zanger 2007: 103), she posits 'that while the referential levels [. . .] do not declare any connection to Joan of Arc, the textual levels reveal a similar surface structure' (Zanger 2007: 108). But contrary to the figure according to Lefebvre, on which the secret remake is based, the notion of surface structure does not take into account any formal aspect of the movies' style. Zanger only dwells on the films' narrative grammar, including a wide range of elements adding to each mytheme: in Joan's case, they are 'voices, the mission, the obstacles on the way to achievement, a change of dress, shaving the head (optional), success, interrogation, betrayal, death by fire and recognition (limited) after death' (Zanger 2007: 111). This lack of aesthetic concern distinguishes secret remakes from ritualistic and disguised ones, highlighting one of the former's traits: a secret remake always involves the minute details of a film in particular and does not follow the constitutive mythemes of a character through each of its screen incarnations, but rather the symbolic and stylistic variations of a unique figure. The secret remake is a specific narrative actually embodied in striking images and not a virtual contour surrounding a well-known mythical figure. It rests upon an acute familiarity, even a fetish, with films. In this respect, my hypothesis is that it stands grounded in the cinephilic approach which stemmed from the Nouvelle Vague in the 1950s and spread around the world as a European perspective, especially since it opposed the so-called low-brow Americans who failed to see Hitchcock and Hawks as the *auteurs* they were according to the young critics at *Les Cahiers du cinéma* (de Baecque 2003).

This film fetish depended on the way in which films were ritually screened, without the possibility of pausing, rewinding, or fast-forwarding the playback. The slipping away of the film as it was screened intensified the desire to possess its plot and shots, if only by memory and imagination, by watching it over and over, each time in its entirety. It explained the very precise knowledge which these eager spectators, soon to be directors, had of an author's style, to the point of summarising his *mise-en-scène* in a single figure, a 'form organising the narrative,' such as Hitchcock's helix according to Rohmer (de Baecque 2003: 17–18). That's why the *jeunes turcs* worshipped Henri Langlois at the *Cinémathèque française* as a potent master of ceremonies sharpening their gaze with every projection, exposing them, like celluloid, to the marks of light, shadow, lasting emotions and deep affects, making them watch movies like smugglers in the dark, bringing their own free associations into the theatre, making them become their own projector by double-exposing every film with many others according to intuitive and sometimes far-fetched family resemblances. For the young Truffaut, as we have seen before regarding the back-to-back screenings of *Paradise Lost* in the continuously running cinema *Le Champo* during the German occupation, the impact of cinema was even greater, encapsulating both the fear and the joy of the movie and of real life. *The Green Room* thus embodies a cinephilic fervour based on the model of the mourning ritual already present in Gance's film. In the dual sense of cinematic apparatus and psychic process, projection is therefore paramount in the creation of a secret remake, as a way of watching films, catching the fluttering glimpse of a virtual *air de famille* without realising that it precisely points out a blind spot, latent trauma, or unaddressed suffering, since according to Freud projection is a defence mechanism denying the existence of unconscious thoughts potentially harmful to the self by attributing them to others. Finally, in its less precise psychological sense of loose associations, projection also explains why, despite all evidence, the fleeting impression of resemblance between two films can indeed eventually be supported by further investigations, or even something of a confirmation bias.

With respect to *The Green Room*, this denial process regarding the film source and the traumatic first encounter with it rests on a literary red herring, since Truffaut claims to have woven various themes by Henry James into a movie. Projection also comes down to what one chooses to consider or ignore in a movie, especially if it is derived from a previous novel behind which the virtual film source can hide. Two final cases – from European and American backgrounds, respectively – can shed light on the relationship between secret remakes and book adaptations as sources or decoys. Kubrick's *Eyes Wide Shut* (1999), officially presented as an adaptation of Schnitzler's *The Traumnovelle*

(1926), was nevertheless considered by Gaspard Delon (2015: 187–99) a secret remake of Kieslowski's *Dekalog: Three* (988). However, Fincher's *Fight Club* (1999), derived from the story by Chuck Palahniuk (1996), only bears resemblance to the famous reflexive motives in Bergman's *Persona* (1966). For one thing, the novel itself was its unconfessed rewriting, first transposing the schizophrenia from a feminine, intimate point of view to a male, political one, then characterising one of its protagonists as a projectionist. Secondly, Fincher, obviously aware of the nod, chose to deepen the *mise-en-abyme* and to punctuate his own film with several allusions to the emblematic plot linking cinematic and psychological projection. For example, Fincher added cigarette marks on the celluloid, as projectionists do to know when to change reels, and he included an almost subliminal shot of an erect penis, as in Bergman's uncensored opening scene. It seems to me that there are two ways to account for these close yet different cases. On one hand, Kubrick's could easily qualify as a secret remake given its uncanny resemblance, both diegetic and figurative, to the impressive arthouse Polish television drama. This is all the more so as it was actually unnoticed except by one scholar, whereas Fincher's rather obvious transposition would fall within postmodern cinema considered as a playful, self-conscious thrill ride of sensations to be 'recognise[d] and enjoy[ed]' (Jullier 1997: 7). On the other hand, flagrancy notwithstanding, there is no denying that in *Fight Club*, book and film alike, the disguising of the figure of *Persona* follows the basic guidelines of secret remakes, including trauma and unconscious processes. According to this second argument, both *Eyes Wide Shut* and *Fight Club* should be considered secret remakes, but their different degrees of 'secrecy' would then be related to their European or American context. A European secret remake such as Kubrick's would appear more twisted, perhaps more unconscious and hidden, whereas an American one tends to show off, which in a way thwarts its very purpose and makes it more of a post-modern eruption of references.

CONCLUSION

To sum up, even if there can be American or Asian ones, secret remakes seem to arise from a European perspective on film, from the Deleuzian time-image to superimposing films upon films in the 'museum without walls' that is a cinephilic memory. Secret remakes thrive in an auteurist visual culture spawned from the 1950s in France and based on the ritual ceremony of projection, in which, according to the complementary meanings of the term, films are taken in, appropriated and modified depending on one's unconscious. But one can also argue that secret remakes seem to have multiplied as new technologies for viewing films have developed and allowed viewers to delve much deeper into their frames, relying not on projection in theatres, but on the rewinding and pausing of the VCR and now the digital-era ATAWAD mindset (Any Time, Any Where,

Any Device) (Gaudreault and Marion 2013: 192–297). While movie theatres provided the strong but fleeting impression that urges a filmmaker to remake a film with all the variations that his shell-shocked memory could create in order not to look it in the eye, so to speak, digital sampling enables viewers to dwell on their obsession for a movie, to repeat its impact on demand and even to quote or re-enact some details exactly. It would then appear that filming a secret remake relies on both an impacted and somewhat fuzzy memory, whereas spotting one benefits from the knowledge tool and control mechanism of freezing the frame. Both cases nevertheless involve projection in either sense of the word, as well as 'movie-made' filmmakers and spectators whose lives have been shaped by film viewing. These two groups tend to meet in yet another film sub-category, thus blurring the boundaries between the American and European contexts, even more so in an age when images are circulating at high speed and embodied by such film buffs as Lynch or Tarantino, both obsessed with repetition as form and as psychological process. A film secretly remaking itself, split in the middle, its second part restaging its first according to the dream- or filmwork and disguising the same seminal obsessions by hybridising with figures from different movies – for instance Wilder's *Sunset Boulevard* (1950) in Lynch's *Mulholland Drive* (2001), or Antonioni's *Zabriskie Point* (1970) and Sarafian's *Vanishing Point* (1971) in Tarantino's *Death Proof* (2007) (Aubron 2015: 55–74), two more films ruled by 'a narrative logic of [the moving image as] commodity based on loss and substitution' (Prouty 1996: 3) – is precisely the universal core of secret remakes.

NOTE

* My deepest gratitude goes to Daniel Morgan (University of Chicago, University of Paris Sorbonne Nouvelle) who proofread this text.

REFERENCES

Altman, R. (1999), *Film/Genre*, Bloomington: Indiana University Press and BFI Publishing.
Aubron, H. (2005), 'Tropical Drive, Mulholland Malady: Trafic d'âmes entre Lynch et Weerasethakul', *Vertigo*, 1: 27, 4–13.
Aubron, H. (2015), 'Les répliques d'une explosion (carambolages et *remake* de soi dans *Death Proof* de Quentin Tarantino)', *CiNéMAS*, 25: 2–3, 55–74.
De Baecque, A. (2003), *La Cinéphilie: Invention d'un regard, histoire d'une culture*, Paris: Fayard.
Brashinsky, M. (1998), 'The Spring, Defiled: Ingmar Bergman's *Virgin Spring* and Wes Craven's *Last House on the Left*', in A. Horton and S. Y. McDougal (eds), *Play It Again, Sam: Retakes on Remakes*, Berkeley: University of California Press, pp. 162–71.
Buiré, J.-F. (2005), 'Hypothèse de film nop: *Mr Klein* et *La Mort aux trousses*', *Cinéma* 10, 87–97.
Cerisuelo, M. (2015), 'Remake secret et univers multiples', *CiNéMAS*, 25: 2–3, 119–37.
Deleuze, G. (1985), *L'Image-Temps*, Paris: Editions de Minuit.

Delon, G. (2015), 'Échange de regards: Schnitzler, Kubrick et Kieslowski', *La Licorne*, 116, 187–99.
Dusi, N (2012), 'Remake as a Practice: Some Problems of Transmediality', *Cinéma & Cie*, 12: 18, 113–28.
Druxman, M. B. (1975), *Make It Again, Sam: A Survey of Movie Remakes*, Cranbury, NJ: A. S. Barnes.
Gaudreault, A. and Marion P. (2013), *La Fin du cinéma? Un média en crise à l'ère numérique*, Paris: Armand Colin.
Greenberg, H. R. (1991), 'Raiders of the Lost Text: Remaking as Contested Homage in *Always*', *Journal of Popular Film and Television*, 18: 14, 164–71.
Jullier, L. (1997), *L'Ecran post-moderne: Un cinéma de l'allusion et du feu d'artifice*, Paris: L'Harmattan.
Kundera, M. (1988), 'Kafka's World', *The Wilson Quarterly*, 12: 5, 88–99.
Kuntzel, T. (1975), 'Le travail du film 2', *Communications*, 23, 136–89.
Lefebvre, M. (1997), *Psycho: de la figure au musée imaginaire: Théorie et pratique de l'acte de spectature*, Paris: L'Harmattan.
Leitch, T. M. (1990), 'Twice-Told Tales: The Rhetoric of the Remake', *Literature/Film Quarterly*, 18: 3, 138–49.
Martin, M. (2007), 'D'un double triptyque: Antonioni/Argento/Greenaway, Cinéma/Peinture/Photographie', *Ligeia*, 77–80, 158–68.
Martin, M. (2009), 'Greenaway avec Starobinski: Le XVIIIe siècle comme espace de résonances imaginaires dans *Meurtre dans un jardin anglais*', in M. Poirson and L. Schifano (eds), *L'Écran des Lumières*, Oxford: SVEC, pp. 133–43.
Martin, M. (2012), 'La poétique du rêve du point de vue d'une théorie des effets: Autour d'une configuration originaire', in M. Martin and L. Schifano (eds), *Rêve et noppo: Mouvances théoriques autour d'un champ créatif*, Nanterre: Presses Universitaires de Paris Ouest, pp. 73–75.
Martin, M. (2014), 'Rêve dans un jardin français: *La Femme de l'aviateur* et *Blow up*', in S. Robic and L. Schifano (eds), *Rohmer en perspectives*, Nanterre: Presses Universitaires de Paris Ouest, pp. 261–76.
Martin, M. (2015), 'Le remake secret: Généalogies et perspectives d'une fiction théorique', *CiNéMAS*, 25: 2–3, pp. 13–32.
Martin, M. and Véray, L. (2015), '*La chambre verte* (1977) de François Truffaut, remake secret de *Paradis perdu* (1938) d'Abel Gance: Du culte des morts à celui du cinéma', *CiNéMAS*, 25: 2–3, 75–95.
Mellier, D. (2015), 'Figure(s) de sang: Amours nopport, troubles fratries et *miscegenation* dans *The Searchers* (Ford, 1956), *The Unforgiven* (Huston, 1960) et *The Missing* (Howard, 2002)', *CiNéMAS*, 25: 2–3, 33–53.
Moine, R. (2007), *Remakes: Les films français à Hollywood*, Paris: CNRS Editions.
Païni, D. (2009), 'Académique, surréaliste? De l'emploi exagéré, sinon nopportune, de certains qualificatifs', *Trafic*, 71, 14–18.
Prouty, R. (1996), 'The Well-Furnished Interior of the Masses: Kirsanoff's *Ménilmontant* and the Streets of Paris', *Cinema Journal*, 36: 1, 3–17.
Ramos Monteiro, L. (2015), 'Remaking a European, Post-Catastrophic Atmosphere in 2000s China: Jia Zhangke's Still Life, Iconology and Ruins', *CiNéMAS*, 25: 2–3, 97–117.
Stam, R. (2000), 'Beyond Fidelity: The Dialogics of Adaptation', in J. Naremore (ed.), *Film Adaptation*, New Brunswick, NJ: Rutgers University Press, pp. 54–76.
Verevis, C. (2006), *Film Remakes*, Edinburgh: Edinburgh University Press.
Zanger, A. (2006), *Film Remakes as Ritual and Disguise*, Amsterdam: Amsterdam University Press.

CHAPTER 3

From 'Mini-Remake' to Open-Ended Coda: How to Make a 'Proper' Homage

Peter Verstraten

In his 'Twice-Told Tales', Thomas Leitch (2002) makes the oft-cited distinction between film homage and 'true remake'. The latter seeks to displace an earlier film version of a similar story; the new film 'takes pains to deny any explicit borrowing' from the older one, in an attempt to show itself off as 'more authentic' (2002: 52). According to Leitch (2002: 53), a film such as Lawrence Kasdan's *Body Heat* (1981) both invokes and denies Billy Wilder's *Double Indemnity* (1944) by pretending that it includes scenes that were too risqué for the sexually repressed era of the 1940s. Kasdan's film offers itself as the definitive version of a familiar film 'that renders its model obsolete'. The (slightly preposterous) tagline of a 'true remake' would run as follows: forget about the 'original', for the copy is superior.

By contrast, the homage renounces 'any claim to be better' (Leitch 2002: 49). Its primary purpose is to pay tribute to earlier films 'which are in danger of being ignored or forgotten' (2002: 47). Leitch cites the example of Werner Herzog's *Nosferatu, the Vampyre* (*Nosferatu: Phantom der Nacht*, 1979), which copies the visual design and stylistic traits of F. W. Murnau's *Nosferatu: A Symphony of Horror* (*Nosferatu, eine Symphonie des Grauens*, 1922) in order to honour what Herzog himself described as 'the most visionary film in all of German cinema'. Moreover, the fact that Herzog's restaging of the vampire myth is not called *Dracula*, after Bram Stoker's novel, but adopts the title of *Nosferatu* is further proof of reverence for Murnau's achievement. And even though Lloyd Michaels points out several crucial alterations, including a much more subversive ending, it is clear to him that Herzog 'has apparently conceived every moment with Murnau's original in mind' (1998: 69).

The most obvious and notorious case of a director's intense admiration for a precursor film is Gus Van Sant's almost frame-by-frame 1998 remake of

Alfred Hitchcock's classic *Psycho* (1960). Unlike the 'true remake', which aims to marginalise the earlier film, Van Sant's *Psycho* is a constant reminder of the existence of the original version and thus a textbook example of an homage. Because of Van Sant's penchant for textual fidelity, the release has spurred a debate over the (few) pros and (many) cons of a close remake. One of the predictable complaints is that the new *Psycho* was only a superfluous exercise: the film only demonstrated the 'technical mastery of a style' and did not create anything new (Leitch 2003: 250). Another one is that all the (small) differences between remake and original were 'bad choices' (Naremore 1999–2000: 10), turning Van Sant's *Psycho* into 'Hitchcock Minus' (Leitch 2003: 254).[1] If the 1998 version has added any value, the sceptics seemed to agree, it is that nothing compares to the genius of Hitchcock. Moreover, Leitch claims that Van Sant's copycat film is inescapably situated in 'a historical limbo' between the 1960s and the late 1990s (2003: 251): It is possible to ask actors to make the same gestures, speak the same lines and so on, but cars, clothes and buildings have become different over a period of almost forty years. If the new film copies such objects, it remains true to the original (in textual terms), but at the same time it immediately reveals itself as a retro movie and not a contemporary picture (in cultural terms).

Slavoj Žižek agrees that the 'unique flair' of Hitchcock's films evaporates with any standard remake (2004: 257), but his grounds for calling Van Sant's *Psycho* a 'failed masterpiece' are different from Leitch's (2004: 268). Van Sant 'failed' because he added some shots, including 'brutal' ones such as Norman's masturbation, and made changes to Hitchcock's precise framing, whereas he should have delivered an exact imitation in order 'to achieve the uncanny effect of the double' (Žižek 2004: 268). The new *Psycho* would then have shown that a repetition never is a repetition. The copy would have served the purpose of articulating that differences 'would have become all the more palpable' despite, or rather on account of, the sameness: the simple fact of casting a different actress already indicates the shift from 1960 to the late 1990s (2004: 268). For Leitch, Van Sant's experiment was doomed to fall short because of an unsolvable historical dilemma, since textual terms will never equal cultural terms. Žižek, however, reverses this logic: Van Sant's film would have been a success, had it been a rigorous exact copy, because then it would have taught us that sameness marks difference.

To answer the question 'Is there a proper way to remake a Hitchcock film?' Žižek gave the exact copy as a first option. As the second way 'to hono[u]r Hitchcock as an artist belonging to our era' (2004: 268), Žižek mentions that we had better ignored the visual and narrative allusions by a usual suspect such as Brian De Palma – whose *Dressed to Kill* (1980) is hyperbolically replaying parts from *Psycho* – and instead be struck by the 'mini-remake' of the tone and atmosphere from *Psycho* in a scene from Francis Ford Coppola's

The Conversation (1974). The protagonist in *The Conversation* is investigating a hotel room, looking for clues to a crime; when he flushes the toilet, blood and other fluids overflow from the sink. This scene from Coppola's movie unobtrusively recalls several scenes from *Psycho*: Lilah and Sam inspecting the motel room; the shower curtain being pulled open; Marion's car being lifted out of the swamp. Rather than the obvious quotations from Hitchcock by De Palma, the term 'homage' is more apt for equivalents to be 'found in unexpected places', since Coppola is 'certainly not a Hitchcockian', as Žižek postulates (2004: 269).

In his study *Film Remakes*, Constantine Verevis (2006) distinguishes three all-encompassing categories of remake (with several sub-divisions). The examples above, in which Hitchcock's *Psycho* functions as a point of reference, help to illuminate this broad classification. Van Sant's film is closest to the industrial category, because by re-using the same title and recycling the script, it is 'pre-sold' to viewers who have knowledge of the original. The pastiches by De Palma belong to the textual category, since his pictures do not tell the same stories as Hitchcock films, but the intertextual relations are unmistakable. The allusions are sufficiently explicit for a ciné-literate audience. There are no such obvious connections between *Psycho* and Coppola's *The Conversation*, but here it is Žižek who ascribes the status of homage to the latter title. In this case, the remake can be conceived as a critical category of reception: a specific viewer recognizes the film as hidden homage.

Taking the different perspectives of Leitch and Žižek as a lead, I aim to examine the conditions of a 'proper' homage, in three steps. The first two steps oscillate between homage as textual and critical category. In its focus on directors deliberately contributing to the 'practice of canon film formation' (Verevis 2006: 26), the first step is primarily rooted in cinephilia, whereas the second one highlights the strategy of using an admired film as a skeleton for sociopolitical purposes. The third step is strictly concerned with the category of reception, much in the vein of Žižek's attitude to see kinship between two films that seem quite unlike each other. By that reading strategy, the newer film can bring to the fore what has remained latent in an earlier film.

HOMAGES MEDIATED BY EUROPEAN (DEBATES ON) CINEMA

According to Leitch, a cinematic homage can only prosper in a culture that takes film seriously as an art form. Homages were made regularly in Europe with its respected legacy of German Expressionism, Italian neo-realism and French *nouvelle vague*, but in the US they were rare, for Hollywood preferred 'true remakes' outdoing previous versions. Americans had commonly discounted film as 'an ethically and aesthetically suspect medium' (Leitch 2002: 48), until the advent of the first phase of New Hollywood (1967–76). This period refers to the shift in the film industry when a young generation of wayward movie brats (Bob Rafelson, Martin Scorsese, Dennis Hopper and Monte Hellman) were able to take over from the studios which were on the brink of bankruptcy: after several considerable flops, studio executives had become doubtful whether the classic formulas could still garner success. Some of these upcoming filmmakers had attended film school and expressed an avidity for cinema, unprecedented among directors from the classic period. With the release of Peter Bogdanovich's *Targets* (1968), made under the wings of B-moviemaker Roger Corman, the homage emerged 'full-blown' in American cinema (Leitch 2002: 48). A few ingredients of this film suffice to hammer the point home that *Targets* is indeed a cinephiliac endeavour: thanks to his famous roles as movie monster, Boris Karloff plays the guest invited to a screening of Corman's *The Terror* (1963) in a drive-in cinema. Karloff has the name of Byron Orlok, a reference to the vampire from *Nosferatu* whose actual name is Count Orlok. While Orlok muses that his breakthrough *The Criminal Code* (1930), broadcast as a late-night movie on television, proves that he has become a 'museum piece', the young director-in-the-film is watching it in total awe – again, because he had already seen it in the prestigious Museum of Modern Art.

Even though Bogdanovich's films are generally couched in terms of reverence to older pictures, something is slightly bothersome. Discussing the 'question of perfect remakes' in his influential *Simulacra and Simulation*, French philosopher Jean Baudrillard qualifies several historical films from the 1970s – such as Bogdanovich's *The Last Picture Show* (1971), Roman Polanski's *Chinatown* (1974) and Stanley Kubrick's *Barry Lyndon* (1975) – as 'disquieting' in their 'very perfection'. These films are immaculate period pieces, but do not let that fool the viewer, so Baudrillard cautions. *The Last Picture Show* remakes 'the atmosphere of the American small town' in the vein of John Ford Westerns,[2] but it is not an original production from the 1950s, for one can sense, as Baudrillard notes, that it is 'a little too good'. Bogdanovich's picture does not offer us the 1950s, but a polished screen image, a 'hyperreal restitution' of the cinema of that era (1994: 45). This brings us to the caveat that, if the point of an homage is to adore 'original' films, is there not always already the risk of surpassing the sources of inspiration? Enchanted by *A Guy Named Joe* (1943) since his adolescence, Steven Spielberg had been eager to remake it, but, as Harvey R. Greenberg argues in his analysis of Spielberg's *Always* (1989), an 'intensely rivalrous spirit' inhabits this 'homage' (1998: 119). Reading Spielberg's biography, Greenberg concludes that his life has been marked by competition with (idealised) father figures. Upon remaking a film by one of his favourite directors, Spielberg is 'simultaneously worshipful and envious' of Fleming (1998: 125). *Always* can be considered a 'contested homage', for Spielberg had wished to both 'honour and eclipse' *A Guy Named Joe* (1998: 126).

If Greenberg attributes a 'dark side' to Spielberg's homage (1998: 120), this is probably due to the fact that *Always*, rooted in Oedipal desires, is predominantly meant to bring a happy childhood memory to life. Although Bogdanovich and other cinephiles are liable to touches of self-promotion as privileged film lovers, the emphasis is slightly different, nonetheless. Bogdanovich's enthusiasm for Hawks, John Ford, Orson Welles and Samuel Fuller is mediated by 'The French Connection', a term coined by Thomas Elsaesser (2004: 45) to describe the New Hollywood affinity with and appreciation for both French critical writing and French cinema. In the late 1950s, the critics of *Cahiers du cinéma* who later became film directors (Jean-Luc Godard, François Truffaut, Jacques Rivette) celebrated many American filmmakers as '*auteur*'. Directors such as Hitchcock, Hawks, Ford, Fuller, Anthony Mann and Nicholas Ray made genre movies, but in the eyes of the French critics their entertaining stories had an artistic appeal. These genre films were marked by a distinctive stylishness: it was possible to recognize their pictures on the basis of thematic preoccupations and, preferably, their *mise-en-scène*. Bogdanovich is a kindred spirit of these French critics: encouraged by their reviews, he appreciates the classic American film directors for their signature style. *Targets* is one of the first films to import French auteurist ideas into (New) Hollywood, and under the influence of the *nouvelle vague* a cinephilia was introduced, which enabled the emergence of the homage in American cinema. Subsequent films by Bogdanovich, such as the above-mentioned *The Last Picture Show*, *What's Up, Doc?* (1972), an ode to Hawks' *Bringing Up Baby* (1938), the oddest of comedies, and *Paper Moon* (1973) confirmed the tendency.

While Bogdanovich's homages were predominantly triggered by European debates on cinema, both Paul Schrader and Martin Scorsese – who collaborated on the New Hollywood film *Taxi Driver* (1976) as screenwriter and director, respectively – are also known as aficionados of cinema, including the work of many European art filmmakers. *Taxi Driver* is one of a number of 1970s films that takes John Ford's *The Searchers* (1956) as its *ur*-text.[3] The narrative skeleton of a restless Civil War veteran who wants to rescue his niece from a Native-American tribe is used for the story of an 'honourably discharged US Marine' (so he says) who wants to rescue a young girl from her pimp. Schrader himself noted a 'tension' in *Taxi Driver* (quoted in Taubin 2012: 23): He himself wrote an 'austere' script, with allusions to the transcendental style of his favourite director Robert Bresson, but Scorsese 'directed in an expressionist way' by using the jump-cut strategies of Godard, the *temps mort* of Michelangelo Antonioni and the 'brutal honesty' of early Rainer Werner Fassbinder films.[4] *Taxi Driver* was not the film Schrader had in mind, but he admitted that his Calvinist austerity and Scorsese's Catholic expressionism happened to create a wonderful synthesis. This mixture gives the film its 'ambiguity of meaning', so that the protagonist remains 'largely a c[y]pher' throughout the movie (Taubin 2012: 24). Due to its myriad influences, *Taxi Driver* could easily have been subjected to the criticism that it is an eclectic hodgepodge, or that it is merely trying to appropriate the aura of the quoted directors, but the film is exempted from such charges because its themes are conveyed, not through character or narrative, but through *mise-en-scène* (Taubin 2012: 24). Because *mise-en-scène* was the cinephiliac criterion par excellence for the French critics, *Taxi Driver* can be said to answer to the condition of a film homage: it is a dedicated accolade to cinema as such and to the discourse of European 'art' cinema and its critical standards in particular.[5]

AN INTERNAL REMAKE RESULTING IN RE-APPRECIATION

In his 'The Future of Allusion', Noël Carroll calls Spielberg's blockbuster *Raiders of the Lost Ark* (1981) an 'homage duly paid to the very source of charm' in the original adventure sagas. However, he argues that there is an aesthetic risk in the 'filmmaker's reverie on the glorious old days'. Ultimately, *Raiders of the Lost Ark* becomes a depiction of 'paradise regained' (1982: 62–63), whereas reminiscences in New Hollywood movies are embedded in either an ironic context – such as *Catch-22* (Mike Nichols, 1970) or *The Long Goodbye* (Robert Altman, 1973) – and/or a social-critical one – deranged ex-veterans in *Targets* and *Taxi Driver*, as well as paranoia in *The Conversation* and, once again, *Taxi Driver*. Adjacent to these 'homages' is the type of film that takes socio-political circumstances as its starting point and grafts its narrative onto an already existing picture.

The clearest example of such a political 'homage' is perhaps Rainer Werner Fassbinder's *Ali: Fear Eats the Soul* (*Angst Essen Seele Auf*, 1974). Even though Douglas Sirk's American melodrama *All that Heaven Allows* (1955) is not credited, every publication on Fassbinder's film mentions it as a source of inspiration, all the more since Fassbinder had expressed in an elaborate essay his admiration for Sirk's cinema. *All that Heaven Allows* is about a middle-aged, suburban widow whose love affair with a young gardener is met with hostility from her high-society surroundings. Because of the major alterations in character, time and setting, *Ali: Fear Eats the Soul* can be regarded as a transformed remake that turns Sirk's melodrama into an indictment of racial prejudices in the petty climate of 1970s Munich, Germany. Salomé Skvirsky even describes the first part of the film as a 'disavowal' of *All that Heaven Allows*, for Fassbinder makes manifest what is absent in Sirk's melodrama: 'the urban space, the working class, and the racial minority' (2008: 98). In *Ali: Fear Eats the Soul*, the sixty-something German cleaning woman Emmi falls in love with the much younger 'Ali', a migrant worker of Moroccan descent. They soon have their wedding ceremony, without any guests. After the wedding, Emmi introduces Ali to her own adult children, who are all very much displeased about their mother's new husband. Worse, with Ali by her side, Emmi is socially rejected by her neighbours and co-workers. Both Emmi and Ali are crestfallen because of the condescending looks cast upon them as a couple, but Emmi does not lose her optimism. In an outdoor café, without any other guests around, Emmi says that they should go on 'vacation', and she predicts that upon their return everyone will be nice to them. Just as the gardener's fall from a snowy hill is a crucial narrative and temporal 'break' in *All that Heaven Allows*, the vacation itself, albeit elided, is a fundamental rupture in Fassbinder's film.

Skvirsky regards the final third as an 'internal remake' of the first hour (2008: 102). Scenes structurally repeat themselves, but with a different response: initially people had acted angrily, but now they approach Emmi in a friendly manner. Their change in attitude is motivated by self-interest, however: her son Bruno needs his mother to babysit his daughter; her co-workers want Emmi to support a petition for a raise; a neighbour hopes to get her storage space; the grocer does not want to lose her as a customer. The nice attitude of Emmi's environment is only pretence, concealing the meanness underneath. She may erroneously believe that the situation has improved, but the goodwill is only superficial; hence, there is neither progress nor moral awakening, as Skvirsky succinctly notes. One of the merits of the last part is that it illustrates how a capitalist logic rules over principles. Another strength is Fassbinder's anti-identity politics stance: underdogs and outcasts who have been treated badly have the right 'to be as mean, inhuman and evil as anyone else' (Elsaesser, 1996: 30). In the first hour, Emmi and Ali are oppressed by short-sighted people, but in the final third the oppression also comes 'from within', as Chris Fujiwara claims. At work, Emmi was excluded from socialising with her co-workers after she started the relationship with Ali, but once a new worker from Herzegovina arrives, she becomes the next scapegoat, and Emmi joins her colleagues in victimising the guest worker. Later, several female colleagues visit Emmi's place, and Emmi is proud to present her husband Ali as an exotic object on display, who is being admired for his 'soft skin'. Emmi also has the habit of talking about Ali in the third person, even in his presence. After this embarrassing exposure, it is clear to Ali that it is not just the two of them against society, but that there is also an 'imbalance of power' among the two (Fujiwara 2014). Ali had already been seeking the comfort of a female pub owner who made him couscous and expected sex in return. Ali's position is as disadvantaged as it had been before: initially, he was rejected together with Emmi, but now he is fetishised, among others by Emmi (Skvirsky 2008: 102). He starts drinking and gambling; in the end, he suffers from a perforated stomach ulcer. Recovering in a hospital, the doctor predicts that Ali will return to the hospital within six months, if the stress, as the cause of his medical problem, will not decrease. Emmi, in tears, holds Ali's hand at his bedside.

While Verevis categorises *Ali: Fear Eats the Soul* as homage (2006: 13), Skvirsky questions this label; according to her, Fassbinder's film only applies 'certain of Sirk's insights to Fassbinder's own, more radical project' (2008: 115). Fassbinder's 'political' film about the urban working class in Munich, so Skvirsky proposes, is too much unlike Sirk's 'moralistic' picture about the suburban upper class in Connecticut, and this difference can be emphasised by pointing at several formal and practical oppositions between Sirk's *All that Heaven Allows* and Fassbinder's reimaging: ample use of extra-diegetic music versus mainly diegetic music from a jukebox; bright colours versus washed-out tones (with a few splashes of red and blue); theatrical performances versus down-to-earth acting; studio shooting versus actual locations. Despite these differences, Sirk's impact on Fassbinder 'cannot be overestimated', as Vance Comeau asserts (2006: 39). In a laudatory essay from 1972, Fassbinder wrote that Sirk's films are descriptive with very few close-ups. *All that Heaven Allows* shows that '[p]eople can't live alone, but they can't live together either'. The atmosphere is 'desperate', but this 'intense feeling' is a result of 'montage and music', of paying attention to 'armchairs and glasses', for 'in Sirk, people are always placed in rooms already heavily marked by their social situation'. Fassbinder learned from watching Sirk how to use *mise-en-scène* to 'tell stories of people caught up in circumstances beyond their control' (Comeau 2006: 38). Fassbinder was greatly impressed by Sirk's custom of meticulously framing his characters when they experience a situation as awkward: they are positioned behind windows, bedposts, or the lattice work of stairways, before mirrors, amid porcelain, and so on, in order to express that they feel trapped. Fassbinder not only copied this trademark, but at times even exaggerated it. When Ali feels depressed and miserable, Fassbinder shows him sitting on the bed in a shot framed by the doorway, just like Sirk would have done. A few moments later, Fassbinder repeats the shot, but this time the camera is almost at the very end of the corridor, hence doubling the framing.

Although Fassbinder very heavily drew on Sirk's tropes of confinement, the 'ideological commentary is never veiled', as it was in Sirk's cinema (Comeau 2006: 55). Sirk made his melodramas in a period determined by the restrictions of the Production Code, at a time when he was expected to produce 'ostensibly light fare for an undiscerning audience' (ibid.). By using Sirk's framing devices, Fassbinder's update not only succeeded as a political commentary on Germany, but it also revealed that there is critical potential in Sirk's use of *mise-en-scène*. On the surface, *All that Heaven Allows* is an entertaining 'weepie'; however, if one focuses on formal devices, a vehement critique of the social veneer can be read between the lines. Upon closer inspection, it becomes clear that this

American suburb is, to quote Fassbinder, 'the last place in the world I would want to go'.

The 'true remake', as mentioned above, aims to surpass the original. A film such as *The Talented Mr. Ripley* (Anthony Minghella, 1999) adds the theme of 'repressed homosexual desires' to both Patricia Highsmith's novel by the same title (1955) and its adaptation *Purple Noon* (*Plein Soleil*, 1960) by René Clément. The 'original' Tom Ripley is a cold and calculating protagonist who experiences no inner turmoil after killing. Minghella's 'true remake', however, tries to 'fill the void' and suggests that Ripley's crimes and misdemeanours are the result of 'psychic traumas' (Žižek 2003: 14). This attempt to humanise Ripley is at odds with Highsmith's novel as well as Clément's adaptation. *Ali: Fear Eats the Soul* has the opposite effect. It articulates narrative aspects that are suppressed in Sirk's melodrama; it either downplayed formal principles (for instance, no lavish interiors, but barren ones) or exaggerated them (double framing), but it did not do so for the sake of eclipsing the 'original'. On the contrary, *Ali: Fear Eats the Soul* has made us see *All that Heaven Allows* anew. Mediated by Fassbinder's refashioning, film scholars came to see the relevance of camera angles, shot compositions, lighting and colour in Sirk's cinema. In the early 1970s, the attitude towards Sirk's films shifted from naive identification to ironic detachment; consequently, the status of his melodramas was transformed. At first derogatorily called 'tear-jerkers', Fassbinder's intervention helped to reread Sirk's films as an extremely critical vision of bourgeois life in small-town America. Fassbinder's reimaging did what should be expected from an homage: it functioned as a catalyst for re-appreciating the 'original'.

UNLIKELY SOUL MATES

If the melodramatic genre had a derivative status in the 1950s and was called 'tear-jerker', Fassbinder contributed to tipping the scales from gratuitous emotion to critical excess. In the wake of his praise for Sirk, many film scholars, especially feminist ones, argued that melodramas were steeped in Brechtian alienation and ironic artificiality rather than sentimentality and pathos. From this perspective, it is relevant to consider here Agnès Varda's *Happiness* (*Le Bonheur*, 1965), for her take on melodrama has divided critics over the years, and it has become Varda's most misunderstood picture. Initially, *Happiness* was disparaged for its seemingly anti-feminist themes (DeRoo 2008: 148). It was considered a disappointment that the two female protagonists meet a sorry fate. Thérèse fulfils the social function of dutiful housewife; yet, instead of showing her gratitude for her sacrifice, her husband François tells her during a picnic in a forest that he loves another woman. When François and the two young children wake up from their afternoon nap, Thérèse is gone. She is found at the bottom of a pond. The mistress Emilie claims that she is happy and free and not of the marrying kind, but she accepts François' proposal after only two months of mourning. Because the housewife dies and the independent woman is domesticated, early critics such as Claire Johnson lamented that *Happiness* perpetuates the conventions of femininity.

However, later critics who emphasised style rather than narrative structure argued that Varda's film subverts and challenges a consumerist-driven bourgeoisie. The colours, such as yellow and pink, are so overtly bright and stylised in their allusion to Pop Art images that their effect is unsettling. Moreover, the palette of autumn colours that matches Emilie's clothing in the closing scene connotes death and dying (Giachetti 2017: 95). In the beginning François walks with his wife Thérèse and his two children in the woods; at the end he does so again, except that Thérèse has been replaced by Emilie. The cyclical plot structure does not suggest a fortunate ending, but rather that the new couple will live 'unhappily ever after'. According to Rebecca J. DeRoo, the visual irony of *Happiness* 'dismantles the sentimental storyline' (2008: 191). She notes that many images echo contemporary advertisements, but the staccato editing and monotonous presentation of household work in Varda's film undermine the glamorous effect propagated by women's magazines. Since the film itself lacks a clear reading guide, and since Varda herself only gave conflicting clues, the favourable judgements were based on the critic's willingness to see the discord between exuberant style and bleak content. The characters remain opaque, and the key question is open to speculation: was Thérèse's death an accident, or was it suicide? As François lifts her body onto firm ground, it seems that her hand 'grabs for a branch, suggesting either her fear or realisation of a mistake made' (Horner 2018: 148). Hence, the film's opacity, as well as its use of highly saturated colours, is emphasised to qualify *Happiness* as alienating as a Sirk film, in a post-*Ali* period.

Žižek's argues that proper remakes of Hitchcock are to be 'found in unexpected places'. He preferred (a scene from) *The Conversation* by non-Hitchcockian Coppola as an implicit homage over any of the direct homages by Hitchcockian De Palma. Similarly, Fassbinder and Sirk turned out to be unlikely soul mates, as I have tried to explain. They are unlikely, because their tones are quite dissimilar, but their kinship is established by the fact that Fassbinder made explicit what was implicit in Sirk. To follow up on this aspect, I would like to introduce a film that solicits a comparison to *Happiness* because of a close parallel in plot. Even though the approaches differ considerably, I will argue that the tones of the two films turn out to be similar.

At the beginning of Valeska Grisebach's *Longing* (*Sehnsucht*, 2006), Markus offers first aid to the victim of a car crash. When it is rumoured that the accident was a possible suicide attempt, Markus is confused, for he thinks he was playing fate: 'I messed up the man's plan'. We then learn that Markus, a locksmith by profession, is a dedicated member of the voluntary fire brigade of a tiny village. His marriage to his first love Ella has so far remained childless. A young nephew regularly visits their place, which indicates that they like children. During a training weekend for firefighters, he meets the waitress Rose. They sleep with each other, but after a couple of encounters he breaks off the affair. When telling this news to Rose, she falls three floors from the balcony of a hotel room. The camera is too close, however, to show whether she jumped out of despair or whether it was an accident. Because of the incident, Ella hears about the romance and leaves him. We then see Markus working in his shed; after caressing a rabbit, he fires his gun.

Several analogies between *Longing* and *Happiness* are obvious. Both films concern a love triangle between a working-class man and two women, told in chronological fashion. There are three apparent suicide attempts, but they could also be accidents. In Varda's case, however, the wife is dead; in Grisebach's case, the husband and his mistress end up in the hospital. Like in *Happiness*, a cause-and-effect logic in *Longing* is missing. Does the accident in the beginning have a bearing on Markus? Why does Ella suddenly cry during a choir rehearsal? Minutes of screen time are devoted to the firefighters' ball, but we do not see any particular contact between Rose and Markus. Did Rose approach Markus, or did he take the initiative? Does he end the romance because he suffers from a guilty conscience? These questions are for the viewer to decide, for Markus remains a closed book (Mukhida 2015: 182). Apart from a similar narrative structure, *Longing* shares a lack of transparency with *Happiness*; yet, once we start to read these two films back-to-back, it becomes particularly striking that their reception has been so different.

There was an overall tendency to interpret Varda's 1965 film according to a yardstick of gender inequality. If the title were taken literally, it could only refer to the husband's happiness. If one, however, chooses to read *Happiness* in an ironic fashion, encouraged by the luxuriant film style, then the husband becomes a potential target of scorn. François is then blamed for his self-absorption: he fails to see that his happiness is at the expense of his beloved, with the serious risk that history will repeat itself. As Linda Hutcheon has explained, irony is neither the said nor the unsaid, but it is both at the same time. Or, in her phrasing, irony 'happens' in 'the space *between* (and including) the said and the unsaid' (1994: 12). Since irony is attributed to a text by an interpreter, it is up to the readers/viewers to determine their evaluative attitude. For viewers for whom the said speaks louder than the unsaid, *Happiness* will perhaps appear as neo-conservative. For those viewers who take an ironic perspective, however, the critical tone in *Happiness* can shift from subtle and teasing to even vehement and harsh.

In comparison to Varda's film with its meticulous framing and vibrant colours, Grisebach has shot her romantic love story in an unromantic and un-melodramatic way. Apart from a few precise and tableau-like images,

Longing has a colloquial style, characterised by a quasi-documentary feel, naturalistic staging and muted tones (Mukhida 2015: 173–75). Grisebach's film has not been subjected to feminist debates to the same extent as *Happiness*. This leniency could be due to Varda's fame as the most prolific female filmmaker in the influential *nouvelle vague*; it could also be because feminist criticism is no longer as fierce as in the 1970s and 1980s. Or, as I would suggest, *Happiness* is the type of film that, instigated by its title, provokes us to judge the characters, for happiness seems an exclusively male affair. Shot in a colloquial style, *Longing* takes a non-judgmental stance in comparison, partly owing to a more inclusive title. Markus and Rose are obviously 'longing', but is the departure of Markus' wife Ella not also a consequence of her desire to 'feel real love', to paraphrase Robbie Williams' song to which Markus dances in a trance during the firefighters' ball? Regardless of this question and despite the ellipses in Grisebach's narrative, the audience of *Longing* is not as confused about their viewing attitude as the spectators of *Happiness*, with its melodramatic style bordering on irony. This adds a more reflexive dimension to Varda's film, which seems to be missing from Grisebach's more pared-down variant of the love triangle.

However, here comes the catch: *Longing* has a four-minute-long epilogue in the form of a children's game. A girl is surrounded by other children hanging out at a playground, and she starts to tell the entire story of the film so far. The response by the children is diverse: one of them calls the actions stupid, another courageous, a third terribly romantic. The girl then reveals that the man survives and asks her listeners: 'Guess with whom he is living right now?' Some children think he lives with the mistress, others guess it is with the wife. The girl smiles, but no answer is given. *Longing* has not only an open ending but, owing to this epilogue the film also explicitly reflects on the phenomenon of open-ended narratives. On account of these concluding moments, the viewer of *Longing* is caught in a position of hesitation. And for the very reason that the film includes this unconventional four-minute coda, I take Grisebach's *Longing* as an unacknowledged homage to Varda's film. They are both exercises in interpretation, the one in terms of style, the other regarding the story outcome.

CONCLUSION

In the majority of cases presented in this chapter, it is quite uncontested that the filmmakers pay homage to cinematic predecessors: Bogdanovich to Hawks and Welles; Scorsese to Ford and Bresson; Fassbinder to Sirk. Regarding Grisebach's film, however, the analysis resonates with Marie Martin's notion of the 'secret remake,' as discussed in this volume. A 'secret remake' differs greatly from an earlier film, but it nonetheless bears an uncanny resemblance to some parts of it. Since the familiarity is hidden, it requires a critical viewer who, quoting Martin, 'brings out its repressed traumatic quality.' Žižek refers to the chilling moment in Coppola's *The Conversation* when the toilet sink produces blood and other fluids as the clue of a possible murder that the protagonist has not been able to prevent. This scene, which Martin might qualify as a 'disguised re-enactment of latent trauma,' is key for Žižek in recognizing the scene from *The Conversation* as a proper 'mini-remake' of the uncanny tone and atmosphere in *Psycho*. Considering Žižek's preoccupation with (Lacanian) psychoanalysis, it is not surprising that he favours remakes/homages which rest upon detecting blind spots and twisted turns; therefore, he privileges *The Conversation* over *Dressed to Kill*.

The unresolved coda in *Longing* is a twisted turn that pays respects to the inherent ambiguity of *Happiness*. Varda's film was described as ambiguous because of the ironic discord between the exuberant style and the heart-rending plot development. Owing to this discord, it is unclear to what extent Thérèse's death in *Happiness* should be taken seriously. *Longing*, however, shifts the focus to the tragic fate of the characters as such. It does so, first, by opting for an unobtrusive rather than excessive style. Second, since the girl's question remains unanswered, the other children in the playground, as well as the viewers are anxious to know what has happened. Because we are left to guess the outcome, we are confronted with the painful choices that the characters have to make. While the trauma in *Happiness* is only latent because Thérèse's demise is quickly glossed over by the enchanting colours and the ironic repetition of the family's walk in the woods, *Longing* emphasises that love triangles hurt and scar. This repressed core at the heart of the overtly aesthetic *Happiness* returns in *Longing* with full force. By acknowledging Grisebach's film as a (secret) ode to the latent traumatic kernel of Varda's picture, the affective impact of the German hidden homage becomes even more effective and enduring.

NOTES

1. Leitch counted no less than 101 differences involving dialogue, sound, credits, the pace of the film and so on.
2. *The Last Picture Show* also features Ben Johnson, known from Ford Westerns such as *She Wore a Yellow Ribbon* (1949), *Wagon Master* (1950) and *Rio Grande* (1950).
3. According to Carroll, allusions to *The Searchers* appear, among others, in *Mean Streets* (Martin Scorsese, 1973), *Ulzana's Raid* (Robert Aldrich, 1972), *Dillinger* (John Milius, 1973) and 'most ruthlessly' in *Hardcore* (Paul Schrader, 1979) (1982: 65).
4. Widely reported is the zoom-in on the Alka Seltzer tablet dissolving in a glass of water, which pays respects to the coffee sequence from Godard's *Deux ou trois choses que je sais d'elle* (1966).
5. Even though *Breathless* (Jim McBride, 1983) embraces the 'enthusiasm for [the] American pop-cultural iconography' of Godard's 'original' *À bout de souffle* (1960) (Verevis 2006: 25), the remake does not meet the criterion of the homage. This embrace was a bold gesture in France of 1960, but it loses this rebellious effect with McBride's remake, since this film is itself a product of American popular culture.

REFERENCES

Baudrillard, Jean (1994), *Simulacra and Simulation*, trans. Sheila Faria Glaser, Ann Arbor: The University of Michigan Press.
Carroll, Noël (1982), 'The Future of Allusion: Hollywood in the Seventies (and Beyond)', *October*, 20: 1, 51–81.
Comeau, Vance (2006). *Melodramatic License: The Re-Imaging of Douglas Sirk's All That Heaven Allows by Rainer Werner Fassbinder and Todd Haynes*, doctoral dissertation, Acadia University, Nova Scotia.
DeRoo, Rebecca J. (2008), 'Unhappily Ever After: Visual Irony and Feminist Strategies in Agnès Varda's *Le Bonheur*', *Studies in French Cinema*, 8: 3, 189–209.
Elsaesser, Thomas (1996), *Fassbinder's Germany: History, Identity, Subject*, Amsterdam: Amsterdam University Press.
Elsaesser, Thomas (2004), 'American Auteur Cinema: The Last – or First – Great American Picture Show', in Thomas Elsaesser, Alexander Horwath and Noel King (eds), *The Last Great American Picture Show: New Hollywood Cinema in the 1970s*, Amsterdam: Amsterdam University Press, 2004, pp. 37–69.
Fassbinder, Rainer Werner (1972), 'Six Films by Douglas Sirk', in Laura Mulvey and Jon Halliday (eds), *Douglas Sirk*, Edinburgh: Edinburgh Festival, pp. 95–108.
Fujiwara, Chris (2014), '*Ali: Fear Eats the Soul*: One Love, Two Oppressions', *The Criterion Collection*, available at: https://www.criterion.com/current/posts/1067-ali-fear-eats-the-soul-one-love-two-oppressions (last accessed 4 July 2019).
Giachetti, Alexis Seccombe (2017), 'Making Sense of the Replaceable Beloved in Agnès Varda's *Le Bonheur*', *Studies in European Cinema*, 14: 2, 91–102.
Greenberg, Harvey R. (1998), 'Raiders of the Lost Text: Remaking as Contested Homage in *Always*', in Andrew Horton and Stuart Y. McDougal (eds), *Play It Again, Sam: Retakes on Remakes*, Berkeley: University of California Press, pp. 115–30.
Horner, Kierran (2018), 'The Art of Advertising Happiness: Agnès Varda's *Le Bonheur* and Pop Art', *Studies in French Cinema*, 18: 2, 133–55.
Hutcheon, Linda (1994), *Irony's Edge: The Theory and Politics of Irony*, London: Routledge.
Leitch, Thomas (2000), '101 Ways to Tell Hitchcock's *Psycho* from Gus Van Sant's', *Literature/Film Quarterly*, 28: 4, 269–73.
Leitch, Thomas (2002), 'Twice-Told Tales: Disavowal and the Rhetoric of the Remake', in Jennifer Forrest and Leonard R. Koos (eds), *Dead Ringers: The Remake in Theory and Practice*, Albany: State University of New York Press, pp. 37–62.
Leitch, Thomas (2003), 'Hitchcock Without Hitchcock', *Literature/Film Quarterly*, 31: 4, 248–59.
Martin, Marie (2020), 'The "Secret Remake": A European Take on the Traditional Remake?' in Eduard Cuelenaere, Gertjan Willems and Stijn Joye (eds), *European Film Remakes*, Edinburgh: Edinburgh University Press, pp. 33–44.
Mukhida, Leila (2015), 'Violence in the Age of Digital Reproducibility: Political Form in Valeska Grisebach's *Longing* (2006)', *German Politics and Society*, 33: 1–2, 172–85.
Naremore, James (1999–2000), 'Remaking *Psycho*', in *Hitchcock Annual*, pp. 3–12.
Skvirsky, Salomé Aguilera (2008), 'The Price of Heaven: Remaking Politics in *All that Heaven Allows*, *Ali: Fear Eats the Soul*, and *Far from Heaven*', *Cinema Journal*, 47: 3, 90–121.
Taubin, Amy (2012), *Taxi Driver*, London: Palgrave Macmillan.
Verevis, Constantine (2006), *Film Remakes*, Edinburgh: Edinburgh University Press.
Žižek, Slavoj (2004), 'Is There a Proper Way to Remake a Hitchcock Film?' in Richard Allen and Sam Ishii-Gonzalès (eds), *Hitchcock: Past and Future*, London: Routledge, pp. 257–74.
Žižek, Slavoj (2003), 'Not a Desire to Have Him, But to Be Like Him', *London Review of Books*, 25: 16 (21 August), 13–14.

CHAPTER 4

Rainer Werner Fassbinder's *Berlin Alexanderplatz* (1980) as Remake?

Mario Slugan

CAN WE SPEAK OF A REMAKE?

When discussing Rainer Werner Fassbinder's 1980 *Berlin Alexanderplatz*, scholars regularly treat it as a film adaptation of Alfred Döblin's 1929 novel *Berlin Alexanderplatz: Die Geschichte von Franz Biberkopf/Berlin Alexanderplatz: The Story of Franz Biberkopf*. There is certainly nothing wrong with that. They both tell the story of Franz who, upon serving time for manslaughter, returns to navigate late-Weimar Berlin where he meets the novel's antagonist Reinhold and suffers by his hand when Reinhold murders Franz's girlfriend Mieze, leading to a mental breakdown and Franz's final re-entry to society. But Fassbinder's is not the first film adaptation of the novel – Piel Jutzi's 1931 *Berlin-Alexanderplatz – Die Geschichte Franz Biberkopfs/Berlin-Alexanderplatz – The Story of Franz Biberkopf* holds that place of honour. With that in mind, it is interesting to pause for a moment and consider how rarely Jutzi's film is mentioned in discussions of Fassbinder's work, let alone how the possibility of treating Fassbinder's production as a remake of Jutzi's is virtually never raised.[1] In the latest companion to Fassbinder (Peucker 2012), for instance, the two pieces that focus on *Berlin Alexanderplatz* mention Jutzi's film altogether once. While for Elena Del Rio (2012) Jutzi's film does not even deserve a single reference, Paul Coates (2012: 413) mentions it in passing only once (and manages to get the production year wrong). Earlier works such as the only monograph study of Fassbinder's *Berlin Alexanderplatz* (Shattuc 1995), as well as the first English-language monograph of Fassbinder's oeuvre (Elsaesser 1996), are no different. Between the two, Jutzi's film is referred to in a single sentence (Elsaesser 1996: 217).

Although the above practice is not uncommon in German-language scholarship either,[2] it appears that including Jutzi in the discussion does come more naturally to scholars writing in German, for they often treat the novel, Jutzi's film and Fassbinder's production together. Matthias Hurst (1996), for example, provides a narratological comparison of the opening of the three works in sequence. Similarly, Hanno Möbius and Guntram Vogt (1990) discuss the three works when analysing the experience of orientation in various artistic representations of the city. Other instances of the three treated side by side include works by Helmut Kiesel (1991), Gabriele Sander (1998) and Christian Schärf (2001). But even these authors primarily understand both films as adaptations ('Verfilmung') of the novel. They certainly do not consider the possibility of treating Fassbinder's production as a remake of Jutzi's film and the potential benefits of doing so.

From this perspective, my own approach has been much in the same vein (Slugan 2017). I focused on a specific device – namely, montage – and although I analysed its perceptual, stylistic and narratological properties across all three works, I did not address the above possibility either. Perhaps this should not come as much of a surprise given my initial interest in demonstrating that the expanded understanding of adaptation (Hutcheon 2012, Leitch 2012) should also include the standard practice of interpretation (Slugan 2014). In other words, my primary interest in adaptation studies there was to argue that interpretation is a form of adaptation; therefore, there was comparatively little to gain by discussing the concept of remake which has already been accepted by scholars of adaptation as one of its types.

The first issue in exploring the possibility of analysing Fassbinder's film version as a remake of Jutzi's adaptation is related to terminology: is the present-day understanding of the term remake applicable to the film in question? According to Constantine Verevis, a remake has been classically understood as 'a film based upon another film' (2017: 268). Although recent developments in remakes have made it necessary to reconceptualise the notion by turning to intermedial perspectives which allow for the transfer of characters and narratives from celluloid to digital media, with our subject-matter firmly in the pre-digital cinema era we can safely stick to the classical definition.[3]

Can we talk about Fassbinder's film, then, as a film based on Jutzi's film? If we consider the existing scholarship, we can find encouragement for such an approach only here and there. Eric Rentschler, for instance, opens his essay on Fassbinder's film as follows: 'Any attempt to sketch a topography of Rainer Werner Fassbinder's expansive and complex *Berlin Alexanderplatz* [...] must take into account the film's textual basis, Alfred Döblin's many-voiced urban epic of 1929, as well as Phil Jutzi's 1930 [*sic*] rendering of the novel starring Heinrich George' (1985: 194).[4] More recently, Alexander Badenoch et al. (2013) have emphasised intermediality, remediation and refashioning in their discussion of the three works and even added a fourth element into the mix – the radio play.[5] Although paving the way for more importance given to Jutzi's film, none of these approaches, however, involve what we really need to speak of as adaptation and remake as its subordinate term – that is, as intentional engagement with the source text. In other words, Fassbinder had to have known Jutzi's film, and the film had to have influenced him in making his own to count the latter as a remake of the former.

Unlike intertextuality and intermediality more generally, adaptation and, by extension, remake is a necessarily intentional phenomenon. It is one thing to make intertextual and intermedial references on which audiences and scholars can pick up and which emphasise their importance, but quite another to produce a remake or an adaptation. For instance, I can say that something sounds like a 'siren's call' and thereby produce an intertextual reference to the *Odyssey* with or without any knowledge of the Greek epic, with or without the intention to be intertextual. For a remake and adaptation more broadly, by contrast, we need a knowing, intentional effort. We cannot make an adaptation or a remake inadvertently. Even if my hypothetical work were an intertext replete with characters such as Penelope and Polyphemus and events such as the captivity on Ogygia and the slaying of the suitors, it would not count as an adaptation/remake if I did not know that those characters and events come from the *Odyssey* – that is, without my intentional engagement with *Odyssey*. Can we find any signs of this type of engagement in Fassbinder?

Fassbinder's non-fictional remarks provide one form of evidence of it. Numerous interviews with Fassbinder, as well as the texts he himself penned, make it clear that we are dealing with an intentional and knowing engagement with Döblin's work. In fact, some months before the original broadcast of the film, in an article he wrote for *Die Zeit*, Fassbinder (1980) emphasised the importance that the novel had for him when he first read it as an adolescent. It was precisely what he perceived as the novel's main subject – the unacknowledged non-sexual love between Franz and Reinhold as its main protagonists – that also helped him deal with his own homosexuality. Given that, next to the engagement on a personal level, Fassbinder (1980, 1982) also articulated his understanding of what it means to make a successful adaptation, we are undeniably dealing with a deliberate reworking of the 1929 novel. But this is clearly nothing new, since numerous discussions of Fassbinder's work which have been interested in how successful the film is as an adaptation are aware of his view on the matter. To speak of Fassbinder's film as a *remake*, we need to ascertain whether Fassbinder knew of Jutzi's film and, if so, whether it influenced him in any way.

There are signs that it did. In the same *Die Zeit* piece, Fassbinder writes:

> Next [after reading Döblin], I saw the 'Alexanderplatz'-film by Piel Jutzi, which, taken for itself, I found to be quite good, by no means a bad film. However, Döblin's novel has been completely forgotten in this film. The book and the movie have nothing to do with each other. Each, even the film by Jutzi, is, of course, art on its own independent of one

another. And since film is the medium with which I identify the most, I decided at that time, one day, and why only one day, that I do not know any more, perhaps, when I could do enough, to attempt with Döblin's 'Berlin Alexanderplatz' a protocol of dealing with this very special literature with my cinematic means as an experiment (Döblin 1980: 39, my translation).

Obviously, Fassbinder was not only aware of the film, but saw it and had a formed opinion about it. At the same time, however, it seems clear that Fassbinder was primarily engaged with the novel, and not with Jutzi's work. But what if we can avoid putting words into Fassbinder's mouth and still claim that Jutzi's film does serve as an important influence for him? And that it does so, not as primary text to be engaged with experimentally in a different medium, but rather as a negative model of what to avoid in such an experiment? For this, we need to expand our pool of evidence by moving away from Fassbinder's non-fictional remarks and include the relationship between the novel, the two films and their critical reception.

NEGATIVE INFLUENCE

Take, for instance, the following paragraph at the beginning of the novel. Here, the titular character has just been released from Tegel prison and has taken the tram to the city:

> He [Franz] shook himself and gulped. He trod on his own foot. Then, with a run, took a seat in the car. Right among the people. Off they went. At first it was like being at the dentist's, when he has grabbed a root with a pair of forceps, and pulls; the pain grows, your head threatens to burst. He turned his head back towards the red wall, but the tram went racing on, and only his head looking towards the prison. The tram took a bend; trees and houses intervened. Busy streets emerged, Seestrasse, people got on and off. Something inside him screamed in terror: Look out, look out, it's going to start now. The tip of his nose turned to ice; something was whirring over his cheek. 'Zwölf Uhr Mittagszeitung', 'B. Z.', 'Berliner Illustrierte', 'Die Funkstunde', 'Any more fares?' The coppers have blue uniforms now. He got off the tram, without being noticed, and was back among people again (Döblin 1978: 13–14).

Jutzi's film transforms this paragraph into a complex two-minute-long montage sequence. Many critics have spoken of it as the sequence that stands out the most, in both a positive (Kracauer 1996) and a negative way (Pinthus 1996,

Ihering 1996). I myself have provided a lengthy analysis of the sequence and its complexity in the attempt to re-evaluate the work (Slugan 2017: 113–25). To evoke the impression of disorientation, the sequence resorts to problematising both spatial and temporal relations of the cityscape. In the former case, it includes the lack of clear spatial motivation for cutting, unmotivated cutting between slightly differing horizontal positions, the problematisation of subjective shots, jump-cutting, canting and so on. The latter includes temporal ellipses, as well as shots which have no clear temporal relations to the rest of the sequence. Moreover, the montage is also so visually intricate and fast-paced that even under repeat viewings (and without access to the original filmstrip) it is impossible to ascertain how many shots it precisely consists of (it may be anywhere between 32 and 34).

Fassbinder's film, by contrast, does not tackle the above paragraph at all. In Fassbinder's version, upon release from Tegel prison Franz never boards the tram, but rather walks away and into the next narrative episode of the novel – the conversation with the Jewish local Nachum. This is even more striking because Fassbinder's work is 15 ½ hours long, which means that there is more than ample time to cover everything in the book. In fact, Fassbinder's work is one of those rare adaptations that has enough time to even add characters and events (such as those involving Franz's landlady who is barely mentioned in the book) on top of all those present in the novel. And despite this luxury, Fassbinder omits this specific episode while claiming that Jutzi's film is the one in which 'Döblin's novel has been completely forgotten'

Arguably, then, we are dealing with an example where Jutzi's film serves as a negative model for the later adaptation. Fassbinder seems to deliberately avoid the most striking sequence from the first film adaptation to set his own work apart. It is as though he is making a point of not doing what Jutzi did. In other words, his remake is so bold that he intentionally jettisons the most discussed sequence from Jutzi's film. This is particularly important in the dominant context in which the novel has been read since its appearance – a 'word film' ('Wortfilm') and an instance of literary implementation of the technique of film montage. Upon its release in 1929, Döblin's novel prompted contemporary German-language critics for the first time to apply the term 'montage' to describe a literary work. In the German milieu, the term was originally popularised with the translation of Vsevolod Pudovkin's *Film Technique* in 1928 and quickly applied to describe a novel type of editing introduced by films coming from the USSR, exemplified by Pudovkin's *Mother* (*Mat'*, 1926), Eisenstein's *October* (*Oktyabr'*, 1928) and Vertov's *Man with a Movie Camera* (*Chelovek s kino-apparatom*, 1929). Once the critics perceived the insistence on the experience of disruption in these films and Döblin's novel alike, they were quick to deploy the term montage to speak of both (Slugan 2020). In this context, it was no surprise that Jutzi would attempt to retranslate literary montage into film montage in the tradition of Soviet-style montage, and especially city montage, something noted by contemporary critics as well (Slugan 2017: 110–12).

This is not to deny that contemporary critics thought that, when compared to the source, there was too little montage-like experimentation in the film overall. Thus, when Fassbinder makes a point that 'the book and [Jutzi's] movie have nothing to do with each other', he clearly writes in this tradition. But at the same time this allows him to dismiss Jutzi's film as a possible (negative) influence on his own work rather too quickly. For Fassbinder, too, is perfectly happy to resort to experimental forms of montage himself. It is just that his experiments are significantly different from Jutzi's. These include both atypical editing patterns and montage proper. Among the former we find asymmetric shot/counter-shot structures, spatiotemporal continuity accompanied by the discontinuity of character placement and the bridging of spatial discontinuity through the continuity of character movement or eyeline matches (Slugan 2017: 147–55). Abrupt flashbacks, alterations between slow motion and normal speed, partial repetition of the content from the previous shot from another angle, introduction of stills and animations, intertitles, disruptive divergence of voice-over and image, and deliberate mismatch between the rear projection and the shot content count among the latter (Slugan 2017: 159–78). Given the abundance of these procedures and the divergence from Jutzi's choices, it makes even more sense to see the omission of the tram sequence and its city-montage type of editing as a sign of what type of montage experiments Fassbinder does *not* want to explore.

The same logic is also at work when we compare the second-most complex montage sequence in Jutzi's film with its equivalent in Fassbinder's – the Alexanderplatz hawking scene in which Franz is selling his wares. In the 1931 production there is not only visual but also sound montage (quite a feat considering the recent introduction of sound). Concerning the former, there are incessant contiguous shots of surroundings characterised by a documentary look, afforded by a lack of staging, hesitant camera movement, chaotic screen composition and increase in image speed. As for the latter, Jutzi includes disruptive shifts in volume depending on the distance of the camera, the alteration of silent and sound shots, as well as the displacement of sound onto a distant image, such as when Franz warns a young man about the traffic while the camera presents an image of a child who must be elsewhere and not in Franz's vicinity (Slugan 2017: 127–34).

In Fassbinder's film, by contrast, the focus of the sequence is Franz, and although there are a number of atypical visual editing patterns – unmotivated camera angle and placement (in one shot it is even placed in a passing bus) and asymmetric shot/counter-shot structures – there is no montage proper. What was a complex editing of documentary footage in relation to staged performance is now replaced by a very different strategy. When it comes to sound, there is also nothing similar to Jutzi – despite differing camera placements, there is no sound volume modulation in Fassbinder. This lack of an attempt at sound montage is even more striking because, in Fassbinder's version, Franz is also heard warning a youngster about the traffic, but the camera remains fixed on Franz and the man who is now keeping him company. Again, Jutzi's film presents itself as a sort of negative model given that the two most important montage sequences in Jutzi's film, as measured by the amount of critical discussion they elicited, are omitted in Fassbinder. We can say, then, that Fassbinder's film is a remake with Jutzi's adaptation serving as a model of what one should *not* do, at least when it comes to how to deal with montage, which remains of crucial importance for the understanding of the novel since its publication.

POSITIVE INFLUENCE

In the preceding pages I have spoken of Jutzi's film as a negative model for Fassbinder's remake, where influence was construed as a knowing intentional engagement with a proximate text. Proceeding with this understanding, can we find any positive influences? Is there something to be found in Jutzi's adaptation and missing from the novel that Fassbinder included in his version? Indeed, when it comes to more generic features, Fassbinder is perfectly happy to follow Jutzi's lead. Both films, for instance, put great emphasis on melodrama. The novel, by contrast, never partakes in that tonality.

Fassbinder, for example, turns his version of the Alexanderplatz hawking episode into an opportunity to heighten emotional engagement with the characters. With keyboards, strings and a zoom-in on Franz's face all setting up the importance of the car parked in the foreground, this sequence for the first time introduces an old romantic interest of Franz's, Eva. What follows is a protracted exchange of glances between Eva and Franz witnessed, crucially, by Franz's current girlfriend Lina. Lina, moreover, is afforded an almost thirty-second-long uninterrupted tracking shot of her approaching Franz (and the camera) during which we can read a range of emotions on her face, from worry to anger in her preparation to confront him.

In Döblin's book, by contrast, neither Lina nor Eva appear in the sequence in question at all. The only role that Lina plays is an earlier one, where she gave Franz the coat he is wearing while hawking. In Jutzi, however, the sequence is once again an opportunity to develop the romantic storyline. Because of the brevity of the film, Lina and Eva do not figure in this version but it is another woman from the novel, Cilly, who plays a role here. At the end of the scene, Franz runs from his stand to embrace Cilly, and the two can be seen giggling happily at the prospect of spending the rest of the day together.

This narrative segment and its versions across the three works are by no means atypical of how melodramatic elements are deployed in the works of Döblin, Jutzi and Fassbinder. In his production, Fassbinder makes his characters wear their heart on their sleeve, allows for long shots in which we can read these emotions, accentuates characters and their emotions with musical leitmotifs, and transforms minor episodes into full-blown emotional roller coasters. To take another example, consider the ending of the first episode, where a joyous meeting between Franz, his friend Meck, Lina and Franz's landlady Frau Bast is cut short by a letter from the authorities.

As Franz first reads the letter silently, he loses his footing and almost falls, having to lean against the door. In an exchange of reaction shots and glances towards each other, both Lina and Meck get visibly upset, and Lina hugs Frau Bast in another demonstration of the gravity of the situation. Only after a long pause, which gives us Franz's shadow-covered and dimly lit profile in a close-up, does he read the letter aloud. As he listlessly trudges through the content of the letter, a sorrowful, sombre tune starts in the background, and the camera moves in, first on the two embracing women and then on Meck letting it all sink in ever so slowly. This is followed by yet another pause, with everybody in silence and framed in a long shot until Lina softly kisses Franz on the lips. At this point, the camera affords another close-up of a visibly shaken and sweating Franz, only to (after a shot/counter-shot exchange with Lina) slowly tilt downwards and reveal the official notice clutched in his hand. General disappointment ensues, with characters slowly sitting down in resignation, until another tune accompanied by a female voice starts and Meck offers a sign of hope by proposing a visit to the prisoner's aid facilities.

An event that in Fassbinder's film lasts approximately 4 ½ minutes is treated only as a minor incident in the novel, in three paragraphs altogether, the second of which is filled by the content of the letter and the first and the last read:

> He was already quite well on his feet in Berlin – he had turned his old furniture into cash, he had a few pennies from Tegel, his landlady and his friend Meck gave him a small loan – then he got another terrible blow. But it turned out later on to be only a slap. One morning, which otherwise wasn't so bad, he found on his table an official yellow paper with printing and typewriting on it.
>
> [. . .]
>
> A staggering blow, that. There was a fine house alongside the city car-line, Grunerstrasse 1, on the Alex, Prisoners' Aid. There they take a look at Franz, ask him this and that, sign: Herr Franz Biberkopf has sought our protective supervision, we will make inquiries whether you are working, and you will have to report here every month. O.K., full stop, everything, everything going slick (Döblin 1976: 40).

The novel undeniably articulates the effect of the letter on Franz treating it as a blow/slap, but this comes out as a matter of fact rather than as an attempt at a deeper empathising with the protagonist. Moreover, no other characters share in this turn of events. By comparison, Fassbinder's treatment looks drenched in emotional excess.

For reasons of brevity, there is no equivalent scene in Jutzi, but this does not mean that he does not capitalise on melodramatic elements, much like Fassbinder. In fact, Jutzi's film invents a very specific first meeting between Franz and Mieze, which sets up a romantic mood from the beginning. As a hitherto unknown voice is heard singing 'Love comes, love goes', the camera descends vertically along the facades of high-rise building and after a few cuts reveals Mieze singing in the courtyard. While she sings, the two giggle and gaze at each other, much like Franz and Cilly did. But this time Mieze's singing continues after a temporal ellipsis as a sonic bridge between this first meeting and the ensuing date. To further the mood, the first shot of the date is an idyllic pan of a fountain; during that pan, as Mieze's singing recedes, Franz's own starts. Opening with an image of greenery overlapping the sight of the luscious water stream, the next shot continues the joyful tone, and finally we cut to Franz and Mieze strolling in a park.

In Döblin's novel there is only the first meeting (arranged by Eva), and this is dealt with in an expedite two-paragraph fashion. Undoubtedly, Franz is infatuated by Mieze, but this is a far cry from the sweetness and the romantic tone conveyed in Jutzi's film. On the relevant pages, although petite and elegant, she is foremost a stunning temptress rather than some girl next-door down on her luck and singing to keep afloat:

> Next day at noon sharp the girl knocks at his door, and Franz is enraptured at first sight. Eva had made his mouth water, and he'd like to please Eva, too. But this one's really a knockout, first-class, a wow, he's never found anything like this in his cookbook. She's a small person, in her little thin white dress with her bare arms she looks like a schoolgirl, she has soft slow movements and in a flash is right beside him. She's been there hardly half an hour, and now he can't imagine his room minus the little minx (Döblin 1976: 269).

Fassbinder retains Döblin's setting of the first meeting – Franz's room – but he also keeps Jutzi's idyllic date. Moreover, the emotional saturation in Fassbinder's versions of both episodes is again on par with the previously described scenes from his film.

The first meeting opens with a close-up of Franz in profile, covered in darkness with his face in the palm of his hand and dreading the encounter that Eva has set up for him. As Mieze's footsteps are slowly approaching, he lifts his head, fingers running down his lips, and cannot help but smile. Cut to Mieze completely in white, lit ever so softly against a gloomy brown interior, while the metallophone starts its melody. It takes them almost a minute to exchange greetings, smitten as they are with each other. A close-up of Mieze with a pink ribbon in her hair follows, fully displaying her innocence and revealing a wide smile. At this point wind instruments join in, and Franz is compelled to blurt out: 'It is like the sun is rising'. As the strings start as well, she sits on his lap, and the camera holds them in a medium close-up with Mieze's back to it and Franz facing forward, only to start rotating slowly and completing a 180-degree turn with a position behind a door glass, thus providing the encounter with an even more ethereal glow. The sequence ends in a flash of light, which reveals an intertitle in black writing over a white surface.

The date in Fassbinder's film, interestingly, starts with a shot of copious amounts of water and closes with a camera moving in on bountiful vegetation, much like in Jutzi's version. The lake on which Franz rows their boat is glistening in the sun, and the forest where they play hide and seek is dappled with strips of sunshine. The pair might not be singing as in Jutzi's version, but the background is a luscious romantic tune accompanied by birds chirping merrily. In both films, in fact, this is the first time that the events take place in nature, outside the city. These formal analyses reveal, then, that in Fassbinder's and Jutzi's versions alike there is undoubtedly an emphasis on melodramatic elements missing in Döblin's novel.

WHAT IS TO BE GAINED?

What are the benefits of considering Fassbinder's film as a remake of Jutzi's production, instead of simply referring to both as adaptations of Döblin's novel? Primarily, it is to talk of influence in terms of knowing intentional engagement rather than only to describe intertextual relations. In other words, although I am certainly not dismissing comparative intertextual studies, if we have multiple film versions of *Berlin Alexanderplatz*, we should surely also be interested in which connections are causal between the two and which are not. Put in yet another way, it is also legitimate to inquire about the proximate source text for Fassbinder's text – not in the sense of the original, but in the sense of the text that was used as the (negative) inspiration for particular aspects and segments of the film.

The first step in doing so was to demonstrate that Fassbinder saw and had good knowledge of Jutzi's film. Fassbinder's non-fictional remarks clearly attest to this. The second step was to argue that Fassbinder's film itself provides further evidence of intentional engagement with Jutzi's work. Here, the argument hinges on treating omissions and inclusions as a deliberate strategy rather than a coincidence, given the history of critical reception.

When it comes to Jutzi's film as a negative model, it is reasonable to read Fassbinder's omission of the most widely discussed and the most experimental sequence in Jutzi's film, as a decision to pursue other experimental means for adapting Döblin's montage technique. Perhaps Fassbinder shared the view of some contemporary critics, such as Kracauer who saw this sequence as a poor emulation of Soviet-style montage. Perhaps such urban montage did not chime with Fassbinder's vision of Berlin set in a studio setting. Whatever the reason might be, however, Jutzi's model is too conspicuous for Fassbinder's version not to be at least partly influenced by it.

From the perspective of positive influence, it is true that Fassbinder has tended to combine *auteur* cinema with melodrama in numerous films preceding *Berlin Alexanderplatz*. Scholars, for instance, regularly emphasise the influence that Douglas Sirk has exerted on Fassbinder – a fact Fassbinder himself has often remarked on (Fassbinder 1971, Rentschler 1984, Shattuc 1995, Elsaesser 1996, Peucker 2012). From this perspective, it could be claimed that the main influence, as far as melodramatic elements are concerned, comes from Sirk rather than Jutzi. But why could the influence on this occasion not derive from both? While Fassbinder is generally interested in melodramatic devices, in large part due to Sirk, the specific way in which he treats both the Alexanderplatz hawking scene and Franz's introduction to Mieze, and especially their first date outside the city, suggests that Jutzi's film played more of a role than Fassbinder is willing to give credit for in his non-fictional remarks. In the latter case, it is not only the case that both Jutzi and Fassbinder introduce an event not represented in the novel, but Fassbinder also opts for an iconography, setting and type of musical background very similar to the ones in Jutzi's film. This is hardly a coincidence. It is the notion of the remake understood as knowing intentional engagement with the proximate source text that allows us to see that.

NOTES

1. There are reasons to refer to the production as both film and TV series, given its subtitle ('A Film in 13 Parts and an Epilogue') and the premiere at the 37th Venice Film Festival, on the one hand, and the original broadcasting pattern (in fourteen weekly instalments from October to December 1980), on the other. For brevity's sake, I refer to *Berlin Alexanderplatz* as a 'film', although more accurately it should be a 'film/TV-series'.
2. Perhaps the most original analysis of Fassbinder's film as an adaptation, Dominique Pleimling's (2010) study does not even give reference to Jutzi.
3. Another term that can be used is re-adaptation, to denote the interaction between the novel, the first and the second adaptation (Leitch 1990). Without dismissing the fact that Fassbinder's film is still an adaptation, I opt for 'remake' for polemical reasons.
4. He goes on to devote only one paragraph to Jutzi's film.
5. Döblin wrote the radio-play adaptation of *Berlin Alexanderplatz*. Although pre-recorded and scheduled to premiere on 30 September 1930, it was cancelled. It was first broadcast only in 1963 (Jelavich 2006).

REFERENCES

Coates, Paul (2012), 'Swearing and Forswearing Fidelity in Fassbinder's *Berlin Alexanderplatz*', in B. Peucker (ed.), *A Companion to Rainer Werner Fassbinder*, Chichester: Wiley-Blackwell, pp. 398–429.
del Rio, Elena (2012), 'Violently Oscillating: Science, Repetition, and Affective Transmutation in Fassbinder's *Berlin Alexanderplatz*', in B. Peucker (ed.), *A Companion to Rainer Werner Fassbinder*, Chichester: Wiley-Blackwell, pp. 269–89.
Döblin, Alfred (1978), *Berlin Alexanderplatz: The Story of Franz Biberkopf*, trans. by Eugene Jolas, Harmondsworth: Penguin.
Elsaesser, Thomas (1996), *Fassbinder's Germany: History, Identity, Subject*, Amsterdam: Amsterdam University Press.
Fassbinder, Rainer Werner (1980), 'Die Städte des Menschen und seine Seele', *Die Zeit*, 14 March.
Fassbinder, Rainer Werner (1982), *Querelle: The Film Book*, Munich: Schirmer/MoseliGrove.
Fassbinder, Rainer Werner (1971), 'Imitation of Life: On Douglas Sirk', in L. Mulvey and J. Halliday (eds), *Douglas Sirk*, Edinburgh: Edinburgh Film Festival, pp. 95–107.
Fickers, Andreas, Jasper Aalbers, Annelies Jacobs, and Karin Bijsterveld (2013), 'Sounds Familiar: Intermediality and Remediation in the Written, Sonic and Audiovisual Narratives of *Berlin Alexanderplatz*', in K. Bijsterveld (ed.), *Soundscapes of the Urban Past: Staged Sound as Mediated Cultural Heritage*, Bielefeld: Transcript, pp. 77–115.
Hurst, Matthias (1996), *Erzählsituationen in Literatur und Film: Ein Modell zur vergleichenden Analyse von literarischen Texten und filmischen Adaptionen*, Tübingen: Niemeyer.
Hutcheon, Linda (2012), *A Theory of Adaptation*, 2nd ed., London: Routledge.
Ihering, Herbert (1996), 'Der Alexanderplatz-Film', in H. Balach and H.-M. Bock (eds), *Berlin Alexanderplatz: Drehbuch von Alfred Döblin und Hans Wilhelm zu Phil Jutzis Film von 1931*. Munich: Edition Text + Kritik, pp. 227–9.
Jelavich, Peter (2006), *Berlin Alexanderplatz: Radio, Film and the Death of Weimar Culture*, Berkely: University of California Press.
Kiesel, Helmuth (1993), 'Döblin und das Kino: Überlegungen zur "Alexanderplatz"-Verfilmung', *Jahrbuch für Internationale Germanistik*, 33, 284–97.
Kracauer, Siegfried (1996), '*Berlin Alexanderplatz*', in H. Balach and H.-M. Bock (eds), *Berlin Alexanderplatz: Drehbuch von Alfred Döblin und Hans Wilhelm zu Phil Jutzis Film von 1931*, Munich: Edition Text + Kritik, pp. 232–34.
Leitch, Thomas M. (1990), 'Twice-Told Tales: The Rhetoric of the Remake', *Literature/Film Quarterly*, 18: 3, 138–49.
Leitch, Thomas M. (2012), 'Adaptation and Intertextuality, or, What Isn't an Adaptation, and What Does It Matter?', in D. Cartmell (ed.), *A Companion to Literature, Film, and Adaptation*, Chichester: Wiley-Blackwell, pp. 85–104.
Möbius, Hanno and Guntram Vogt (1990), *Drehort Stadt: Das Thema 'Grossstadt' im deutschen Film*, Marburg: Hitzeroth.
Peucker, Brigitte, ed. (2012), *A Companion to Rainer Werner Fassbinder*, Chichester: Wiley-Blackwell.
Pinthus, Kurt (1996), '*Berlin Alexanderplatz:* Capital am Zoo', in H. Balach and H.-M. Bock (eds), *Berlin Alexanderplatz: Drehbuch von Alfred Döblin und Hans Wilhelm zu Phil Jutzis Film von 1931*, Munich: Edition Text + Kritik, pp. 224–26.
Pleimling, Dominique (2010), *Film als Lektüre: Rainer Werner Fassbinders Adaptation von Alfred Döblins Berlin Alexanderplatz*, Munich: Martin Meidenbauer.
Rentschler, Eric (1984), *New German Film in the Course of Time*, Bedford Hills: Redgrave.

Sander, Gabriele (1998), *Erläuterungen und Dokumente: Alfred Döblins 'Berlin Alexanderplatz'*, Stuttgart: Reclam.
Schärf, Christian (2001), *Alfred Döblins 'Berlin Alexanderplatz': Roman und Film*, Stuttgart: Steiner.
Shattuc, Jane (1995), *Television, Tabloids, and Tears: Fassbinder and Popular Culture*, Minneapolis: University of Minnesota Press.
Slugan, Mario (2014), *Montage Aesthetics: Narrative, Adaptation and Urban Modernity in Alfred Döblin's* Berlin Alexanderplatz, doctoral dissertation, University of Warwick, available at: http://wrap.warwick.ac.uk/67648/ (last accessed 2 August 2020).
Slugan, Mario (2017), *Montage as Perceptual Experience:* Berlin Alexanderplatz *from Döblin to Fassbinder*, Rochester: Camden House.
Slugan, Mario (2020), 'The role of Montage for the Understanding of Nature and Technology in *Berlin Alexanderplatz*', in D. Midgley and S. Davies (eds), Special Issue of *Jahrbuch für Internationale Germanistik – Reihe A*, 133, 183–95.
Verevis, Constantine (2017), 'Remakes, Sequels, Prequels', in T. M. Leitch (ed.), *The Oxford Handbook of Adaptation Studies*, New York: Oxford University Press, pp. 267–84.

CHAPTER 5

Remakesploitation: Exploitation Film Remakes and the Transnational *Giallo*

Iain Robert Smith

In my 2016 monograph *The Hollywood Meme: Transnational Adaptations in World Cinema*, I developed a methodology for studying the unlicensed reworkings of Hollywood movies that have appeared in film industries around the world. Building upon Dawkins' (1989: 192) use of the term 'meme' as a cultural equivalent of the biological gene, I argued that we could use a memetic model to track how films are adapted and reworked as they circulate globally. Analysing how Hollywood blockbusters such as *The Exorcist* (1974), *Star Wars* (1977) and *E.T. the Extra-Terrestrial* (1982) were reworked in various different national film industries, the book utilised the concept of the 'Hollywood meme' to explore the politics of cultural globalisation and to trace how individual reworkings such as *The Man Who Saves the World* (*Dünyayı Kurtaran Adam*, 1982, aka The Turkish Star Wars) were shaped by their specific sociohistorical contexts. Most importantly, the concept of the meme offered a method to track how film ideas evolve and mutate as they are reworked globally, with some memes dying out in their new context while others adapt and flourish. Moreover, it allowed for comparisons to be made between different national contexts to see how factors such as governmental policies, industrial conditions and copyright regimes impacted the kinds of remakes that were being produced.

In this chapter, however, I want to address two potential weaknesses within the model of the 'Hollywood meme', or to at least clarify how the model may be applied beyond the case-studies in this monograph. First of all, it is clear that the model of the meme appears to privilege major blockbuster films that have had a significant level of global impact. By its nature, a meme is unsuccessful if it is only adapted once and then dies out; hence, this kind of model focuses attention on texts that have had numerous adaptations, especially given that this level of transnational proliferation helps facilitate global comparisons. There are therefore questions to be asked about how useful this model is for examining individual remakes of films that did not have the global impact of a Hollywood blockbuster, such as *Star Wars* or *E.T. the Extra-Terrestrial*. This then raises the second potential weakness with the model – the focus on Hollywood itself. It is important to recognize that Hollywood is not the only national cinema that has inspired these kinds of transnational adaptations within world cinema. We could easily apply a memetic model to the various international remakes of Akira Kurosawa's *Seven Samurai* (1954), for example, or to the global reworkings of Bruce Lee's 1970s Hong Kong martial arts films. There is clearly a danger that a model that focuses specifically on the 'Hollywood meme' neglects these other transnational cultural flows and ultimately reproduces a problematic binary in which Hollywood appears to produce the 'original' material, while other popular cinemas just adapt and rework that material. I still stand by the position outlined in my book, where I argued that it is vital to address the dominance of Hollywood within these processes of cinematic cultural exchange, but it is clear that we also need to supplement this analysis of Hollywood's transnational impact with memetic studies of the numerous cultural flows that do not centre on Hollywood. Indeed, in an insightful review of my book from one of the editors of this very collection, Cuelenaere asks whether the model of the 'Hollywood meme' implies an interdependence between the concept of the meme and the international presence of Hollywood cinema. He asks: 'Is there only a Hollywood meme? Or could there also be a European meme? Or even a broader transnational meme?' (2017: 2).

This chapter responds to that query, as well as to the two potential weaknesses I have outlined, by applying the concept of the meme to a relatively little-known European remake – the Italian *giallo The Strange Vice of Mrs. Wardh* (*Lo strano vizio della Signora Wardh*, 1971) and its unlicensed Turkish remake *Thirsty for Love: Sex and Murder* (*Aşka Susayanlar: Seks ve Cinayet*, 1972). Part of a broader trend of reworkings of popular Italian cinema within Turkish cinema of the period, *Thirsty for Love: Sex and Murder* is an invaluable case-study for exploring the utility of this memetic model for analysing cultural flows that do not centre on Hollywood. This case-study also facilitates a discussion of the broader phenomenon of 'remakesploitation' – a term I use to describe the international subgenre of unlicensed exploitation film remakes – and, thereby, establishes how the study of low-budget reworkings can help us to interrogate the transnational exchanges between global popular cinemas. This chapter therefore explores the implications that this model has for our understanding of the transnational influence of popular cinematic forms such as the Italian *giallo* and demonstrates the applicability of a memetic model beyond major Hollywood franchises.

GLOBAL EXPLOITATION CINEMAS

It is clear that much of the existing scholarship on international exploitation cinema has positioned the American variant as the dominant norm. Clark's *At a Theater Or Drive-in Near You: The History, Culture, and Politics of the American Exploitation Film* is representative of this attitude in his claim that, '[a]lthough other nations, particularly Italy and England, have produced some noteworthy exploitation pictures, this sort of cinema originated in the United States, and the exploitation films of other countries largely adhere to the conventions of those made in America' (1995: 9–10). Indeed, much of the existing scholarship on exploitation cinema builds on the insights in Schaefer's (1999) discipline-defining monograph *Bold! Daring! Shocking! True!: A History of Exploitation Films, 1919–1959*. However, it is important to remember that Schaefer explicitly focused his study on the classical exploitation film in pre-1959 American cinema and that his definitions are based on the historical usage of the term in the US by figures such as exploitation producer David F. Friedman. This specific use of the term grounds Schaefer's study in a particular historical conjuncture and therefore avoids some of the slippages apparent in other discussions of exploitation cinema. Yet, this also means that his insights are not necessarily easily applied to other national contexts. It is important that we pay attention to the specificities of different international exploitation film traditions and not treat them merely as variations on a US norm. Thankfully, in recent years there have been several attempts to provide a more international perspective on exploitation film traditions,[1] even if scholarship has clearly still tended to privilege the US context. In their own brief survey of exploitation cinema, Mathijs and Sexton reflect on this bias: '[T]he sheer number of films produced in America, and the wealth of research on American production and the reception of films in this country, has inevitably led to our current survey of exploitation cinema being skewed towards this country' (2012: 150). There is a danger, therefore, that discussions of international exploitation cinema tend to skew towards the US and use that country as the normative model. It is essential that we work to identify those aspects of exploitation cinema practices that are consistent, but also distinct, across different national film industries.

One characteristic of international exploitation cinema that is identifiable across numerous different industries is an emphasis on imitating success. In her pioneering work on exploitation film practices, Cook addressed this reliance on reworking existing material and the economic factors underpinning this action, arguing that 'exploitation is a derogatory term, implying a process of "ripping off"' and that it also 'implies an economic imperative [. . .] exploiting, or capitalising on the success of more up-market, mainstream productions' (1985: 367). It is this phenomenon of unlicensed exploitation film reworkings capitalising on the success of their sources that I am terming here 'remakesploitation'. This ranges from US direct-to-video films such as *Snakes on a Train* (2006) and *Transmorphers* (2007), which deliberately utilise soundalike titles to capitalise on the popularity of a Hollywood blockbuster release, to transnational exploitation films such as the Indonesian thriller *Revenge of the South Seas Queen* (*Pembalasan Ratu Pantai Selatan*, 1988, aka Lady Terminator) and the Mexican wrestling film *The Batwoman* (*La mujer murciélago*, 1968), which localise elements borrowed from *The Terminator* (1984) and *Batman* (1966), respectively. There are also numerous examples of remakesploitation that are neither produced in the US, nor based on a US source text, such as the Turkish remake of the Hindi classic *Vagabond* (*Awaara*, 1951), titled *Avare* (1964), or the disco-themed Bollywood remake of the Italian spaghetti western *God Forgives . . . I Don't!* (*Dio perdona . . . Io no!*, 1967), titled *Wanted: Dead or Alive* (1984) (see Smith 2016b). This abundance of reworkings across international exploitation cinema reflects Hunter's (2009: 8) suggestion that exploitation cinema can itself be 'usefully thought of as a mode of adaptation'. Illustrating his argument through the numerous international reworkings of *Jaws* (1975), he observes that . . .

> . . . exploitation films often explicitly imitate other movies, cannibalising their titles, concepts and publicity gimmicks. Sometimes this gives rise to a tightly defined cycle of films inspired by a mainstream or exploitation success [. . .] but it may involve aping, more or less faithfully, the most exploitable elements of a specific high-profile movie (Hunter 2009: 9).

While the majority of Hunter's examples of 'Jawsploitation' are from the US, such as *Grizzly* (1976) and *Piranha* (1978), he also includes various international exploitation films such as the Turkish film *Desert* (*Çöl*, 1983) and the Italian film *The Last Shark* (*L'ultimo squalo*, 1981).[2] This is hardly surprising, since Turkey and Italy had thriving popular film industries throughout the 1970s and 1980s and since both engaged heavily in these remakesploitation practices of capitalising on the success of mainstream and exploitation releases. Nevertheless, there are also some significant differences between the remakesploitation produced in Italy and that produced in Turkey, and it is important that we attend to the specificities of each context. This is not about identifying some ineffable cultural 'Italianness' or 'Turkishness' within the films themselves, but about exploring the ways in which exploitation film practices are shaped by the distinct industrial contexts in which they are produced.

To understand the specific ways in which Italian exploitation cinema functions, therefore, it is essential to understand the Italian concept of the '*filone*', which describes the specific production model that underpins popular Italian filmmaking practices. As Baschiera and Hunter explain, . . .

... [l]iterally translating as vein (or thread), [*filone*] is best conceptualised as a trend or a current. In filmic terms, a keen awareness of commercially popular filone meant that producers would look to see what genre was current and try to exploit its popularity. The concept of the filone is a particularly Italian notion that lies close to, but is not the same as, Anglo-American ideas surrounding exploitation cinema (Baschiera and Hunter 2016: 6).

Within the model of the *filone*, producers would seek to capitalise on whatever was popular at that current moment; this would lead to highly productive but often short-lived cycles of particular *filone* such as spaghetti westerns, *mondo* films, peplums, cannibal films and *gialli*. This model of a popular film industry devoted to emulating recent successes is encapsulated in a statement from Italian director Luigi Cozzi who famously claimed: 'In Italy [. . .] when you bring a script to a producer, the first question he asks is not 'what is your film like?' but 'what *film* is your film like?' That's the way it is, we can only make *Zombi 2*, never *Zombi 1*' (Newman 1986b: 92). Cozzi is here referencing the fact that Lucio Fulci's *Zombi 2* (1979) was released as an unofficial sequel to George A. Romero's *Dawn of the Dead* (known in Italy as *Zombi*, 1978). It is important to note that Cozzi himself was very much involved in remakesploitation practices, with his films *Star Crash* (1979) and *Contamination* (1980) being specifically designed to capitalise on the international success of *Star Wars* (1977) and *Alien* (1979), respectively. The Italian industry of this period was infamous for these kinds of unlicensed imitations, ranging from relatively high-profile reworkings such as Ruggero Deodato's *The House on the Edge of the Park* (*La casa sperduta nel parco*, 1980), which shared its star David Hess with its source text *Last House on the Left* (1972), to Bruno Mattei's notorious low-budget remakesploitation titles such as *Shocking Dark* (1989), which reworked elements of both *Aliens* (1986) and *The Terminator* and was even released in many territories with the title *Terminator 2*. As Baschiera and Hunter note, this emphasis on capitalising on success was built into the Italian production regime of the time:

> The aim was always to copy genres that were currently popular – genres that 'sold' – and exploit this popularity by making cheap, low-end, rip-offs [. . .] [T]he whole enterprise of exploitation filmmaking was based on the ability to successfully 'piggy-back' on the popularity of currently successful trends. To be effective, therefore, exploitation filmmakers had to work quickly (and on low budgets) in order that their products tap into currently popular genres (Baschiera and Hunter 2016: 7).

The similarities with the popular Turkish cinema of the period are rather telling. As Arslan notes in his history of cinema in Turkey, the Turkish industry was also constituted by a proliferation of small production companies that 'sought their fortune in quickies, reminiscent of Hollywood's B-movies or independent exploitation films' and that the 'practice of producing quickies [. . .] closely resembles the history of Italian cinema' (2011: 109). These conditions helped stimulate a booming Turkish industry in the early 1970s, with over 300 films being produced in 1972, the same year as *Thirsty for Love: Sex and Murder*. This 'quickie' production model in the Turkish context also produced numerous examples of remakesploitation, including unlicensed reworkings of Hollywood titles such as *Star Wars*, *The Exorcist*, *Star Trek* (1966-) and *Some Like it Hot* (1959) (see Smith 2016a). Yet, it is significant that the Italian and Turkish industries were not simply borrowing from Hollywood, but also from each other. Director Çetin Inanç, for example, not only directed *The Man Who Saves the World* and *Fearless* (*Korkusuz*, 1986), which infamously reworked *Star Wars* (1977) and *Rambo: First Blood Part II* (1985), but he also directed *Steel Wrist* (*Çelik Bilek*, 1967) and wrote the screenplay for *Killing in Istanbul* (*Kilink Istanbul'da*, 1967) which reworked the Italian comic characters 'Il Grande Blek' and 'Killing'. Indeed, there were numerous Turkish reworkings of Italian comic strips and photo novels throughout the period (see Broughton 2014), and this practice of Turkish remakesploitation even extended to Italian sex comedies such as *Homo Eroticus* (*Man of the Year*, 1971) that was remade in Turkey as *Five Chicks One Rooster* (*Beş Tavuk Bir Horoz*, 1974).[3]

However, despite the many similarities between Turkish and Italian exploitation cinemas, and the many exchanges between these two industries over this period, there were some significant differences. Italian exploitation cinema was constituted by a proliferation of small production companies competing with each other, often working in co-production agreements with production companies in other European countries and pre-selling films to international distributors on the basis of a concept and title, often before the screenplay had even been written (Koven 2014: 207). While popular Turkish cinema was similarly made up of numerous small production companies producing 'quickies' on low budgets to capitalise on recent successes, the films were seldom produced as co-productions with other European countries and were hardly ever pre-sold to international distributors. Whereas the majority of Italian exploitation films were being 'produced with a global market in mind' (Koven 2006: 15), the Turkish exploitation films were instead primarily intended for distribution on the domestic market only, relying on the *Bölge İşletmeleri* (literally 'Regional Operations', or 'regional system') where producers would presell their films to seven distribution areas across Turkey. This crucial difference shaped the prevalent forms of remakesploitation in these two countries, as I will now explore in my comparison of *The Strange Vice of Mrs. Wardh* and its unlicensed Turkish remake *Thirsty for Love: Sex and Murder*.

STRANGE VICES AND *THIRSTY FOR LOVE*

Director Sergio Martino worked across numerous different *filone* in his career, from *mondo* documentaries such as *Mondo Sex* (1969) and *Naked and Violent* (1970), to remakesploitation films such as *2019: After the Fall of New York* (1983), which was part of a briefly flourishing Italian post-apocalyptic *filone* inspired by *Mad Max* (1979) and *Escape from New York* (1981). He is most celebrated, however, for his work in the *giallo* genre, with iconic titles such as *All the Colors of the Dark* (*Tutti i colori del buio*, 1972), *Your Vice Is a Locked Room and Only I Have the Key* (*Il tuo vizio è una stanza chiusa e solo io ne ho la chiave*, 1972) and *Torso* (*I corpi presentano tracce di violenza carnale*, 1973). His first *giallo* and first major commercial success was *The Strange Vice of Mrs. Wardh* in 1971. The film follows Julie Wardh (Edwige Fenech), a woman who is haunted by memories of the sadomasochistic relationship with her former lover Jean (Ivan Rassimov). She suspects that he may be the serial killer who is murdering young women across Vienna. While the film itself is not an example of remakesploitation, the central murder plot is nevertheless partly inspired by *Les Diaboliques* (1955),[4] and there are various borrowings from other films such as a murder scene at Schönbrunn Palace that pays homage to the Maryon Park scene in *Blow Up* (1966) and a triple twist ending that resembles the conclusion to *The Feast of Satan* (*Las amantes del diablo*, 1971).

Scholars of Italian popular cinema have often had to struggle with the notion that these films are highly derivative. From a survey of this literature, I would argue that there are two primary strategies that have been used to defend against this accusation: (1) emphasising the exceptions to this rule, or (2) highlighting the Italianness of the cycle as a way to argue for its cultural specificity. Reflecting the first strategy, Newman, for example, attempts to separate the superior examples of each *filone* by arguing that, '[w]hile it is undoubtedly true that many Italian genre films are simply worthless carbon copies with a few baroque trimmings, the best examples of most cycles are surprisingly sophisticated mixes of imitation, pastiche, parody, deconstruction, reinterpretation and operatic inflation' (1986a: 20). Yet, it is the second strategy that is particularly instructive. The term *giallo* derives from the yellow covers that adorned the series of detective novels published by Mondadori, and it is significant that the majority of these publications were Italian translations of English whodunits from authors such as Agatha Christie and Arthur Conan Doyle and American hard-boiled detective novels by figures such as James M. Cain and Dashiel Hammett. The filmic *giallo* has even been called 'Italian film noir' (Wood 2007), reflecting the sense of this *filone* being derivative of Anglo-American detective novels and films. While the issue of cultural (in)authenticity is not as prominent as with the Italian 'spaghetti' western, it is nevertheless a significant part of the scholarly debate surrounding the *giallo* – especially given that the films often feature international casts and are shot in locations around the world. The Italianness of the *giallo* is not always self-evident.

Many critics have therefore attempted to emphasise the Italianness of the *giallo*, either by tracing the influence of specifically Italian detective fiction – such as Olney's argument that the *giallo* is 'defined by its narrative debt to postwar Italian anti-detective fiction' (2013: 115) – or by asserting that the films reflect the specific cultural concerns of post-war Italian audiences. Koven, for example, has argued that the single theme that binds together the entire cycle is that they 'display a marked ambivalence toward modernity' (2006: 16). Yet, I would contend that what is especially interesting about the *giallo* is the notion that the films deal with 'a particularly delicate relationship between local and global culture [and] with the permeability of national borders' (Baschiera and Di Chiara 2010: 104). Most of these Italian exploitation films resulted from international co-productions and were explicitly designed to appeal to a global market; this complicates any claims of their underlying 'Italianness'. *The Strange Vice of Mrs. Wardh* is no exception.

The film was an Italian-Spanish co-production, shot primarily in Austria and Spain in locations including the Schönbrunn Palace in Vienna, the Semmering ski resort in Lower Austria and the Platja de la Fragata in Sitges. Moreover, these sites were filmed with a remarkably touristic lens, reflecting Needham's argument that Italian popular cinema generally has a 'tendency to exaggerate and exploit the "foreign" through the tropes of travel and the tourist's gaze' (2002). Indeed, it is notable that the *giallo filone* is particularly well suited to offering a touristic view of pan-European locations. As Baschiera and Di Chiara argue, '[i]nstead of "hiding" the international involvement in the production of the films (pretending to be "fully foreign", as happened in the horror and western, or "fully Italian", as in the comedies), the *giallo* completely exploited the possibility offered by co-production agreements to shoot in suggestive international locations – a possibility seldom exploited in other Italian genres' (2011: 34). As we can see in an over-the-shoulder shot of Edwige Fenech looking out over the Platja de la Fragata in Sitges (Figure 1), the film clearly took advantage of the opportunities offered by its co-production agreement to film in visually appealing Spanish tourist sites.

The film also features an international cast, bringing together Edwige Fenech, George Hilton, Ivan Rassimov, Manuel Gil and Alberto de Mendoza – stars who were born in Algeria, Uruguay, Italy, Spain and Argentina, respectively. Furthermore, the characters that they are playing are similarly international, from George Hilton's Australian love interest, to Carlo Alighiero's German detective.[5] Baschiera and Di Chiara argue that the representation of foreignness is distinctive to Sergio Martino's *gialli*; they suggest that it is presented with three aims in mind:

Figure 5.1 Edwige Fenech looking out over Platja de la Fragata in *The Strange Vice of Mrs. Wardh* (*Lo strano vizio della Signora Wardh*, 1971).

[I]t gives a cosmopolitan touch to the haute bourgeois characters, who manage to merge with and confront the outsiders; it allows the representation of imported foreign trends and customs, in particular among the young generations (from music to sexual liberation), thus showing the consequences that a modern activity such as tourism has on a traditional world; and finally, it shows the touristic *mondo* movie's gaze through a sexual exoticism (Baschiera and Di Chiara 2010: 117).

The cosmopolitanism of *The Strange Vice of Mrs. Wardh* is therefore tied to its depiction of international locations, foreign characters and imported trends and customs – which, as we will see, is quite distinct from what we find in the Turkish remake *Thirsty for Love: Sex and Murder*. Before turning to the remake, however, it is important to first acknowledge the emphasis on aesthetic style within *The Strange Vice of Mrs. Wardh* and the Italian *giallo* more generally. While the plot of the *giallo* is often relatively similar to Anglo-American detective fiction, what particularly makes it stand out from other national cycles are its aesthetics. Scholarship on the *giallo* tends to highlight this specific emphasis on visual style, with Olney observing that 'story often takes a backseat to style [and] the plot can frequently seem like little more than an excuse to present a series of extravagantly staged sequences' (2013: 104). Moreover, Bondanella argues that the 'Italian *giallo* film represents a profoundly cinematic product [. . .] built around the set-piece extravaganza' (2009: 376). With its spectacular cinematography and elaborately choreographed set-pieces, such as the iconic murder sequence in the park of Schönbrunn Palace and the suspenseful chase sequence through an underground car park, *The Strange Vice of Mrs. Wardh* exemplifies this emphasis on visual style within the *giallo*.

What we find in *Thirsty for Love: Sex and Murder*, however, is a film that closely replicates the plot of *The Strange Vice of Mrs. Wardh*, albeit with a significantly lower budget and with few of the visual flourishes that we see in Martino's *giallo*. The film stars Meral Zeren and Kadir Inanir in the roles made famous by Edwige Fenech and George Hilton in the original, and director Mehmet Aslan sticks relatively closely to his source, even recreating moments that are largely irrelevant to the plot such as a sequence where two female party-goers remove each other's clothing. While there are minor tweaks to some of the murder sequences, and while the ending is altered to include an additional shootout and fight sequence in a warehouse, *Thirsty for Love: Sex and Murder* is at times close to being a shot-for-shot remake. This is remarkable given that the film is only 58 minutes in length, as compared to the 100 minutes running time of *The Strange Vice of Mrs. Wardh*. The primary reason for this difference in length is that Aslan's direction privileges brevity at the expense of visual flourishes. The elaborately choreographed sequences of sex and violence that characterise Martino's film are replaced with much shorter, often clumsily staged set-pieces. For example, the initial dream sequence in which the central female protagonist is violently ravished by her former lover is under a third of the length in the Turkish remake,[6] with the highly aestheticised use of slow-motion replaced with a more pedestrian, unembellished visual style.

It is nevertheless important to note that director Mehmet Aslan was not a novice, but a highly prolific filmmaker who directed eleven feature films in 1970 alone and had worked across numerous genres, including comic book adaptations, adventure films, historical films and crime dramas. While the visual style in this remake is relatively unpolished, this is actually representative of popular Turkish cinema of the period. The film exemplifies the production methods of Yeşilçam – a term that refers to a street off Istiklal Avenue that originally housed the production offices of the Turkish film industry, but more generally evokes a particular mode of popular filmmaking. As Arslan has observed, 'Yeşilçam films, in comparison to Western popular cinemas, had undeniable problems with technical quality and narration due to the economic conditions of filmmaking' (2011: 110). In other words, the technical failings in *Thirsty for Love: Sex and Murder* were relatively common in Turkish popular cinema of the period and reflect the conditions under which they were produced. As Arslan explains, 'In Yeşilçam [. . .] all films were shot very quickly (in a period ranging from a couple of days to a few months), and all involve a seemingly endless number of technical "mistakes" when compared to contemporary notions of "proper" filmmaking' (2011: 15). Moreover, the production methods in Yeşilçam rarely extended to composing an original soundtrack, instead reusing cues from other films without licensing.[7] *Thirsty for Love: Sex and*

Murder, for example, makes use of Ennio Morricone's score for *The Burglars* (1971) and John Barry's soundtrack for *Diamonds are Forever* (1971). This is due to the copyright regime in Turkey of that period, which allowed filmmakers to make use of music, storylines and sometimes even footage from imported films, with little fear of legal action (see Smith 2016a) – quite distinct from the Italian situation where remakesploitation films were generally very careful to comply with international copyright laws.

The other key difference between the two films regards their cosmopolitan outlook. While *The Strange Vice of Mrs. Wardh* features an international cast and was shot in Austria and Spain, *Thirsty for Love: Sex and Murder* has all the major roles played by Turkish actors and was shot entirely in Turkey. This was shaped by the *Bölge İşletmeleri* distribution circuit in Turkey, which was aimed primarily at appealing to the domestic market. This is not to say that *Thirsty for Love: Sex and Murder* is not cosmopolitan on various levels, but simply that this is less overt. As we can see in Figure 2, the remake retains the emphasis on the fashions, sexual liberation and decadence that proliferated across 1970s European cinema. Indeed, the film contains many of the cosmopolitan themes that Baschiera and Di Chiara identified in the Italian *giallo* – including

Figure 5.2 1970s European fashions and interior design reflecting a domestic cosmopolitanism in *Thirsty for Love: Sex and Murder* (*Aşka Susayanlar: Seks ve Cinayet*, 1972).

the representation of imported foreign trends and customs among the youth of Turkey. Rather, it differs in that this is largely a domestic form of cosmopolitanism – incorporating imported influences and gesturing towards international trends, but within a film that features a largely Turkish cast and crew and is aimed primarily at a domestic audience. Therefore, while the fact that Turkey produced a near shot-for-shot unlicensed remake of an Italian *giallo* is clearly indicative of the multiple convergences between the two exploitation film industries, *Thirsty for Love: Sex and Murder* also demonstrates the significant differences in terms of aesthetic style, cosmopolitan outlook and the use of copyrighted material.

CONCLUSION

In his study of the influence of the Italian *giallo* on 1970s Spanish films such as *The Blue Eyes of the Broken Doll* (*Los ojos azules de la muñeca rota*, 1974) and León Klimovsky's *A Dragonfly for Each Corpse* (*Una libélula para cada muerto*, 1974), Willis claims that, 'whilst it is possible to argue that a number of these films can be considered as part of the internationalization of the *giallo*, to fully understand them one needs to place them into the particular context of Spanish culture and society in the early to mid-1970s' (2015: 103–4). This relationship between the international influence of the *giallo* and the cultural specificity of its various adaptations is crucial. In this chapter, I have used the case-study of a low-budget Turkish remake of an Italian *giallo* to explore what a memetic model can tell us about the phenomenon of remakesploitation and the transnational dynamics of global popular cinemas more broadly. While it is clear that Italian and Turkish exploitation cinema traditions are remarkably similar in many ways, it is essential that we pay attention to the specificities of these different exploitation film traditions and to the ways in which they are shaped by the material conditions in which the films are produced and by industrial factors such as coproduction agreements, distribution pre-sales and copyright regimes.

By studying this specific Turkish reworking of an Italian *giallo*, I have attempted to demonstrate the applicability of the model I used in *The Hollywood Meme* beyond major Hollywood franchises. Future scholarship could take this further and explore the transnational influence of the *giallo* more generally. Indeed, the advantage of a memetic model is that it allows us to place these specific individual remakes within a wider framework of intertextual exchange. The *giallo* may often be analysed in terms of its culturally specific 'Italianness', but it is also known for its international influence – not only within the Turkish and Spanish industries, but also famously influencing the American slasher films of directors such as John Carpenter and Brian De Palma, as well as the British thrillers of directors such as Freddie Francis and Nicolas Roeg. A memetic model would allow us to trace how elements from the Italian *giallo* were borrowed and adapted in exploitation film industries all around the world and, thus, help us move beyond a model of exploitation cinema that still too often takes the US situation as the norm.

NOTES

1. Publications such as Shipka's *Perverse Titillation: The Exploitation Cinema of Italy, Spain and France, 1960–1980* and Ruétalo and Tierney's *Latsploitation, Exploitation Cinemas, and Latin America* exemplify this attempt to broaden the study of exploitation cinema beyond the US context. Moreover, the Bloomsbury 'Global Exploitation Cinemas' book series, launched in 2016 by series editors Johnny Walker and Austin Fisher, is focused specifically on international exploitation film production and reception.
2. *Desert* has become known within fan circles as 'The Turkish Jaws', although it actually uses relatively little from the Spielberg film, whereas *The Last Shark* was famously blocked from release in North America due to its close similarity to *Jaws*.
3. This relationship was partly established by a number of Italian films shot in Turkey in the 1960s, such as Umberto Lenzi's *Kriminal* (1966) and Riccardo Freda's *Coplan FX 18 casse tout* (*The Exterminators*, 1965).
4. The murder plot in *Les Diaboliques* also inspired *Il dolce corpo di Deborah* (*The Sweet Body of Deborah*, 1968) which shared the same screenwriter (Ernesto Gastaldi) and producer (Luciano Martino) with *The Strange Vice of Mrs. Wardh*.
5. Interestingly, Sergio Martino claims on the DVD extra 'Thrills, Chills and Cleavage' that the decision to have a German detective and to set the film outside of Italy was because this was felt to be more credible for audiences – both within Italy and internationally.
6. The sequence in *Thirsty for Love: Sex and Murder* is 32 seconds long, whereas it is 100 seconds long in *The Strange Vice of Mrs. Wardh*. All timings in this chapter are taken from the Shameless Blu-ray release of *The Strange Vice of Mrs. Wardh* and the Onar Films DVD release of *Thirsty for Love: Sex and Murder*.
7. This process is captured in Cem Kaya's documentary *Remake, Remix, Rip-Off* (2014) where Turkish filmmaker Kunt Tulgar details how he would duplicate the music from vinyl releases of Hollywood film soundtracks.

REFERENCES

Arslan, Savaş (2011), *Cinema in Turkey: A New Critical History*, Oxford: Oxford University Press.
Baschiera, Sergio and Francesco Di Chiara (2010), 'A Postcard from the Grindhouse: Exotic Landscapes and Italian Holidays in Lucio Fulci's Zombie and Sergio Martino's Torso', in Robert G. Weiner and John Cline (eds), *Cinema Inferno: Celluloid Explosions from the Cultural Margins*, Lanham: Scarecrow Press, pp. 101–23.
Baschiera, Sergio and Francesco Di Chiara (2011), 'Once Upon a Time in Italy: Transnational Features of Genre Production 1960s–1970s', *Film International*, 8: 6, 30–39.
Baschiera, Sergio and Russ Hunter, eds (2016), *Italian Horror Cinema*, Edinburgh: Edinburgh University Press.
Bondanella, Peter (2009), *A History of Italian Cinema*, London: Continuum.
Broughton, Lee (2014), 'Captain Swing the Fearless: A Turkish Film Adaptation of an Italian Western Comic Strip', in Lúcia Nagib and Anne Jerslev (eds) *Impure Cinema: Intermedial and Intercultural Approaches to Film*, London: I. B. Tauris.

Clark, Randall (1995), *At a Theater or Drive-in Near You: The History, Culture, and Politics of the American Exploitation Film*, New York: Garland.
Cook, Pam (1985), 'The Art of Exploitation, or How to Get Into the Movies', *Monthly Film Bulletin*, 52: 623, 367–69.
Cuelenaere, Eduard (2017), 'Book Review: I. R. Smith: The Hollywood meme: Transnational adaptations in world cinema', *Communications: The European Journal of Communication Research*, 42: 3, 387–9.
Dawkins, Richard (1989), *The Selfish Gene*, Oxford: Oxford University Press.
Eleftheriotis, Dimitris (2002), *Popular Cinemas of Europe: Studies of Texts, Contexts and Frameworks*, London: Continuum.
Hunter, Ian (2009), 'Exploitation as Adaptation', *Scope: An Online Journal of Film & TV Studies*, 15, 8–33.
Koven, Mikel J. (2006), *La Dolce Morte: Vernacular Cinema and the Italian Giallo Film*, Lanham: Scarecrow Press.
Koven, Mikel J. (2014), 'The Giallo and the Spaghetti Nightmare Film', in Peter Bondanella (ed.), *The Italian Cinema Book*, London: BFI, pp. 203–10.
Mathijs, Ernest and Jamie Sexton (2012), *Cult Cinema: An Introduction*, Malden: Wiley-Blackwell.
Needham, Gary (2002), 'Playing with Genre: An introduction to the Italian Giallo', *Kinoeye*, 2: 11, available at: http://www.kinoeye.org/02/11/needham11.php (last accessed 2 August 2020).
Newman, Kim (1986a), 'Thirty Years in Another Town: The History of Italian Exploitation', *Monthly Film Bulletin*, 53, 20–24.
Newman, Kim (1986b), 'Review of Contamination', *Monthly Film Bulletin*, 53, 92.
Olney, Ian (2013), *Euro Horror: Classic European Horror Cinema in Contemporary American Culture*, Bloomington: Indiana University Press.
Ramos Arenas, Fernando (2016), 'Towards a Generic Understanding of the Giallo: Crime-Horror Hybrids in Italian Cinema of the 1970s', in Ivo Ritzer and Peter W. Schulze (eds), *Genre Hybridisation: Global Cinematic Flow*, Marburg: Schüren, pp. 81–91.
Ruétalo, Victoria and Dolores Tierney, eds (2009), *Latsploitation, Exploitation Cinemas, and Latin America*, New York: Routledge.
Schaefer, Eric (1999), *Bold! Daring! Shocking! True! A History of Exploitation Films, 1919–1959*, Durham: Duke University Press.
Shipka, Danny (2011), *Perverse Titillation: The Exploitation Cinema of Italy, Spain and France, 1960–1980*, Jefferson: McFarland.
Smith, Iain Robert (2016a), *The Hollywood Meme: Transnational Adaptations in World Cinema*, Edinburgh: Edinburgh University Press.
Smith, Iain Robert (2016b), 'Cowboys and Indians: Transnational Borrowings in the Indian Masala Western', in Austin Fisher (ed.), *Spaghetti Westerns at the Crossroads: Studies in Relocation, Transition and Appropriation*, Edinburgh: Edinburgh University Press, pp. 185–210.
Willis, Andy (2015), 'Violence, Style and Politics: The Influence of the Giallo in Spanish Cinema of the 1970s', in Elena Oliete-Aldea, Beatriz Oria and Juan A. Tarancón (eds), *Global Genres, Local Films: The Transnational Dimension of Spanish Cinema*, London: Bloomsbury.
Wood, Mary P. (2007), 'Italian Film Noir', in Andrew Spicer (ed.), *European Film Noir*, Manchester: Manchester University Press, pp. 236–72.

Part II
Historical Perspectives: Continuity and Change

CHAPTER 6

Re-forming *La Maternelle*: Socio-Cultural Continuity and the Remake

Jennifer Forrest

When discussing remaking practices during the Golden Age of French sound cinema (1930–60), we cannot interpret French filmmakers' recourse to remaking as an industry practice along the same lines as Hollywood studios, which would maximise the investment in a film property. In contrast to the American industrial model, the French film industry, 'particularly at the level of production, was unstable, [and] fragmented' (Flitterman-Lewis 1990: 170). This fragmentation – the creation of short-lived studios and *ad hoc* production companies – meant that theoretically filmmakers had more freedom to choose unconventional subjects, implement non-standard camera and editing techniques, as well as pursue more personal projects. Not all directors had ambitions to explore the expressive qualities of the art of cinema, however, and certainly not all French studios and independent producers readily supported such pursuits. Indeed, given studios and financial backers' keen interest in returns on investments, most filmmakers, even those whom film history has designated as *auteurs*, felt pressure to make above all commercially successful films. In most instances, this translated into productions with conventional narratives and – in some instances, especially in the transition from silence to sound – twice-told tales. When French filmmakers did remake during the first decade of the classic era, it was often simply in the interest of updating successful productions using the new sound technology.[1] It is unusual, however, that (outside the early sound practice of multi-language films and the re-adaptation of works from canonical and best-selling literature) filmmakers would remake a film a second time.[2]

Léon Frapié's *La Maternelle* (1904), winner of the Prix Goncourt from the same year, was for a good part of the first half of the century one of those beloved novels found on the bookshelves of families of all classes.[3] However, unlike the novels of Honoré de Balzac, Gustave Flaubert and Émile Zola, to name a few, La Maternelle has ceased to be relevant either as social critique or as literature that has stood the test of time.[4] Nevertheless, it was the source of three films bearing the same title: Gaston Roudès' adaptation from 1925, Jean Benoit-Lévy and Marie Epstein's remake from 1933, and Henri Diamant-Berger's from 1949.[5] One advantage to retaining the novel's title in all three films, of course, was that their filmmakers could count on audience familiarity with and fondness for the Frapié work.[6]

While the directors of both the adaptation and the remakes updated the general historical conditions of the novel to make the story relevant to their viewing public, they also chronicled stages in the state of the Republic. Indeed, the shared title invokes the *maternelle* or nursery school as the pivotal government institution charged with initiating the inculcation of the notion of and belief in the legitimacy of the Republic. Roudès' film advances it as a metaphor for a France unable to recover from the massive loss of life incurred during World War I, a situation from which an already declining birth rate seemed unable to recover. Benoit-Lévy and Epstein's film betrays a conviction of the cinema's ability to educate and thereby bring about social change. And Diamant-Berger's film encourages a climate of forgiveness and solidarity in order to effect the transition from a republic destroyed by the German Occupation to a new one rebuilt on the solid foundations of the preceding one.

While these significant historical differences serve to distinguish one film clearly from the other, each participates in an underlying continuity revealed precisely in the filmmakers' retention of the same title and the liberal adoption of the narrative changes and additions made by their predecessors. Not once do the remakes credit their sources for elements incorporated from previous films into their own versions; yet, their silence does not register easily as cases of disingenuous disavowal. As Leitch notes regarding the typical position of a re-adaptation toward a previous adaptation, the former usually 'ignores or treats' the latter 'as inconsequential' (2002: 45). In contrast, here, the climate of competition that one normally senses between a re-adaptation and previous adaptations – being more faithful to the original written source – seems oddly absent. Indeed, while the novel appears as the source work in each film's credits, as per French copyright law,[7] the 1933 and 1949 films are not true re-adaptations but remakes, hewing closely to the narrative structure and focal shift established by Roudès. If the 1933 version was silent about its relationship to Roudès' film, as was the 1949 version about the two earlier productions, the guiding spirit behind that silence was less competition and more collaboration. The resulting continuity springs from the novel and films' setting – a nursery school – as *a*, if not *the* republican institution best suited for putting into practice and sustaining the core democratic principles and objectives of the Revolution, and as an essential building block in the physical, moral and intellectual well-being of the Republic. The *maternelle* is the site of a child's introduction to the greater educational apparatus identified and exploited by both republican progressives and conservatives during the first years of the Third Republic (1870–1940) for being singularly positioned to inculcate a sense of loyalty to and thereby ensure the stability of France. *La Maternelle* – novel, film adaptation and remakes – enacts (acts out *and* puts into action) democratic solidarity as well.

LÉON FRAPIÉ'S *LA MATERNELLE* AND THE FAILINGS OF THE SECULAR MORALITY OF THIRD REPUBLIC EDUCATION

Upon marrying in 1888 the primary school teacher Léonie Mouillefert, Frapié discovered the milieu in which he would place many of his novels' and short stories' characters, mostly female school teachers. His wife's profession and experiences were a great source of material, and he took advantage of it for the rest of his life. If he continued to draw from that well, it was also, as Guy Thuillier suggests, because his publishers pushed him to continue to tap this commercially rewarding vein (1970: 510).

The target of the novel was the still relatively new educational system that came about through the Jules Ferry laws of 1881 and 1882, the first providing for free primary education for all French children and the second for mandatory attendance and secular instruction, with the latter provision being finalised in 1905 with the Law on the Separation of Churches and the State. The trickiest part in the initial application of these laws was determining just what constituted secular morality, especially since there was still strong conservative opposition to replacing the entrenched religious model. It took roughly ten more years for legislators to agree on a pedagogical programme for training teachers who would mould the youngest French citizens into responsible voters, patriotic soldiers and defenders of the Republic. This was an objective that targeted primarily boys, but that by default included girls, since legislators realised that girls were integral to the success of inculcating republican secular morality. Women were targeted as the instructors best suited to directing and teaching in nursery and primary schools because of their maternal ability to touch children's hearts. According to this rationale, once the seeds of republican secular morality were firmly planted by women teachers, male teachers would step in to shape children's minds.

The intrigue of Frapié's novel takes place in a nursery school in a working-class section of Paris, Ménilmontant; in it, he reveals the mismatch of curricular secular morality and the experience of the children of the urban poor. Through his heroine Rose, he criticises an educational system that fosters conformity (principally unquestioning obedience towards family, but also towards nation and God) rather than explores the individual potential of its disadvantaged students, trapping them hopelessly within the class into which they are born. The nursery school, its personnel and its wards are observed and critiqued through the eyes of an outsider who comes from the class that wielded the authority to carry out reforms. Rose is a bourgeois woman, whose father dies leaving her destitute, whose fiancé abandons her upon the disappearance of her dowry and who has to hide all signs of her class (advanced education degrees, fine clothes, cultured manners and elegant speech) in order to get employment as a lowly all-purpose cleaning lady and aide in a nursery school. The uselessness of her degrees is testimony to the specialised normal school training and diplomas required for working in the new curriculum. After a year, Rose is torn between a marriage proposal, ostensibly from the regional school superintendent Dr Libois, and staying on at the school to devote herself entirely to the children. We never learn what she decides, although in the final paragraph one disabused mother tells her in so many words to 'get out' of Ménilmontant, vowing that 'you will not have my kid for your school that dooms us to starvation' (Frapié 1904: 304). The author does not explicitly state what option Rose chooses. The film adaptation and remakes, however, offer an unequivocal resolution: Rose will marry Dr Libois, and the couple will adopt little orphaned Marie Coeuret, a character that does not exist in the novel. Both Rose and Dr Libois subordinate their personal needs to those of this child, who is by extension the bigger concept of the nation and its future.

Frapié challenged the compromises and biases of the legislators who enacted the Ferry laws. While the latter saw the importance of allying all French citizens to the cause and health of the fragile Republic (since the Revolution, France had gone through two republics, two empires and the reigns of three constitutional monarchs, although not in that order), they erred in attributing minimal importance to the education of the lower classes beyond primary school. Frapié's novel critiques the inculcation of a secular morality that does not give underprivileged children the tools for improving their lives, condemning them by official edict to perpetuating the failings of their class. What good does it do to teach these children to submit and conform to the example of their parents, for instance, as the novel's heroine Rose points out, if 'the parents are not perfect, quite the contrary' (1904: 111). This thinking presupposes that these parents 'possess the highest virtues *along with lots of money*' (1904: 117). Operating under the assumption that lower-class children will not (and should not) continue to secondary school, these 'progressive' republican statesmen betrayed a conviction of the naturalness of class stratification. Under this program, the critical years of nursery and primary school instruction validate the bourgeoisie's most grievous social prejudices, dooming its most vulnerable group – the children of the urban poor – to perpetuating the cycle of misery and poverty.

GASTON ROUDÈS AND THE ORPHAN GENRE

While the novel clearly had a reformist agenda, equally clearly it was Frapié's portraits of the children of Ménilmontant and Rose's interactions with them that appealed most to readers over the span of half a century. In making his 1925 adaptation of *La Maternelle*, Roudès clearly banked on audience familiarity with the novel, as well as on the popularity of the orphan genre, which Monaco situates in the years 1921–6, but which clearly enjoyed continued popularity into the early 1930s with Jean Vigo's *Zero for Conduct* (*Zéro de conduit*, 1933), the sound remakes of *La Maternelle*, Julien Duvivier's *Poil de carotte* (1925 and 1932), as well as the different versions of *Crainquebille* (1922 and 1934) and *The Two Girls* (*Les Deux gamines*, 1921 and 1936), to name a few (1976: 85). 'No national cinema of any other land at any other time,' so Monaco contends, 'has been so singularly obsessed with this particular thematic material' (1976: 89). Monaco attributes the relevance of orphan story films to a combination of two peculiarly French collective psychological preoccupations, for which the abandoned children of the films are metaphors: first, for post-World War I depopulation and, second, for France as a 'diplomatic orphan', deserted by England and the United States in their failure to follow through on the security provisions of the Versailles Treaty (1976: 101). The orphan genre addresses fears for an already depopulated France that due to the war 'lost proportionately the most of any nation in human as well as in material terms', and it plays out a national wish fulfilment dream to '[r]egain the protectors of 1917/18, England and the United States' (1976: 98, 101).

In two articles on Benoit-Lévy and Epstein's *Maternité* (1929) and *La Maternelle*, Koos (2003, 2009) argues that these films were influenced by the pro-natalist and familialist movements that warned of an increasingly invigorated and menacing German neighbour threatening a weak France. At the time when she wrote these articles, Koos was apparently aware neither of the 1925 adaptation of Frapié's novel, nor of the 1949 remake, but her contention regarding the 1933 film pertains more aptly to the earlier one. It was during this period that pro-natalist and familialist reform groups carried out relentless and strategically effective lobbying of legislators, the press and educators to fight depopulation, in particular through an attempt to have a pro-natalist and familialist programme piggy-back onto secular morality instruction in primary and secondary schools. Indeed, it was through the principal channel of schools that the objectives of the right and the left met, wedding leftist and centrist secular morality's formation of young minds in an allegiance to the Republic to the right's quest to inculcate a sense of urgency and responsibility for becoming fathers and mothers of large families and thus reverse the disturbing declining birth trend. This ideological cohabitation explains the enthusiastic responses to the 1933 film by groups on both sides of the political spectrum.

However, it was the generic narrative structure of the orphan story that Roudès grafted onto his adaptation which, in countering the fragmentation of Frapié's novel, provided the narrative template for all subsequent film versions: a child loses her mother to death (1925 and 1949) or abandonment (1933), despairs to the point of attempting suicide (1925 and 1933), or risks being lost to Child Protective Services (1949), but is finally welcomed into a nurturing family composed of a mother *and* a father. The ability to unite opposing political agendas in support of a strengthened republic begins, not with the 1933 remake, as Koos contends, but with the 1925 adaptation.

The nursery school is the culturally privileged site for determining the fate of the French Republic. It is here that future republicans are trained. It is also here that future mothers and fathers heed the call to counter the declining birth rate. The message of the films is not principally anti-feminist, yet traditional gender roles are central to the beneficial effect of love on children, which in turn would be the foundation of the family unit, symbol of a reinvigorated nation (1925), a healthy society (1933) and an enduring republic (1949). Each film strives to awaken, therefore, the maternal instinct in Rose and a paternal bond in Dr Libois. An example is provided in the 1949 film's parable of the chickadee, whose care of a baby cuckoo bird along with her own is rewarded when he saves the mother bird and his stepbrothers and stepsisters from a snake. Rose, however, does not need a parable for her maternal instinct to be awakened. Nor does the burden of social responsibility rest solely on her shoulders. The desired stability that the family unit can bring means that the male protagonist also must accept his social duty to care, not only for their own future children, but for the abandoned ones who need love and attention now.

DOCUMENTING REALITY IN *LA MATERNELLE*

Critics and scholars find in Frapié's novel a descendant of nineteenth-century Realism and Naturalism, and in many respects this realist component visually translates into the adaptation and remakes' semi-documentary approach to filming the activities of the children. In the 1925 film, it is this blend of the conventions of the orphan genre with semi-documentary detachment which validates Monaco's conclusions regarding the genre as a metaphor of an abandoned France. Here, documentary objectivity substitutes for Frapié's social commentary.

While Roudès' adaptation blends location and studio shooting, it was in the studio where the director was able to catch the children seemingly unaware of the camera. He filmed them at play or congregated in groups in the schoolyard and in the nursery school lobby or in their classrooms. There is little information on the production, but given that Roudès was clearly counting on audience familiarity with the novel and exploiting the popular orphan genre, it is likely that he also sought to ramp up audience pleasure and the recognition effect by reproducing the picturesque liveliness and spontaneity of Francisque Poulbot's illustrations for the 1904 edition and Théophile Steinlen's for the 1908 edition. Given the remakes' replication of the semi-documentary component of Roudès' film, it is also likely that the palpable freshness and sense of lively movement that comes from the rapidly sketched glimpses of impoverished and vulnerable children in their milieu and at play, which Poulbot and Steinlen caught on the fly in their illustrations, led the director to focus on the natural behaviour of the largely non-professional child actors, an effect that the silence of the medium facilitated.

The 1933 sound remake had to work considerably harder to achieve similar results. Epstein said of the making of the film that Benoit-Lévy had conceived the project ten years prior to their production, and that it took three years to get it off the ground. It is clear, however, from the repetition of the basic storyline, from the word-for-word reappearance of entire bits of dialogue, and from the many visual borrowings that the writing-directing team had seen and studied Roudès' adaptation and that it fell into the class of films they liked to make: films possessing an educational thrust.[8] Indeed, Benoit-Lévy devoted ten years (1922–32) to the making of scientific and educational documentaries, the latter of which often covered hygiene for new mothers, the education of children and the betterment of children's lives in slums. For example, among his fictional films with an educational objective, in *La Future maman* (1925), he addressed pre- and post-natal hygiene; in *L'Ange du foyer* (1928) and *Le Nid* (1928), he proposed ways to combat deleterious life in slums. His first four feature films, co-written and co-directed with Epstein, equally had social objectives: first, he examined urban poor children and their access to education, their health and welfare (*Peach Skin*, *Peau de pêche*, 1928, *Âmes d'enfants*, 1928, and *Heart of Paris*, *Le Coeur de Paris*, 1931); second, he addressed women and the raising of children (*Maternité*, 1929). Benoit-Lévy felt keenly that the cinema has the 'moral imperative' to inform and educate its audience (Flitterman-Lewis 1990: 152).

In order to capture the same sense of unselfconscious spontaneity on the part of the children achieved by Roudès in the silent adaptation, Benoit-Lévy and Epstein had to get the children to accept the camera as a natural part of their daily life. The two directors did extensive location research, spending at least one month observing a nursery school in an impoverished Parisian neighbourhood, building a set in Courbevoie that replicated in every detail the very school that the children attended, transporting all 200 of them daily to the set where actors and teachers ensured the children's perception that they were in *a*, if not *their*, nursery school.[9]

Epstein, who was the sister of director Jean Epstein, brought the French Impressionistic style to the teamwork in this film – namely, optical techniques and rhythmical camera movement – to express little Marie's unique subjective experience as her need for maternal love becomes increasingly intense. The visual impression of the child's inner experience reproduced the sketched-from-daily-life feel of Poulbot's and Steinlen's illustrations, images with which a new generation of spectators was perhaps unfamiliar. The objective semi-documentary comes to the service of the subjective camera here, intensifying by its depiction of real life and thereby making more immediate the audience's experience of the child's emotional trauma. The result is that we are compelled to respond to her need for maternal nurturing. Our response should be Rose's: to get married – which Dr Libois obligingly offers – and adopt the orphaned Marie Coeuret.

From the reappearance of shots/scenes from the earlier films and from the reproduction of the general narrative outline and dialogue from both predecessors, it is clear that Diamant-Berger was very familiar with both the 1925 adaptation and the 1933 remake.[10] Indeed, he adopts Roudès' positioning of Rose and the nursery school head mistress in a love triangle. The attempt at semi-documentary realism is less successful: the non-professional child actors awkwardly deliver rehearsed dialogue and mug at the camera. Like Benoit-Lévy and Epstein *vis-à-vis* Roudès' film, Diamant-Berger seemingly disavows knowledge of his immediate predecessors' production process, marking his disavowal as thoroughly and shamelessly disingenuous. Indeed, in a 2012 interview, his grandson Jérôme extols the degree of authenticity that his grandfather sought to create in the recreation of a nursery school in the studio at Épinay: 'In fact, they reconstructed – that, too, was a tour de force – [. . .] a school with the children [. . .] in the studios of Épinay [. . .] where the children came for two months to continue their classes in fake classrooms. And so, this entire world was reconstituted from "a" to "z"' (Ollé-Laprune 2012).

That Diamant-Berger took credit for the semi-documentary practice introduced by Benoit-Lévy and Epstein seventeen years earlier defies credulity. The filmmakers' methods were well known, having been over two years the subject of interviews and film reviews in France and New York, where he often travelled in his capacity as producer for Pathé and later Pathé-Natan. However, his seemingly brazen 'theft' is neither indicative of the director's treatment of the earlier versions as unworthy of his consideration, nor just another instance of the director's habit of taking credit for a number of historical details from film history.[11]

LA MATERNELLE AND THE CONTINUITY REMAKE

Diamant-Berger did not make any movies during the German Occupation of France (1940–44). As a Jew, he was first exiled to the United States, where he became involved with the Free French Forces, which led later to an appointment in Algiers. *La Maternelle* represented his post-war return to commercial cinema; like Roudès, who had counted on a certain measure of box-office success in 'adapting' the novel precisely for its lasting popularity and for the possibility of simultaneously exploiting the vogue for the orphan genre, Diamant-Berger trusted in the continued currency of the novel's appeal to audiences to revive his own dormant career. In remaking *La Maternelle*, he reminded the French public of his relevance as a *cinéaste*, hitching his own history in the profession to a turn-of-the-century story that still resonated with readers.

In his consultations with Frapié, however, the two decided that the film's context needed to be updated. He chose to set the film, not in the 18th arrondissement of Montmartre like the 1933 version, but in Ménilmontant in the 20th arrondissement, still a working-class section of Paris at the time and the original setting for Frapié's tale (Ollé-Laprune 2012). Regardless, we cannot interpret this reversion as a simple sign of competition with Benoit-Lévy and Epstein's film by means of greater fidelity to the novel, since Diamant-Berger hewed to the basic story structure established by the 1925 film and reprised in the 1933 version. His is a gesture expressing resolve and resilience, his own and, perhaps unintentionally, the nation's. He deliberately opened his film with a montage of street shots of the neighbourhood, not in an attempt to set the movie's tone amid the dirt and squalor reminiscent of Frapié's Ménilmontant, but on the contrary to reveal the improvements made in the nearly fifty years since the first publication of the novel, an urban renewal revealed in clean, uncluttered streets – we even notice a garbage collection truck and a street cleaner in two separate shots – and building fronts.

Diamant-Berger's scriptwriters were Alexis Daban and Marcelle Capron, the latter the former director of a secondary school for girls in Cannes. It is to Capron that we can attribute the updates regarding the educational system. In 1949, nursery school teachers no longer needed a special pedagogical degree from the École Normale Supérieure; accordingly, once the principal realises that Rose has advanced diplomas, she promotes her to teacher. And, contrary to the earlier versions in which Rose takes Marie home with her and keeps her there for the duration of the story, the 1949 film depicts state welfare agencies intervening quickly in situations such as parental abuse (the boy Prosper) and the death of parents (orphaned Marie Coeuret) to place these children in *L'Assistance publique* (Child Protective Services).

In a strategy to compete with the American movies inundating the market after the war, French filmmakers returned to the pre-war approach of appealing to French nationalism in the adaptation of works from France's literary patrimony. Although Diamant-Berger worked with a relatively low budget, preventing him from making a historical drama – the genre most associated with French cinema's Tradition of Quality (1946–59) – he chose to 're-adapt' a work that tapped into an expression of the 'national Spirit' (Williams 1992: 278). This remake permitted Diamant-Berger to jumpstart his stagnant commercial career. The updating of the source texts' setting – novel, adaptation (1925) and remake (1933) – also served to celebrate regime continuity, building on a pre-World War past (both wars) embodied in a familiar nursery school tale that stood as incontrovertible evidence of the legitimacy and resilience of the French Republic. The story may get tweaked with the passage of time in order to engage with current socio-cultural conditions and preoccupations, but the skeleton and basic muscular structure remain intact. For Diamant-Berger the remake was a bridge between the pre- and post-war periods that served to restore him to his place in French cinema. *La Maternelle* as remake is a bridge also between the Third and the Fourth Republics, symbolised by the *maternelle* as an institution that survived the Occupation. In this light, the remake is a re-forming, a gesture of forming or shaping the Republic anew.

The thrust of the 1949 film is professional (for Diamant-Berger) and sociocultural continuity (for the Republic). Nowhere is this more evident than in the general call to forgiveness, which happens on two levels. On the level of story, the financial scandal of the novel, the adaptation (1925) and the 1933 remake is garden-variety socio-economic disgrace: Rose's father dies from suicide or remorse, her fiancé jilts her and she must now earn her own living. In the 1949 film, however, no one states the nature of the scandal, but it is serious enough for Rose to change her last name and to seek to lose herself in a community where no one knows either her or her family. Given that this film expressly addresses the post-war period, we can conjecture that Rose's father may have been a collaborator. When they discover Rose's background, the nursery school principal and personnel accept her among them, refusing to associate the sin of the father with the daughter.

On another level, the film appeals to the nation to come together through the figure of the mother with a child born out of wedlock. It explicitly entreats women not to abandon their babies, many of whom may be war children, a circumstance that in the immediate post-war period had doomed their mothers to harsh social censure. Women who had fraternised with Occupation soldiers were arrested, judged and/or subjected to public humiliation, the most common form of which was shaving the head. A scene late in Diamant-Berger's movie takes place in a child welfare services building where orphaned Marie Coeuret has been remanded after the killing of her prostitute mother by the police. Rose tries to find Marie and stumbles upon a room where a nun is explaining to a young mother how abandonment works: if she leaves her child, she may be unable to reclaim her when she is better positioned to care for her. The objective of child welfare services is to arrange for the adoption of such children. We see a sign above the head of the nurse that pleads, 'Mommy... mommy, don't abandon me!' Another mother with an infant in the waiting room overhears this explanation and promptly leaves with her baby, apparently persuaded to keep her child.

A first reflex is to interpret the appeal to mothers to assume their maternal function as propaganda against single working women, of which the film offers two examples. In the final scene of the film, we see a despondent principal who is paying the price for her aspiration to have a family *and* a job: her future promises loneliness. Earlier, the film presents the school's cold and masculine social worker as a working woman who has suppressed, along with her femininity, any trace of maternal tendencies. As she prepares to take custody of the child Prosper in the name of the state, the principal asks her rhetorically if she has ever even held a child.

Another, equally valid, target materialises in *L'Assistance publique* as a social institution that not only wrested children from unfit parents, but that also doomed its orphan wards to precarity in adulthood. Marie Coeuret's mother, who had gone through the foster-care system, turned to prostitution when all other efforts at obtaining employment failed. When her orphaned daughter finds herself in the care of the state, the cycle threatens to repeat itself. Dr Libois intimates that he, too, grew up in a state orphanage. If he was successful in overcoming his social disadvantages, it was only because he also surmounted the anger that consumed him, often a vestige of life in foster care. As in the 1933 version, the 1949 film proposes the nuclear family – a working father, a housewife and mother, and their children – as the cure for a fragmented post-Occupation France. This is essentially the message that Dr Libois imparts to a group of children who have 'quarantined' (in other words, ostracised) a class/playmate: they need to unite and work/play together. No one – neither men, nor women and children – are spared the film's schooling.

CONCLUSION

An interesting dynamic of disavowal and invocation emerges in this series of adaptation and remakes. With the last remake, the interplay of the two positions is reminiscent of post-war Hollywood films in which wartime wayward women are forgiven their transgressions. The disavowal that one finds in all three films responds to changing historical conditions. Still, there is an effort to provide continuity between all of them. Citing from the novel and from the previous filmed versions works to reaffirm the endurance of secular democracy and the French Republic. The last film, taking place in the immediate post-World War II period, adds forgiveness for past transgressions and the spirit of inclusiveness as ingredients in a recipe for moving the nation forward. The 1949 remake is a symbol of France in the same way in which the 1925 adaptation was a symbol of the nation as orphan child, a wish-fulfilment dream in which a previously divided country, split between collaborators and Resistance fighters and sympathisers, reconciles and reunites. These remakes serve less to rewrite cinematic history than to 'induce a climate of overall moral as well as historical continuity' (Forrest 2002: 195).

NOTES

1. Two of the three directors discussed in this chapter made silent to sound remakes. In 1932, Gaston Roudès remade Louis Feuillade's *Le Gamin de Paris* (1923). Roudès also remade in 1937 Alfred-Francis Bertoni's *Enfants de Paris* (1924). As for Henri Diamant-Berger, he remade his 1923 silent film *Jim Bougne, boxeur* in 1935, and he turned his 1921 twelve-episode serial *Les Trois mousquetaires* into a feature-length sound production in 1932.
2. Protopopoff and Serceau attribute the systematic adaptation of French literature to the screen beginning in the teens to the 'desire to promote cinema to the status of art in its own right' (1989: 22). Perhaps more precisely, however, France's inability to compete with American film after the onset of World War I necessitated a strategy that could counter, however minimally, the flooding of its market by Hollywood product. One response was to appeal to French audience chauvinism with distinctly French product. All translations from the French are my own.
3. With some gaps in publication, *La Maternelle* was reprinted and republished almost every year until the 1960s.
4. Indeed, film critic Pierre Ducrocq qualified Frapié as a 'second-rate Zola' (1949: 1).
5. Frapié served as consultant for the 1933 and 1949 films. Although I have been unable to determine whether he was involved in the 1925 film's production, Frapié would have had direct knowledge of its existence through Roudès' application for licensing. For his part, Benoit-Lévy would have at the very least learned of the 1925 production through Epstein, since her work with her brother Jean overlapped with the early stages of her collaboration with Benoit-Lévy. Indeed, Roudès produced Jean's *Sa Tête* (1929), starring France Dhélia, the actress who featured in roughly twenty-five films directed by Roudès from 1923 to 1939.
6. Future references to these films will be indicated by directors or the year of production.
7. French copyright law accorded with the Berne Convention for the Protection of Literary and Artistic Works (1886) to which the 1908 revision added film.
8. Surprisingly, in over twenty film reviews, newspaper articles and interviews with Frapié, Benoit-Lévy and the star Madeleine Renaud, not one mentions the 1925 adaptation.
9. When one remakes, one often does so in a bigger way. The 1925 film's roughly twenty students multiplied by ten in the 1933 version.
10. Benoit-Lévy and Epstein's remake was a huge international success: It ran for nine months straight in Paris and was dubbed into five languages (Koos 2003: 12–13). Claude Lazurick of *L'Aurore* described the 'new version' of Frapié's novel as being a 'decent' production that nevertheless milks the material for all its sentimental potential (1949: 1). Ducrocq of *Carrefour*, however, who recalled with fondness the 1933 film, chastised Diamant-Berger for having 'ruined a nice memory' (1949: 1). Ducrocq's explanation for why the director remade the 1933 movie – with which he was most certainly familiar – was that, for him, '[i]t was not about making a good film as much about making a good business deal' (1). Jeander of *Libération* echoed Ducrocq, stating that the film as remake 'belongs to the "commercial" genre par excellence' (1949: 1).
11. Among his many boasts, he claimed to have invented the words *photogénie* and *script-girl* as well as the practice of movie trailers (1977: 30, 31).

REFERENCES

Diamant-Berger, Henri (1977), *Il était une fois le cinéma*, Paris: Jean-Claude Simoën.
Ducrocq, Pierre (1949), 'Les Mineurs avec nous! . . .', *Carrefour*, 1 June, p. 1.
Flitterman-Lewis, Sandy (1990), *To Desire Differently: Feminism and the French Cinema*, Urbana and Chicago: University of Illinois Press.

Forrest, Jennifer (2002), 'Sadie Thompson Redux: Postwar Reintegration of the Wartime Wayward Woman', in Jennifer Forrest and Leonard R. Koos (eds), *Dead Ringers: The Remake in Theory and Practice*, Albany: SUNY Press, pp. 169–202.
Frapié, Léon (1908), *La Maternelle*, Paris: Librairie Universelle.
Jeander (1949), 'Le Cinéma: La Maternelle', *Libération*, 24 May, p. 1.
Koos, Cheryl A. (2009), 'The Good, the Bad, and the Childless: The Politics of Female Identity in *Maternité* (1929) and *La Maternelle* (1933)', *Historical Reflections/Réflexions historiques*, 35: 2, 3–20.
Koos, Cheryl (2003), 'True Women and Social Demons: *La Maternelle* (1933) and the Politics of Gender in Interwar France', *Film & History CD-ROM Annual*, pp. 1–17.
Lazurick, Claude (1949), 'La Maternelle', *L'Aurore*, 21 May, p. 1.
Leitch, Thomas (2002), 'Twice-Told Tales: Disavowal and the Rhetoric of the Remake', in Jennifer Forrest and Leonard R. Koos (eds), *Dead Ringers: The Remake in Theory and Practice*, Albany: SUNY Press, pp. 37–62.
Monaco, Paul (1976), *Cinema and Society: France and Germany During the Twenties*, New York, Oxford, Amsterdam: Elsevier.
Ollé-Laprune, Jean (2012), 'Jérôme Diamant-Berger nous parle de son grand-père Henri Diamant-Berger', Entretien/Henri-Diamant Berger/FilmoTV, available at: https://www.youtube.com/watch?v=SrXveoffO2c (last accessed 1 September 2019).
Protopopoff, Daniel and Michel Serceau (1989), 'Du cinéma comme bibliothèque idéale', in Michel Serceau and Daniel Protopopoff (eds), *Le Remake et l'adaptation*, Paris: CinémAction, pp. 21–28.
Thuillier, Guy (1970), '"Marcelin Gayard" de Léon Frapié', *La Revue administrative*, 137, 510–15.
Williams, Alan (1992), *Republic of Images: A History of French Filmmaking*, Cambridge, MA, and London: Harvard University Press.

CHAPTER 7

Screening Transformation Processes: Post-War Remakes of Nazi-Era Films

Stefanie Mathilde Frank

German cinema of the Adenauer era (1949–63) has always suffered a bad reputation. *Heimatfilme* were written off as mere escapism. War films, meanwhile, glamourised German soldiers and trivialised the country's guilt about World War II. The same directors and technicians who had served the National Socialist film industry could continue their careers unabated. Indeed, the German film industry as a whole underwent little to no artistic or political renovation during this time (Hake 2002, Rentschler 1998). The multitude of remakes that emerged in the 1950s would appear to confirm this assessment at first glance. More so as, by my estimate, 106 of the 154 remakes produced between 1949 and 1963 were based on films that were first released under the Nazi regime and had been popular in the years between 1933 and 1945.

It is within this context of regression that film historians have firmly situated the post-war remakes. Already in 1961, Joe Hembus noted in his fundamental critique of German cinema:

> The cinema season without a remake is unthinkable in Germany. Of course, this repetitiveness does not have criminal traits in all cases. [. . .] Sometimes it can prevent damage. For as long as the manpower of certain filmmakers is bound to these innocuous tasks, they are prevented from working on more challenging subjects. It really only becomes questionable when the producers believe they can put old film successes originally created for the cinema through the same remake-grinder that only just recently devoured *Im weißen Rössl* (Hembus 1961: 95).

The author's damning tone is clearly apparent here. Interestingly, the fundamental argument against the 'remake grinder' is not aimed at the lightweight subject matter represented here by *The White Horse Inn* (*Im weißen Rössl*, 1935 DE, 1952 FRG, 1960 AT), but rather at the 'questionable' remakes of 'original cinematic creations'. The post-war German remakes were not considered problematic for social or political reasons, but mainly for reasons of aesthetics. Incidentally, this argument already dominated the contemporary journalistic discourse on remakes in the 1950s, as well as the subsequent opinions of German film historians (see Faulstich and Korte 1990: 23, Hake 2004: 190).

My own interest in the remake phenomenon of the 1950s is not merely limited to aesthetic considerations, but also includes their role within a wider sociological context. It is the ambiguity of the remakes that interests me particularly. On the one hand, they drew on existing popular subjects, screenplays and films. On the other hand, they represented new productions with new actors, new music and revised scripts. This is precisely what makes remakes ideal subjects when trying to determine the relationship between feature filmmaking in the National Socialist and post-war periods. In this way, remakes can be seen to provide information from a diachronic perspective on those elements of Nazi-era filmmaking that continued unchanged after the war and those that were altered or dropped altogether. The corpus of remakes produced in the 1950s encompasses a variety of popular genres. This diversity and the ambiguity between old and new following processes of change lies at the centre of the ensuing examination. From a diachronic perspective, questions concerning typical and idiosyncratic themes become virulent, as do questions about changes that occur over time. Thus, it is possible to extend the *Heimatfilm*-centric genre historiography of the 1950s,[1] as re-evaluated by Von Moltke in his ground-breaking work. With his notion of 'nostalgic modernisation', which both historically expands and refines Herf's theory of 'reactionary modernism' during the Nazi era (1984), Von Moltke argues that the function of the post-war *Heimatfilm* represents an 'imaginary compromise between radical change and radical conservatism' (Von Moltke 2005: 151).

Following this notion, I would argue that the references and changes inherent in the post-war remakes cannot simply be described dichotomously. These references and changes, moreover, unfold and manifest themselves over the course of the decade. Using some of the most popular remakes from the early and late 1950s as examples, I intend to accentuate diachronic and synchronic research perspectives in turn. Through questions about the recreation of time periods, contemporary discourses, music and stars/actors, I can refine Von Moltke's theory beyond the limits of any one genre as it relates to the content of the individual films. As a basis for possible transnational comparisons, I will first define the body of films as a whole, before presenting the films themselves, as well as the political and legal conditions behind their production. In doing so, I will put the peculiarities of post-war German film history in focus and be able to provide answers to some of the questions that remain open after the close readings: are there any specific structural conditions under which the film remakes were produced in the fledgling Federal Republic of Germany? How does the production of remakes develop over the course of the 1950s? How can their demise at the start of the 1960s be explained? Can remakes really be understood in purely economic terms as a means of minimising risk by falling back on prior successes?

DEFINING REMAKES

The fundamental question from the outset concerns the definition of a remake. With reference to Oltmann, remakes could be defined as 'all those productions that repurpose the story of an earlier film (hereinafter referred to as a "premake") for cinema exploitation' (Oltmann 2008: 26). But what precisely does it mean to 'repurpose a story'? The German remakes of the 1950s range from films which essentially recycle the first scripts verbatim to those which deviate so heavily from the predecessors that only their titles, the names of the principal characters and essential plot points are recognisable. To determine the precise body of films that would serve as the basis of the examination, I established four essential, defining criteria: (1) consistency of the basic plot, (2) verifiable transfer of author's rights, (3) common source materials (novels, operettas, plays) and (4) reference to an earlier film as source (for example, in the opening credits, in production or distribution materials or in reviews). By fulfilling one or another of these criteria, a film could be classified as a remake for the statistics (Frank 2017: 27). The first criterion concerns narrative according to established and critically evaluated taxonomies or definitions (Druxman 1975, Leitch 2002). The second point is related to the specific nature of copyright law in the Federal Republic of Germany from 1949 to 1963. The third is by far the broadest and, from an international und theoretical perspective, most problematic: I would argue that contemporary cinema-going audiences' knowledge of the premake played a larger and more significant role than their knowledge of the source material. The distinction between adaptations and remakes of earlier films seems to be of secondary importance. Indeed, both remakes and premakes were screened concurrently in West German cinemas in the 1950s.[2] Like the third, the fourth criterion considers remakes as a reception phenomenon (Schaudig 1996, Simonet 1987).

All four criteria draw on Verevis' (2006) considerations of remaking as industrial, textual and critical categories, as applicable to the location and time-period under examination. It is important to highlight here that the corpus of films analysed systematically did not include those films based on earlier unfinished and/or unreleased projects, as contemporary cinema-going audiences would not have perceived these films as remakes. Also included in the analysis were thirty-three remakes and their corresponding premakes that were made in Austria. The Austrian and German markets were closely linked in the entire period under examination (Loacker 1999, Wauchope 2007), and German cinema throughout its entire existence has benefited from input from Austrian artists and performers. Moreover, many of the most successful films released in Germany during this time were Austrian productions. While a division is thus inappropriate in this specific context, I by no means wish to insinuate that all Austrian films should be considered synonymous with German films.

GERMAN REMAKE PRODUCTION IN NUMBERS

Significantly, the first film to be shot in the newly founded Federal Republic of Germany (FRG) was a remake (of sorts): Director Helmut Weiß reshot his film *Sag die Wahrheit* (1949),[3] which he had begun during the war but soon abandoned. Between 1949 and 1963, a total of 1,375 feature films were produced in the FRG, 154 of which were remakes. Of these 154 remakes, 106 were based on films originating in the 'Third Reich' (Frank 2017: 31). Of the 241 imported Austrian films, meanwhile, thirty-eight can be identified and defined as remakes (Frank 2017: 130). The production of remakes in the FRG increased in tandem with film production as a whole. Remakes accounted for an average 10 percent of the entire West German film production between 1949 and 1963, increasing to a maximum 15 percent in the years in which film production was at its highest in the FRG (1953–57). In 1953, 104 feature films were produced, twenty-one of which were remakes of earlier German films, including fourteen that were first released between 1933 and 1945. Of the 123 feature films produced in 1956, meanwhile, seventeen were remakes (sixteen from the Nazi era). The number of remakes declined after 1955, falling more steeply than the overall film production, and by the early 1960s very few remakes were being produced. When *Autorenkino* (*auteur* cinema) came to dominate West German film production following the signing of the 'Oberhausen Manifesto' in 1962, remakes largely disappeared from German cinema screens.

The average percentage of German films produced in the 1950s that could be classified as remakes was double of what it had been in the period following the transition from silent to sound film. Between 1930 and 1941, only 5.5 percent of all German productions were remakes of earlier films: 106 of the 1,585 feature films produced during this time were remakes of German and international silent films (Frank 2017: 42). In no other period in the history of German cinema have so many remakes been produced as in the 1950s.

As the examples analysed in this paper will show, it was not only remakes of earlier hits that proved to be the biggest box office draws, but rather the remakes of lesser known films from the Nazi era. Throughout the 1950s, remakes proved to be both critical and commercial successes, as well as flops. According to the polls carried out by the magazine *Film-Echo*, remakes on average performed adequately but not outstandingly at the box-office.[4]

GERMAN FILM POLITICS

To assume that remakes were a 'safe bet', as the contemporary film press put it, would seem to be short-sighted. The problem mainly had to do with the complicated copyright situation in Germany. For one, there was no sure-fire way to outright purchase authors' rights under German copyright law. In the case of remakes, the rights had to be cleared on three different levels: adaptation rights (originated by the premake), the rights to original literary or theatrical sources and music rights, if popular hits were to be reused. At the same time, a vast number of records documenting proof of copyright were destroyed in World War II. The former state-run film company Ufa-Film (UFI),[5] which was liquidated in the 1950s, was practically the only constant claimant. This was not only because it had a robust network of lawyers working for the company prior to 1945, but also because the slow liquidation process resulting from German federal policy tended to play out in the company's favour. Article 5 of the German Constitution of 1949 protected films from state influence. However, thanks to the legal requirements of the UFI-liquidation as well as the guarantee schemes of the early 1950s, both the federal government and parliament intervened quite actively in the film market until the mid-1950s: in March 1950, the German parliament agreed to provide 20 million Marks to subsidise feature film production. Incidentally, a small number of remakes can be found among these so-called 'guarantee films' such as *Der letzte Walzer* (1953) and *Stern von Rio* (1955). As the following examples illustrate, the German remakes of the 1950s in essence were neither politically forced nor a mere economic phenomenon; rather, they can be described as a popular practice in a period of social transition.

REMAKES IN THE EARLY 1950S

At the beginning of the decade, remakes mainly consisted of comedies and operettas, as well as a few examples that can be attributed to the *Heimatfilm* genre. The films are mostly of the same technical standard as the films of the Nazi era. Comedies play frequently in bourgeois interior spaces and were moreover often shot in black and white. Marital conflict is a dominant theme in the films. In *Spatzen in Gottes Hand* (1950), a remake of *Kleiner Mann, ganz groß* (1938), poverty and misunderstanding threaten to break up a recent marriage. Money goes to the head of Heinz Rühmann's eponymous character in *Briefträger Müller* (1953), increasingly alienating him from his wife and children. What can be observed in these films above all are visual allusions to the post-war period. For instance, in *Muss man sich gleich scheiden lassen?* (1953) the betrayed wife has her old drawing table converted into a *Nierentisch* (kidney-shaped table) while renovation work is being carried out on her house.

The remakes of *Heimatfilme* from the early 1950s were set in a seemingly timeless Germany of neither past nor present and, from 1950 onwards, photographed exclusively in colour. Two successful examples of this genre, both of which premiered in 1953, illustrate the range of contemporary references as well as changes in diachronic and synchronic perspectives. *Der Klosterjäger* (1935, 1953) is a film adaptation of the 1892 novel by Ludwig Ganghofer, Germany's most popular author from the Wilhelmine period right up to the 1950s. The story takes place in the Middle Ages. The conflicts and the ensemble characters would have been rendered obsolete, had the story been updated. Later Ganghofer adaptations use both discrete and offensive means to update the plot, for instance, by adding cars and city footage, as in *Das Schweigen im Walde* (1955, 1937), or featuring contemporary brands such as the Martini ashtray seen in *Schloss Hubertus* (1954, 1934). Bernhard Eichhorn's soundtrack to *Der Klosterjäger* shares a common trait with Marc Roland's music to its premake in its orchestrated musical accompaniment to the shots of the landscape.

At the centre of the plot is the monastery hunter Haymo, who is in love with the orphan girl Gittli. Poverty and fear for his terminally ill daughter drive Gittli's brother to poaching, and he ends up seriously injuring Haymo. Gittli takes care of the injured Haymo, and her brother repents. By chance, it transpires that Gittli is the kidnapped daughter of Count Dietwald and, being of noble blood, cannot marry Haymo. In both cases, a final twist makes the happy ending possible: in the 1935 version, the monastery hunter is appointed game master, and the pair can marry. In the remake, the couple announces that they will leave together. The father overcomes his initial shock and ultimately gives the couple his blessing: 'Follow your heart, my child'. A final insert interprets the story of Haymo and Gittli as a 'symbol of eternally victorious love'. In the remake, the happy ending no longer needs to be achieved through the intervention of state authority. but through the blessing of the father. Thus, it can be interpreted as a form of de-politicisation.

Gittli's father is portrayed in the 1953 remake by Austrian actor Paul Richter, who became a star thanks to his performance as Siegfried in Fritz Lang's *Die Nibelungen* (1924) and who acted in all Ganghofer adaptations from 1934 onwards. In the 1935 version of *Der Klosterjäger*, he had portrayed the young eponymous character. This recasting of former male leads in older parts can otherwise only be observed in the remakes of films starring Willy Fritsch.

Interestingly, both actors had risen to stardom already in the silent era, their careers continuing seamlessly into the Nazi era.

In comparison to the earlier film, the remake of *Der Klosterjäger* seems strikingly discreet and de-historicised: the stories of battles and Germanness characteristic of the source novel are far more prevalent in the 1935 version. In his speech delivered in the film's opening scene, the church dignitary Heinrich declaims pointedly: 'For me, every man should be a German first and an ecclesiastic second'. This line is a direct quotation from the novel, but the quotation does not continue beyond this point (see Ganghofer 1985: 288). In the 1953 remake, the destruction of the count's castle and the loss of his family are no longer attributed directly to warfare. All the more conspicuous is the space afforded to the suffering father in the remake. In the 1935 version, his master had ordered him to become a monk, and he obeyed. In the remake, the count almost obsessively searches for his lost child, thus possibly offering the audience a projection surface for their own experiences of loss in the context of escape and expulsion after 1945. The film was the fifth-most successful feature film released in the FRG in the 1953/54 season (Garncarz 2013: 188).

The most successful film was *When the Village Music Plays on Sunday Evening* (*Wenn am Sonntagabend die Dorfmusik spielt*, 1953, 1933), a *Heimatfilm*, which tells the story of Kathi and Martin, a poor lumberjack. Displaced persons had been established as characters in post-war German feature films with the so-called 'rubble films' (see Tiews 2017: 56–86). Rarely, however, do their stories play such a significant and positive role in the dramaturgy. In the 1933 version of *When the Village Music Plays on Sunday Evening*, Martin is merely a poor lumberjack, and it is a female writer who comes to the village. In the 1953 version, however, the character is a trumpeter who flees from the tax office and his consumerist girl-friend, another reference to the money-theme of early remakes. The opening scene of the remake – a trumpeter's jazz concert in which the local community can be seen doing the boogie-woogie – already refers to the changes which German popular cinema was about to undergo. This scene occurs directly after the opening titles accompanied by the German folk song from which the film takes its title.

With its depiction of a crowd of young people and its exuberant, undisciplined dance scenes free from the carefully choreographed revue framework, *When the Village Music Plays on Sunday Evening* breaks from the traditional image of the pre-1945 German musical. The break is concealed, however, by the ensuing plot lacking in visual and musical references to modernisation: after the concert, the action leads to a countryside ideal complete with horse breeding, a forest and lumberjacks.

Visual and musical references to the contemporary present, and particularly brands and consumer culture, are noticeable in many remakes from the mid-1950s onwards. Signboards advertising Coca-Cola, for example, can be found in two *Heimatfilme*. Coca-Cola itself was nothing new at that time, as the company had been active on the German market already before 1945 (Schaefer 2009: 17). New, however, is the recurring presence of the product in feature films.

The most significant changes to the premakes are to be noticed in the soundtracks to the films. Throughout the 1950s, the musical spectrum becomes increasingly broad and, with the inclusion of popular hits (called 'Schlager'), ever more up-to-date. While folk music and lush orchestral scores initially dominated the *Heimatfilm* genre, a form of opening-up is apparent already in 1953 with *When the Village Music Plays on Sunday Evening* and its depiction of youth music. Over the course of the decade, various Rock'n'Roll numbers would be featured in numerous remakes. Feature films, therefore, picked up on popular youth culture, represented incidentally on more than a few occasions by the hit songs of Bill Haley. However, the Rock'n'Roll numbers are just details in complex plots, as much influenced by the use of folk songs in *Heimatfilm* or classical film music, as well as by conservative family images. Thus, the different strategies of integration in musical comedies reveal themselves. *Die unentschuldigte Stunde* (1957 AT) also shows that dance and bodies are frequently related to specific media practices and by no means linked exclusively to concerts or dance events, as one would expect. The film centres on a high school girl who falls in love with a doctor. Before he comes to visit her again, she is depicted in a short sequence enjoying leisure time at home: the girl reads while seated on a chair, then turns on the radio. A fanfare sounds. She turns the radio off, puts on a record instead, indicates a few dance steps, lies down with a magazine on the floor and nibbles chocolate pralines. Here we see music and youth in connection with mass media, depending on the different physicality and sensual pleasure. The chocolates are significant here; the combination of media consumption, pleasure and sensuality had been one of the main criticisms by youth protection agencies against the cinema in the time of the German Empire and in the 1920s (Maase 2012). It is thus possible to observe a change in the physicality of young protagonists, who act with less restraint and more freedom. The changes in male physicality at the end of the decade can be observed particularly in the performances of actor and singer Peter Alexander in remakes of two films that had previously starred Heinz Rühmann.

FROM COMEDY TO SCHLAGERFILM

Peter Alexander played the main role in one of the most successful German remakes from the latter half of the 1950s. *That Will Work* (*Das haut hin*, 1957) is a remake of the Austrian comedy *The Man One Talks About* (*Der Mann, von dem man spricht*, 1937). In the earlier film, Heinz Rühmann (one of the most popular actors of the 1930s and 40s) had played a zoology student who has to win the heart of a circus performer, Bianca. The remake retains the plot and most of the dialogue from the earlier film. When the protagonist is ex-matriculated after he oversleeps and misses an important exam, his rich family tries to force him to get married. While in the 1937 film it is the grumpy uncle played by Hans Moser who tries to force the nephew to marry, in 1957 the role is reassigned to the character of a strict, comical aunt played by Grethe Weiser. Interpreting this reassignment of roles historically as the symbol of a shift in the family image is not sufficient, however. This film is an exception among all the remakes examined. A line of dialogue in the remake even refers back to the first casting: the aunt laments her anger at the 'Reblaus' (a vine louse, phylloxera) – the title of the 1940 Viennese song and one of Hans Moser's most popular hits.

Despite its repetitions and allusions, the remake differs considerably from the 1937 premake where music is concerned. Already in the opening scene, the star of the film sings the hit 'Das tu' ich alles nur für dich', a foxtrot, in a 1950s interior backdrop made recognisable by the presence of the kidney table and its colour scheme. While Rühmann had only drunkenly staggered out of a restaurant, Alexander sings an ode to 'Ole Babutschkin', later revealed by a billboard to be a brand of vodka. He finally beguiles his beloved with the song 'Ein bisschen mehr' (A little more), during which a corpulent man is depicted in front of a gigantic sausage platter – an ironic comment on the West German 'Fresswelle' (food binge) of the time.

The differences in performance are even more noticeable in the next film to star Peter Alexander in a role previously played by Heinz Rühmann, *Blow Upon Blow* (*Schlag auf Schlag*, 1959 FRG), a remake of *Bachelors' Paradise* (*Das Paradies der Junggesellen*, 1939 DE). The film is a comedy revolving around the character of registrar Hugo Bartels who, after his second divorce, promises his boss that he will not marry again. With two male friends, he moves into a flat which no woman is permitted to enter. Bartels soon falls in love again, however, while his two friends end up marrying his ex-wives. In April 1958, following the success of *That Will Work*, producer Kurt Ulrich successfully acquired the rights to the original film.[6]

The cast and crew of *Blow Upon Blow* is similar to that of *That Will Work* and reflects both continuity and transition. Director Géza von Cziffra was a seasoned veteran of popular German cinema and a household name at the time. The soundtrack, however, was assigned to a younger generation of artists. Heinz Gietz composed the music, while Kurt Feltz, who had translated many English-language hits such as Elvis Presley's 'Are you lonesome tonight' into German (Schulz 2012: 141), provided the lyrics. The remake held on to the old character constellations and plot lines, as well as the focus on the all-singing, all-dancing star. At the same time, it modernised the source material in several respects. For example, the time that the three friends had spent together on a battleship during the war was changed to time spent together in a football club. While the protagonist's passion for railways was retained from the premake, it is worth noting the differences in the respective posture of the two actors. In the 1939 film, Rühmann sits disciplined, upright, cross-legged while he plays with the trains. In the remake, Alexander lies comfortably stretched out on the floor. As with *That Will Work*, the remake depicts post-war German consumer society in the form of the design of the furniture, the lushly furnished apartment, eye-catching illuminated advertisements and women's dress.[7]

Here, too, the music can be seen to have undergone an 'upgrade'. The earlier film was dominated by a single hit, 'Das kann doch einen Seemann nicht erschüttern' (That can't unsettle a sailor), which is used as a leitmotif throughout the film following its first performance. In 1939, when the German submarine 47 sunk the *Royal Oak*, the song was turned into a battle anthem with new, overtly anti-British lyrics (see Jockwer 2002: 222). In the remake, the musical repertoire is much broader and more up-to-date. The numerous singing numbers no longer need to be motivated by the plot. Through these show values, the film, much like *That Will Work*, becomes a revue, a contemporary genre hybrid: a comedy mixed with elements of the pop musical ('Schlagerfilm'). A prime example of the film's diversity is the scene that takes place during a celebration at the football club. Peter Alexander in his role as Hugo Bartels parodies famous singers. His repertoire includes the above-mentioned Hans Moser song 'Reblaus' from the film *Sieben Jahre Pech* (1940), as well as popular numbers by Johannes Heesters and Vico Torriani. At one point, a woman in the audience requests a song by 'Peter Alexander'. With a self-ironic hint, he states that he does not know Peter Alexander and instead performs 'See you later alligator', a song popularised by Bill Haley. The boys dancing in the room refer to contemporary German youth culture as influenced by Rock'n'Roll and American films such as *Rebel Without a Cause* (1955), as well as German 'copycat films' like *Die Halbstarken* (1956). In this case, it is integrated within the decent environment of family entertainment with more than just a hint of parody. These images of youth culture in the remakes of the 1950s can be considered the post-war transformation of a form of cross-generationally appealing cinema.

In this context, Peter Alexander can be interpreted as a star of integration. Having not been involved in the cinema during the Nazi era, his reputation was untarnished, and he was a well-trained all-round talent that was able to attract a young audience. As a clean-cut, married man who was not embroiled in any scandals, he embodied the traditional 1950s norms of consolidation and transition. At the same time, his musical repertoire proved popular across different generations. Comparing his performances to those of other male actors in the remakes of the mid- to late 1950s, one tendency can clearly be observed:

male protagonists often act much more physically, less disciplined and with a wider emotional range. My own detailed analyses of the films *Schloss Hubertus* (1954, 1934) and *Before Sunrise* (*Vor Sonnenuntergang*, 1955, a remake of *The Ruler* [*Der Herrscher*, 1937]) even demonstrated a change in the physicality of authority figures (Frank 2017: 315–92). This, in turn, can be interpreted as the de-heroising of male figures after World War II. Here the portrayal of heroic, active protagonists is replaced in some remakes by processes of reflection and cognition.

CONCLUSION

The inclusion of Rock'n'Roll music, youth culture and the change in corporeality can be understood as part of the popular dialogue with the processes of Americanisation and Westernisation – remakes as hybrid forms between tradition and innovation. These post-war 'hybrid forms' also probe 1950s historiography (see Kießling and Rieger 2011: 12). Looking back at the *Heimatfilm* remakes from 1953, hints of these processes can be clearly discerned. However, there also exist examples of earlier remakes in which the dialogue with American culture can be found, as in the comedy *Spatzen in Gottes Hand* and the *Heimatfilm* titled *Ferien vom Ich* (1953). Yet, this is not a common motif or theme shared by all remakes, not even throughout the entire course of the 1950s. The body of films does not reveal the entire history of the progress of pluralisation, but rather demonstrates the simultaneity of different strategies of actualisation and recourse.

The popular musical films discussed here show how, despite having almost identical scripts, the staging of the contemporary present, music and youth culture becomes more offensive by the end of the decade. They also reveal the impact of set design, music and performance over screenplay. Each individual remake, however, displays its own references to continuity and social change, and at the same time they remain, through their similarities and differences, amalgams of past and present.

This makes it all the more important to be able to situate and examine the analyses of individual films within a broad, yet clearly defined corpus. Comparisons with systematic, large-scale studies of remakes from other countries could provide clues as to which of the findings presented here are specific to 1950s West German cinema. At the same time, such comparisons could aid to refine and differentiate the social function of remakes within social transformation processes. Research from English-speaking countries, which is primarily dominated by studies of American remakes (see Verevis 2006, Forrest and Koos 2002, among others), also notes and analyses an increasing number of remakes produced in the US in the period following World War II (Forrest

2002). Following this, I would like to argue that remakes should be understood and researched as cultural phenomena of social transition. At least for as long as cinema was a mass medium in the truest sense, remakes represented a means of expression and negotiation space for social transformation processes.

The remakes of the Adenauer era are part of a process of transference. Nazi-era popular culture is transferred by way of changed images of masculinity, corporeality and pluralisation of music that connect different generations and their experiences in cinemas. The transformation of conflicts back to families, as the example of the happy ending in the *Heimatfilm* showed, is in fact a de-politicisation of popular film. It can be interpreted as escapism, as well as distrust of state and community in the wake of the damage caused by the 'Third Reich'. Understanding remakes as cross-generational popular culture may also help explain their demise in German cinema after the 1950s. From the early 1960s onwards, the cinema increasingly became the medium of the younger generation in Germany, while older generations turned to television where the analysed remakes as well as 'new' remakes (or adaptions?) appeared.[8]

NOTES

1. Heimatfilm is an Austrian and German film genre established after World War II as a replacement for the 'Volksfilm'. As a result of the success of *Schwarzwaldmädel* (1950), a vast number of films were produced in the 1950s, characterised by German landscapes and love stories. Because of their popularity, German film historians tend to label Heimatfilme the typical genre of the decade.
2. After 1945, older German films approved by the Allies were screened in cinemas by licensed distributors. The so-called 'Reprisen' were dominant and important at the beginning of the decade. In the 1950/51 season, there were 174 'Reprisen'. After 1955, however, SPIO declared them 'irrelevant' (Roeber and Jacobi 1974: 283). On Reprisen and remakes in the 1950s, see also Frank 2017: 51–52.
3. For many of the films discussed in this chapter, there is no English title known.
4. Every year, the magazine *Film-Echo* conducted a survey among cinema owners to determine which films had been the most successful at the box office. An overview of all German films was later published (Axtmann and Herzberg 1960).
5. In 1942, the German film industry was monopolised under state ownership. The new concern, which incorporated all German production companies, distributors and exhibitors, was abbreviated 'UFI' (Ufa-Film GmbH) to distinguish it from the production company Universum Film AG or 'UFA'.
6. Vermerk Willy Söhnel über Reise nach Berlin am 1.4.1958 [Memo by Willy Söhnel about his trip to Berlin on 1 April 1958], BArch R 109 R 109-I, 1867. For other copyright deals, see Frank 2017: 92–113.
7. For a detailed comparison and images, see Frank 2015.
8. For instance, *Blow Upon Blow* (1958) was in the top of films in television in 1972; *Briefträger Müller* (1953) was the most successful film on German TV screens in 1974. See Garncarz 2012: 203–4.

REFERENCES

Axtmann, Horst and Georg Herzberg (1960), *Film-Echo-Verleihkatalog 1960/61*, Wiesbaden: Verlag Horst Axtmann.
Druxman, Michael B. (1975), *Make it Again, Sam*, New York: A. A. Barnes.
Faulstich, Werner and Helmut Korte (1990), *Fischer Filmgeschichte*, Frankfurt am Main: Fischer.
Forrest, Jennifer (2002), 'Sadie Thompson Redux', in Jennifer Forrest and Leonard R. Koos (eds), *Dead Ringers*, Albany: State University of New York Press, pp. 169–202.
Forrest, Jennifer and Leonard R. Koos (2002), *Dead Ringers: The Remake in Theory and Practice*, Albany: State University of New York Press.
Frank, Stefanie Mathilde (2015), 'Varianten verkehrter Welt', *WerkstattGeschichte*, 65, 103–15.
Frank, Stefanie Mathilde (2017), *Wiedersehen im Wirtschaftswunder*, Göttingen: Vandenhoeck & Ruprecht Unipress.
Ganghofer, Ludwig (1985 [1892]), *Der Klosterjäger*, München: Droemersche Verlagsbuchhandlung.
Garncarz, Josef (2013), *Hollywood in Deutschland*, Basel: Stroemfeld.
Hake, Sabine (2002), *German National Cinema*, London: Routledge.
Hake, Sabine (2004), *Film in Deutschland*, Hamburg: Rowohlt.
Hembus, Joe (1961), *Der deutsche Film kann gar nicht besser sein*, Bremen: Carl Schünemann Verlag.
Jockwer, Axel (2004), 'Unterhaltungsmusik im Dritten Reich', doctoral dissertation, University of Konstanz, Germany, available at: http://nbn-resolving.de/urn:nbn:de:bsz:352-opus-14740 (last accessed 1 September 2019).
Kießling, Friedrich and Bernhard Rieger (2011), *Mit dem Wandel leben*, Köln: Böhlau.
Leitch, Thomas M. (2002), 'Twice-Told Tales: Disavowal and the Rhetoric of Remakes', in Jennifer Forrest and Leonard R. Koos (eds), *Dead Ringers*, Albany: State University of New York Press, pp. 37–62.
Loacker, Armin (1999), *Anschluss im Dreivierteltakt*, Trier: WVT.
Maase, Kaspar (2010), 'Leute beobachten in der Heimat', in Kaspar Maase (ed.), *Was macht Populärkultur politisch?* Wiesbaden: Verlag für Sozialwissenschaften, pp. 189–212.
Maase, Kaspar (2012), *Die Kinder der Massenkultur*, Frankfurt am Main: Campus.
Oltmann, Katrin (2008), *Remake/Premake*, Bielefeld: Transcript.
Rentschler, Eric (1998), 'Das "Dritte Reich" und die Folgen', in Geoffrey Nowell-Smith (ed.), *Geschichte des internationalen Films*, Stuttgart: Metzler, pp. 338–47.
Schäfer, Dieter (2009), *Das gespaltene Bewusstsein*, Göttingen: Wallstein.
Schaudig, Michael (1996), 'Recycling für den Publikumsgeschmack? Das Remake', in Michael Schaudig (ed.), *Positionen deutscher Filmgeschichte*, Munich: Diskurs Verlag, pp. 277–308.
Schulz, Daniela (2012), *Wenn die Musik spielt . . . Der deutsche Schlagerfilm der 1950er bis 1970er Jahre*, Bielefeld: Transcript.
Simonet, Thomas (1987), 'Conglomerates and Content', in Bruce A. Austin (ed.), *Current Research in Film*, 3, pp. 154–62.
Tiews, Alina Laura (2017), *Fluchtpunkt Film: Integration von Flüchtlingen und Vertriebenen durch den deutschen Nachkriegsfilm 1945–1990*, Berlin: be.bra wissenschaft.
Verevis, Constantine (2006), *Film Remakes*, Edinburgh: Edinburgh University Press.
Von Moltke, Johannes (2005), *No Place Like Home: Locations of Heimat in German Cinema*, Los Angeles: University of California Press.
Wauchope, Mary (2007): 'The Other German Cinema', in John E. Davidson and Sabine Hake (eds), *Take Two: Fifties Cinema in Divided Germany*, New York: Berghahn Books, pp. 210–22.

CHAPTER 8

The Colour Remakes of Swedish Classics in the 1950s: Production, Promotion and Critical Reception in the Context of Technological Innovation*

Kamalika Sanyal and Eduard Cuelenaere

INTRODUCTION

Between the late 1910s and 1920s, the practice of adaptation gained traction in Sweden. During this 'golden age' of Swedish cinema (Furhammar 2003), many silent films were produced based on the works of renowned Nordic authors most prominently the Swedish Nobel laureate Selma Lagerlöf, Swedish author and playwright Hjalmar Bergman and other well-known writers from Scandinavia. Later, in the 1950s, two major Swedish production companies, AB Svensk Filmindustri (SF) and AB Sandrews (Sandrews) decided to remake some of the film classics of the 1910s and 1920s, which were already based on Swedish literary texts. Yet, this time, these film remakes would have sound – which saw swift progress in the 1930s – and colour, the latter being a relatively new development. This all happened during a highly transformative era of Swedish film history, known for its international advancements in every stage of the filmmaking process, as well as for its developments regarding the mobility of technology and professionals (Stenport 2019). The advancements in the film technology of that time – most importantly sound, colour and screen aspect ratio – offered new opportunities for re-adaptations and remakes (Eberwein 1998; Forrest and Koos 2002; Verevis 2006). Although there exists a clear theoretical line between a film remake (that is, generally understood as a film based on another film; see Verevis 2017) and a film re-adaptation (that is, a new film adaptation of a literary text which had already been adapted before to the filmic medium; see Leitch 2002), this chapter will use both terms interchangeably. The main reason for this is our agreement with Verevis' statement that film remakes are 'created and sustained through the repeated use of terminology [implying that] the very limited direct intertextual referentiality between the remake and its original is organized according to an extratextual referentiality, located in historically specific discursive formations' (2006: 28). Hence, while a purely theoretical distinction between a film remake and re-adaptation might be possible, from a discursive standpoint, the understanding of cultural artefacts and their labels is dependent on the surrounding discourses.[1]

Even though it is known that the filmic adaptations of the 1910s and 1920s were critically acclaimed and commercially successful (Furhammar 2003), and now are arguably considered as 'classics', not much research has been done on the re-adaptations and remakes that were released three to four decades later. Therefore, this chapter focuses on the practice of the Swedish film industry in the 1950s to release colour remakes of film classics based on literary works. In doing so, this chapter deviates from the Hollywood-centric modus of the field of remake studies (Smith and Verevis 2017), while expanding the existing scholarly discussions on Swedish remakes and Nordic narrative mobilisation on a global stage at the turn of the twenty-first century (Bondebjerg and Novrup Redvall 2011; Mazdon 2017; Stenport 2016). Moreover, this chapter agrees with Cuelenaere's (2020) plea to broaden the limited methodological toolbox of the field and Herbert's (2017) suggestion that mainstream criticism offers novel aspects of analysis that could inform and improve the scholarly study of film (remakes).[2] Building on archival research (conducted at the Svenska Filminstitutet, or the Swedish Film Institute), we look into the promotion as well as (journalistic) critical reception of these Swedish colour remakes. More specifically, our archival research looks at the promotional materials (for example, film programme booklets) and critical reviews published in daily Swedish newspapers and weekly or monthly film journals: *Aftonbladet, Aftontidningen, Svenska Dagbladet, Ny Dag, Arbetaren, Morgontidningen, Svenska Morgonbladet, Veckojournalen, Dagens Nyheter, Upsala Nya Tidning, Bonniers Litterära Magasin* and *Göteborgs Handels- och Sjöfartstidning*.

The overarching aim of this chapter is to reconstruct and understand the position of film remakes in the context of colour and the audio-visual culture of Sweden in the 1950s. In this vein, we want to investigate if and how the use of colour is employed as a promotional strategy for these remakes. Moreover, the chapter focuses on the possible incentives behind the decision to remake classics in colour. Apart from the colour aspect, we wish to learn how these remakes at that time were received, interpreted and labelled by critics and journalists, and what impact this might have had on their judgements – and, therefore, on the cultural value of these films.

RE-ADAPTATIONS AND REMAKES AS ECONOMIC STRATEGY?

Even though it was the first Scandinavian country to venture into it, Sweden was rather late in exploring natural colour film (Hjort and Lindqvist 2016) – a technique where colour is recorded photographically. The first Swedish colour feature film, *The Bells in Old Town* (*Klockorna i Gamla Sta'n*), was released in 1946, many years after countries such as the US, France, Germany and the UK initiated their experiments with colour. Colour's popularity in Sweden, however, did not rise immediately, as only three feature films were produced between 1946 and 1952, none of them successful. Also, the post-production colour film processing had to be done in laboratories outside Sweden. Still, the slow adoption of the colour technique does not strike one as odd, given that Sweden was a small industry in terms of revenues and number of yearly produced films – especially when compared to other major European industries (Elton 1950) which were already innovating with various types of colour film systems.

In 1948, the Swedish film industry was confronted with an entertainment tax, leading to an industry-wide strike or 'film stop' in 1951 (Soila 1998; Larsson and Marklund 2010). After the film industry came to an understanding with the government, the entertainment tax only gradually decreased during the 1950s, still causing financial difficulties (Soila 1998). Following several hits and misses over the previous two decades and right after the 'film stop', in the 1950s SF and Sandrews tried every available strategy to achieve financial stability. It is in this context of economic difficulties that the biggest production house, SF, decided to invest in colour remakes of film classics based on earlier literary texts. This is in line with the findings of Ross – namely, that 'in periods when the film industry has suffered a malaise, companies have resorted to the tactic of acquiring long-term rights to films and producing multiple remakes based on the same literary property, rather than inventing new material' (2017: 137). The projects in which SF invested were, on the one hand, *Sir Arne's Money (Herr Arnes pengar*, 1919), which was remade into *Sir Arne's Treasure* (*Herr Arnes penningar*, 1954) and, on the other hand, *Song of the Red Flower* (*Sången om den eldröda blomman*, 1919, alternative title *The Flame of Life*), which was remade in 1956 under the same Swedish title.[3] Mauritz Stiller directed both 1919 film adaptations, while the remakes were directed by Gustaf Molander. Sandrews, the second-largest Swedish film production company, did not stop there either. In 1956, it produced *Girl in Tails* (*Flickan i Frack*, 1956), which was a remake of *Girl in Tails* (*Flickan, i frack: En sommarlätt filmhistoria*, 1926), also based on a novel titled *Flickan i Frack*, written by Hjalmar Bergman. The following year, AB Sandrew-Ateljéerna and AB Artistfilm jointly produced *A Girl of Solbakken* (*Synnöve Solbakken*, 1957), the re-adaptation of a Norwegian novel by Nobel laureate Bjørnstjerne Bjørnson, which was adapted under the same title in 1919 and then re-adapted in 1934.

Following Ross (2017), Stern notes a commercial 'paradox' of remaking: the industry is inspired by an economic imperative to repeat confirmed successes, but in order to maintain viability 'remakes are also compelled to register variation and difference to incorporate generic developments' (2000: 226). For SF and Sandrews this arguably holds true, as they devoted large budgets to re-adapt and remake well-known, successful narratives with a technological update. Likewise, Leitch (2002) argues that, typically, while the producers of a film remake purchase the adaptation rights of the property (that is, the source text), they pay no remake fees to the makers of the first film adaptation, even though the remake is often the direct successor of the first film adaptation, rather than of the source text. Interestingly, this does not seem to be the case for *Song of the Red Flower*, as SF made two agreements with AB Wivefilm, the producer of Stiller's film. These agreements were made to acquire the rights for a colour remake of *Song of the Red Flower*, with both of them stating that 'Filmindustri intends to record a film in colour based on the work in question, but a prerequisite for this is that a manuscript acceptable for recording can be produced' (Svensk Filmindustri 1955a, 1955b).[4]

COLOUR AS PROMOTIONAL STRATEGY?

Colour seemed to play an important role in the promotion of these remakes, and this was quickly picked up by both journalistic articles and critical reviews. *Dagens Nyheter*, for instance, published an article eight months before the release of *Sir Arne's Treasure*, about the last day of on-location shooting. It mentioned that, because the film was a production in colour, cinematographer Åke Dahlqvist was measuring the light's brightness to find out that it was 'great with colour' (Malice 1954). In *Veckojournalen*, the journalist reported that *Sir Arne's Treasure* was one of the most lavish productions in all of Swedish cinema. He also noted how Dahlqvist was moving around with an exposure meter because Gevacolor needed twice the light exposure in comparison to a black-and-white film (Sellermark 1954). The promotional materials for the four films all mention, on the front page and in highlighted font, that the film was in colour. The programmes used phrases such as 'färgfilm' ('colour film'), 'färg' ('colour'), 'i färgfilmen' ('in the colour film'), along with the names of the colour film system, such as Eastmancolor and Gevacolor (Sandrews - Flickan i frack 1956; Sandrews - Synnöve Solbakken 1957; SF - Sången om den eldröda blomman 1956; SF reklamråd - Herr Arnes penningar 1954). *A Girl of Solbakken*'s programme, however, does not highlight its film system, but recounts that it is a 'vidfilm' or widescreen film in colour. Finally, all pamphlets for *Song of the Red Flower* mention that the format is widescreen Agascope – this technology was the latest trend worldwide around the mid-1950s (Belton 1992).

Examining the excerpts of various reviews mentioned in the programmes, we found that they were all positive; this does not surprise us, given that the programmes served as promotional materials. It became apparent that colour was a prominent factor there too. For example, the programme for *Sir Arne's Treasure* quotes that it is the 'first absolutely flawless colour film in Sweden' and the 'best Swedish colour film to date' (SF reklamråd - Herr Arnes penningar 1954). Moreover, the programme quotes the Swedish newspaper *Östgöten*, which stated that *Herr Arnes* is 'an interesting film where the colour gives an artistic touch to everything'. The programme of *A Girl of Solbakken* acknowledges in detail that it is the third rendition of the novel, but this time as colour and widescreen film. It also quotes Staffan Tjerneld of *Expressen*: 'without doubt, [this is] the nicest Swedish film since the colour film came out'. Another review quote claims that this is '[p]erhaps the most beautiful Swedish film ever created' (Sandrews - Synnöve Solbakken 1957). Finally, the trailer of the new version of *A Girl of Solbakken* contains the on-screen text 'in the modern film version' – again a nod to the earlier Swedish adaptation and its remake (Synnöve Solbakken Trailerlista 1957).

Overall, our archival analysis shows that the new colour technique was generally used as a unique selling point for these recycled films. In some of the promotional programmes, the fact that these films were based on older source material was also clearly mentioned. As such, one could argue that the promotional material for these films tried to keep a balance between repetition (meaning, the film being based on already existing material) and novelty (that is, the use of the new colour technique), which is emblematic for sequential filmmaking (Jess-Cooke 2009). In order to grasp the discourses around these colour re-adaptations or remakes more fully, we analysed journalists' and critics' opinions and pieces. Hence, we want to find out whether Stern's (2000) commercial 'paradox' of remaking also holds true for the practice analysed in this chapter, by investigating whether the above-mentioned relationship between the recognizable and the innovative was found to be balanced or not. Yet, before analysing these critical discourses, we will first elaborate on how the status or label of the film remake and re-adaptation relates to the notion of cultural value, and what role the new colour technique might have played in this relationship.

JUDGING COLOUR RE-ADAPTATIONS/REMAKES AND ASSERTING THEIR CULTURAL VALUE

Mee (2017) argues that 'both [as] a category of text and [. . .] an industrial phenomenon, remakes (and the industry trend for remaking) are especially vulnerable to criticism rooted in preconceived notions of cultural value' (2017: 194). Hence, remakes or other '"imitative" types of film are in danger of being assigned a low cultural status, or even of eliciting critical opprobrium, because they are copies of "culturally treasured" originals' (Naremore 2000: 13). Oftentimes, this disdain 'is rooted in the neoromantic belief that art should somehow not be concerned with making money' (Klein and Palmer 2016: 12). This same neo-romantic belief, stemming from the 1950s – a time when *auteur* theory was highly influential – also relies on the idea that the creator of a film is 'a heroic, visionary, and idiosyncratic artist [. . .] [which] would appear to conflict with the apparent lack of "originality" in remakes' (Herbert 2008: 189). As claimed by Mazdon (2000), in the case of a film adaptation (thus not a remake) of a classic text, a new set of audience members is introduced to an often 'essential' product of a (national) culture. Furthermore, the resulting film adaptation gains the cultural capital of the source text, which increases even more if the person who adapts the classic work also enjoys a culturally iconic status, thus helping it to become a classic in itself (Mazdon 2000). Given the complex status or label of our Swedish cases (see note 1), we want to find out whether the Swedish critics' discourses show traces of such a neo-romantic understanding of originality, how this relates to their labelling of these films and what role the new colour technique plays in all of this.

Yet, before elaborating on the critical discourses of the re-adaptations and remakes, a quick look at the status of some of the earlier adaptations (and its creators) will help us understand the reception of the 1950s colour remakes. In fact, the 1919 films *Sir Arne's Money* and *Song of the Red Flower* are appropriate examples of Mazdon's argument: Stiller is one of the most eminent film directors of Swedish cinema, hailed as one of its pioneers. Moreover, by adapting a classic text (and thanks to his own status as a classic director) his film was eventually transformed into a classic. For instance, critic Bengt Idestam-Almquist literally declared Stiller's adaptation of *Sir Arne's Treasure* a classic (Hood 1950). In 1954, critic Uno Asplund suggested that Stiller's film had a place among the best classic films of the world (Asplund 1954). Since the early days of Swedish cinema, producers had always shown a predominant ambition to achieve artistic or 'culturally valuable' film (Soila 1998). *A Girl of Solbakken* (1957) was also the third rendition of a popular Norwegian novel, the first one being made in the silent era (*A Girl of Solbakken* [*Synnöve Solbakken*], 1919) and the second being a talkie version *A Girl of Solbakken* (*Synnöve Solbakken*, 1934) starring Victor Sjöström. Unfortunately, the reviews of the 1957 *A Girl of Solbakken* were unavailable in the archives of the Swedish Film Institute; therefore, a comparison with reviews of the earlier version was not possible.

Apart from the 'classic' status of these earlier film adaptations and their directors, we would argue that in Sweden successful and critically admired silent films of the 1910s and 1920s – which had not yet reached the technical superiority of the 1950s – became ideal representatives of a 'golden' Swedish cultural past worthy of cherishing. *Girl in Tails*, for instance, presents an excellent example that depicts an idyllic Swedish suburb of Hjalmar Bergman's time, with a simple small-town narrative. *Song of the Red Flower* is another contender, as it is a love story set in the heart of Lapland, featuring the journey of a man trying to find himself. SF and Sandrews reintroduced these films to the public imagination, while updating them for the contemporary audience. By modifying silent films with toned-down acting and screenplay, as well as colourful visuals, the new remakes tried to look back at the old times and re-establish the Swedish classics as an entertaining genre. Hence, in these Swedish cases, it is highly likely that the process of remaking and the nostalgia cycle (Le Sueur 1977) of the creative industry constituted an overlapping phenomenon.

Analysing the critical reviews, we found that many of the critics did praise the films' use of colour. For *Sir Arne's Treasure*, the consensus was that the cinematographer Dahlqvist did an excellent job with his 'mechanical perfection' in colour photography (Oldin 1954). The nature shots in colour also received praise. In Pir Ramek's (1954) opinion, this was the first 'fullgoda' ('satisfactory') Swedish colour film. Another critic viewed the colour as sober – the essence of the 1500s, albeit artificial, was captured well in Gevacolor (Filmson [Sven Jan Hanson] 1954); however, he also felt that the film itself was boring and that the colour added nothing to the story (A. K sk. 1954). Interestingly, apart from the colour aspect, other technologies such as sound were, at times, less welcome. One critic even wished that someone would 're-invent the silent films again' (Filmson [Sven Jan Hanson] 1954), while another claimed that Lagerlöf's narrative would work better with silent film's storytelling style (Beyer 1954). Asplund (1954) of the *Göteborgs Handels- och Sjöfartstidning*, conversely, liked the usage of Lars-Erik Larsson's music that according to him reminded viewers of the *Pathétique* by Tchaikovsky. Asplund also commented that Molander's version boasted extremely thorough detail and offered a pompous visual impression of the 1500s.

Others were more critical about the use of film colour in these remakes: *The Song of the Red Flower* was rejected by the critics, and the fact that the remake was in colour did not help. Beyer remarked that the film colour showed 'how red the flower is, how green the forest is and how blue the water is' (1956), but that this did not contribute to the film itself. It was also claimed that the wilderness within the story was toned down (Lill [Ellen Liliedahl] 1956b): 'Yes, the flower is red in Eastmancolor [. . .] however, it is a pictorial wilderness story that does not impress anyone' (Sången om den eldröda blomman 1957). Ramek disliked the technical quality of the colour cinematography, stating that many scenes had dirty grey images with 'irritating' blue tints (Ramek 1956b). *Aftonbladet*'s reviewer Karl Ekwall even went so far as to claim that the film was a testament to SF's bankruptcy and nothing else (Ekwall 1956b).

The latter statement brings us to the critics' interpretations and/or judgements of the films themselves, or, more specifically, their status or label of a remake or re-adaptation. With the exception of Ramek (1954) – who defended the remake status of the film itself, saying that many of the audience members might not have seen Stiller's version and that, hence, Molander's film 'should of course be reviewed as "new"' – the fact that SF was trying to remake its golden age films did not sit well with most critics. In the case of Molander's re-adaptations, almost all of the reviews presented a comparative analysis between him and the director of the preceding film adaptations, Stiller.[5] Generally, Molander's remake of *Sir Arne's Treasure* and *The Song of the Red Flower* received bleak criticism: the artist was not willing to seriously devote himself to his work, and the films did not do justice to Stiller's artistic literacy. This reflects the typical neo-romantic critique of remakes. The question was openly raised as to how Molander and Dahlqvist, in spite of their well-known talent, could 'dare to take up competition with the dead master?' (Beyer 1954). Ekwall (1954) held a similar opinion, stating that Molander could not add an inch to Stiller's work despite having all the aids of modern film technology. Furthermore, Bengt Gunnäs of *Ny Dag* wrote that 'the choice is hardly a conscious endeavour to consolidate a national tradition, but rather the ambition to try to surpass the reputable works from *guldåder* ["golden age"] of Swedish cinema' (Gunnäs 1954). He further explained that it was an unnecessary proof of poor judgement to repeat *The Treasure* (*Herr Arnes penningar*) when several of Selma Lagerlöf's most important works were still out there waiting to be adapted. What becomes clear from these judgements is that, apart from their neo-romantic critique, most of the critics complained about the use of colour purely in relation to the fact that these films are re-adaptations or remakes. Indeed, for most of the commentators, the addition of colour to these stories did not make up for the recycling of these materials. In general, while the use of colour was often lauded, it did not compensate for these films' status as remakes or re-adaptations. This not only confirms the (especially in journalistic and critical circles) common negative bias towards the film remake (Mazdon, 2000: 4), but also expands this finding to the context of a small film industry such as that of Sweden in the 1950s.

The importance of the status or label of the remake/re-adaptation is confirmed when analysing the discourses surrounding the case of *Girl in Tails*. The first film adaptation of *Girl in Tails* in 1926 was considered a gem of a comedy film from the silent era (Kindblom 2011). Moreover, the general feedback of the 1956 remake was equally positive. Yet, notably, none of the reviews compared the colour remake with the 1926 film, but only with the literary text by Bergman. Following Leitch's (2002) categorisation, this suggests that the 1956 film was rather regarded as a re-adaptation of the original text instead of a remake of the first film adaptation. Some critics called it a satisfactory adaptation from literature to screen (Flickan i frack 1956), while others recognized the film as director Arne Mattsson's finest directorial work (Flickan i frack 1956; Ramek 1956a). In terms of technicality and colour, a reviewer compared it with another colour feature of the previous year, *The People of Hemso* (*Hemsöborna*, 1955) – also directed by Mattsson – and remarked that *Girl in Tails* was worse. Again, Filmson perceived the colour tones of the re-adaptation as artistically conscious (Filmson [Sven Jan Hanson] 1956). For Ekwall (1956a), the colours were better in the exterior scenes and usually less so in the interiors. The film was perceived as a pastiche that constituted 'a picture book of extremely delicious colour posters' (Lill [Ellen Liliedahl] 1956a). Perceiving this film as a re-adaptation rather than a remake and comparing these films only with their literary (and not filmic) predecessor resulted in more positive judgements. This also happened in the case of *The Song of the Red Flower*: almost all of the critical reviews compared the 1956 remake only to Stiller's film adaptation, and not to the classic text.[6] As a result, the film was negatively received.

CONCLUSION

For its remakes, SF tried to use the allure of a well-known Scandinavian narrative, updated film technology and the director's reputation to draw the attention of contemporary audiences and garner profits in a stagnating economy. Sandrews did likewise, although none of the directors of their remakes were on par with Molander's status. Nevertheless, the grand plan of SF and Sandrews failed. The complexity of shooting with large colour cameras and the post-production of the colour film made these remakes very expensive (Zetterström 1956). Thrashed by the critics, SF's remakes did not perform well at the box office. After making *The Song of the Red Flower*, Gustaf Molander quit the directorial profession for a while, returning only after more than a decade (Qvist and Von Bagh 2000). Sandrews' *Girl in Tails*, however, was successful, as critics and audiences liked the light-hearted story and pretty suburbia visuals.

Our analysis of the press reviews revealed that the Swedish industry of the 1950s was yet to explore the multifaceted aspect of film colour in order to improve on films considered classics. The principal aim was to re-tell famous stories so as to reap financial benefits. A probable consequence is that the companies utilised colour film systems as a modern means to update the narrative in a new package and in an apparent trial of making the films more accessible to the masses. The journalistic discourse surrounding these films clearly shows that the critics were mostly interested in a strict comparison between the *auteur*s; they noted that the filmmakers had little interest in exploring film colour as an element that could have significantly contributed to the creative treatment of the narrative. The reviews show that black-and-white Scandinavian imagery still had a stronghold over the industry, being considered artistic and of substance, with the backing of critics. The discussions within film critic circles is thus significant for understanding the contemporary perception of film colour and classic film remakes.

Apart from elucidating the process of introducing colour technique to the Swedish film industry (its employment as a strategy to recycle existing material), our analysis has pointed at the connotative power of labels such as remakes and re-adaptations. Our findings confirm that there existed a general critical disdain towards remaking practices also in Sweden of the 1950s. The analysed critiques not only showed clear signs of a neo-romantic take on originality, but also suggested that critics found that the novelty (the new technique of colour) of these films did not compensate for their repetitive character (that is, their status as remake). In other words, the two aspects of Stern's (2000) commercial 'paradox' (innovation versus recognition) were found to be out of balance, resulting in an overall negative stance towards these films. Lastly, we found that, generally, when a film was regarded as a remake (that is, based on an already existing film), its critical reception was overall negative, while a film considered a re-adaptation received more positive reviews. Apparently, today's tolerance for filmic adaptations (and, by extension, re-adaptations) and intolerance for film remakes dates back at least to the 1950s. While this notion necessitates further research, it might point towards the existence of a less critical stance towards intermedial adaptations (for example, from book to film), when compared with intramedial ones (for instance, from film to film). As such, this chapter indeed gives further weight to Herbert's (2017) assertion that critical reviews are necessary if one wants to more holistically understand the workings of a creative industry, but clearly wishes to expand this plea to the field of remake studies.

NOTES

* Sanyal wishes to express her gratitude to the Academische Stichting Leuven (Academic Foundation Leuven), Belgium, for awarding her the grant that made a research stay and archival research in Sweden possible.
1. As will become clear by looking at the (critical and journalistic) discourses about the films under analysis in this chapter, specific terms such as 'adaptation' and 're-adaptation' did not appear in the reviews of that time. Yet, many of the reviewers did indirectly suggest that these films were re-adaptations, calling them the 'third Swedish version' or 'third Swedish recording'. The label 'remake', however, was mentioned twice in the case of *Song of the Red Flower* (Ekwall 1956b; C.B-n. 1956). Although we decided to use both terms interchangeably, we do not underestimate the power of the connotations that both carry, as will become clear in our analysis itself.
2. We hesitate to depict the Swedish film journalist circle as entirely 'mainstream' in the narrow sense of the word, however, as we have also considered reviews penned by famed film critics and authors such as Bengt Idestam-Almquist and Uno Asplund.
3. The film was released under different titles in different European countries. Its English title is *The Song of the Red Flower*. The English programme booklet featured this title on the front page, while programmes of other countries had different titles. In Danish it was *Den Blomrøde Blomst* and in Finland *Laulu tulipunaisesta kukasta*. In West Germany, it was released, accompanied by two separate programme booklets, under two different titles: (1) *Das Lied von der roten Blume* and (2) *Heiss war meine Sehnsucht* (Das Lied von der roten Blume 1958; Den Blomrøde Blomst 1958; Heiss war meine Sehnsucht 1958; The Swedish picture: The Song of the Red Flower [n. d.]).
4. All translations from Swedish to English are by Kamalika Sanyal.

5. Interestingly, a young Molander was also involved in Stiller's *Sir Arne's Money*, as one of the screenplay writers, along with Stiller.
6. Except for one critic in *Stockholms Tidningen* who compared the film's ethos with the original novel (and understood it as a re-adaptation). This, again, resulted in a positive reading of the film: 'They treat Linnankoski's book and its film traditions with a deeply touched reverence, much like you treat an old inherited plush furniture: you cut off the longest tassels but leave the furniture otherwise' (1956).

REFERENCES

A.K sk (1954), 'Röda Kvarn: Herr Arnes penningar', *Svenska Morgonbladet*, 27 December, AB Biografernas Filmdepôt, (n.d.), available at: http://www.svenskfilmdatabas.se/sv/item/?type=company&itemid=500058 (last accessed 10 September 2019).
Asplund, Uno (1954), 'Herr Arnes Penningar', *Göteborgs Handels- och Sjöfartstidning*.
Belton, John (1992), *Widescreen Cinema*, Harvard: Harvard University Press.
Beyer, Nils (1954), 'Röda Kvarn: Herr Arnes Penningar', *Morgontidningen*, 27 December.
Beyer, Nils (1956), 'Röda Kvarn: Sången om den eldröda blomman', *Morgontidningen*, 27 December.
Bondebjerg Ib and Eva Novrup Redvall (2011), *A Small Region in a Global World: Patterns in Scandinavian Film and TV Culture*, Copenhagen: Centre for Modern European Studies-CEMES, University of Copenhagen.
C.B-n (1956), 'Sången om den eldröda blomman', *Dagens Nyheter*, 27 December.
Cuelenaere, Eduard (2020), 'Towards an Integrative Methodological Approach of Film Remake Studies', *Adaptation* online first.
Das Lied von der roten Blume (1958), Stockholm: Svensk filmindustri.
Den Blomrøde Blomst (1958), Stockholm: Svensk filmindustri.
Eberwein, Robert (1998), 'Remakes and Cultural Studies', in Andrew Horton and Stuart Y. McDougal (eds), *Play it Again, Sam: Retakes on Remakes*, Los Angeles: University of California Press, pp. 15–33.
Ekwall, Karl (1954), 'Herr Arnes Penningar', *Aftontidningen*, 27 December.
Ekwall, Karl (1956a), 'Flickan i frack', *Aftontidningen*, 16 October.
Ekwall, Karl (1956b), 'Sången om den eldröda blomman, Röda Kvarn', *Aftontidningen*, 27 December.
Elton, Arthur (1950), 'The Small Countries', in Film Centre London (ed.), *The Film Industry in Six European Countries: A Detailed Study of the Film Industry in Denmark as Compared with that in Norway, Sweden, Italy, France and the United Kingdom*, Paris: Unesco, pp. 17–84.
Filmson [Sven Jan Hanson] (1954), 'Herr Arnes Penningar: Röda Kvarn', *Aftonbladet*, 27 December.
Filmson [Sven Jan Hanson] (1956), 'Flickan i frack, Royal', *Aftonbladet*, 16 October.
'Flickan i frack' (1956), *Bonniers Litterära Magasin*, IX.
Forrest, Jennifer and Leonard R. Koos (2002), 'Reviewing Remakes: An Introduction', in Jennifer Forrest and Leonard R. Koos (eds), *Dead Ringers: The Remake in Theory and Practice*, Albany: State University of New York Press, pp. 1–36.
Furhammar, Leif (2003), *Filmen i Sverige: En historia i tio kapitel och en fortsättning*, Stockholm: Dialogos and Svenska Filminstitutet.
Gunnäs, Bengt (1954), 'Herr Arnes Penningar', *Ny Dag*, 27 December.
Heiss war meine Sehnsucht (1958), Stockholm: Svensk Filmindustri.
Herbert, Daniel (2008), 'Transnational Film Remakes: Time, Space, Identity', doctoral dissertation, University of Southern California.

Herbert, Daniel (2017), 'The Transnational Film Remake in the American Press', in Iain R. Smith and Constantine Verevis (eds), *Transnational Film Remakes*, Edinburgh: Edinburgh University Press, pp. 210–23.
Hjort, Mette and Ursula Lindqvist (2016), *A Companion to Nordic Cinema*, Chichester: John Wiley & Sons.
Hood, Robin [Bengt Idestam-Almquist] (1950), 'Stiller, A Pioneer of the Cinema', *Biografbladet*, 31: 3, 133–40.
I.S. (1956), 'Sången om den eldröda blomman', *Ny Dag*, 27 December.
Jess-Cooke, Carolyn (2009), *Film Sequels*, Edinburgh: Edinburgh University Press.
Kindblom, Mikaela (2011), 'Karin Swanström', available at: http://www.svenskfilmdatabas.se/en/item/?type=person&itemid=58282#biography (last accessed 11 September 2019).
Klein, Amanda Ann and Robert Barton Palmer (2016), *Cycles, Sequels, Spin-offs, Remakes, and Reboots: Multiplicities in Film and Television*, Austin: University of Texas Press.
Larsson, Mariah and Anders Marklund (2010), *Swedish Film: An Introduction and Reader*, Lund: Nordic Academic Press.
Le Sueur, Marc (1977), 'Theory Number Five: Anatomy of Nostalgia Films, Heritage and Methods', *Journal of Popular Film*, 6: 2, 187–97.
Leitch, Thomas (2002), 'Twice-Told Tales: Disavowal and the Rhetoric of the Remake', in Jennifer Forrest and Leonard R. Koos (eds), *Dead Ringers: The Remake in Theory and Practice*, Albany: State University of New York Press, pp. 37–62.
Lill [Ellen Liliedahl] (1956a), 'Flickan i frack', *Svenska Dagbladet*, 16 October.
Lill [Ellen Liliedahl] (1956b), 'Röda Kvarn: Sången om den eldroda blomman', *Svenska Dagbladet*, 27 December.
Malice (1954), 'Filmare kämpade mot våren, räddade "Herr Arnes pengar"', *Dagens Nyheter*, 5 April.
Mazdon, Lucy (2000), *Encore, Hollywood: Remaking French Cinema*, London: British Film Institute.
Mazdon, Lucy (2017), 'Disrupting the Remake: The Girl with the Dragon Tattoo', in Iain R. Smith and Constantine Verevis (eds), *Transnational Film Remakes*, Edinburgh: Edinburgh University Press, pp. 21–35.
Mee, Laura (2017), 'The Hollywood Remake Massacre: Adaptation, Reception, and Value', in Colleen Kennedy-Karpat and Eric Sandberg (eds), *Adaptation, Awards Culture, and the Value of Prestige*, Cham: Palgrave Macmillan, pp. 193–209.
Naremore, James (2000), *Film Adaptation*, New Brunswick: Rutgers University Press.
Oldin, Gunnar (1954), 'Herr Arnes penningar', *Arbetaren*, 27 December.
Oldin, Gunnar (1956), 'Royal: Flickan i frack', *Arbetaren*, 16 October.
Qvist, Per Olav and Peter Von Bagh (2000), *Guide to the Cinema of Sweden and Finland*, Westport: Greenwood.
Ramek, Pir (1954), 'Herr Arnes penningar', *Upsala Nya Tidning*, 27 December.
Ramek, Pir (1956a), 'Flickan i frack – ett lyckokast', *Upsala Nya Tidning*, 16 October.
Ramek, Pir (1956b), 'RÖDA KVARN: Sången om den eldröda blomman', *Upsala Nya Tidning*, 27 December.
Ross, Jonathan (2017), 'Factors Behind Retranslations: What can We Learn from the Scholarly Discourse on Film Remakes?' *Journal of Translation Studies*, 23, 129–46.
Sandrews – Flickan i frack (1956), Sandrews.
Sandrews – Synnöve Solbakken (1957), Stockholm.
'Sången om den eldröda blomman' (1957), *Veckojournalen*, 2.
Sellermark, Arne (1954), 'Selma Lagerlöf i Naftalin', *Veckojournalen*, 16.
SF – Sången om den eldröda blomman (1956), Svensk filmindustri.
SF reklamråd – Herr Arnes penningar (1954), Stockholm: Svensk Filmindustri.

Smith, Iain R. and Constantine Verevis (2017), 'Introduction: Transnational Film Remakes', in Iain R. Smith and Constantine Verevis (eds), *Transnational Film Remakes*, Edinburgh: Edinburgh University Press, pp. 1-18.
Soila, Tytti (1998), 'Sweden', in Tytti Soila (ed.), *Nordic National Cinemas*, London: Routledge, pp. 135–220.
Stern, Lesley (2000), '"Emma" in Los Angeles: Remaking the Book and the City', in James Naremore (ed.), *Film Adaptation*, New Brunswick: Rutgers University Press, pp. 221–38.
Stenport, Anna Westerståhl (2016), 'Nordic Remakes in Hollywood: Reconfiguring Originals and Copies', in Mette Hjort and Ursula Lindqvist (eds), *A Companion to Nordic Cinema*, Chichester: John Wiley & Sons, pp. 436–56.
Stenport, Anna Westerståhl (2019), 'Opening up the Postwar World in Color: 1950s Geopolitics and Spectacular Nordic Colonialism in the Arctic and Africa', in Anna Westerståhl Stenport and Arne Lunde (eds), *Nordic Film Cultures and Cinemas of Elsewhere*, Edinburgh: Edinburgh University Press, pp. 105–25.
Svensk Filmindustri (1955a), Avtal, Stockholm.
Svensk Filmindustri (1955b), Avtal, Stockholm.
Synnöve Solbakken Trailerlista (1957), AB Sandrew-Ateljéerna; AB Artistfilm, available at: http://www.svenskfilmdatabas.se/sv/item/?type=film&itemid=4544#holdings-scripts (last accessed 10 September 2019).
The Swedish picture: The Song of the Red Flower (n.d.), Stockholm: Svensk Filmindustri.
Tjerneld, Staffan (1956), 'Flickan i frack på Royal', *Expressen*, 16 October.
Verevis, Constantine (2006), *Film Remakes*, Edinburgh: Edinburgh University Press.
Verevis, Constantine (2017), 'Remakes, Sequels, Prequels', in Thomas Leitch (ed.), *The Oxford Handbook of Adaptation Studies*, New York: Oxford University Press, pp. 267–84.
Zetterström, Marianne (1956), 'Går pa bio: Flickan i frack', *Idun*, 44.

Part III

Contemporary Perspectives: European Film Remakes in the New Millennium

CHAPTER 9

Remakes *à la polonaise*: From National Re-Adaptations to Internationally Inspired Rom-Coms

Kris Van Heuckelom

> *For the time being,*
> *the umbilical cord that connects our cinematography*
> *to our library continues to hold tight* (Chełminiak 2001: 42).

The introductory quote to this chapter is the concluding sentence of what is perhaps the first journalistic piece devoted to remake practices in Polish cinema. Written and published almost twenty years ago, the article provides a general introduction to the phenomenon of remaking – which it vaguely defines as the 'reworking of old films' – and then goes on to explain why Polish filmmakers have been so reluctant to engage in remake projects.[1] Although the overall tone of the article is quite pessimistic, the author simultaneously suggests that 'all signs in heaven and earth indicate that we will witness a real breakthrough in the domain [of remaking] in the twenty-first century' (Chełminiak 2001: 43). In this chapter, I seek to investigate – with the obvious benefit of hindsight – the validity of this assertion, by taking a closer look at the development of Polish remake practices over the past two decades, with particular attention to the critical discourses and marketing strategies that have surrounded these practices. Since there are no other scholarly texts that have the Polish context of film remaking as their central focus, this study charts hitherto largely unexplored territory.[2]

By way of contextualisation, I begin with a brief historical investigation of a specific kind of remake that has tended to dominate Polish cinematography throughout the twentieth century – namely, re-adaptations of (Polish-language) literary and theatrical fiction. The central part of the chapter, in turn, is taken up by a discussion of four Polish film productions from the past fifteen years:

Jan Hryniak's *The Third* (*Trzeci*, 2005), Piotr Wereśniak's *Oh, Charles 2* (*Och, Karol 2*, 2011), Michał Kwieciński's *Love Is All* (*Miłość jest wszystkim*, 2018) and Tadeusz Śliwa's *(Un)familiar People* (*[Nie]znajomi*, 2019).[3] As I will show, inasmuch as the first decade of the new millennium was largely dominated by speculations about possible (and potential) remakes of Polish features, the following decade saw a shift towards the actual realisation and finalisation of remake projects. At the same time, the four films examined in this chapter mark a significant transition in terms of temporal and geographical scope: whereas the first two productions embody a particular form of 'diachronic remaking' within a distinct Eastern Bloc context by offering contemporary variations on communist-era film classics, the two most recent projects (which take their cues from a Dutch and an Italian screenplay, respectively) indicate that Polish film professionals are becoming increasingly active in the field of transnational (synchronic) film remaking, even if – with an average cinematographic output of more than forty feature films per year – the actual number of film remakes in Poland remains relatively low.

THE 'UMBILICAL CORD' OF POLISH CINEMA: RE-ADAPTATIONS OF LITERARY FICTION

The particular backdrop against which the above-mentioned article about remakes appeared in the Polish press was far from trivial: in the early 2000s, the Polish film industry saw a growing and strongly mediatised rivalry between two production teams, both of which had started to work on a re-adaptation of the classical novel *The Teutonic Knights* (*Krzyżacy*, 1900) by the Polish Nobel Prize winner Henryk Sienkiewicz. Although, quite ironically, neither of these competing high-budget projects eventually made it to the screen, the rather grotesque circumstance of having two Polish crews working simultaneously on a very similar literature-derived film project points to the long-standing inclination of (some) Polish filmmakers to draw inspiration from the country's rich literary output. A few statistics may help to indicate the scale of this phenomenon. The Wikipedia entry on 'polskie adaptacje filmowe' ('Polish film adaptations') offers a list of nearly 500 productions; with more than 90 percent, the overwhelming majority takes its narrative cues from Polish-language literary sources. The reputability of the literary heritage among not only filmmakers, but also domestic spectators is neatly indicated by the fact that two cinematic charts – the list of greatest Polish box office successes of all time (Haltof 2007: 299) and the list of attendance rates for Polish films screened in domestic movie theatres since 1990 (Haltof 2018: 429–30) – continue to be headed by three literary adaptations.

One more remarkable indicator of the persistent influence of the national canon – along with some notable 'second-rate' literary works – on Polish screenwriting and filmmaking practices is the number of literary works that have been adapted for the Polish screen multiple times: while there are at least eighteen cases of so-called re-adaptation (or double adaptation), no less than four Polish literary works have been turned into a Polish-language film production three times. At the same time, the very fact that one more instance of triple adaptation – the above-mentioned 'millennial' attempts to re-adapt Sienkiewicz's *Teutonic Knights*, after Aleksander Ford's first feature in 1960 – ultimately did not come to fruition points to the conjunctural character of the Polish audience's interest in screen versions of 'lektury szkolne' ('compulsory school readings'). As Haltof (2018: 397–98) observes, the 'national heritage' peak from the turn of the millennium has increasingly given way to more popular forms of mid-budget genre filmmaking (most notably romantic comedies). This shift does not imply, however, that adaptations of literary works have ceased to appear altogether (Lubelski 2014).

From a strictly textual perspective, one could, of course, argue whether these repeated re-adaptations of Polish literary fiction should be labelled 'film remakes' in the first place. In his nuanced critique of Leitch's four-part taxonomy of the remake (2001), Verevis (2006: 11–22) rightly observes that it is often very difficult – and even pointless – to identify one singular (literary or cinematic) text as the actual ('original') precursor of the remake. Meanwhile, in the vast majority of Polish cases, there is a considerable time-span of at least four decades separating the first adaptation from the next one, which urges us to assume that the canonised literary source text (and not its cinematic derivative) typically came to serve as the primary frame of reference (and identification), for makers and viewers alike. This state of affairs applies in particular to those times before the introduction of television and the home video market, when literary texts circulated much more easily and systematically than film productions. There are, however, some notable cases that counter this all too simple assumption. Take, for instance, Stefan Żeromski's controversial novel *The Story of a Sin* (*Dzieje grzechu*, 1910), which was adapted for the Polish screen no less than three times (1911, 1933 and 1975). While this triple adaptation seems to offer a typical example of technology-induced remaking – from silent through sound to colour film – the very fact that the director of the third version (*enfant terrible* Walerian Borowczyk) decided to cast the main actress from the second version (Karolina Lubieńska) in the role of the mother of the female lead character in the 1975 adaptation establishes a direct intertextual connection between the two films. A slightly different example of a triple Polish adaptation that equally complicates the triangular relationship between literary source, adaptation and re-adaptation is Tadeusz Dołęga-Mostowicz's popular interwar novel *The Career of Nikodem Dyzma* (*Kariera Nikodema Dyzmy*, 1931), the first two screen versions of which were made by the very same director, Jan Rybkowski, in 1956 and 1979.

WAITING FOR A (REAL) REMAKE: FROM *KNIFE IN THE WATER* (1962) TO *THE THIRD* (2005)

As the reverse side of the same coin, the dissatisfaction which some Polish film critics have voiced about the 'umbilical cord' tightly connecting 'our cinematography' to 'our library' is supplemented by the repeatedly expressed desire to have a 'real' remake (without any literary interface whatsoever). The most often quoted anecdote in this respect is the story of Roman Polański's obstinate refusal to shoot – at the request of 20th Century Fox – a Hollywood remake of his acclaimed feature debut *Knife in the Water* (*Nóż w wodzie*, 1962).[4] In the late 1990s, the discourse surrounding Polish cinema's incapacity to 'remake' (or to be 'remade') was given a new boost (and a reflexive twist) when American director Barry Sonnenfeld expressed his interest in Juliusz Machulski's popular comedy *Kiler* (1997), up to the point of acquiring the rights for a Hollywood remake. In the 1999 sequel to his film – *Two Kilers* (*Kiler-ów 2-ów*) – Machulski made himself appear on screen as an extra in the arrival hall of Warsaw airport, ostentatiously holding a piece of cardboard with the name 'Barry Sonnenfeld' on it. In the following years, Polish critics and journalists would repeatedly rake up this scene, emblematic as it became of the long-awaited, but ultimately failed project of *Kiler*'s American remake. More or less in the same time frame, Polish film critic Zdzisław Pietrasik (2002) published a lengthy article in a Polish weekly – under the telling title 'Let's Shoot It One More Time' – complaining about Polish cinema's negligence (and considerable backlog) in the field of remakes, prequels and sequels and, at the same time, offering a playful list of suggestions about which Polish films should be considered for remaking.[5]

Quite ironically, however, the Polish film field of the day – producers and critics alike – did not turn out to be fully prepared to 'welcome' its first real (non-literary) remake. In March 2004, a couple of Polish newspapers (*Dziennik Zachodni* 2004; *Gazeta Wrocławska* 2004) briefly informed their readers about a new Polish film-in-the-making, sensationally announced in the paper headlines as '*Knife in the Water* for the second time'. The film production hinted at in the articles – Jan Hryniak's second feature film *The Third* – would premiere at the Gdynia Film Festival in September 2004 and receive a nation-wide cinematic release in the spring of 2005. Two elements immediately catch the eye in these early news reports on Hryniak's alleged remake of *Knife in the Water* (referred to under the film's apparent working title *The Hitchhiker* [*Autostopowicz*]). First of all, although the articles involved correctly identify the three actors who were invited to play the leading roles in Hryniak's film, they turn out to be much worse informed when it comes to assigning specific roles to specific actors (based on the false assumption that the older male actor, Marek Kondrat, would fill the slot of the older man from Polański's film, whereas the younger actor, Jacek Poniedziałek, would play the part of Polański's juvenile hitchhiker). What is more, a very strong normative discourse pervades the articles involved. Not only do they foreground the masterpiece status of the (Oscar-nominated) Polański film, but they also explicitly express the hope that Hryniak's film will at least equal its 1960s source text in terms of quality ('Is *The Hitchhiker* going to be better than *Knife in the Water*? Because if that is not the case, what would be the sense of it?' *Gazeta Wrocławska* 2004).

In hindsight, the normative (remake-oriented) media discourse that started to surround Hryniak's film already at the production stage turned out to have a substantial impact on the critical reception of the film. Although screenwriter Wojciech Zimiński and director Jan Hryniak were very well aware of the fact that some obvious parallels between both films at the outset of the story would invite comparison with Polański's feature debut (Hryniak, personal communication, 5 August 2019) the status of *The Third* as a 'remake' would run as a thread through most of the – predominantly negative or unenthusiastic – reviews of the film. One journalist directly blamed the production team for misleading the audience in that they explicitly marketed the film as a contemporary version of Polański's feature debut.[6] What is more, whereas some critics addressed the remake issue in a more or less neutral way[7], for others it became an evident pretext to dismiss Hryniak's film altogether.[8] As a result of a quite unfortunate – and perhaps ill-prepared – marketing campaign, a film production that was not intended to be a remake in the first place became identified as a remake after all (and was, consequently, evaluated as a failed one).[9]

NAVIGATING BETWEEN REMAKE AND SEQUEL: *OH, CHARLES* 2 (2011)

As one may suspect, Hryniak's lukewarmly received *The Third* did not quench the Polish audience's thirst for a remake. In the spring of 2006, the monthly review *Cinema Polska* launched an online poll among Polish movie-goers to rank those Polish feature films considered worthy of remaking (Zagraj to jeszcze raz, Juliusz' 2006). The top twenty list was headed by three communist-era cult comedies, with the already mentioned literary adaptation *The Teutonic Knights* and Polański's *Knife in the Water* at a relative distance. Among the three top-ranked comedies, it was Marek Piwowski's *Rejs* (*The Cruise*, 1970) that would become the most frequent subject of rumours about advanced remake plans (*nota bene* initiated by Piwowski himself). Surprisingly, however, it was another communist-era comedy – missing altogether from the top twenty issued by *Cinema Polska* – that eventually became the actual object of a remake, namely Roman Załuski's *Oh, Charles* (*Och, Karol*, 1985). Based on an original screenplay by first-time screenwriter Ilona Łepkowska, Załuski's 'erotic comedy' offers the story of a Warsaw-based architect, Karol Górski, who has a mesmerising effect on women and succeeds in cheating on his wife with three different mistresses at the same time. Realised and released in a period of socio-economic scarcity and lingering political tension, the film became an instant box office success in the Polish People's Republic, attracting more than three million viewers, and it remained popular with Polish TV audiences even after the fall of communism.[10]

Interestingly, the news about the planned remake of *Oh, Charles* was disseminated in a textual form that immediately brings to mind the sensationalist headlines announcing back in 2004 the Hryniak film ('Oh, Charles, one more time!'). In this case, however, the information about the remake-in-progress did not appear as a news item in a badly informed Polish daily, but as a blog, dated 13 May 2010) on the personal website of Piotr Wereśniak, director of the film and – together with the above-mentioned Ilona Łepkowska – author of the new screenplay. Wereśniak's strong involvement in social media would become one of the hallmarks of the intensive media campaign surrounding the release of *Oh, Charles 2*. As early as in July 2010, six months before the actual premiere of the film, a Facebook page was launched to gather and disseminate news about the film-in-progress, taken from both traditional and digital media and presented in carefully measured doses.

Taxonomically speaking, *Oh, Charles 2* can be classified as an acknowledged close remake, borrowing from the hypotext not only many 'syntactic elements (plot structure, narrative units, character relationships, . . .)' (Verevis 2006: 84), but also some important semantic features, most notably the names of most of the main (and some of the secondary) characters. At closer investigation, the dynamics of 'repetition' and 'novelty' that are central to remaking as a process and the remake as a product came to play a central role in the pre-release marketing strategy developed by the production team. As early as in July 2010, various details about the shooting process were complemented by a series of day-to-day teasers related to the cast of the new *Oh, Charles* production. After separate posts introducing every single actor and their corresponding roles – 'Meet Irena', 'Meet Paulina' and so on – the Facebook page was gradually supplemented with photo albums named after each character. In view of the fact that most roles were given to well-known Polish soap actors and actresses, this strategy could appeal to both older and younger viewers, inviting the former to associate new faces with familiar characters (from the original film) and the latter to connect familiar faces (from Polish TV) with new characters. This marketing method even extended to the use of props in the film, when it was announced (on 11 August) that Karol's Volkswagen Golf from the original film would be replaced by a Peugeot RCZ (foreshadowing the ostentatious role of product placement in *Oh, Charles 2*).

The marketing campaign about the cast came full circle in mid-August, when after the final shooting day it was announced that Jan Piechociński (who had played Karol in the original film) was granted a cameo appearance in the remake (*nota bene* in the role of a priest). In the months that followed, Piechociński and his successor, the popular actor Piotr Adamczyk, regularly appeared side by side in various Polish media, forging further identification between the communist-era comedy and its post-communist remake. Therefore, all the way from pre-production to the actual release, *Oh, Charles 2* was recognizably and consistently advertised as a remake (which puts it in sharp contrast to the rather ambivalent media attention generated by Hryniak's *The Third*).[11] Interestingly, while the production team clearly intended to capitalise on the cult status of the communist-era original and on the nostalgic reflexes it would stir in older viewers, they remained hesitant about the actual name of the film, doubting whether the title terms should be followed by a '2' or not (Wereśniak, personal communication, 18 August 2019). On a general level, this hesitation may be said to pinpoint the rather fluid boundary between practices of remaking (repetition) and sequelisation (continuation) (Perkins and Verevis 2012: 2–3). On a more specific level, the eventual decision to add the serial number to the title is in line with the makers' overarching intent to overwrite, but not to erase the original film and to turn the targeted audience – not only older viewers with a background in the People's Republic, but also the younger ones – into a (more or less) 'knowing audience' (Hutcheon 2006: 120–27). Significantly, however, apart from being part of a commercially driven audience-building effort, *Oh, Charles 2* exposes this sense of intergenerational continuity (and communal coherence) also within the story world. Particularly symbolic in this respect is the appearance of

Figure 9.1 The priest (played by Jan Piechociński) addresses his 'son' (Karol 2) during a wedding ceremony in *Oh, Charles 2*

Jan Piechociński in the guise of a priest in the closing sequence of the film, set in a church. For the 'knowing' viewers, this narrative thread introduces an element of plot progress, suggesting that the communist-era Karol has ultimately done penance for his sins (polygamy and adultery). Even more significant, however, is the way in which the priest addresses his polygamous post-communist successor at the very end of the same wedding scene: while the young Karol is literally knocked off his feet at the first glance of the woman with whom he is likely to spend the rest of his life, the priest bends over him and comments on the monogamous life that lies ahead of him in the following way: 'Better late than never, my son'. The parent-child dyad turns both Karols into the kindred representatives of two successive generations, which is symbolically reinforced by the time-span that separates *Oh, Charles 2* from its source film – that is, a quarter of a century, which is the average period for a generation to come of age.

Drawing further on Kathleen Loock's research into the social function of 'diachronic remaking' – as a 'mode of timekeeping' and 'generationing' (Loock 2019) – *Oh, Charles 2* may be said to engage in a specific form of 'post-communist generationing', as it gears itself towards a double target audience (the pre- and the post-1989 generations) and projects the generational passage of time onto the sociological rift between state socialist and capitalist Poland.[12] This rupture closely relates to the distinctly different treatment which the topic of 'abundance' (Karol's struggle with 'too many women') is given in both films: while Załuski's daring portrayal of polygamy (and on-screen nudity) mainly helped the communist-era viewer to escape from the omnipresent atmosphere of grayness and scarcity – a much needed 'headache tablet', as it was aptly called by the director (Bątkiewicz 1985) – Wereśniak's remake, for its part, foregrounds the dangers of hedonism (and lack of marital commitment) at a time when material abundance is actually in reach (at least for privileged upper-middle-class men like Karol Górski). Although finding only lukewarm reception by most critics (not least because of its sexist portrayal of women), *Oh, Charles 2* ultimately reached a staggering number of more than 1,700,000 viewers, as a result of which the film (temporarily) entered the top ten of greatest box office hits on Polish screens since the fall of communism.[13]

THE POLISH OFFSPRING OF *LOVE ACTUALLY*: FROM *LETTERS TO SANTA* (2011, 2015, 2017) TO *LOVE IS ALL* (2018)

A predictable side-effect of the buzz surrounding the making of *Oh, Charles 2* was the resurgence of the remake debate in the Polish media. On 21 July 2010, the major daily *Rzeczpospolita* published a long article under the telling title 'Oh, Charles, is Kloss going to return now?' (Świątek 2010). The name

Kloss referred to the lead character of the popular 1960s TV series *Stawka więcej niż życie* (*More Than Life at Stake*). Throughout the article, the story of three aborted Polish film projects – the two competing *Teutonic Knights* re-adaptations and Władysław Pasikowski's attempts to turn the TV series about Kloss into a feature film – served to illustrate the journalist's (under)statement that 'remakes are not a Polish speciality'. At the same time, the topical case of the *Oh, Charles* reboot made the author wonder 'whether the film's success will set in motion an avalanche of remakes'. In the years that followed, these speculative musings about the 'return of Kloss' and 'an avalanche of remakes' took quite an unexpected turn. The popular Kloss did make his comeback on the Polish screens, but in a production that turned out to be a sequel to (rather than a remake of) the communist-era serial, namely Patryk Vega's *More Than Death at Stake* (*Stawka więcej niż śmierć*, 2012). *Oh, Charles 2*, for its part, did not become a model of domestic (diachronic) film remaking worth imitating, but it gathered a following in a different way, as one of the first examples of sequelisation practices in the ever more popular (and commercially viable) genre of the romantic comedy. In times when re-adaptations of the literary canon increasingly lost attraction and appreciation among Polish audiences, this type of films provided domestic production companies with a tried-and-tested formula for box office success.

The Polish variation of the genre did not further develop, however, without taking some of its cues from well-known foreign examples. Its perhaps most prominent example is the *Letters to Santa* (*Listy do M.*) cycle, the first part of which came out at the end of 2011 (with its omnipresent Christmas décor, offering a cross between two film genres, the romantic comedy and the holiday movie). Along with the Polish ensemble cast, the mosaic Christmas narrative and a poster campaign almost identical to that of Richard Curtis's *Love Actually* (2003), *Letters to Santa* was immediately and easily recognized as a rip-off of its famous British forerunner (Wałkiewicz 2011). Yet, in spite of some obvious syntactic similarities, the semantics of the film differed significantly enough to avoid any issues with the legal departments of the European and American production companies involved. After two equally popular sequels released in 2015 and 2017, the *Letters to Santa* cycle was supplemented at the end of 2018 by what may be called a 'distant cousin' of the successful franchise, namely Michał Kwieciński's romantic Christmas comedy *Love Is All*. With its winter holiday setting, its ensemble cast and its interlocking narratives of love, betrayal and reconciliation, it equally reaches back to *Love Actually*, but it does so in a roundabout way, through its strong syntactic reliance on another foreign film loosely inspired by the Curtis film – namely, the Dutch production *All Is Love* (*Alles is Liefde*, 2007). As the first officially licensed Polish-language remake of a foreign film, Kwieciński's film has undeniably opened a new chapter in Polish remaking practices, pointing to Polish cinema's participation in wider European (and global) industrial trends, a move that Polish TV producers had made already in the preceding decades.

Generally speaking, the case of *Love Is All* confirms some of the main findings of recent (Europe-focused) research in the domain of synchronic remaking practices, in terms of both industrial dynamics (Labayen and Morán 2019) and cultural and textual adaptation strategies (Cuelenaere, Joye and Willems 2019). As transpires from a long interview with the director (and co-producer) of the film (Kwieciński, personal communication, 25 July 2019), the Polish remake project was set in motion at the annual film market in Cannes, where the producers got in touch with the manager of the Brussels-based distribution company Crazy Cow, Michel Daemen, one of the European pioneers in the trade of film remake rights. One particular film in the Crazy Cow catalogue turned out to fulfil the needs of the Polish producers who were actively soliciting screenplays for a new winter holiday film that would deviate enough from the *Letters to Santa* franchise. What followed then was an intensive process of localisation, as a result of which *Love Is All* could be presented as an original to the Polish viewers.[14]

Along these lines – and in obvious contrast to the domestic remake of *Oh, Charles* – the Polish audience was kept entirely uninformed about the film's remake status, which can be amply testified by a perusal of the marketing and the critical reception of the film, in digital and traditional media alike. Likewise, the fact that the authorship of the screenplay at the outset of the end credits is attributed exclusively to the Polish production team allows to label *Love Is All* as a strongly disguised remake, albeit a credited one (with some information about the Dutch source film appearing at the very end of the closing credits). Although Kwieciński himself does not avoid using the label 'remake', he prefers to call his film a 'creative adaption' (Kwieciński, personal communication, 25 July 2019). What is more, not unlike other recent examples of 'manufacturing proximity' through remaking (Labayen and Morán 2019), the 'creative adaptation' of the source film also extends to the level of production strategies, including the creative appropriation of funding methods and practices (Cuelenaere, Joye and Willems 2019). This applies in particular to the role of city marketing and product placement throughout the film, with the harbour city of Gdańsk offering an ideal equivalent for Amsterdam and serving as both a postcard-like film location and one of the major investors in the project.[15]

(UN)FAMILIAR PEOPLE (2019), OR THE REMAKING OF TRANSNATIONAL FLOWS

This brings us, finally, to Tadeusz Śliwa's and Katarzyna Sarnowska's very recent Polish reworking of the Italian box office hit *Perfect Strangers* (*Perfetti sconosciuti*, 2016). When treated in tandem with Kwieciński's *Love Is All*, the release of another Polish-language remake of a foreign film in less than one year suggests that a new trend – that is, Polish producers exploring the international remake rights market in search of interesting screenplays – is indeed taking shape. At the same time, the Polish remake is part and parcel of an exceptionally global phenomenon. The Italian source film's ever-expanding track record in terms of remakability – covering countries as diverse as Turkey, Russia, Mexico, China and South Korea – undoubtedly renders it an intriguing case for cross-cultural analysis, both from an industrial perspective and through the lens of localisation practices. In terms of storytelling, the worldwide appeal of *Perfect Strangers* at least partly relies on its original engagement with a globally recognizable (and applicable) phenomenon – namely, our increasingly intimate dependence on the 'black boxes' of our smartphones.

That said, the Polish version, ambiguously titled *(Un)familiar People*, appears to take up a particular position within the expanding body of local-language remakes of *Perfect Strangers*, which directly relates to the Polish film's strong investment in self-reflexive references and tropes. Whereas many remakes of the transnational type tend to obscure – by way of localisation – their foreign provenance, *(Un)familiar People* implicitly and explicitly inscribes various aspects of transnationalism into the local Polish context. Its most prominent manifestation is the migration thread that runs like a motif through the film: the hostess Ewa is portrayed as a professional expatriate who spends most of her time between Italy and Warsaw, where her husband and her daughter live. What emerges then from this addition is a range of Italian motifs cropping up within the narrative and *mise-en-scène* of the film: Italian cuisine and clothing, Italian speech, a phone call from Italy and so on. This approach is also discernible in the intensive online marketing surrounding the film (for instance, on Facebook), which – apart from self-reflexively engaging with the impact of social media and applications on our daily lives – repeatedly exposes the Polish-Italian connection underlying the remake project.

On a reflexive level, the various instances of transnational mobility and communication highlighted within the diegesis help to foreground the status of the film remake itself as a product of transnational flows and exchanges (in this case, between Italy and Poland). Co-producer Katarzyna Sarnowska – who initiated the project and co-adapted the screenplay – indicates that from the outset of the project there was the intention to have a subtle, but overt point of connection between the Italian and the Polish version, because 'we do not run away from the fact that this is a remake nor are we ashamed of it' (Sarnowska, personal communication, 17 September 2019). As in the case of Wereśniak's *Oh, Charles 2* – which was explicitly advertised and marketed as a remake – this statement defies the widespread negative reputation of the remake label (Cuelenaere, Joye and Willems 2016). Moreover, there are two particular circumstances that make the Polish case stand out from the other remakes of *Perfect Strangers*. First of all, although the Italian original had a cinematic release in more than twenty European countries, the attendance rates in Poland with some 160,000 viewers were exceptionally high, which means that Poland offered a much larger reservoir of 'knowing' viewers potentially interested in a local-language version (but making it simultaneously very difficult to fully erase the existence of a source text). Another noteworthy element is the fact that the original Italian cast included a well-known actress of Polish extraction, Kasia Smutniak. As a result, when the migration thread began to take shape during the adaptation of the screenplay, the most obvious way of establishing a close bond between the Italian and the Polish version was to cast Smutniak in the role of the hostess (Ewa), the character which she also played in the source film (Eva) (Sarnowska, personal communication, 12 September 2019). Self-evidently, the very fact that Ewa's secret lover calling from Italy carries the same name as Eva's lover in the original film (Cosimo) provides 'an optional bonus of pleasure to those in the know' (Leitch 2001: 42). Through the combined process of localisation (transplanting the action from Rome to Warsaw) and interlocalisation (foregrounding the transnational flows between Italy and Poland), *(Un)familiar People* interestingly complicates the existing taxonomic models of film remakes: while altering the semantics and – to a lesser extent – the syntactics of the source film, it uses some of these transformations precisely to reinforce the bond with the Italian original. Ultimately, it is the film's highly ambiguous title that captures most powerfully the makers' reflexive take on transnational remaking practices and their sophisticated engagement with both 'knowing' and 'unknowing' audiences: although the notion of '(un)familiarity' primarily refers to the character relationships depicted within the story world, it also brings the viewers' own position into play, as well as their awareness – or lack thereof – of a precursor film and precursor characters. Inasmuch as the expression of 'a playful self-reflexive attitude towards the remake phenomenon' is a widespread practice in film remakes (Cuelenaere, Joye and Willems 2019, 273), the makers of *(Un)familiar People* positioned it at the very core of their creative project.

CONCLUSION

As the film projects discussed in this chapter indicate, Polish cinematography seems to be drifting away from its long-standing reliance – through adaptation and re-adaptation – on literary source texts, moving slowly into the direction of 'real' (film-based) remakes. Over the past two decades, speculations about domestic film remakes have tended to revolve around cult or classical films that belong to the accumulated popular cultural heritage of the communist era (of which *Oh, Charles 2* offers the first successfully realised example). The case of Hryniak's *The Third*, for its part, indicates that engaging with the sacrosanct catalogue of Polish national cinema is not without risk. As it transpires, a much safer (and commercially attractive) venue for Polish remake projects is offered by the expanding international market of remake rights sales, a domain that is increasingly being explored by Polish film producers, who do not eschew actively engaging in the process of 'creative adaptation', either as a director – as in the case of Kwieciński – or as a screenwriter – as in the case of Sarnowska. So far, however, as the diverging cases of *Love Is All* and *(Un)familiar People* show, these transnational flows have been exclusively import-oriented, and it remains to be seen if (and when) Polish cinema – after having shown its ability to 'remake' both domestic and foreign productions – will eventually actualise and realise its potential (and desire) to 'be remade'. The very reason for which Polish producers are increasingly exploring the foreign market – that is, the scarcity of high-quality screenplays in the segment of Polish middle-of-the-road cinema – suggests that the export-oriented flow will manifest itself later rather than sooner.

NOTES

1. The author of the article mentions two main reasons for this situation – namely, the lack of state funding for remake projects and Polish filmmakers' fear of being accused of a lack of originality (which does not apply, however, to adaptations of the literary canon). Interestingly, throughout the article, two Polish near-synonyms are used interchangeably with the English word 'remake' (*powtórka* and *przeróbka*). When taken in tandem, both terms point to the dynamics of iteration (*powtórzyć*) and transformation (*przerobić*), which are crucial to the remaking process.
2. The only notable exception is Paweł Sitkiewicz's recent historical research into a series of 'Polish-language remakes' of Paramount productions from the 1930s, in the heydays of what is usually called the multiple-language version film (Sitkiewicz 2017).
3. I am greatly indebted to the following film professionals for sharing with me their thoughts on the film projects in which they have been directly involved: Jan Hryniak, Piotr Wereśniak, Michał Kwieciński, Katarzyna Sarnowska and Oleg Fesenko.
4. See his own account of this story in Polanski (1985: 205–6).
5. Much less known is the fact that in the early 1990s Polish screenwriter Cezary Harasimowicz and director Jacek Skalski started working on a remake of Tadeusz Konwicki's acclaimed feature film debut *The Last Day of Summer* (*Ostatni dzień lata*, 1958). Harasimowicz's screenplay has been archived at the library of the National Film Archives in Warsaw. I am greatly indebted to the director of the archives, Adam Wyżyński, who shared with me this and other invaluable information.
6. 'The producer misused the audience's patience by guaranteeing that *The Third* would evidently draw on Polański's *Knife in the Water*' (Bubin 2005).
7. '*Knife in the Water* AD 2004' (*Warszawski Informator Kulturalny* 2005), 'A contemporary *Knife in the Water*' (Kądziela 2005), 'A 21st-century *Knife in the Water*' (*Polityka* 2005), 'Knife in the car' (Jagielski 2005).
8. 'Old knife in a new Lexus' (Reszka 2005), 'A failed reworking of Polański's film' (Żurawiecki 2005), 'This is, unfortunately, a failed attempt' (*Tygodnik Solidarność* 2005), 'Against the backdrop of *Knife in the Water*, Jan Hryniak's film makes a pale impression' (Hollender 2005).

9. In an interview that appeared between the shooting process and the first festival screening of the film, Hryniak clearly attempted to steer attention away from the alleged remake character of *The Third*, indicating that 'while working on the film we moved away from *Knife in the Water* ever more' (Hollender 2004).
10. Another exemplification of the film's cult status is the special *Oh, Charles – 30 years later* (*Och, Karol – 30 lat później*) that was broadcast by Polish public television at the end of 2015.
11. Tellingly, while the various screenplay versions of *The Third* stored at the National Film Archives (FINA) in Warsaw do not contain any paratextual reference whatsoever to Polański's feature debut, the title page of the *Oh, Charles 2* screenplay stored in the FINA archives prominently contains the label 'remake'.
12. With the exception of Russia (see the chapter by Noordenbos and Souch in this volume), most post-communist cinemas do not tend to engage (systematically) in the remaking of communist-era films. This state of affairs may not only be related to the size of the respective film industries, but also to a different form of post-communist nostalgia (which, at least in the case of Poland, relies on an enduring attachment to communist-era films, mostly comedies, that foreground in a subtly critical way the absurdity and downsides of state socialism). Remarkably, there is also one notable example of a contemporary Russian film that takes its cues from a communist-era Polish source text, Oleg Fesenko's 2006 psychological drama *Rush Hour* (*Chas pik*). According to the director, however, the film was not based on Jerzy Stawiński's eponymous film (*Godzina szczytu*, 1974), nor on Stawiński's original novel (Warsaw 1968), but on the Russian-language theatrical adaptation that was very popular in the Soviet Union in the early 1970s (Fesenko, personal communication, 17 August 2019).
13. As another marker of the 'overwrite, not erase' strategy, both films were released in a DVD box at the end of 2011 (including a digitally remastered version of the 1985 film).
14. In terms of cultural adaptation, there existed two main challenges for the production team. First of all, although the figure of Saint Nicholas has its historical place in Polish culture, the action of the film had to be moved from the beginning of December (when Saint Nicholas is celebrated in the Netherlands and Belgium) to the week preceding Christmas (which is a much more established holiday in Poland). As a result, by portraying the peripeteias of a Saint Nicholas stand-in against a Christmas backdrop, the Polish version of the film positioned itself in between the Flemish remake from 2010 (which eventually stuck to the original Saint Nicholas feast) and the German one from 2014 (which had it replaced by Santa Claus in a Christmas setting). In contrast to the three earlier versions of the film, however, the Polish production team decided to 'heterosexualise' the gay marriage that occupies a central place in the picture's mosaic narrative – in Kwieciński's words, because 'this is impossible in Poland – now even more so – and nobody would want to put money into that'. While this intervention in the original screenplay is, obviously, a case of perceived cultural differences (Cuelenaere, Joye and Willems 2019), it should be stressed that there is no legal framework whatsoever for same-sex marriage in Poland – let alone that such a wedding could be portrayed as 'normal' and 'accepted', which the earlier versions of the film manifestly do. At the same time, Kwieciński maintained the gay identity of one of the minor characters – the manager of the local shopping mall – and added some minor jokes that spread confusion about the actual sex of the wedding couple, as a wink to those viewers who are familiar with the original film and its 'normalising' engagement with same-sex marriage (Kwieciński, personal communication, 25 July 2019).
15. Significantly, one of the returning positive elements in the reception of the film was exactly the fact that it breaks away from the prototypical settings of the Polish rom-com, Warsaw and Cracow.

REFERENCES

Bątkiewicz, Andrzej (1985), 'Pastylka od bólu głowy', *Panorama*, 24 November.
Bubin, Stanisław (2005), 'Trzeciorzędny knot', *Dziennik Zachodni*, 23 March.
Chełminiak, Wiesław (2001), 'Znacie? To obejrzyjcie!' *Nowe Państwo*, 7 December.
Cuelenaere, Eduard, Stijn Joye and Gertjan Willems (2016), 'Reframing the Remake: Dutch-Flemish Monolingual Remakes and Their Theoretical and Conceptual Implications', *Frames Cinema Journal* 10 [online, no pag.].
Cuelenaere, Eduard, Stijn Joye and Gertjan Willems (2019), 'Local Flavors and Regional Markers: The Low Countries and Their Commercially Driven and Proximity-Focused Film Remake Practice', *Communications*, 44: 3, 262–81.
Dziennik Zachodni (2004), '"Nóż w wodzie" po raz drugi. Czy "Autostopowicz" dorówna dziełu Polańskiego?' 5 March.
Gazeta Wrocławska (2004), '"Nóż w wodzie" po raz drugi', 5 March.
Haltof, Marek (2007), 'Adapting the National Literary Canon: Polish Heritage Cinema', *Canadian Review of Contemporary Literature*, 34: 3, 298–306.
Haltof, Marek (2018), *Polish Cinema: A History*, Oxford, New York: Berghahn Books.
Hollender, Barbara (2004), 'Trójkąt z inną pointą', *Rzeczpospolita*, 21 July.
Hollender, Barbara (2005), 'Banał zamiast prawdy', *Rzeczpospolita*, 10 March.
Hutcheon, Linda (2006), *A Theory of Adaptation*, New York, London: Routledge.
Jagielski, Sebastian (2005), 'Trzeci. Nóż w samochodzie', *Cinema Polska*, 3: 70.
Kądziela, Agnieszka (2005), 'Rola trzeciego', *Metropol*, 13 March.
Labayen, Miguel Fernández and Ana Martín Morán (2019), 'Manufacturing Proximity through Film Remakes: Remake Rights Representatives and the Case of Local-Language Comedy Remakes', *Communications*, 44: 3, 282–303.
Leitch, Thomas (2001), 'Twice-Told Tales: Disavowal and the Rhetoric of the Remake', in Jennifer Forrest and Leonard R. Koos (eds), *Dead Ringers: The Remake in Theory and Practice*, Albany: State University of New York Press, pp. 37–62.
Loock, Kathleen (2019), 'Remaking Winnetou, Reconfiguring German Fantasies of Indianer and the Wild West in the Post-Reunification Era', *Communications*, 44: 3, 323–41.
Lubelski, Tadeusz, ed. (2014), *Od Mickiewicza do Masłowskiej: Adaptacje filmowe literatury polskiej*, Kraków: Universitas.
Perkins, Claire and Constantine Verevis (2012), 'Introduction: Three Times', in Claire Perkins and Constantine Verevis (eds), *Film Trilogies: New Critical Approaches*, New York, London: Palgrave Macmillan, pp. 1–34.
Pietrasik, Zdzisław (2002), 'Nakręćmy to jeszcze raz', *Polityka*, 21 December.
Polanski, Roman (1985), *Roman by Polanski*, New York: Ballantine Books.
Polityka (2005), 'Trzeci', 12 March.
Reszka, Jarosław (2005), 'Stary nóż w nowym Lexusie', *Express Bydgoski*, 16 March.
Sitkiewicz, Paweł (2017), 'Polskojęzyczne remaki filmów z Hollywood: Powrót do Joinville', *Kwartalnik Filmowy* 97–8, 83–93.
Świątek, Rafał (2010), 'Och, Karol, czy teraz wróci Kloss', *Rzeczpospolita*, 21 July.
Tygodnik Solidarność (2005), 'Trzeci'.
Verevis, Constantine (2006), *Film Remakes*, Edinburgh: Edinburgh University Press.
Wałkiewicz, Michał (2011), 'Miłość i świąteczna gorączka', *Film*, 56: 12, 80.
Warszawski Informator Kulturalny (2005), 'Trzeci'.
Wereśniak, Piotr (2010), 'Och Karol – jeszcze raz!' *Piotr Wereśniak* (blog), 13 May, available at: https://piotrweresniak.com/2010/05/13/och-karol-jeszcze-raz/ (last accessed 28 September 2019).
'Zagraj to jeszcze raz, Juliusz' (2006), *Cinema Polska*, 7, 14.

'Znacie? To obejrzyjcie!' (2001), 7 December, available at: https://kultura.onet.pl/wiadomosci/znacie-to-obejrzyjcie/yc7677p (last accessed 28 September 2019).

Żurawiecki, Bartosz (2005), 'Nóż w młodzież: Nieudana przeróbka filmu Polańskiego', *Przekrój*, 10 March.

CHAPTER 10

Nostalgic Mediations of the Soviet Past in Nikolai Lebedev's Remake *The Crew* (2016)

Boris Noordenbos and Irina Souch

> The Crew *is the first remake [. . .] of a Soviet film that does not look like a parody, or a glamourised copy.*
> (Film historian Andrei Plakhov, commenting on the release of *The Crew* in 2016)

NOSTALGIA AS A 'RE-MAKING' PRACTICE

The process of remaking the Soviet cinematic canon started soon after the demise of the Soviet Union, with Gleb and Igor' Aleinikov's 1992 film *Tractor Drivers 2* (*Traktoristy 2*), a parodic fantasy remix of no less than three Soviet classics: the comedy drama *Tractor Drivers* (*Traktoristy*, 1939), the musical comedy *Wedding in Malinovka* (*Svad'ba v Malinovke*, 1967) and the television thriller mini-series *The Meeting Place Cannot Be Changed* (*Mesto vstrechi izmenit' nel'zia*, 1979). Aleinikov's project was promptly followed by many similar endeavours, encompassing a wide array of filmic genres.[1] From the start, the remakes were received with considerable sarcasm by Russian critics and audiences alike, who tended to agree on these films' inferiority in relation to their originals in every possible way. Their plots, casting, visual imagery, technological innovations (or lack thereof) and their alleged kowtowing to Hollywood invariably caused public contempt.[2] Paradoxically, this negative reception has by no means curtailed the production of ever new remakes. It appears that the intensive reuse of the domestic canon (instead of lesser-known foreign material) is not just an instance of the capitalist 'commodification of Soviet culture' (Usmanova 2004), nor is it merely a symptom of the pitiable shortage of authentic ideas, as online viewer forums tend to claim. While acknowledging the audiences' desire 'to see whether the new film can re-create the magic of the former' (Todd 2016), we argue that contemporary remakes are involved in the larger process of reassessing Soviet (cultural) heritage, often understood in terms of nostalgia.

It is widely observed in Russian Studies that the wholesale rejection of everything Soviet – a dominant sentiment immediately after the demise of the Soviet order (Smith 2002: 3) – was soon replaced by a renewed Russian interest in (an eclectic set of) nostalgically cherished Soviet symbols and values (Dubin 2007: 297–311; Boym 2001: 57–71). By the twenty-first century, elements from Soviet history came to operate as prevalent focal points of collective self-identification, adding to an image of the (late) Soviet era as a period of existential values that are felt to be lacking in Russia's reformed society (Dubin 2010: 187; Khapaeva 2007: 95). If nostalgia, in its original meanings, is the desire to return to a lost home (Boym 2001: xiii), for many former Soviet citizens the notion of 'home' is inseparable from the idea of Soviet-era stability, solidarity and sincerity (Lankauskas 2014: 39; Nadkarni and Shevchenko 2004: 510). Accordingly, public opinion surveys in the year 2000 show that in the Russian cultural imagination Soviet film classics, especially those produced between the early 1960s and the late 1980s, appear as objects of collective reverence. They epitomise the essence of a perceived Soviet Golden Age, conceived as an unspecified *époque* that conflates a number of divergent historical periods, including the Khrushev-era Thaw and Brezhnev-era Stagnation (Dubin 2010).[3] Anna Novikova, critically commenting on this renewed, rose-tinted fascination with the (cinematic) past, observes that '[t]he idyllic view of Soviet everyday life that was typical for films made under the strict control of communist censorship now seems truthful even to those who should have remembered those years well' (2010: 287). By offering a way to revisit, relive and rethink the past, post-Soviet remakes, so it appears, help assuage the public's nostalgic yearnings and recreate, albeit temporarily, the structures of feeling which are now experienced as irretrievable.

Cultural expressions of nostalgia are often seen as indicative of a (potentially dangerous) desire to return to communist ideology or Soviet authoritarianism. Yet, the rekindled interest in older cultural *forms* does not automatically amount to reactionary aspirations to rehabilitate normative systems from the past (Oushakine 2007: 453–54; Boele et al. 2019: 6; Nadkarni and Shevchenko 2004: 504). Therefore, instead of conceiving of nostalgia as a misguided sentimental fixation on the Soviet era, here we approach it as an affective 'practice' or 'activity' (Smith and Campbell 2017: 612; Stewart 198: 227; Pickering and Keightly 2006: 937), one that negotiates ruptures and continuities (Atia and Davies 2010: 184). While dramatising historical breaks, nostalgia also helps to establish connections between different epochs and, thus, to replenish a sense of self and belonging, especially in times when social identities are felt to be under threat (Davis 1979).

The above views provide a valuable background for our discussion of Nikolai Lebedev's 2016 remake of the canonical disaster film *The Crew* from 1979. The relation between the two films is made particularly evident through their shared Russian title *Ekipazh*, which is often obscured in the varying English translations, such as *The Crew*, *Air Crew* and *Flight Crew*. To emphasise the historical and ideological links between these works, here we deliberately use *The Crew* for both. We discuss Lebedev's film as a cultural text that not only illuminates the issues involved in the contemporary remake industry in Russia, but also, and more importantly, helps to understand the cultural 'work' of nostalgia in Russian society today. Capitalising on the public's nostalgic feelings towards the Soviet order to procure the highest possible audience figures, the film also consciously cultivates the 'memories of transition' and seeks to emphasise the cultural continuities that exist, despite the alienating ruptures brought about by the all-encompassing societal changes of the past decades.

THE CREW AND ITS STATUS AS A REMAKE

As the epigraph to this chapter indicates, *The Crew* occupies a special position among a large number of post-Soviet remakes produced by the Russian film industry over the last twenty-five years. The film is the coming-of-age story of a young pilot, Alexei Gushchin (Danila Kozlovskii). The narrative commences when Alexei finds a position as an intern at a private passenger airline company in Moscow after being discharged from military service for disobeying his corrupt superior's orders. Alexei's new supervisor, Leonid Zinchenko (Vladimir Mashkov), frequently reprimands him for recalcitrant behaviour, but acknowledges the young man's exceptional talent as pilot. Alexei has a chance to prove himself when Zinchenko's crew faces the challenging task of evacuating the survivors of a volcanic eruption at a faraway oceanic island.

Upon the film's premiere in spring 2016, it was critically acclaimed as a 'surprisingly fun action blockbuster' (Corbet 2016) that confidently emulated Hollywood's similar genre successes, but did so with a twist to cater to domestic audiences (Todd 2016).[4] The same year the Russian cinephile site *Kinopoisk* estimated the box-office receipts over 24 million dollars. Yet, *The Crew* also provoked an avalanche of negative comments from pundits and viewers alike. Perhaps not surprisingly, most discussions revolved around its relation to the source, Alexander Mitta's film from 1979.[5] The comparison was further fuelled by the fact that in various interviews Lebedev emphasised his long-lasting admiration for Mitta's classic, declaring his work to be an homage and even ensuring the previous director's cameo appearance in the new story. Remarkable therefore is Lebedev's simultaneous dismissal of his project's status as a remake: 'Remaking the Soviet-era film *The Crew* is just as meaningless as remaking Fellini's *Amarcord*. These are unique films. Also, it is impossible to transfer the problems and people of the 1970s to the post-Soviet landscape' (Lebedev, quoted in Kichin 2016).

The latter view was supported by critic Nina Tsyrkun who in the influential Russian film journal *Iskusstvo Kino* observed that the modern version of *The Crew* is 'cast in a different mould' and is incomparable to the original: '[T]he former [film] belongs to the period of developed socialism, the latter – to the post-industrial capitalism. And each one is constructed according to its own laws' (Tsyrkun 2016). Yet, after having rejected the analogy Tsyrkun immediately sets out to establish connections between the two productions. She states that, although Mitta had excelled in his creative use of the limited contemporary technologies to depict a natural catastrophe in a realistic manner, his major strength lies in the true-to-life portrayal of the characters and their private ordeals. Conversely, while Lebedev succeeds in producing a disaster movie according to Hollywood standards, he painfully fails to infuse the individual storylines with the veracity necessary to engage the audience affectively. Other reviewers did not share Tsyrkun's reservations and, not in the least because of the identical titles, perceived Lebedev's film as a remake of sorts (Gorelov 2016; Plakhov 2016; Styshova 2016; Todd 2016; Tyrkin 2016). The initial disagreement about *The Crew*'s relation to its predecessor arguably stems from critics' divergent views on the notion of remake itself. While it can be seen as a full replica of the original text, contemporary remake theory privileges a much broader understanding, identifying the remake as a film based on an earlier, usually successful, work which 'accept[s] the original text's authority on its own terms, by attempting to disclose and valorize those terms' (Leitch 1990: 144).[6] Such definition sees the sequel and homage as particular types of the remake. This is why the more informed analyses of *The Crew* indeed characterise it as a 'loose remake' of Mitta's earlier film (Shavlovskii 2016; see also Dolin 2016; Kuzmina 2016; Stepanov 2016).

While the above discussions illuminate the context of *The Crew*'s production and reception, we take our cue from Leitch's conceptualisations of the remake to consider the film's broader cultural implications. In his seminal article 'Twice-Told Tales: The Rhetoric of the Remake', Leitch points out that remakes tend to treat their cinematic sources as 'forerunners instead of true originals' and engage in a 'ritual invocation/denial of [their] discursive features', reasserting some of them as timeless, while devaluing others as outdated (1990: 148). *The Crew* employs this evaluative potential in a markedly self-conscious way, which makes it an outstanding case for the exploration of the concerns that the present reproduction of the Soviet cinematic canon brings in relief. We will argue that, by incorporating a series of recognizable generic, thematic and aesthetic correspondences, Lebedev's film effectively encourages a (nostalgic) revisiting and examination of cinematic and discursive connections between two distinct historical epochs, helping viewers reassess their relations to Soviet-era social values. Through this evaluative work, the film ultimately proposes a multifaceted 'reconciliation with the Soviet', which according to the sociologist Boris Dubin constitutes 'one of the leading characteristics of collective life in Russia under Putin's regime' (2010: 187).

IDENTIFYING POST-SOVIET RUPTURES

In his discussion of Hollywood disaster films from the 1970s, Roddick notes that the genre taps into 'a widespread contemporary phobia that traditional values are somehow threatened, if indeed they have not already collapsed' (1980: 255). Interweaving the destinies of individual characters who often function as markers of social types, disaster films typically start from a portrayal of the protagonists' daily lives in ways that invoke such social anxieties. Following this first, melodramatic stage, the subsequent catastrophe functions, in Roddick's words, as 'a catalyst, enabling a transition [. . .] and justifying the societal transformation which is characteristic of [. . . the film's] final stage' (1980: 258). Notwithstanding the deviations from the Hollywood tradition, both Lebedev's and Mitta's films work with these formulas. Especially in Lebedev's story, the pre-disaster scenes suggest the necessity of 'a certain kind of societal reorganisation' (Roddick 1980: 250). The catastrophe that follows not merely causes destruction, but also paradoxically instigates a process of social reparation. As one pundit perceptively noted, *The Crew*'s narrative appears to advance the idea that 'we need a big calamity [. . . since in the face of] calamity, war, catastrophe we are united and invincible' (Maliukova 2016).

The social 'phobias' exhibited in *The Crew* are all premised on a temporal and cultural rift, a perceived rupture which operates as the precondition for the rhetoric of nostalgia (Boym 2001: 25; Nadkarni and Shevchenko 2004: 492; Tannock 1995: 459–61). Being a tribute to Mitta's heritage, *The Crew* not only directly refers to a forever perished tradition of Soviet cinema, but also reveals the fraying fabric of social life, in particular the loss of the authority once held by a generation of biological or surrogate fathers. As Goscilo and Hashamova demonstrate in a volume devoted to what they call 'cinepaternity', fraud father-son relations are a strikingly ubiquitous motif in recent Russian film. The recurring concern with troubled generational relations, so the scholars assert, was 'triggered by the radical rupture in Russia's historical continuity and the concomitant crisis in masculinity and paternity' (2010: 5).

The Crew, at least initially, falls in step with this 'cinepaternal' tradition: father-son disagreements and their detrimental effects on masculine authority are its thematic pivot. This theme is introduced when Alexei Gushchin, dismissed from his post in military cargo aviation, visits his father, a retired aircraft engineer. We see an aerial shot of the protagonist, standing on a crowded Moscow street, his feet fixed on a compass rose laid into the pavement. Subsequently, the camera spirals downward from above the crowds and traffic, as if mimicking Alexei's social 'fall'. Then, a sequence of quick-cut point-of-view shots zero in on the faces of random passers-by, implying Alexei's lack of orientation in the modern metropolis. The following scenes in his father's apartment contrast sharply with the chaotic cosmopolitan life outside. Here time has frozen. The camera lingers on the Brezhnev-era interior and on the numerous black-and-white photographs that adorn the walls. Seated behind his typewriter, Gushchin Senior works on a document dramatically entitled 'Memoirs of the Last Aircraft Designer'. If the capitalist realities of present-day Moscow disoriented Alexei, his father's antiquated lifeworld is equally alien to him. Yet, against his better judgement, the old man helps Alexei find an intern position in a 'small but solid' air company.

There, intergenerational alienation immediately takes on more conflictual forms. The reckless Alexei constantly clashes with his supervisor Zinchenko, an experienced pilot, who serves as an authoritarian mentor figure to him. Alexei's rebellious nature reveals itself with renewed force when during one of their flights a wealthy business class customer refuses to put out his cigarette, ignoring the repeated requests of the cabin crew. Violating the regulations, Alexei leaves the cockpit and resolutely puts out the passenger's cigarette in his glass of cognac. The ensuing scuffle is filmed by other passengers with their smartphones. The situation escalates later, when, upon the videos going viral on social media, the businessman turns out to be one of the air company's shareholders. Anticipating forced resignation, Alexei visits his father again. Less welcoming now, Gushchin Senior is eager to point out that sometimes 'one has to step back in life' and rebukes this prodigal son for belonging to a generation who 'has torn apart the country', who are incapable of building, and 'can only destroy'. This concern is echoed in many other plotlines, most notably in Zinchenko's vexed relationship with his wayward teenage son Valera, who disrespectfully compares his father's job as a pilot to that of a 'taxi driver'.

Thus, in *The Crew* the social fears inherent in the disaster film genre take the form of an almost obsessive concern with ruptured filial lineages. Insubordinate young men, grown up in a post-Soviet age of loose morals and wild capitalism can no longer bond with their real and symbolic fathers who have been drilled by Soviet discipline. In dramatising these damaged ties, the film advances the notion of 'a cut, a Catastrophe, a separation or sundering, the Fall' that is so typical of the nostalgic outlook (Tannock 1995: 456). It also implicitly imagines a prelapsarian situation, before post-Soviet upheaval struck, when the succession of (male) generations was, supposedly, more harmonious.

Intertwining the theme of a calamitous flight with the generation conflict, *The Crew* relies on subtle references (whether intentional or not) to the myth of Icarus. As noted earlier, Alexei' s discharge from the army is visually presented as a 'fall' into Moscow's modern realities. Later, following the incident with the drunk shareholder, Zinchenko unexpectedly attempts to exonerate Alexei in the company director's eyes by claiming that 'that rookie' is a stellar pilot with 'wings instead of arms'. Being a retired aircraft designer, Alexei's father, in turn, incarnates the builder and inventor Daedalus when he rejects the reckless behaviour of his son, telling him, in words reminiscent of the Icarus myth, that he has 'his head in the clouds'. In *The Crew*, this classic trope becomes infused with a specific post-Soviet significance. Alexei's hubris consists not only in his challenging the physical laws of nature – Zinchenko regularly reprimands him for his risky manoeuvres – but also in his constant violation of the social norms dictated by (surrogate) fathers. The film thus echoes the subtext of the 'patrilinear conflict' (Goscilo and Hashamova 2010: 7) present in many versions of the Icarus story, in which the boy ignores (or rebels against) the restraining admonitions of Daedalus. Building on the Icarus tradition, Lebedev represents the discord between father-inventors and their courageous but disobedient sons as the crucial problem that impedes adequate responses to the inequities of the new Russia. The Soviet fathers' conformism to old and new figures of authority deprives them of the ability to take risks and assert themselves in an unjust world of oligarchy and corruption, while the unchecked rashness of post-Soviet sons repeatedly results in violence and destruction. The troubles in the air dramatically foreground the pressing need to re-align the generations' divergent codes of conduct.

THE RECONCILIATORY FORCES OF DESTRUCTION

An hour into the film, the protagonists, underway to their planned destination, are asked by the Moscow flight operators to redirect their aeroplane to the (fictional) Pacific island of Kanwoo, in order to evacuate the survivors of a volcanic eruption. The crew includes an experienced female pilot, Alexandra Kuz'mina (Agnė Grudytė), who happens to be Alexei's love interest, albeit no longer reciprocated. Incidentally, Zinchenko's son Valera is also on board. After their arrival on the island, the initial eruption is followed by an earthquake that destroys most of the airport's buildings. Even more threatening are the unstoppable torrents of lava that begin to creep towards the landing strips. Zinchenko and Alexandra manage to evacuate some of the international scientists and miners that make up Kanwoo's population, leaving the island in a heavy cargo plane. Meanwhile Alexei, Valera and one of the flight attendants proceed to rescue another group of people whose mini-buses have been trapped by streams of lava on a mountain road. In a thrilling scene, the three young men evacuate these residents in a passenger airliner seconds before Kanwoo is wiped out by the forces of natural destruction. Both planes are damaged, and the nearest landing runway is hundreds of miles away in Petropavlovsk. Leaking fuel, Zinchenko's cargo plane is about to fall into the ocean. Radio contact is established with the traffic controllers in Moscow and with Alexei's cockpit. Dramatic moments follow when Zinchenko learns that his son Valera has escaped the island. The latter, initially upset about his father abandoning him on Kanwoo, sets his grudge aside when he learns about the impending crash.

The desperate situation further accentuates the different orientations of Soviet fathers and post-Soviet sons. The middle-aged personnel in the Moscow control tower are, at least at first, characteristically inert, their main concern being 'what the protocols are in situations like this'. The admittedly 'foolish' rescue plan, which in the end saves almost everyone, comes from the post-Soviet misfits Valera and Alexei, who propose to hoist Zinchenko's passengers in a cargo net to Alexei's plane via a cable. Ignoring the flight company's veto on the plan, the protagonists manage to transfer passengers from one plane to the other with minimal loss of lives. Finally, after losing a wing during a protracted skid across the landing strip of Petropavlovsk, the aircraft comes to a halt, its passengers unharmed.

The acrobatic rescue scenes in mid-air may appear less absurd when seen in light of *The Crew*'s fixation with patrilinear ruptures. The cable between the two planes (an umbilical cord of sorts) symbolically spans the rift between overly disciplined fathers, who cannot think of solutions outside 'the protocols', and hubristic sons who impulsively seize on any 'foolish idea'. The film leaves no doubt that the rescue mission devised by the sons would fail if it was not backed up by the fathers' expertise. Crucial during the tribulations in the air is the intervention of Gushchin Senior, who has been summoned to assists the flight operators in Moscow with his technical knowledge. When Alexei fails to open the aircraft's main door to grab the cable coming from Zinchenko's cargo plane, the old Gushchin interferes via radio, putting his invaluable experience at the disposal of the rescue operation. No longer holding on to anachronistic Soviet convictions, Guschin Senior suddenly sees value in the 'foolish' reasoning and quixotic behaviour of the generation he had condemned earlier. He instructs his son to lift the floor of the passenger cabin in order to gain access to the aircraft's exterior and attach the cable coming from Zinchenko's plane. When, in a striking reversal of roles, Alexei objects that this procedure would be 'against protocol', his father confidently replies that he had written those protocols himself decades before for a standard situation, sarcastically adding: 'But this is not a standard situation, is it?' Seeking rapprochement with his post-Soviet offspring, while reclaiming his authority and social value, Gushchin Senior performs the role of what Alexander Sekatskii, in reference to a prevalent motif in late- and post-Soviet cinema, calls a 'prodigal father' (2005), just as Alexei, twice 'returning' to his father's apartment, was a 'prodigal son'. In the film's non-partisan plea for an intergenerational 'reconciliation with the Soviet' (Dubin 2010), these are two sides to the same coin.

In Lebedev's version of the final stage of the disaster film (Roddick 1980: 258), Valera has developed renewed respect for Zinchenko Senior ('pap, you're really cool!'), and Alexei visits *his* father again and is now lovingly received. Despite their heroic feats, the scandalous incident with the shareholder is not forgotten, and the company's director is pressed to discharge both Alexei and Zinchenko. They find employment with Aeroflot, the country's 'best airline company'.[7] Alexandra, who has rediscovered her affection for Alexei, joins them and in the film's final scene the three pilots are shown in a well-lit, modern hangar, climbing ropes as part of their physical training. Under Aeroflot's welcoming wings, all conflicts have been dissolved, and the protagonists – regardless of age, experience and gender – start their careers anew as perfect equals.

In *The Crew*'s predecessor from 1979, the natural disaster and the evacuation of men, women and children from an imaginary locale similarly set in motion a process of social reparation. To that extent, the 'original' film's protracted build-up to the calamitous situation was designed for an in-depth exploration of the individual characters' tribulations. Zooming in on three male pilots, the pre-disaster scenes displayed their coming to terms with different set-backs in their private lives. The chief pilot has health issues and clashes with his obstinate daughter who refuses to marry the man who has impregnated her. Another protagonist fails to sustain romantic relationships and breaks the heart of the stewardess Tamara, who later happens to be on board of the disastrous flight. The third pilot loses custody over his young son after particularly contentious divorce proceedings with his unreasonable wife. Here, too, in the wake of the disaster, characters recalibrate their attitudes and repair (some of) these disturbed relations. With an eye to our current argument, it is important to note that this gamut of social ills (the portrayal of which also bore marked misogynistic overtones) has been almost entirely reduced to father-son trouble in Lebedev's version of the story. In the new film, even the relatively progressive plotline of the female pilot Alexandra Kuz'mina, who struggles with sexist prejudice in this male-dominated environment, is ultimately overshadowed by the all-encompassing motif of patrilinear conflict and reunion.

Apart from its pertinence to the plot, this central motif is also performed through *The Crew*'s casting choices. Most evocative in this respect is the early scene that mimics a similar moment in Mitta's film, by depicting Alexei's training in a flight simulator. Testing the young man's capacities, his supervisor Zinchenko lowers the 'visibility' and raises the 'turbulence' to unmanageable levels. Alexei's virtual flight is doomed, and the simulator shakes and jolts in all directions. Next to the machine sits an elderly watchman, played by Mitta, who looks up in surprise, staring at the simulator's wild movements. It is hard not to see in this character yet another father figure, metaphorically appraising the behaviour of an audacious son (director Lebedev, in this case). With this nod to Mitta, Lebedev's production appears to highlight its own status as a hubristic ('foolish') post-Soviet alternative to an authoritative Soviet classic, anticipating the criticism of a generation of viewers who cherish memories of the original film. As one commentator wrote: 'It is perfectly clear that [Lebedev's] alter ego in the film is [. . .] that very intern [Alexei] arrogantly embarking on a task that is beyond his power' (Dolin 2016). Yet, here, too, the emphasised differences between the generations paradoxically function to highlight the hoped-for reconciliation that the film also expresses. As the production history shows, Mitta was engaged in Lebedev's project as a consultant, which is respectfully acknowledged in the closing credits: 'We would like to express our gratitude to Aleksandr Mitta for the lessons in creativity and for inspiration'. Mitta's puzzled glance at the jolting simulator invites a view of Lebedev's film as the product of a thrill-seeking generation. At the same time, the older director's cameo appearance marks Lebedev's intention to create an homage to his predecessor and teacher. Another noticeable (re)appearance in the new story is that of flight controller Tamara Igorevna, played by Alexandra Iakovleva, who performed in the role of stewardess Tamara in Mitta's film. Subtle hints suggest that Tamara, who is among the staff in the Moscow air control tower, can handle this air calamity so expertly because of her first-hand experiences with a similar situation almost four decades earlier. Such allusions open up an interpretation of *The Crew* as not only a remake or homage, but also a sequel to Mitta's classic.

CONCLUSION

Our discussion of Nikolai Lebedev's *The Crew* showed that the director, while certainly capitalising on the success of Mitta's production, emphatically conceives of his film not as a replacement or an 'update', but as a tribute (occasionally even a sequel) to the Soviet classic. On the level of plot as well as casting, the new film thus sets out to create a cultural space for the Soviet legacy within an ostensibly uninterrupted Soviet/Russian (cinematic) history. Turning the relationship between the 'old' and the 'new' into its central concern, *The Crew* mobilises the remake for a practice that we have described as nostalgic. Rather than being an unreflective fixation on the days of yesteryear, nostalgia, in the definition used here, appears as a process of signification premised on a perceived temporal break and involved in a recalibration of the relationship between past and present. Freed from its negative connotations, nostalgia can, in the cogent words of Ritivoi, be understood to 'signal the breach and inaugurate a search for the remedy' (2002: 39). Indeed, before exploring the possibility of repaired social, cultural and cinematic continuity, *The Crew* spectacularly stakes out the post-Soviet ruptures that threaten it, and the scenes of (natural) disaster contribute to this exuberant dramatization of 'damage'. Severed or disturbed relationships, broken (real and symbolic) infrastructures, demolished material markers of civilisation – all these elements add to a pervasive sense that the country, as Gushchin Senior phrases it, 'has been torn apart'. Yet, it is precisely the multifaceted portrayal of post-Soviet loss and destruction that provides a necessary background to the quest for repaired homeliness and familiarity.

The Crew's obsession with restored cohesion and continuity, as well as its self-conscious play with its own intertextuality, point to a curious paradox in the Russian film industry's current investment in remake production. Remaking Soviet cinema tangibly gains in significance at the very moment when the Soviet epoch can no longer be 'remade' – that is, when the classics of Soviet cinema, together with the values, worldviews and social norms they epitomised, are perceived as irretrievably belonging to the past. If the nostalgic person imaginatively returns, as Pourtova asserts, 'to a moment *before* the loss in order to recover what can be saved and mourn what cannot be' (2013: 42, italics original), *The Crew* overtly cultivates the evaluative potential of such an undertaking. Thematising loss and rupture, while probing the possibilities of recuperation and reconciliation, the film exhibits a nostalgic practice that may latently exist in many other post-Soviet remakes.

NOTES

1. The examples include, to name but the few most notorious ones: *Sky. Plane. Girl.* (*Nebo. Samolet. Devushka.* 2002) based on the 1968 existential realist drama *Once More About Love* (*Eshche raz pro liubov*); *Another Year* (*Eshche odin god*, 2014) based on the 1970 melodrama *Don't Leave Your Lovers* (*S liubimymi ne rasstavaites'*); the 2007 remake/sequel *The Irony of Fate 2* (*Ironiia sud'by*) of the romantic comedy by the same name from 1976; and, finally, the updated version of another comedy, *Office Romance* (*Sluzhebnyi roman*, 1977), now titled *Office Romance. Our Time* (*Sluzhebnyi roman. Nashe vremia*, 2011).
2. For example, after the release, in 2014, of Maksim Voronkov's remake of the famous Soviet comedy *Kidnapping, Caucasian Style* (*Kavkazskaia plennitsa*, 1967) one of the participants of the online forum Kinopoisk exclaimed: 'Why has this film been made? Why are we, the viewing public, treated as morons? Why do such projects receive financial support? And when will the 're-makers' finally run out of money?' 'Kinopoisk, 'Kavkazskaia plennitsa!', available at: https://www.kinopoisk.ru/film/689077/ (last accessed 1 August 2019). All translations from Russian are ours.
3. Aleinikov Brothers' *Tractor Drivers* invoked at the start of this article ironically reflects on this tendency by simultaneously establishing intertextual relations with three films produced in 1939, 1967 and 1979, exemplary of rather different sociohistorical conditions.

4. Produced by Studio TriTe, owned by Nikita Mikhalkov, with a budget of 10.3 million dollars, the film was shot in the 3D IMAX format on elaborately designed sets and expensive real-life locations. The films also received financial support from the Central Partnership subsidiary of Gazprom Media Holding, TV Channel Russia, the Russian government's funding body for the screen production industry Fond Kino and the distributor Paramount Pictures (Solntseva 2016).
5. It is obvious that Mitta's project was inspired by George Seaton's disaster-drama *Airport* made in 1970 and based on Arthur Hailey's 1968 novel of the same name. Soviet audiences, however, had no access to Seaton's film, and to date Mitta's *The Crew* is treated in Russia as the only true original. More remarkable still is the fact that, at the time, the translated version of Hailey's novel enjoyed great popularity amongst the Soviet readership, but we could not find evidence suggesting that contemporary cinephiles recognized the novel as the source of their favourite film.
6. In relation to the Russian context, scholar Marina Zigidullina even sees the re-affirmative ability as the most important and necessary function of remakes. She conceives of remakes as 'sign[s] of the utmost prestige (or popularity . . .) of the original text, its maximal diffusion, and inscription in the cultural horizon of the nation' (Zigidullina 2004).
7. As the critic Nataliia Grigor'eva (2016) observed, this is one of multiple instances of product placement in *The Crew*.

REFERENCES

Atia, Nadia and Jeremy Davies (2010), 'Nostalgia and the Shapes of History', *Memory Studies*, 3: 3, 181–86.
Boele, Otto, Boris Noordenbos and Ksenia Robbe (2019), 'Introduction', in Otto Boele, Boris Noordenbos and Ksenia Robbe (eds), *Post-Soviet Nostalgia: Confronting the Empire's Legacies*, London: Routledge, pp. 1–17.
Boym, Svetlana (2001), *The Future of Nostalgia*, New York: Basic.
Davis, Fred (1979), *Yearning for Yesterday: A Sociology of Nostalgia*, New York: The Free Press.
Corbett, Justin (2016), '*Flight Crew* (The 2016 Russian Resurrection Film Festival)', available at: https://filmink.com.au/reviews/flight-crew-the-2016-russian-resurrection-film-festival/ (last accessed 23 November 2016).
Dolin, Anton (2016), '"Ekipazh" Nikolaia Lebedeva: ogon' v illuminatore', available at: https://daily.afisha.ru/cinema/1216-ekipazh-nikolaya-lebedeva-ogon-v-illyminatore/ (last accessed 23 November 2016).
Dubin, Boris (2007), *Zhit' v Rossii na rubezhe stoletii: sotsiologicheskie ocherki I razrabotki*, Moscow: Progress-Traditsiia.
Dubin, Boris (2010), *Klassika, posle I riadom. Sotsiologicheskie ocherki o literature I kul'ture*, Moskva: Novoe literaturnoe obozrenie.
Grigor'eva, Nataliia (2016), 'Krov'iu, potom, samoletom: V rossiiskii prokat vykhodit novyi "Ekipazh"', available at: http://www.ng.ru/cinematograph/2016-04-21/8_airplane.html (last accessed 9 September 2019).
Gorelov, Denis (2016), 'Pochemu fil'm "Ekipazh" tak I ne vzletel', available at: http://www.gq.ru/blogs/revizor/148825_pochemu_film_ekipazh_tak_i_ne_vzletel.php (accessed 25 October 2016).
Goscilo, Helena and Yana Hashamova (2010), *Cinepaternity: Fathers and Sons in Soviet and Post-Soviet Film*, Bloomington: Indiana University Press.

Ivanov, Boris (2016), 'Ekipazh: Spasenie uletaiushchikh', available at: https://www.film.ru/articles/spasenie-uletayuschih (last accessed 23 November 2016).
Khapaeva, Dina (2007), *Goticheskoe obshchestvo: morfologiia koshmara*, Moscow: Novoe literaturnoe obozrenie.
Kichin, Valery (2016), 'Can a Low-Budget Russian Disaster Film Look Like a Hollywood Blockbuster?', available at: http://rbth.com/arts/movies/2016/07/22/can-a-low-budget-russian-disaster-film-look-like-a-hollywood-blockbuster_614009 (last accessed 20 November 2016).
Kuzmina, Lidia (2016), 'V bezvozdushnom prostranstve. "Ekipazh", rezhisser Nikolai Lebedev', available at: http://kinoart.ru/archive/2016/04/v-bezvozdushnom-prostranstve-ekipazh-rezhisser-nikolaj-lebedev (last accessed 20 November 2016).
Lankauskas, Gediminas (2014), 'Missing Socialism Again? The Malaise of Nostalgia in Post-Soviet Lithuania', in Olivia Angé and David Berliner (eds), *Anthropology and Nostalgia*, New York: Berghahn, pp. 35–59.
Lebedev, Nikolai, dir. (2016), *Ekipazh*, Three T Productions, Russia-1. DVD.
Leitch Thomas (1990), 'Twice-Told Tales: Disavowal and the Rhetoric of the Remake', *Literature/Film Quarterly*, 18: 3, 138–49.
Maliukova, Larisa (2016), '"Ekipazh" vyshel v prokat: "nu ne za pravdoi zhizni ty zhe siuda prishel?"' *Novaia Gazeta*, 43, 22 April.
Mitta, Alexander, dir. (1979), *Ekipazh*, Mosfilm. DVD.
Nadkarni, Maja, and Olga Shevchenko (2004), 'The Politics of Nostalgia: A Case for Comparative Analysis of Post-Socialist Practices', *Ab Imperio*, 2, 487–519.
Novikova, Anna (2010), 'Myths about Soviet Values and Contemporary Russian Television', *Russian Journal of Communication*, 3: 3–4, 280–94.
Oushakine, Serguei (2007), '"We're Nostalgic But We're Not Crazy": Retrofitting the Past in Russia', *The Russian Review*, 66: 3, 451–82.
Pickering, Michael and Emily Keightley (2006), 'The Modalities of Nostalgia', *Current Sociology*, 54: 6, 919–41.
Plakhov, Andrei (2016), '"Ekipazh" poshel na vtoroi krug. Fil'm Alexandra Mitty dozhdalsia remeika', available at: http://kommersant.ru/doc/2969195 (last accessed 20 November 2016).
Ritivoi, Andreea (2002), *Yesterday's Self: Nostalgia and the Immigrant Identity*, Lanham: Rowman & Littlefield.
Roddick, Nick (1980), 'Only the Stars Survive: Disaster Movies in the Seventies', in D. Brady (ed.), *Performance and Politics in Popular Drama: Aspects of Popular Entertainment in Theatre, Film, and Television 1800–1976*, Cambridge: Cambridge University Press, pp. 243–69.
Sekatskii Alexandr (2005), 'Otsepriimstvo', *I*, 21–22, 199–205.
Smith, Laurajane and Gary Campbell (2017), 'Nostalgia for the Future: Memory, Nostalgia and the Politics of Class', *International Journal of Heritage Studies*, 23: 7, 612–27.
Solntseva, Alena (2016), 'Smena ekipazha', available at: https://www.gazeta.ru/comments/column/solnceva/8179895.shtml (last accessed 29 October 2016).
Stepanov, Vasilii (2016), '"Ekipazh": A teper'—krutoe pike', available at: http://seance.ru/blog/reviews/equipage/ (last accessed 20 November 2016).
Stishova, Elena (2016), 'Razbor poleta. Nebo, baba I sud'ba. "Ekipazh", rezhisser Nikolai Lebedev', available at: http://kinoart.ru/blogs/razbor-poleta-nebo-baba-i-sudba (last accessed 24 October 2016).
Tannock, Stuart (1995), 'Nostalgia Critique', *Cultural Studies*, 3: 9, 453–64.
Todd, Laura (2016), 'Nikolai Lebedev: *Flight Crew* (*Ekipazh*, 2016)', available at: http://www.kinokultura.com/2016/54r-ekipazh.shtml (last accessed 20 August 2019).

Tsyrkun, Nina (2016), 'Liker "shassi". "Ekipazh", rezhisser Nikolai Lebedev', available at: http://kinoart.ru/blogs/liker-shassi-ekipazh-rezhisser-nikolaj-lebedev (last accessed 23 November 2016).

Tyrkin, Stas (2016), 'Kryl'ia vmesto ruk, ili kak Timchenko stal Zinchenko', available at: http://www.kp.ru/daily/26517/3533781/ (last accessed 25 October 2016).

Usmanova, Al'mira (2004), 'Povtorenie I razlichie, ili "Eshche raz pro liubov"' v sovetskom I postsovetskom kinematografe', *Novoe literaturnoe obozrenie*, 5: 69, available at: https://magazines.gorky.media/nlo/2004/5/povtorenie-i-razlichie-ili-eshhe-raz-pro-lyubov-v-sovetskom-i-postsovetskom-kinematografe.html (last accessed 9 August 2019).

Zagidullina, Marina (2004), 'Remeiki, ili ekspansiia klassiki', *Novoe literaturnoe obozrenie*, 5: 69, available at: https://magazines.gorky.media/nlo/2004/5/remejki-ili-ekspansiya-klassiki.html (last accessed 9 August 2019).

CHAPTER II

Mistaken Identities: Millennial Remakes, Post-Socialist Transformation and Hungarian Popular Cinema

Balázs Varga

Distance makes beauty, so the saying goes. Even if it is not a spatial distance, but a temporal or cultural distance (or a mixture of these), remake studies certainly often focus on broad questions of proximity (Leitch 1990; Forrest and Koos 2002; Verevis 2006; Cuelenaere, Joye and Willems 2016; Smith and Verevis 2017). Cultural proximity – that is, the shaping of the codes, patterns and structures of an adapted product in order to appeal to local audiences – is a characteristic feature of adaptations and remakes (Straubhaar 1991). Recent studies of transnational film remakes have highlighted the performative power of 'manufacturing proximity' and discussed remaking as a shaping process of culture and national identity, inevitably raising the question of localisation (Cuelenaere, Willems and Joye 2016). But what about intra-national remakes and their specificities in the remaking practices? In a recent article about remaking *Winnetou* for the German audience, Loock claimed that intra-national and transnational remakes are distinguished by the presence or absence of local context. While intra-national remakes have a past in their national cultural context, transnational remakes usually have to adapt their contents to the given national background. Furthermore, Loock stated that '*diachronic remaking* (relating to the production of remakes over a decade-spanning period of time) seems less common that *synchronic remaking* (relating to the production of remakes that takes place at roughly the same point in time as the production of the predecessors)' (Loock 2019: 326–27).

In the following analysis, I will examine a case of intra-national remakes: a series of Hungarian millennial remakes of classic interwar comedies (four films were made one after the other, between 1999 and 2006). The production of these remakes is an interesting example of the diachronic remake, as there is generally a time span of sixty to seventy years between the source film and the remake. The sample consists of four film tandems: *Hippolyt* (original version in 1931, remake 1999), *Car of Dreams* (original 1934, remake 2000), *One Skirt and a Pair of Trousers* (original 1943, remake 2005) and *One Fool Makes a Hundred* (original 1942, remake 2006). The source films are prominent examples of Hungarian entertainment cinema of the 1930s and 1940s. Although the remakes were domestic box office hits, their overall reception was quite negative. This critical antipathy might be one of the reasons behind the lack of scholarly discussion of these Hungarian remakes.

As this chapter will be the first detailed study on the topic, in addition to focusing on the textual and industrial practices of intra-national remakes, it is necessary to provide some information regarding the cultural context and aspects of the series of Hungarian millennial remakes. Thus, the aim of this study is twofold: firstly, to shed light on aspects of intra-national remakes, such as canonisation, the function of genre patterns and acting performances. Secondly, in the specific context of post-socialist transformation, my aim is to show the unique potential of remaking in the shaping and discussion of the traditions of local popular cinema by focusing on the case of Hungary.

Remaking was and is not a typical feature of post-war and contemporary Hungarian film culture – contrary to the pre-war period, when the powerful local film culture (with a dynamic transnational dimension) was firmly built on different kinds of repetition practices (Balogh and Király 2000; Cunningham 2004; Gergely 2017). As in the case of smaller European film industries, the emergence of sound film production in Hungary was closely related to the production of films with multi-language versions (Frey 2018). The trend of producing multi-version films survived in the Hungarian film industry until the late 1930s. Since then, especially during the decades of socialism, remaking has not at all constituted a typical feature of Hungarian cinema. It might be called paradigmatic that, alongside the wave of nostalgia which swept over the region in the 1990s (Pehe 2015), sequels, re-adaptations and remakes of previously successful films have proliferated in Eastern European film cultures (Varga 2018). The series of millennial remakes thus represents a novel phenomenon in the post-socialist Hungarian film ecosystem, forging an interesting link between pre-1945 and post-1989 film culture. In what follows I will discuss the novelty of Hungarian millennial remakes and the diachronic dynamics of intra-national remaking in the framework of the concepts of risk management and cultural memory.

REMAKES, RISK MANAGEMENT AND THE TRANSFORMATION OF HUNGARIAN POPULAR CINEMA

Hungarian millennial remakes can be linked to discourses on risk in two ways: first, as attempts to repair the film-ecological imbalance (Hjort 2015) during the hectic decade of post-socialist transformation and, second, as examples of economic pragmatism (in other words, minimising risk) which Constantine Verevis (2006) describes as the basic function of remake practices.

The end of socialism drastically changed the cultural ecosystem of Eastern Europe. During the decades of state-socialism, political control of the film studio system and financial protection constituted the structural framework. With the end of state-funded film culture, filmmakers were not only unshackled from censorship, but they also had to leave the haven of stable state funding. Newly gained freedom obviously brought new challenges and risks for filmmaking. Following Hjort's argument that 'one way of understanding what counts as being in a state of transition is to consider the extent to which the relevant risk environment has changed' (2015: 49), post-socialist transition unquestionably changed the whole 'risk environment' of Eastern European cinemas and made the region a unique example of small cinemas in transition. According to Mette Hjort's and Duncan Petrie's (2007) parameters (population, territory, GNP and political independence), many of the Eastern European national cinemas might be identified as 'small cinemas'. In that respect, Hjort (2015) listed several 'systemic risks' that might threaten small national cinemas such as the risk of a film-ecological imbalance. Here, Hjort refers to the asymmetry of mainstream (typically non-state-funded) and arthouse (usually heavily funded) films which was illustrative of the post-socialist transformation of Eastern European cinemas as the sustainability of popular mainstream films was a vital aspect of the industry and funding systems' transformation. After all, the greatest beneficiaries of the transition were arthouse and *auteur* films. Popular films not only had to contend with the flood of Hollywood blockbusters on the domestic markets, but also had to struggle for funding. The emergence of commercial televisions as potential (co)producers of comedies and mainstream genre films was an important step in redressing the film-ecological imbalance.

After the passing of the media law in 1997, two nation-wide commercial broadcasters appeared on the market: TV2 (owned by ProsiebenSat1) and RTL Klub (owned by the RTL Group). These channels soon took an extremely strong position in terms of market share and cultural impact, rapidly and completely transforming the mediascape of Hungarian popular culture (Kaposi 2007). Regarding film, they provided new sources and platforms for financing and broadcasting Hungarian films. As the media law required them to support Hungarian film production, this requirement was met by financing projects that suited their entertainment profile. The first example of Hungarian millennial remakes was one of the early flagship projects of RTL Klub. The producer and director of the first remake, *Hippolyt*, was Barna Kabay, an acknowledged Hungarian arthouse filmmaker.

The idea of producing a remake of an emblematic Hungarian classic film comedy by said director was illustrative of the increasing attention paid to the tradition of local popular film culture. At the same time, it was perceived by most of the critics as a foreign practice, alien to the local film culture. Nevertheless, after the success of the first remake, another interwar classic comedy was remade the next year, with two subsequent remakes in the following years. All of them were made under the auspices of commercial television companies, produced and directed by the same tandem of filmmakers, Barna Kabay and Bence Gyöngyössy. The films served the public image of commercial television stations as safeguards of domestic film culture, since they included the most popular Hungarian comedians from film, theatre and cabaret, together with emblematic personalities of commercial television's shows. The series of Hungarian millennial remakes not only show the pre-eminent role and function of remakes within the risk environment of small cinema (risk-minimising and the film-ecological imbalance), but could also be viewed as a powerful gesture of revitalising the cultural memory of local popular narratives.

REMAKES, NATIONAL IDENTITY, CULTURAL MEMORY AND CANONISATION

Recently, Loock (2019: 327) discussed the way in which remakes bring back 'popular narratives from a national storytelling repertoire' and function as a 'mode of timekeeping'. However, as she elaborates her arguments on the dynamic of cultural memory, generationing and remakes, she claims that new versions of culturally stored experiences not only bring back popular narratives, but also add new interpretations to their reception history and provide fresh perspectives for their audience. With the appearance of new generations and the extension of the audience, the variety and dynamic of the interpretative communities of the film evolves. Furthermore, Loock shows how shared knowledge and experiences might help to stabilise 'imagined communities' (Anderson 1983) and demonstrates the potential of remakes for the (re)negotiation of shared and established imaginations concerning the definition of a nation.

The claim that encounters with emblematic stories preserve familiar cultural manifestations and products can be linked to the oft-discussed role of remakes in the formation of a canon. Verevis, for example, views film remakes as 'a function of cinematic and discursive fields that is maintained by historically specific practices, such as copyright law and authorship, canon formation and media literacy, film criticism and re-viewing' (2006: VII). Yet, there are still many variations of remaking and canonisation. Remakes can be based on (and canonise) already canonized texts, and it may also happen that source films become established and acknowledged as 'classic' and 'original' pieces after they have been remade (Quaresima 2002, Loock 2012). Introducing the remake into the process of cultural memory and canon formation may involve changes in the memory of the original (Kelleter and Loock 2017: 127).

Questions of cultural memory, canonisation and the legacy of former popular narratives of shared experiences are no less complicated in the case of Hungarian millennial remakes. We have seen that all four source films are emblematic works of 1930s' and early 1940s' Hungarian popular cinema. However, the temporal order in which the remakes were produced clearly represented the differences in the canonical influence and power of the source films.

The first film to be remade in 1999, *Hyppolit the Butler*, is an iconic work of early Hungarian sound film culture. Székely's comedy from 1931 was such an instant hit that it is regarded as having established 'the tone of Hungarian bourgeoise [sic] comedy that came to define Hungarian filmmaking throughout the 1930s' (Balogh 2019). The source film of the second remake, *Car of Dreams* (2000), was a romantic comedy from 1934, made by another star director of the era, Béla Gaál. As a Hungarian version of Frank Capra's myth of the 'common man', its story about the love of a bank director and a low-ranking bank clerk became the basic model of comedies of the early 1930s – the film even received an English remake by the same title (directed by Graham Cutts and Austin Melford in 1935). Gaál's film was the greatest box office hit and became a symbol of the period. *Hyppolit* and *Car of Dreams* are canonical films of 1930s Hungarian commercial filmmaking; they are remembered as exemplary works, emerging from the commercial film production of the period. Their remakes bear the characteristics of homage, in the sense in which Leitch (1990) uses the term in his taxonomy of remakes. The source films of the third and fourth remake (made in 2005 and 2006, a couple of years after the first two remakes) are also memorable pieces of interwar Hungarian popular cinema, but represent a different era (the early 1940s), a different genre (farcical comedy, as opposed to romantic comedy) and, last but not least, a different position in the local cultural memory. *One Skirt and a Pair of Trousers* and *One Fool Makes a Hundred* are memorable comedies due to their star comedian's popularity, but they are not canonical films.

Another important feature of interwar Hungarian film culture, which provides the key to understanding the process of cultural memory of these films, is the close embedment of the domestic popular film culture in the local entertainment culture of the period, especially cabaret. Discussing the cultural memory of Hungarian entertainment film culture of the era, Manchin (2013) argued that these films were forgotten for political reasons in the decades of socialism and rediscovered by the public with resounding success only after 1989. Manchin rightly describes as a cause the ideological and political resentment towards bourgeois popular culture during socialism, but even then these films were not completely invisible: they saw various adaptations and re-runs at that time. After 1945, during the decades of socialism, the tradition of Hungarian interwar entertainment film culture was rejected. From an ideological and political point of view, Hungarian films of the earlier period were treated as representatives of bourgeois, commercial culture, detached from social reality. However, these films cannot be said to have completely disappeared from cultural memory. For instance, in 1956 the weekly *Hungarian Film Newsreel* commemorated the twenty-fifth anniversary of the production of *Hyppolit, the Butler*. In 1957, a year after the repression of the Hungarian revolution, the newly established Hungarian Film Archives opened their cinematheque with the re-release of *Car of Dreams*, attracting a large audience. *Hyppolit* was staged in theatres many times during the socialist decades. Furthermore, interwar classics were often broadcast on television, especially in the 1980s. Following the political changes, the revival of interwar Hungarian entertainment culture in the 1990s received a new impetus. In short, the memory of these films and their star-comedians was vivid and present during the decades of socialism. Moreover, the influential series of stage adaptations of these stories maintained and reinforced the interconnectedness, strong dynamics and internal relationships between Hungarian popular theatre and cinema. Traditions and trends of Hungarian popular cinema may have been weakened and transformed during socialism, but the legacy of interwar popular culture and cinema found a way to make itself manifest. The series of remakes, which began in 1999, succeeded in activating both the popularity and cultural memory of these films and comedians, as well as in building on the legacy of cabaret and popular theatre (Varga 2016b).

ALTERED WORLDS, REPLAYED SITUATIONS

Mistaken identities and disguise, the leading motifs of comedies, are central to all the four film tandems investigated in this chapter. The first two source films, *Hyppolit* and *Car of Dreams*, revolve around the topics of modernisation, generational conflict and upward social mobility. Since these are canonised and well-known films, the millennial Hungarian audience was well-acquainted with the stories. Both films followed local cabaret traditions and focused on witty dialogue, sarcastic catchphrases, comic situations and emblematic acting performances. These were their most important and memorable characteristics, which supposedly made audiences expect that the remakes would repeat and replay these memorable motifs. The remakes had to face the challenges of close adaptation or transformation (see Verevis 2006) – namely, staying as close as possible to the originals and at the same time effecting a fundamental change while transferring the stories to contemporary Hungary. Given temporal distance of seventy years between the source films and the remakes, as well as the fundamental difference of the social and cultural context, maintaining cultural proximity was an essential challenge. In the following, I will argue that both remakes used the strategy of deliberate anachronism to resolve this challenge.

Regarding Verevis' (2006) textual descriptions of remaking techniques, both films (especially *Hippolyt*) kept syntactic elements, such as their accurately reconstructed plot structure, dialogue and character relationships. They also kept fundamental semantic elements from the original films, although at this point incoherency became bothersome, since important semantic elements and motifs were obviously anachronistic in the contemporary milieu. The main difference between the adaptation and transformation strategies of the first two remakes consisted of the way in which they integrated these anachronistic motifs into their overall narrative-semantic system. The first remake, *Hippolyt*, was a closer adaptation, although the most important alteration was a symbolic one: it left the butler out of the title and changed the place of the letters y and i in Hyppolit/Hippolyt's name. Nevertheless, this accurate repetition in *Hippolyt* led to a more coherent reinterpretation of the original film. The second remake, *Car of Dreams*, exhibited more effort in replaying the most emblematic situations from the source film (which are connected to the secondary plot line) and left the central romantic plot loosely motivated and situated in the social realities of 2000s Hungary. This resulted in a culturally and politically more conservative and incoherent interpretation of the story.

The basic conflict of *Hyppolit* focuses on a wealthy transportation entrepreneur and the newly hired butler who tries to set standards of manners that the wealthy nouveaux riches cannot meet. On one hand, the target of ridicule is the entrepreneur's wife, while on the other hand the source of the comedy is the husband's subversive compliance (against the butler's efforts) (Balogh and Király 2000). As the source film sets the story in the interwar period's modernisation context, the remake retells the story against the backdrop of the post-socialist transformation. In this context, the winners of the rapid transition from socialism to market-driven capitalism were the new entrepreneurs who sensed the winds of change and took advantage of the opportunities. Thus, the problem it confronts, of rapid enrichment and social advancement, or more precisely, the nouveaux riches versus the traditional elite, served as an analogy. However, the figure of the title character, the butler, was anachronistic by the 1990s. By keeping the occupation of the butler, the film intensified the contrast between the protagonist's values and the rigid aristocratic rules. Another possible explanation of why the butler's character was still important lies in the fact that the story updated the initial conflict by rearranging the socio-political dynamics. Now the entrepreneur-versus-Hippolyt-conflict represented the clash of pre-war and post-war Hungary: the legacy of the (post) socialist heritage and the pre-1945 (conservative, Christian-national) social order. The entrepreneur and his friends are survivors of the decades of socialism. They observe various careers around them with jovial serenity. In the carnivalesque closure of the film, the fireworks celebrate the failure of Hippolyt and hypocrisy – perhaps the similarity between the character's name and the word is not by chance – and the victory of small communities, self-acceptance and hedonist pleasures. Thus, the remake's focal point is the legacy of socialism and the mockery of efforts to bring back the pre-1945 aristocratic and elitist middle-class culture and worldview.

In contrast to *Hyppolit/Hippolyt*, where the conflicts between the old and new elites and the question of the change of habits provided a kind of connecting point between the source film and the remake, in the case of *Car of Dreams* socio-cultural inconsistencies and anachronisms are much more typical to the plot. The remake preserved the romantic storyline of the rich man in disguise and the ambitious poor girl. Yet, the central motif and symbol of the story, where a girls receives as a gift a luxury dream car and a volunteer driver accompanying it, is almost as anachronistic as the butler was in *Hippolyt*. In the 1930s, the car was a symbol of modernity – a desired new product, accessible only to a few. Seven decades later, it was still be a luxury commodity, but not for a cool roller-skater courier – the young female protagonist works as a courier in the remake. However, she seems quite happy to be transported around the city by the handsome driver in the elegant car. The remake simply leaves out all the story motifs from the source film that make her an active, autonomous, ambitious person. As a result, regarding the representation of gender and the possibilities of social mobility, the new version is more conservative than the source film. The remake presents a flat romantic comedy as its central plotline and puts its focus on the secondary romantic plot, which runs parallel with the love story of the bank director and the assistant. This subplot explores the relationship between the director's secretary and a middle-rank bank manager. While the central plot shows the realm of dreams, the subplot deals with comic everyday romance. As the source film's most comic and memorable situations originate in the subplot, the remake tries to repeat and carefully re-stage these emblematic scenes, situations and dialogues. This is where the importance of acting and re(en)acting lies. The 'texture of performance', as Alex Clayton put it (2011) in his analysis of the differences of acting between *Psycho* and its remake, is a significant issue in the case of Hungarian millennial remakes. *Hyppolit* and *Car of Dreams* provide an especially interesting case, as the star comedian of the era, Gyula Kabos, played in both films, and his role and performance was repeated in a completely different way by Róbert Koltai in *Hippolyt* and Imre Bajor in *Car of Dreams*. Koltai, who regained his popularity as the clumsy protagonist in bittersweet comedies, presents a jolly and hedonistic character (different from Kabos' more ambiguous figure, who always seems to vacillate). Imre Bajor, however, echoes and imitates the gestures and expressions (even the fine details, or the 'texture' as Clayton calls it) of Kabos. Here, in *Car of Dreams*, the main source of humour revolves around how much the actor in the remake can re-enact the performance of the comedian in the source film. What makes the comparison and game of matching even more compelling is the physical and physiognomic difference between the two actors.

Thus, instead of social commentary, the appeal of the second remake is rather a combination of homage and rivalry in which a popular comedian from the 1990s tries to imitate and re-enact memorable acts from the source film. However, this aspect can be more generalised. Not only *Car of Dreams*, but all other Hungarian millennial remakes provide an intriguing combination of respect and exploitation in their attitude towards their source films. While they admire the classic comedies for their popularity, narrative and stylistic excellence, they simultaneously exploit this popularity. Thus, appreciation and appropriation go hand in hand, resulting in the ambivalent strategy of a 'parasite remake' which admires and at the same time exploits its original.

Deliberate anachronism as a stylistic-textual tool is absent from the third and fourth remake, as these films modified and altered the stories of their source films more effectively to fit a contemporary milieu. As mentioned above, these changes could be connected to the usage of different genre patterns, since these source films were not romantic comedies, but less story-centred absurd and farcical comedies with the extremely popular dancer-comedian Kálmán Latabár. Although the personality of the comedians and their acting performances were crucial in every interwar Hungarian comedy, absurd and farcical comedies of the early 1940s were even more centred on the leading comedian and his/her character. It is precisely because of these films' distinctiveness that they were comedian comedies; this made their remakes focus not on their story, but on the absurd situations and uncontrolled comic performances. Comedian comedies – that is, comedies organised around the persona of the comedian – constitutes a special trend or tradition in classical Hollywood films, as Steve Seidman (1981) describes it. Seidman argues that in these films the performing skills of the performer are more important than character construction; instead of realistic acting and a homogenous fictional world and diegesis, the focus moves to 'the maintenance of the comedian's position as an already recognizable performer with a clearly defined extrafictional personality' (Seidman 1981: 3). In comedian comedies, the comedian is often an eccentric individual who is dysfunctional from the perspective of social conventions and the normative parameters of cultural identity (Krutnik 1995). The last two instalments of Hungarian millennial remakes take full advantage of the comedian comedy's potential to ridicule social order and present an eccentric and crazy comedy.

The eccentric acting style dominates these films. Every member of their ensemble cast is characterised by unconventional and unusual acting and behaviour, and (in line with their exaggerated farcical and absurd character) basic dynamics of comedian comedies (the weakening of narrative cohesion, the conflicted relationship with social conventions) result in the incoherent and weird character of these films.

One Skirt and a Pair of Trousers (1943) was a variation on a cross-dressing comedy. The story used (gender) disguise and transgression to celebrate the performative power of acting. Its protagonist, a star-actor, dresses as a woman to seduce an actress who chooses a count over him. The actor then decides to dress like the wealthy Spanish widow whom the count would like to marry. The story's motivation is twice-injured vanity, since the actor wants to take revenge both as a man (for being rejected by the actress) and as an actor (for the count calling him a ham actor). As opposed to the widespread use of the cross-dressing scheme, in which the reason for crossing the gender line usually is due to an existential crisis – eluding some existential danger or reacting to the loss of a job (Lieberfeld and Sanders 1998) – *One Skirt* focuses on the reinforcement of identity and self-esteem. Nevertheless, the problem of social mobility has a significant role in the story. The actress seeks the count's company in the hope of wealth and a career. Over the course of the story, we learn that the count is not a poor, degraded aristocrat who sees the actress as just a bit of fun before entering a marriage motivated by wealth; rather, he turns out to be a crook who is only pretending to be a count.

The remake of *One Skirt and a Pair of Trousers* keeps the initial situation of the plot regarding wounded masculinity, but it places the story in the present-day world of Hungarian show business. The world of commercial television was a familiar milieu for the makers of the film, which renders the ironical references and allusions quite comprehensible. However, the preoccupation with the transgressive and eccentric permeates the whole plot. The remake features several significant changes to the plot of the source film. While in the original the actor and the actress find each other as a romantic couple, the remake ends with love between the actor and the widow. The remake, then, ultimately accomplishes the perfect reparation of injured masculinity and the actor's vanity, with all its consequences. Not only is traditional, heteronormative masculinity reinforced with its attributes of conquest, dominance, charm and irresistibility, but the protagonist also wins the love of the Mexican woman. Moreover, the remake not only uses various orientalist tropes to deliver its story about wounded (post-socialist, Eastern European) masculinity (Imre 2009), but it also offers a slightly elitist critique of its production background – that is, the commercial television entertainment industry – in a paradoxical and divisive way.

The fourth source film from the early 1940s, *One Fool Makes a Hundred*, also follows the patterns of classic comedies with disguise and mistaken identity. Its protagonist, a lazy head waiter, is fired from his workplace. When he discovers his shocking similarity with a famous lion-hunting count, he transforms himself into the count. Because the count seems to be in Africa, his double can safely move into the aristocrat's castle and have fun with his new acquaintances – until the true count returns home unexpectedly. Thus, the remake retains only the initial idea of the source film and turns the plot into a series of absurd gags and nonsense situations. Instead of centring on a count, the remake takes a millionaire and repositions the story to a luxury villa, a troubled business and the love interests of this representative of society's nouveaux riches. Of all the films from the remake series, this is the most obvious representation of post-socialist transformation as a crisis of traditional, heteronormative masculinity. By dint of his occupation, the protagonist represents the state and is fired after just fifteen years of employment. Thus, considering when the film is taking place (the mid-2000s), he had been working at the registry since about 1990 – that is, since the change of the regime. This hyper-saturated thematisation of the nation (Hjort 2000) and the staging of post-socialist transformation concludes with casting the fifteen years of post-socialism into a binary opposition of clumsy losers and idiotic winners, while the film's exploitative humour and farcical approach make every character ridiculous. Nevertheless, the film, again with the help of orientalist patterns, construes a new, post-socialist Hungarian (masculine) identity, which is to be defined around the even more ridiculous Eastern tricksters and losers (Chinese mafioso, Ukrainian mechanics and debt collectors). The story proceeds toward complete absurdity and self-destruction. In the end, post-socialist Hungary's new equilibrium has been restored. Winners and losers can swap places; success and failure are not a question of skill or social background but depend purely on blind chance. Everything and everybody are interchangeable, identical and unique. In the very last shot of the film, a pizza delivery man (a lookalike of one of the protagonists) arrives at the villa, closing the cycle of remakes, duplicates, counter-parts and doubles with a final destabilising joke.

CONCLUSION

This chapter started its analysis with questioning the specificities of intra-national remakes. Accepting Loock's proposition that locally remade stories are different from transnational remakes in that they have a past in the given nation's local cultural context, the analysis focused on the textual strategies and cultural aspects of Hungarian millennial remakes. The specificity of this group of films, which consists of four remakes of interwar classic comedies, is the unusually long time-period of sixty to seventy years between the source films and their remakes. Differences over time raise questions of cultural memory and canonisation. The chapter formulated its argument around the relationship and interconnectedness of the original films' canon position and the textual strategies of their remakes. The more canonical the original, the greater the challenge and attraction in evoking its most memorable scenes. The chapter describes a dual, parallel process of intertwining industrial and textual practices. On the one hand, the success of the first remake led to the production of another remake; therefore, within two years each of the two most important Hungarian interwar comedies was released in a new version. A couple of years later this was followed by another two remakes, this time based on two memorable but not canonised comedies, which are primarily remembered for their star comedian. On the other hand, as the chapter argued, after the first remake's close and accurate adaptation strategies, the next remakes followed their own vision more freely. This tendency partly resulted from the fact that the latter two instalments of the film tandems were originally farcical comedies – a special subgenre which is less organised around narrative coherency and provides more freedom for acting performances. Re-enacted emblematic scenes and dialogues have a significant role in both the source films and the remakes, providing a continuity of the tradition of comedian comedies in Hungarian cinema. This tradition of Hungarian popular entertainment culture held great importance in the period of post-socialist transformation, as a tried-and-tested local cultural practice which might be reused in the revision of the film-ecological balance and in the revitalisation of local popular cinema. Eventually, the millennial remakes of interwar Hungarian classic comedies turned out to be absurd comedies of mistaken, false and uncertain identities, connected to and representing the social-cultural ambiguities and confusion of the post-socialist transformation of Hungary.

NOTE

This paper was supported by the Hungarian National Research, Development and Innovation Office (no. 135235).

REFERENCES

Anderson, Benedict (1983), *Imagined Communities*, London: Verso.
Balogh, Gyöngy and Jenő Király (2000), *'Csak egy nap a világ . . .' A magyar film műfaj- és stílustörténete, 1929–1936*. Budapest: Magyar Filmintézet.
Balogh, Gyöngyi (2019), 'From Hyppolit to Hollywood – István Székely Born 120 Years Ago', National Film Institute Hungary, Film Archive, 2 March, available at: http://filmarchiv.hu/en/news/from-hyppolit-to-hollywood-istvan-szekely-born-120-years-ago-1 > (last accessed 7 February 2020).
Clayton, Alex (2011), 'The Texture of Performance in *Psycho* and its Remake', *Movie: A Journal of Film Criticism*, 3, 73–9.
Cuelenaere, Eduard, Stijn Joye and Gertjan Willems (2016), 'Reframing the Remake: Dutch-Flemish Monolingual Remakes and Their Theoretical and Conceptual Implications', *Frames Cinema Journal* 10: 1, 1–19.

Cuelenaere, Eduard, Gertjan Willems and Stijn Joye (2019), 'Local Flavors and Regional Markers: The Low Countries and Their Commercially Driven and Proximity-Focused Film Remake Practice' *Communications*, 44: 3, 262–81.
Cunningham, John (2004), *Hungarian Cinema: From Coffee House to Multiplex*, London and New York: Wallflower Press.
Forrest, Jennifer and Leonard R. Koos, eds (2002), *Dead Ringers: The Remake in Theory and Practice*, New York: SUNY Press.
Frey, David (2018), *Jews, Nazis and the Cinema of Hungary. The Tragedy of Success, 1929–1944*, London: I. B. Tauris.
Gergely, Gábor (2017), *Hungarian Film, 1929–1947: National Identity, Anti-Semitism and Popular Cinema*, Amsterdam: Amsterdam University Press.
Hjort, Mette (2000), 'Themes of nation', in Hjort and Scott Mackenzie, eds (2000), *Cinema and Nation*, London and New York: Routledge, pp. 103–17.
Hjort, Mette and Duncan Petrie, eds (2007), *The Cinema of Small Nations*, Edinburgh: Edinburgh University Press.
Hjort, Mette (2015), 'The Risk Environment of Small-Nation Filmmaking', in Janelle Blankenship and Tobias Nagl (eds), *European Visions: Small Cinemas in Transition*, Bielefeld: transcript Verlag, pp. 49–64.
Imre, Anikó (2009), *Identity Games: Globalization and the Transformation of Media Cultures in the New Europe*, Cambridge: MIT Press.
Kaposi, Ildikó (2007), 'The Hungarian Media Landscape', in George Terzis (ed.), *European Media Governance*, Bristol: Intellect, pp. 363–74.
Kelleter, Frank and Kathleen Loock (2017), 'Hollywood Remaking as Second-Order Serialization', in Frank Kelleter (ed.), *Media of Serial Narrative*, Columbus: Ohio State University Press, pp. 125–47.
Krutnik, Frank (1995), 'A Spanner in the Works? Genre, Narrative and the Hollywood Comedian', in Kristine Brunovksa Karnick and Henri Jenkins (eds), *Classical Hollywood Comedy*, New York and London: Routledge, pp. 17–38.
Leitch, Thomas (1990), 'Twice-Told Tales: The Rhetoric of the Remake', *Literature/Film Quarterly*, 18: 3, 138–49.
Lieberfeld, Daniel and Judith Sanders (1998), 'Keeping the Characters Straight: Comedy and Identity in "Some Like It Hot"', *Journal of Popular Film and Television*, 26: 3, 128–35.
Loock, Kathleen and Constantine Verevis, eds (2012), *Film Remakes, Adaptations and Fan Productions*, Basingstoke: Palgrave Macmillan.
Loock, Kathleen (2019), 'Remaking Winnetou, Reconfiguring German Fantasies of Indianer and the Wild West in the Post-Reunification Era', *Communications*, 44: 3, 323–41.
Manchin, Anna (2013), 'Cabaret Comedy and the Taboo of "Jewishness" in Twentieth-Century Hungary', *Comedy Studies* 4: 2, 167–78.
Pehe, Veronika (2015), 'The Colours of Socialism: Visual Nostalgia and Retro Aesthetics in Czech Film and Television', *Canadian Slavonic Papers*, 57: 3-4, 239–53.
Quaresima, Leonardo (2002), 'Loving Texts Two at a Time', *Cinémas* 12: 3, 73–84.
Seidman, Steve (1981), *Comedian Comedy: A Tradition in Hollywood Film*, Ann Arbor: UMI Research Press.
Smith, Iain Robert and Constantine Verevis, eds (2017), *Transnational Film Remakes*, Edinburgh: Edinburgh University Press.
Straubhaar, Joseph (1991), 'Beyond Media Imperialism', *Critical Studies in Media Communication*, 8: 1, 39–59.
Varga, Balázs (2013), 'Tradition and Modernization: Contemporary Hungarian Popular Cinema', *Images*, 22, 175–87.

Varga, Balázs (2016a), *Filmrendszerváltások*, Budapest: L'Harmattan.
Varga, Balázs (2016b), 'The Missing Middle: Trends, and Genres in Hungarian Popular Cinema after the Political Changes', in Jana Dudková and Katarína Misiková (eds), *Transformation Processes in Post-Socialist Screen Media*, Bratislava: Academy of Performing Arts, Institute of Theatre and Film Research – The Slovak Academy of Sciences, pp. 97–116.
Varga, Balázs (2018), 'Quest for Coherence and Continuity: Sequelization in Central European Popular Cinemas in the Late 1980s and Early 1990s', *Studies of Eastern European Cinema*, 9: 1, 15–32.
Verevis, Constantine (2006), *Film Remakes*, Edinburgh: Edinburgh University Press.

CHAPTER 12

Refashioning the Remake: *A Bigger Splash*

Constantine Verevis

Luca Guadagnino's *A Bigger Splash* (2015) remakes the 1969 French-Italian production *The Swimming Pool* (*La Piscine*) by Jacques Deray, a film that showcased four of the then biggest names in European cinema: the (once) golden couple Alain Delon and Romy Schneider, supported by Maurice Ronet and Jane Birkin. Described as 'a glossy *Cote d'Azur* thriller' (Vincendeau 2009), the narrative image of *La Piscine* owes much to Delon's high profile, glamorous lifestyle and the distinctly chic Parisian 'look' of the female lead characters, Marianne (Schneider) and Pénélope (Birkin), whose wardrobes were provided by the high-profile French designer André Courrèges. *A Bigger Splash* was instigated by Studiocanal (which owned the rights to *La Piscine*) together with director Luca Guadagnino, who employed the talents of costume designer Giulia Piersanti (formerly of Fendi and Balenciaga) along with (then) Artistic Director at Dior, Raf Simons, to re-fashion the film's costumes, with particular attention given to the clothing worn by the star-character Tilda Swinton (playing Marianne Lane). The presentation of Swinton-Lane as a fashion icon was forged through Swinton's early collaborations with experimental filmmakers Derek Jarman and Sally Potter. More recently, her trans-European (and trans-national) brand has been extended through her work with high-profile directors (such as Wes Anderson, Jim Jarmusch and Bong Joon-Ho), as well as her collaborations with Guadagnino – in particular, *I Am Love* (*Io sono l'amore*, 2009) and *A Bigger Splash*, which along with *Call Me by Your Name* (2017) make up Guadagnino's 'Desire Trilogy', and recently Guadagnino's 2018 remake of Dario Argento's *Suspiria* (1977).

This chapter focuses on *A Bigger Splash*, drawing on some ideas around remaking as commercial *refashioning* and authorial *branding* to argue that Guadagnino's film – an English-language, European co-production – exhibits some features typical of the 'new millennial remake' (Verevis 2017). This phrase is used to describe a distinct media-historic period in which film remakes – most often, digital adaptations of earlier analogue films – are understood by way of four interrelated characteristics: namely, new millennial remakes are *intermedial, transnational, post-authorial* and *characterised by proliferation and simultaneity* (see Verevis 2016). In particular, this essay works with the proposition that *A Bigger Splash* is a European 'style film' – that is, a remake in which fashion and music focus the energy of each character like a single-minded prism. In doing so, the chapter pulls a thread not only from *The Swimming Pool* through to *A Bigger Splash*, but also to David Hockney's pool painting 'A Bigger Splash' (1967) and Jack Hazan's pseudo-documentary *A Bigger Splash* (1974).

THE SWIMMING POOL

Set in the verdant hills overlooking Saint-Tropez, Deray's version of *The Swimming Pool* looks in on the passionate couple Jean-Paul (Delon) and Marianne (Schneider) who have retreated to a friend's grand villa, where they idle away the summer days lounging around the swimming pool. Jean-Paul is a failed writer and reformed alcoholic who now earns a frustrated living in advertising, while his mistress, Marianne, is a one-time journalist who seems happy enough to neglect her professional career for love. Their blissful isolation is disrupted when Harry (Ronet), an old friend of Jean-Paul and Marianne's former lover, arrives with his shy teenage daughter, Pénélope (Birkin). Jean-Paul, depressed and directionless since his failure as a writer, is envious of Harry's success and suspicious of his renewed attraction for Marianne. During a party at the villa (populated by a group of strangers that Harry has brought along from the local village), Harry and Marianne once again enjoy each other's embrace, while Jean-Paul and Pénélope are mutually, if tentatively, attracted. Late the following night, Harry, drunk and angered by Jean-Paul's budding sexual relationship with his teenage daughter, takes a wild swing at his friend and accidentally falls into the swimming pool. Rather than help Harry out of the water, Jean-Paul holds him under until he drowns and then makes it look like a drunken accident. Suspicious of the circumstances, a police detective questions Marianne, who in turn learns the truth from Jean-Paul but admits nothing to the authorities. At the end, Pénélope is returned home, leaving Jean-Paul and Marianne (in the film's final shot) in guilty embrace, to an uncertain future together.

The Swimming Pool has been described as 'a frozen moment of perfect 1960s bossa nova cool' (James 2016: 43) and an 'icily elegant *pas de quatre* [that] involves four of the most outrageously photogenic actors to ever appear on screen' (Melville 2010). An adored celebrity couple, Delon and Schneider had met a decade earlier, during the filming of *Christine* (Pierre Gaspard-Huit, 1958);

although their highly publicised romance lasted only four years, the friendship endured and the film seemed to promise a romantic reunion. Following his breakout role in *Plein soleil* (René Clement, 1960), Delon had become one of France's biggest stars, known internationally for his roles in films by renowned European directors such as Jean-Pierre Melville, Michelangelo Antonioni and Luchino Visconti. Schneider, having left behind both her role as Elizabeth of Bavaria in the popular *Sissi* trilogy of the mid-1950s and her native Austria to live with Delon in Paris, had developed her own international profile, after she had worked with directors such as Orson Welles, Vittorio De Sica and Otto Preminger. An established star of the French new wave, Maurice Ronet had his breakthrough role in *Ascenseur pour l'échafaud* (Louis Malle, 1958) and had previously appeared alongside Delon in *Plein soleil*. Jane Birkin, however, was an emerging star, recently seen as Penny Lane in *Wonderwall* (Joe Massot, 1968), but better known for her then controversial song duet with Serge Gainsbourgh, 'Je t'aime . . . moi non plus' (1969) and their first on-screen performance together in *Slogan* (Pierre Grimblat, 1969). The combined celebrity power – and *The Swimming Pool*'s emphasis on wealth and glamour – underwrote the film's box office potential. More particularly, *The Swimming Pool* invested in the erotic spectacle of Delon's semi-clad body and, through its close attention to costume, in two contrasting versions of womanhood – sophisticated (Marianne) and gauche (Pénélope) – and the respective star personas of Schneider and Birkin (Chaplin 2015).

The Swimming Pool's reputation as a fashion classic was not only established by its star performers, but also through its precise production design (Penz 2014: 116–17) and the striking outfits provided by André Courrèges, one of the emblematic designers of the 1960s. Courrèges had opened his first couture house in Paris where in 1961 he launched the Courrèges brand for the 'active woman' and created his 'Moon Girl' (1964) line, one of the most significant collections of the period. As Laverty writes:

> Taking inspiration from the clean mod silhouettes of Swinging London, particularly those of designer John Bates, Courrèges created a stripped-down intergalactic Utopia that would go on to be referenced for the rest of the decade. [. . .] If Courrèges cannot individually lay claim to inventing the miniskirt – an honour he shares with Bates and fellow British designer Mary Quant – he did bring it to affluent Paris (Laverty 2016: 15).

The sole credited costumier for *The Swimming Pool*, Courrèges developed looks for the film's female leads, Schneider and Birkin, that register as 'nothing less than a capsule retrospective of the designer's entire sixties back catalogue: everything from a dropped-waist flared shift with contrast piping, to a swirly print halter-maxi, to blue cigarette pants and upturned collar shirt, plus a sizeable quota of

Courrèges's speciality, swimwear' (Laverty 2016: 16). The ongoing influence of Courrèges' designs can be found in the work of contemporary designers and the fashion press which recently raided *The Swimming Pool*'s styles to illustrate its shopping pages (Rees-Roberts 2012: 93).

The enduring appeal of *The Swimming Pool* was further secured by a 2010 Dior Perfume communication strategy that invested in the Delon myth, promoting its *Eau savage* line with a 25-second advertising spot that recycled a series of images from the film. A kind of limited remaking, the Dior advertisement consists of six glossy shots of Delon sunbathing at the edge of the pool, re-cut from the film's opening sequence and accompanied by an excerpt of Michel Legrand's jazz saxophone score. As Rees-Roberts (2012) points out, the near perfect colour coordination of the excerpts – the actor's deeply tanned skin in graphic contrast to the translucent blue water – situates the tonal coding of *The Swimming Pool* in the territory of glamour advertising. Adduced to Delon's 'virility' (Vincendeau 2014), the sensorial, narcissistic focus of the shots on the actor's body perfectly fits with the advertising brief for the perfume, the sequence edited together so as to construct an approving exchange of looks: 'a series of Delon clones assembled to appear to be cruising one another' (Rees-Roberts 2012: 92). The sequence opens with two shots – an extreme long shot and a mid-shot – of Delon laying on his back, sunning himself by the side of the pool. As he tilts his head poolside, an eyeline match shows (another) Delon emerging from the water before cutting back to Delon, now in close-up, apparently admiring himself. The final two shots – a long shot and a mid-shot – repeat the two opening shots, but this time around the second one ends with Delon startled by a splash: he raises his head and upon removing his sunglasses is caught in freeze frame. The overall effect of the short advertisement – including Delon being splashed by an unseen diver – is achieved by editing out Schneider who (in the film) calls his name off-screen before splashing him and then swimming across the pool's length to join him.

Brown and Hirsch write that 'it is difficult to conceptualize swimming pools without thinking of David Hockney' (2014: 1); the unseen diver of the Dior advertisement seems to draw a line to Hockney's pool painting, 'A Bigger Splash' (1967), the largest and most striking of his three 'splash' paintings of the 1960s. Emptied of human presence, Hockney's painting presents a view across a swimming pool towards a 1960s modernist building, the intense blue of the water interrupted by the lighter blue and fine white lines of a splash. Guadagnino's remake not only takes its title from Hockney's work, but was also initially planned with a framing scene at the Tate Gallery in London featuring Hockney's actual painting.[1] The painting also lends its name to Jack Hazan's *A Bigger Splash* (1974), a hybrid documentary film work that focuses on the creation of Hockney's 'Portrait of An Artist (Pool with Two Figures)' (1972) and (like Guadagnino's film) deals with the breakdown of a relationship, in this case between Hockney and his lover Peter Schlesinger (Keska 2014: 148). As Massey points out, the portrait of Hockney at this early 1970s juncture is achieved through a combination of real events and unscripted reenactments, 'the accoutrements of [Hockney's] self-perpetuating myth [providing] a brand of ironic glamour – the gold lame jacket, the peroxided Artful Dodger haircut, Le Corbusier specs, etc.' (2012: 24). The film's depictions of gay lifestyles and bohemian glamour are played out in particular through fashion sequences, including Hockney, Schlesinger and textile designer Celia Birtwell seated in the front row audience of an Ossie Clark fashion show, as well as another sequence of Andrew Logan's 'Alternative Miss World' contest in which Derek Jarman, identified as the 'Ascot of radical drag', struts down the aisle in 'gay-liberationist drag' (Massey 2012: 25). Guadagnino's film directly remakes *The Swimming Pool*, but also draws on the atmosphere of both versions of 'A Bigger Splash', at once investing in Hazan's interest in the cult of personality – the thrall of high-fashion photography and its world of surfaces – and in Hockney's rendering of the mystery of the broken surface – of what lies beneath in the depths of desire.

A BIGGER SPLASH

A Bigger Splash broadly follows the narrative template of *The Swimming Pool*, relocating the story from the Riviera to the island of Pantelleria, situated between Sicily and Tunisia. Rock star Marianne Lane (Swinton) has retreated to a friend's villa on the island – together with her lover Paul (Matthias Schoenaerts), who is a documentary filmmaker and recovering alcoholic – to convalesce from throat surgery, speaking only rarely in a hoarse whisper to protect her larynx. Their idyll is interrupted by the surprise arrival of rock impresario Harry Hawkes (Ralph Fiennes), Marianne's former lover and Paul's music-industry associate, who is accompanied by his taciturn American daughter, Penelope (Dakota Johnson). Despite Harry's raucous behavior and Paul's disapproval, Marianne asks them to stay, and the following day Harry invites his friends, Mireille (Aurore Clément) and Sylvie (Lily McMenamy), to visit the villa. Later that day, at the island's San Gaetano festival, Harry tries to convince Marianne to rekindle their relationship, while the (sexually) aggressive Penelope assails Paul with invasive questions. The next day, each couple – Marianne and Harry, Paul and Penelope – has an intimate encounter, and following a tense dinner back at the villa Harry goes out drinking. Upon returning, Harry provokes a fight with Paul, and in the course of their struggle Harry is held down and semi-accidentally drowned in the pool. During the police investigation, it emerges that Penelope is a minor, and she is sent home to her mother. Marianne and Paul fear that suspicion of murder might fall on them, but when their car is stopped by the island's bumbling police investigator, it turns out he only wants Marianne to sign a copy of her album.

Guadagnino's version of *The Swimming Pool* retains the same basic narrative structure and the 'centrality of the swimming pool', but the filmmaker insisted that – in his collaboration with screenwriter David Kajganich – it was more 'important to see *behaviour* rather than drama unfolding on the page' (James 2016: 43–44, emphasis added). This interest in *performance* (over plot) is played out not only through the contrast between Harry's voice-movement and Marianne's silence-stasis, but just as evidently in the 're-fashioning' of each character, Marianne in particular. Gilligan takes note of the 'pivotal and disruptive role' played by fashion in *A Bigger Splash* and of the way in which 'attention is continually drawn to the clothes that adorn the cross-media star-celebrity body of Swinton' (2017: 697). Essential to this is Swinton's status as a fashion and general style icon, developed initially through collaborations with Jarman (*Caravaggio* [1986], *The Last of England* [1987], *War Requiem* [1989], *The Garden* [1990] and *Edward II* [1991]), Potter (*Orlando* [1992]) and more recently Jarmusch (*The Limits of Control* [2009], *Only Lovers Left Alive* [2013], *The Dead Don't Die* [2019]) and David Bowie (*The Stars [Are Out Tonight]* [2013]).

Swinton's collaboration with Guadagnino dates back to his first feature *The Protagonists* (1999), but their breakout film was *I Am Love*, in which she played the character of Emma Recchi, the stylish Russian émigré wife of a wealthy Milanese textile industrialist. Swinton's carefully chosen wardrobe was provided by costume designer Antonella Cannarozzi, who worked in collaboration with Raf Simons and his team at Jil Sander to create a look of understated elegance (Laverty 2016: 171–72). By the time of *A Bigger Splash*, Simons had moved to Dior and, in collaboration with Guadagnino and first-time costume designer Guilia Piersanti, created a 'more elegant than her surroundings' look for Marianne: 'through [a] stylishly understated capsule wardrobe [. . .] *A Bigger Splash* demonstrates its exclusivity through attention to detail, drape, movement, and coordination' (Gilligan 2017: 674). Although Marianne's 'nostalgic resort wardrobe' (McColgin 2016) is sometimes reminiscent of Courrèges' designs for *The Swimming Pool*, Heller (in conversation with Piersanti and Guadagnino) explains:

> For Swinton's role, Piersanti and Guadagnino looked to Ingrid Bergman [in *Journey to Italy* (*Viaggio in Italia*, 1954)]. 'Even though she's on an island, she's purposely overdressed – she's still a big star', Piersanti says. Schoenaerts's character [Paul], on the other hand, sticks to a uniform of T-shirts and jeans: 'He's trying to disappear in a way, and survive'. Johnson's character [Penelope] was dressed with teenage insouciance, in clashing tops and bottoms and Lolita-like white shades; her father

[Harry] was made to appear scattered yet refined. For one sequence, they had Charvet, the empyrean French tailor, re-create a polka-dotted shirt once worn by [French author] Jean Giono – 'because if you want to tell the story of that guy [Harry], he only wears, for sure, Charvet shirts', says Guadagnino (Heller 2016).

As described here, the costumes of *A Bigger Splash* inform each characterisation, the film's credits even blurring the distinction between character and personage: 'Marianne Lane's shoes created by Francesco Russo, Paris; Harry Hawkes's wardrobe created by M. Bardelli, Milan; Harry Hawkes's shirts created by Charvet, Paris; Marianne Lane, Penelope Lannier and Paul de Smedt wear jewels and watches by Damiani [Valenza]'. But it is in particular Swinton's multi-faceted and transformative 'brand-image' that produces, as Radner describes, a persona that circulates as 'the expression of a new plastic European identity [. . . blurring] boundaries between her life and her work, between art and "being"' (2016: 402). Stacey similarly refers to the significance of Swinton's figure within shifting transnational landscapes, referring to the actor's 'off-gender flux', less in order to signal the 'in-between-ness of [her] androgyny and more [to describe her] capacity to move across, to embody the mobility of temporal flux' (2015: 267). This includes Swinton's capacity to cross 'genres', most evidently mainstream and art house, but also to move between cinema and fashion, fact and fiction, original and remake. This fluidity, which is typical of the migratory movements of the new millennial remake, is evident in 'A/W15: Real/Unreal', an article for the international fashion and culture magazine *AnOther*. Co-authored by Swinton, Guadagnino, Kajganich and Glenn O'Brien, the piece features a (*faux*) interview with and 'backstage' photos of Swinton posed as 'musician Marianne Lane, [who, following the events on Pantelleria] talks [candidly about her] career crisis, recovery from substance abuse and the mysterious death of her producer [and former lover] Harry Hawkes' ('A/W15' 2015).

This flux or mobility is amplified in and through Swinton's ongoing work with Guadagnino, a filmmaker whose approach to *A Bigger Splash* seems consistent with those accounts of new millennial remakes in which authorial agency and brand name vision are understood as key elements in the promotion and reception of new film versions (Verevis 2017: 156). *A Bigger Splash* was initiated by Studiocanal, and Guadagnino insisted that he had little enthusiasm for Deray's film, saying it was 'not exactly his "cup of tea"', and therefore found it 'liberating' to use the property as the basis for a new film (quoted in Pulver 2016). The fact that Guadagnino had little personal investment in the property suggests that the remake was in the first instance led by commercial rather than creative imperatives, and the film's press notes state that Guadagnino self-consciously drew (authorial) inspiration not from Deray's work, but from that of Roberto Rossellini, in particular *Stromboli* (1950) and *Journey to Italy*. Furthermore, Guadagnino's re-fashioning of the property suggests that the remake works as an instance of 'commodity auteurism' (Rees-Roberts 2018: 56–63) and as globally 'branded entertainment': a product that reflects the 'new cartographies of taste and consumption' which have emerged in a transnational culture 'where traditional boundaries between media industries, texts and audiences have grown ever more difficult to maintain' (Grainge 2008: 42). In this way, Guadagnino's work in commercial advertising, undertaken through his company Frenesy, provides a foundation for the (intermedial) refashioning of *The Swimming Pool*. As James describes, 'with Guadagnino, you get the sense that his precise and exquisite work in luxury videos for brands such as Cartier, Ferragamo and Sergio Rossi et al. operates as a sketchbook for the bigger ideas on display in *A Bigger Splash*' (2016: 43).

The post-authorial, cross-media brand value with which Guadagnino invests *A Bigger Splash* further extends to the film's performance strategies. As Rayns observes, 'Guadagnino is much more interested in giving his cast room to "perform" than in honing a plot: the storytelling is languorous [. . .]. A thriller it is not' (2016: 71). Guadagnino nonetheless retains from *The Swimming Pool* the triangulation of its four principal characters – Marianne, Paul and Harry, on the one hand; Marianne, Paul and Penelope, on the other – but he shifts the balance away from *The Swimming Pool*'s insecure (sometimes sado-masochistic) couple Marianne and Jean-Paul, to focus instead on the stark contrast and interaction between the motor-mouth Harry and the near silent Marianne. Harry dominates his environment and the characters within it – his arrival by plane literally casts a dark shadow over Marianne and Paul – and he frequently takes on the role of orator, or performer. An early conversation provides a quick sketch of Harry's attitude (and even anticipates his fate in the pool). Prompted by Paul, Harry tells him:

> I've been teaching myself some Italian finally. . . .
> *Vaffanculo*. Go fuck yourself. Go take it up the arse, in fact.
> *Cacasentenze*. Someone who pretends to be very smart, who won't stop talking, one who shits sentences.
> And my favourite is *vomitare l'anima*. To puke your guts up. Literally, to vomit your soul.

The coordinates of Harry's character are further established in two 'scene-stealing' musical set-pieces (Rayns 2016: 72). In the first of these, Harry comes upon Paul, Marianne and Sylvie relaxing, listening to some music, only to exclaim: 'Why are we listening to this? You want to end up in a padded room? Fuck'. Flicking through the collection of record albums by the turntable, he comes across a copy of the Rolling Stones' *Voodoo Lounge* (1994), whereupon he sets about telling the story of how he produced the double album, specifically providing a commentary on the track 'Moon Is Up'. Acknowledging that Marianne has heard it all before, he asks Sylvie:

> Do you know this album? I can tell you a little story about my contribution to Rolling Stones history: Just after Darryl [Jones] came in and I was working with Don Smith, who'd done a lot of Keith's solo stuff with me and we were at Windmill Lane in Dublin and it was raining. [. . .] And this song, which you are going to hear, it just wasn't fucking working. Keith is insisting no drums, you know? [. . .] So I'm thinking 'What the fuck!' So I give Mick castanets. So you've got Chuck Leavell on the harmonium and everyone is folding in all this beautiful shit, but this song is not taking off, so I say to Keith, 'Do you trust me?' He goes yeah. 'If I promise no drums, can we do a percussion track?' He says, 'What's Charlie going to play?' And I'm thinking, 'What *is* Charlie going to play?' But I'm asking myself what's the sound, something, not too crisp and I look over and I see in the corner. . .

Now in full *cacasentenze* mode, Harry proceeds to lower the stylus on to the track, asking of the distinctive beat about to be heard: 'What is it? . . . Wait, listen, what is it? It's not a drum. What is it?' Clearly delighted with himself he tells an astonished Sylvie: 'It's a trash can. . . . It's an aluminium fucking trash can'. However, as the track plays on, he admits: 'Yeah, all that and you still can't fucking move to it, you know'. He continues to look through the records whereupon he finds the Rolling Stones' earlier album *Emotional Rescue* (1980). Triumphantly he declares: 'This is tops. I didn't know it then, but I do now'. He plays the title track. Announced by extreme close-ups of the gleaming vinyl and the Ortofon cartridge, there follows a long shot in which Harry sings along with and exuberantly dances to 'Emotional Rescue', pointedly directing its first verse at Marianne:

> Is there nothing I can say, nothing I can do?
> To change your mind, I'm so in love with you
> You're too deep in, you can't get out
> You're just a poor girl, in a rich man's house
> Ooh ooh ooh ooh ooh ooh ooh
> Ooh ooh ooh ooh ooh ooh ooh
> Yeah, baby, I'm crying over you.

As the song continues, he beckons Sylvie who, dressed in a tiny blue bikini top and leopard-print sarong, gyrates before him. Marianne and Paul groove along, until Harry, constrained by the interior space of villa, bursts out onto the rooftop. Shot from a low angle, arms outstretched to encircle his domain and dressed in a distinctive white, green and gray short-sleeve shirt from Christophe Lemaire, Harry – like some ancient, pagan deity – continues his display under the haze of the scorching midday sun.

In the following sequence, Sylvie and Mireille ask the group, now assembled for an *al fresco* lunch, if they plan to attend the San Gaetano festival which will be held in the local village that afternoon and into the evening. At the festival, the parading of the Madonna presents a stark contrast to the satanic majesty of Harry's earlier performance, and as Harry and Marianne walk together (apart from the others), drinks in hand, he immediately sets in on her, telling Marianne: 'Frankly, it's sentimental to think you can help Paul by not drinking in front of him. [. . .] And people *talk* about addiction, they talk about suicide. It happens. You know, I doubt he wanted to kill himself anyway. [. . .] What's the point of Paul in your life now?' Literally pushed up against a wall, Marianne's response is: 'I'm happy, Harry. Can't you stand that?' As evening comes, Harry and Marianne enter a bar looking for a table, only to find that it is karaoke night. The impulsive Harry tells Marianne that they should find something they would be embarrassed to sing anywhere else. In the bathroom, they share a pill and then proceed to seduce the local crowd, first with a karaoke cover of Metropole's 'Miss Manhattan' (1981) and next with Harry directing another message to Marianne, this time by way of the Rolling Stones' song 'Worried about You', from *Tattoo You* (1981):

> Sometimes I stay out late, yeah I'm having fun
> Yes, I guess you know by now that you ain't the only one
> Oh, baby, sweet things that you promised me, babe
> Seem to go up in smoke
> Yeah, vanish like a dream
> 'Cause I'm worried
> I just can't seem to find my way.

The sequences at the village festival represent Harry's first deliberate attempt to insert himself into the relationship between Marianne and Paul. His endeavour is further abetted by Penelope whose youthful presence, provocative attire and deliberate mimicry of Harry's (bad) behaviour also works to destabilise the couple's equilibrium. At the same time as Harry and Marianne stroll through the village, Penelope pursues Paul, asking about his suicide attempt: 'You must have been really desperate to crash your car like that. [. . . Harry says] you didn't leave a note or anything. [. . .] He thinks it's the most interesting thing you've done'. The morning after the karaoke, Penelope aims her sneering at Marianne, telling her: 'You're pretty domesticated for a rock star'. And, upon being told that Marianne and Paul have been together for six years, the same period Marianne spent with Harry, Penelope says: 'I heard that there used to be six songs on either side of a [vinyl] record album. You'd hear six and then you'd have to flip the thing over to hear more'. Although younger and not (yet) expert in the type of manipulation exercised by Harry, Penelope nevertheless exhibits her father's influence – most obviously in the Rolling Stones T-shirt she wears by the pool – but also in her adoption of his language. Specifically, in an early flashback, in which Harry is trying to set Paul up with Marianne, he tells him: 'She's the woman of the century, and I'm talking about her soul now'. He then adds: 'On top of all of that, she's a trumpets-of-Jericho, white-hot fuck. [. . .] She fucks and she fucks and she fucks'. Although not privy to the conversation, Penelope later exactly mimics Harry's provocative and pitiless language. Upon her return from a swimming excursion she pointedly tells all: 'Paul took [me] to the cliffs. [. . .] We dived and dived and dived'. These provocations of the first afternoon and evening at the San Gaetano festival are acted upon the following day.

Unlike *The Swimming Pool* which 'obey[s] the unities of time and space [to] develop a claustrophobic atmosphere' (O'Donoghue 2016: 51), *A Bigger Splash* opens up its action to allow the island of Pantelleria to play a part in the energy of the film. On the second day, Harry takes Marianne to the village to pick up groceries, while Paul and Penelope take a two-mile hike to the rock pools at the edge of the island. It is during these excursions that the wind – in housekeeper Clara's description – 'fast first and then slow, one doesn't understand what it wants' – picks up, gusting through the streets and stirring up tension. In the village scenes, as Gilligan describes, '[Marianne's] clothes wildly flutter, flap and billow in the powerful wind [. . .] the angry, violent movement of the fabric speak[ing] for Marianne, as the destructive passions of Paul and Penelope's desire rise' (2017: 675–76). The same wind gusts as Paul and Penelope silently make their way across the rugged island toward the water, a mist hanging over the landscape like a shroud. Pausing briefly, Paul opens up, telling Penelope that 'I did leave a [suicide] note', but one that only contained Marianne's name: 'I wanted to write it down one last time'. As if on cue, Penelope runs ahead, Paul's disorientation registered in a sequence of three close-up shots of Paul (looking left, right and centre) intercut with shots of the rocky landscape, before revealing Penelope, naked at the rock pool: first standing defiantly, next reclined and beckoning. Commenting on these figures in the landscape, Guadagnino observed:

> Pantelleria is a strange, unsettling place. It's a volcanic island off Sicily, and it's rough, hot, windy and sunny. There's a strong energy that comes off the volcano, which gives the island a distinctive atmosphere. When I began imagining a story about four people on holiday, trying to find a way to come back to each other, I wanted their inner souls to be reflected in the landscape (quoted in Lack 2016).

Back in the village, Harry takes Marianne to a local house, where the villager Rosa demonstrates her generation-old way of preparing – gently stirring, skimming and draining – ricotta. If Penelope finds a direct way of seducing Paul, then Harry's strategy is more oblique, opening up Marianne's senses through the experience of taste. In this way, Guadagnino closely follows a technique employed in *I Am Love* where the carefully constructed persona of Swinton's character, Emma Recchi, begins to unravel when she swoons at the taste of a dish prepared by her (soon-to-be) lover, Antonio. As described by Radner, 'taste is the sense that serves as the trigger that [. . .] reawaken[s] "Emma" to the world of feeling, a world against which fashion has constituted an elaborate defence throughout her [cold and loveless] marriage' (2016: 409). In a similar way, Marianne samples the ricotta from a tablespoon, throwing her head back in ecstasy. Harry tastes from the same spoon, and then two exterior shots of the island follow ahead of Marianne emerging, shot from a low angle in medium long shot, with her clothing – a Dior black silk body and cotton white silk skirt – billowing in the hot wind. Sitting on a step, she is joined by Harry, whereupon she puts her arm around his shoulder. Whispering inaudibly in Harry's ear, he replies by telling her: 'You don't need to apologise . . . ever'. Upon arriving back at the villa, an elaborate panning shot registers Paul's and Penelope's absence. As Marianne and Harry prepare dinner, taking the ricotta fetched from Rosa from its bag, the silent question posed that afternoon is answered by the strains of the Rolling Stones' song, 'Heaven' (1981):

> Smell of you baby, my senses, my senses be praised
> Smell of you baby, my senses, my senses be praised
> Kissing and running, kissing and running away
> Kissing and running, kissing and running away
> Senses be praised
> Senses be praised.

Like some passages in Hazan's film, the music and sentiment of the lyrics render the sequence 'almost oneiric' (Keka 2014: 148). Repeating an earlier action, Harry pushes Marianne up against the wall. They begin to have sex. Harry tells her 'Come on, this is happening. [Paul] put a bell on your neck', but her reply – 'I'm glad he did . . . Don't be angry' – brings his advances to a devastating close.

When Penelope and Paul return, the tension reaches its highest point. Harry announces that he and Penelope will leave the following day, but before doing so takes the car to the village. When he returns in the early hours of the morning, the drama reaches its operatic climax (Verdi's 'Falstaff' now plays on the soundtrack). Harry asks Paul: 'Did you fuck [Penelope] or not?' Paul responds: 'Did you fuck Marianne?' Eventually the two, once close friends, come to blows. Harry slaps Paul. Paul pushes Harry. Harry pulls Paul into the pool where they wrestle until Harry is held under and drowned. As the sun rises, the porcelain faces of the statues around the pool and garden stand as mute witnesses to the night's tragedy. Clara raises the alarm, and Marianne frantically runs to the pool, while Nilsson's 'Jump into the Fire' (1972) plays. Heard earlier in the film, as Paul and Harry race each other in the pool, the song not only underscores their rivalry and struggle for the attentions of Marianne, but also foreshadows their inevitable fate. The race in the pool is punctuated by telling flashbacks. In one, Harry and (the younger) Paul meet for the first time when the latter films a documentary interview in which Harry says: 'That was when the Stones came into their own. They killed their fathers, so to speak, in front of millions of people, and the first real casualty of that was Brian Jones [the band member who mysteriously drowned in his pool]'. In another, Harry introduces Marianne to Paul during a studio session in which Marianne is laying down a cover of The Rolling Stones' 'Worried about You', the song Harry directs at Marianne during the karaoke night. Returning to the present, the race in the pool concludes. Paul is the winner, by a narrow margin, and he embraces his prize, Marianne, as Harry and Penelope look on.

As in *The Swimming Pool*, the final panel of *A Bigger Splash* consists mainly of the police investigation into Harry's death but – indirectly addressing the issue of the near-daily drownings of North African refugees seeking asylum on the island – the film forces a shift in perspective and a possible reassessment of the calamity at the villa. On the morning after the drowning, Marshall Carmelo La Mattina (Corrado Guzzanti) arrives. Seen already on two occasions – on Harry's first evening, Mattina recognizes Marianne and gives up his table in an otherwise full restaurant, and the next day he is one of the onlookers at Harry and Marianne's karaoke performance – Mattina is decidedly more abrupt and distracted by the many other drownings on the shores of the island. Clara provides limited assistance in translating for Mattina but is hampered by the language barrier; he requests the presence of Marianne, Paul and Penelope at the police station later that afternoon. Although Mattina seems to pick up on some clues that Harry's death was not accidental, Marianne almost immediately realises the truth and opportunistically tells Mattina that it might be the work of the island's refugees: 'There is a path. To the house. It comes up behind the pool. You saw it. And anybody could . . . come up there, when Mr Hawkes was swimming and . . . we would never have heard them'. Although Mattina apparently sees through the ruse – saying he will question the asylum-seekers but adding 'they cannot be more offended than they already are' – he also sees no grounds for laying charges. At the very end of the film – after Marianne and Paul have dropped off Penelope at the airport – their car is chased down by Mattina's squad car. With rain falling, Marianne apprehensively approaches Mattina who – starstruck and with umbrella held aloft – asks her to sign a CD of her album. Returning to her car, the near-hysterical Marianne hoarsely tells Paul (in the final words of the film): 'He's a fan'.

Commentators have said, in reference to the conspicuous absence of any mention of the contemporaneous events of May 1968, that *The Swimming Pool* is a 'bourgeois dream [. . . of] luxury, calm and sensuality' (Michel Boujut, quoted in Penz 2014: 117). Like its predecessor, *A Bigger Splash* combines sex and death, and the swimming pool is the instrument of murder, but Guadagnino says his remake is also a response to the 'new conservatism that is [. . .] ruling us today' (quoted in Sragow 2016). Swinton goes even further, suggesting that *A Bigger Splash* began as 'a sick satire [. . .] about a kind of solipsistic bubble-life': 'the overbearing and incessant babbling of the narcissist, the disengagement of the bereaved and disenchanted, the resentful cowering of tamed (suppressed) violence and the lethal allure of the undereducated, surface-sampling, oversaturated young' (quoted in Shoard 2016). Writing for *Cineaste*, O'Donoghue adds that it was, 'perhaps, inevitable' that Guadagnino – 'a director of glossy promos for high-end fashion houses' – would remake *A Bigger Splash* in such a way as to suggest that 'the exhausted art-house tradition' of European cinema 'cannot cope with the new socio-economic realities of global financial crisis, mass migration, and political corruption' (2016). Such an evaluation withers, however, in the face of the film's high-end fashions – 'all elevated shirt-dresses, swimsuits and scene-stealing sunglasses' (Carolan 2016) – and a narrative image that applauds the filmmaker's brand and plays to its transnational market. While Guadagnino's remake gestures toward a socio-political context are largely absent from *The Swimming Pool*, in the final analysis *A Bigger Splash* cannot help but reflect and celebrate the view of mobility, leisure-class relaxation and desire found in the pool painting from which it takes its title.

NOTE

1. The four-shot sequence – which culminates in a slow zoom on to the painting – is now available as an extra on the DVD release.

REFERENCES

'A/W15: Real/Unreal' (2015), *AnOther*, 11 September, available at: https://www.anothermag.com/fashion-beauty/7765/marianne-lane-for-another-magazine-a-w15 (last accessed 23 December 2018).
Brown, Christopher and Pam Hirsch (2014), 'Introduction: The Cinema of the Swimming Pool', in Christopher Brown and Pam Hirsch (eds), *The Cinema of the Swimming Pool*, Oxford: Peter Lang, pp. 1–20.
Carolan, Nicholas (2016), 'Tilda Swinton's Dior Costumes Will Make "A Bigger Splash" Than Usual On Your Wardrobe Aspirations', *Grazia*, available at: https://grazia.com.au/articles/tilda-swinton-costumes-dior-a-bigger-splash-luca-guadagnino-raf-simons/ (last accessed 28 May 2019).

Chaplin, Felicity (2015), 'The Sophisticate and the *Ingénue*: Two Visions of *la Parisienne* in Jacques Deray's *La Piscine*', *Colloquy: Text Theory Critique*, 29, 48–65.
Gilligan, Sarah (2017), 'Sun, Sex, and Style in Smart Cinema: Tilda Swinton in *A Bigger Splash* (Luca Guadagnino, 2015)', *Fashion Theory*, 21: 6, 667–87.
Grainge, Paul (2008), *Brand Hollywood: Selling Entertainment in a Global Media Age*, London: Routledge.
Heller, Nathan (2016), '*A Bigger Splash* Brings High-Fashion Glamour to the Big Screen', *Vogue*, available at: http://www.vogue.com/13433353/bigger-splash-la-piscine-high-fashion-glamour/ (last accessed 28 May 2019).
James, Nick (2016), 'Island of Lost Souls', *Sight and Sound*, 26: 3, 42–45.
Keska, Monika (2014), 'Filming the Splash: David Hockney's Swimming Pools on Film', in Christopher Brown and Pam Hirsch (eds), *The Cinema of the Swimming Pool*, Oxford: Peter Lang, pp. 145–55.
Lack, Hannah (2016), 'Luca Guadagnino on the Inspiration Behind *A Bigger Splash*', *AnOther*, 12 February, available at: https:ß//www.anothermag.com/design-living/8361/luca-guadagnino-on-the-inspiration-behind-a-bigger-splash (last accessed 23 December 2018).
Laverty, Christopher (2016), *Fashion in Film*, London: Laurence King.
McColgin, Carol (2016), 'The 6 Pieces You Need to Pack for Summer Vacation', *Hollywood Reporter*, 5 December, available at: https://www.hollywoodreporter.com/news/tilda-swintons-a-bigger-splash-892962 (last accessed 28 May 2019).
Massey, Ian (2012), 'Magnificent Obsession', *Sight and Sound*, 22: 3, 24–25.
Melville, David (2010), 'Writing on Water From the Depths of *La Piscine*', *Cinematheque Annotations on Film*, 55, available at: http://sensesofcinema.com/2010/cteq/writing-on-water-from-the-depths-of-la-piscine/ (last accessed 28 May 2019).
O'Donoghue, Darragh (2016), '*A Bigger Splash*', *Cineaste* 41: 3: 49–51.
Penz, François (2014), 'Atmosphère *d'Eau Sauvage*: Reflections on *La Piscine* (1969)', in Christopher Brown and Pam Hirsch (eds), *The Cinema of the Swimming Pool*, Oxford: Peter Lang, pp. 101–19.
Pulver, Andrew (2016), '*A Bigger Splash* Director: "Italian Cinema is Mostly a Bureau for Tourism"', *Guardian*, 5 February, available at: https://www.theguardian.com/film/2016/feb/04/bigger-splash-director-luca-guadagnino-italian-cinema-is-mostly-a-bureau-for-tourism (last accessed 28 May 2019).
Radner, Hilary (2016), 'Transnational Celebrity and the Fashion Icon: The Case of Tilda Swinton, "Visual Performance Artist at Large"', *European Journal of Women's Studies*, 23: 4, 401–14.
Rayns, Tony (2016), '*A Bigger Splash*', *Sight and Sound*, 26: 3, 71–72.
Rees-Roberts, Nick (2018), *Fashion Film: Art and Advertising in the Digital Age*, London: Bloomsbury.
Rees-Roberts, Nick (2012), 'Men of Mode: Alain Delon, Christian Dior and Brand Heritage', *Film, Fashion and Consumption*, 1: 1, 81–99.
Shoard, Catherine (2016), 'Tilda Swinton: "Our Film Started as Sick Satire – Now It's a Recognisable Portrait"', *Guardian*, 16 December, available at: https://www.theguardian.com/film/2016/dec/15/tilda-swinton-a-bigger-splash-interview (last accessed 28 May 2019).
Sragow, Michael (2016), '*A Bigger Splash*', *Film Comment*, 52: 3, 69–70.
Stacey, Jackie (2015), 'Crossing Over with Tilda Swinton – The Mistress of "Flat Affect"', *International Journal of Politics, Culture, and Society*, 28: 3, 243–71.
Verevis, Constantine (2016), 'The Cinematic Return', *Film Criticism*, 40: 1, available at: https://quod.lib.umich.edu/f/fc/13761232.0040.134/--cinematic-return?rgn=main;view=fulltext (last accessed 7 December 2019).

Verevis, Constantine (2017), 'New Millennial Remakes', in Frank Kelleter (ed.), *Media of Serial Narrative*, Columbus: Ohio State University Press, pp. 148–66.

Vincendeau, Ginette (2009), 'Shackled by Beauty', *Sight and Sound*, 19: 12, 25.

Vincendeau, Ginette (2014), 'The Perils of Trans-National Stardom: Alain Delon in Hollywood Cinema', *Mise au Point*, 6, available at: https://journals.openedition.org/map/1800#article-1800 (last accessed 7 December 2019).

Part IV

Industrial Perspectives: Practices of Production and Circulation

CHAPTER 13

Remake and Decline in Scottish Cinema: *Whisky Galore!* 1949 and 2016

Robert Munro and Michael Stewart

INTRODUCTION

Released during a period of austerity following World War II, *Whisky Galore!* (Mackendrick 1949) has become a canonical example of Ealing Comedy, that most iconic of classic British film genres, and one of the best-loved 'Scottish' films of all time. Yet, as the hesitancy to claim it as Scottish in the preceding sentence alludes to, it has also become a frequent object of study for those interested in cinematic representations of Scotland, as well as their allegedly problematic ideological address. The remake of the film, which premiered at the Edinburgh International Film Festival in 2016 before receiving its general release in May of 2017, offers an opportunity to reflect on the re-articulation of particular discourses on Scottishness and Britishness in a very different socio-political historic context, albeit one which shares the austerity politics of 1949. Furthermore, *Whisky Galore!* is in the first instance adapted from the novel by Compton Mackenzie (1947), which was itself a fictionalised retelling of real events during World War II. The basic plot is the same in all four real-life and fictional variations. On a remote Scottish island, a cargo ship containing thousands of cases of whisky runs aground. A campaign by the locals to retrieve the whisky is undertaken against the wishes, and under the noses, of Customs and Excise men and the comedically pompous English commander of the home guard on the island, Captain Wagget.

In what follows we address the 1949 and 2016 films through the three categories identified by Verevis (2006) in his work on film remakes: industrial, textual and critical (although, of course, there are spillages between the three). In terms of the industrial, any reading of the original film must take into account the peculiarities of the film's production by Ealing Studios towards the beginning of its very successful and fondly remembered series of comedies, which included films such as *Passport to Pimlico* (1949), *Kind Hearts and Coronets* (1949), *The Lavender Hill Mob* (1951), *The Ladykillers* (1955) and, most pertinently for our purposes here, *The Maggie* (1954). The 2016 remake, directed by Gillies Mackinnon, makes clear the realities of film production in the UK in the present moment. It was entirely financed with private capital raised by producer Iain Maclean over the course of fourteen years, receiving no public funding through the BBC, BFI or Creative Scotland – a bone of contention for Mackinnon (Ferguson 2016). Finally, we move on to consider the differences and similarities between the two films, and how the distance between them can be understood through the respective critical discourses of their eras of production.

'TO THE WEST THERE IS NOTHING . . . EXCEPT AMERICA': *WHISKY GALORE!* AND THE SCOTTISH DISCURSIVE UNCONSCIOUS

Whisky Galore! has made many of the tensions of Scottish film criticism readily apparent. The view expressed most persistently by Colin McArthur (1982; 2003) is that *Whisky Galore!* reiterates the image of Scotland on the fringes of the British imperial project: a Celtic, romanticised wilderness on the edge of modernity where the uncouth yet canny locals are able to entrance civilised visitors (primarily American and English) through the use of the remote Scottish wilderness as a space of fantasised sanctuary from the harsh realities of modern, urban life. Indeed, one of the earliest lines of the film – and its most famous – identifies this geographical remoteness: 'To the west there is nothing . . . except America'. McArthur's approach, seminal in initially theorising Scotland and the cinema, has since been criticised for its trenchant neo-Marxist impulses which, it is argued by Petrie (2000), perhaps obscure some of the qualities and popular appeal of films like *Whisky Galore!* and *Local Hero* (1983), which may offer their own knowing takes on representing Scotland. As Murray's (2019) recent summary of Scottish film criticism details, debates about national representativeness have arguably been detrimental to widening the frame of analysis. McArthur's project is undoubtedly political, and his reading of Scottish film culture places it inextricably within the power relations made apparent through film production, which not only place Scotland as a geographical 'postcard' periphery, but locate the nation both economically and politically as a voiceless limb of the Anglo-American imperial and military complex: something made apparent, McArthur would no doubt voice, by the use of Scotland as a site for their nuclear arsenal.[1] This situation is parodied, although not successfully according to Petrie (2000), in the sequel to *Whisky Galore!* – that is, *Rockets Galore!* (1958) – where Todday is used as a site for nuclear rockets by the British government.

For McArthur (2003), *Whisky Galore!* is an escapist dream where the Scots achieve superiority over their English overlords – in this case embodied by Captain Wagget – even though such superiority remains impossible in the realms of the political. Brown (1983: 41) offers a similar reading of the film, noting that the dismissal of *Whisky Galore!* and similar films is 'a form of political revulsion against the cultural/industrial institutions [. . .] which by their very mode of operation create such images of Scotland and then impose them on the international consciousness to the exclusion of other more authentic images'. For McArthur (2003), the fact that films like *Whisky Galore!* are popular with Scottish audiences – the film broke box office records for the Highlands and Islands Film Guild as their most popular touring film – is beside the point. McArthur (2003: 12) believes that the film is an example of the Scottish discursive unconscious from which 'a dream Scotland emerges which is highland, wild, 'feminine', close to nature and which has, above all, the capacity to enchant and transform the stranger'. McArthur (1982) argues that the pervasive influence of this type of cinematic representation has also become the discursive grid through which Scots view themselves on screen and, indeed, in the case of *Local Hero*, make their own cinema. Brown (1983) succinctly calls this the 'Whisky Galore syndrome' where Scots identify with the kidnappers of their image (in this case the British and Hollywood film industries). What such analyses point towards is a sort-of-false consciousness, in which the proletariat (in this case the Scots) have been so indoctrinated to the hegemonic narratives of the ruling ideology that they can only see themselves through it. In this sense, the original *Whisky Galore!* might be enduringly popular with Scottish audiences, but only because they do not know what is good for them.

The same accusation cannot be made against the 2016 remake, which has been neither commercially nor critically successful. *Whisky Galore!* (2016) was also released in an era of austerity, this time brought about by the crash of de-regulated financial markets in 2008, rather than World War II. Beyond this similarity the two films' socio-political and historical contexts differ greatly. In the late 1940s, Scottish identity was very much subservient to British identity, despite the brief resurgence of Scottish nationalism and cultural renaissance in the 1920s and 1930s. The primary ways of thinking about national identity in the aftermath of World War II (and perhaps specifically because of the war) was to think as a British whole. Scotland and England voted, mostly, in the same way – for the Conservative Party – yet by the end of the twentieth century, McCrone (2001: 28) notes: 'Being British is a secondary identity to being Scottish [. . .] Feeling British is becoming a matter of memory, of history, rather than of the future'. What then, of the 2016 remake? Its release came two years after a referendum on independence for Scotland from

Britain returned a narrow vote in favour of remaining British and one year after another referendum found that British voters wanted to leave the EU (although Scotland voted to remain European). In this sense, the film's representation of the union between the English Sergeant Odd and the Scottish islander Peggy Macroon may have offered an updated insight into contemporary Anglo-Scottish relations. In the 1949 version, when Sergeant Odd is proposing to Peggy, she remarks: 'It's a pity you haven't the Gaelic' He responds: 'It's clear what I'm saying in any language'. Subsequently Sergeant Odd reveals that he has learned Gaelic when he once again asks Peggy to marry him. She still does not give him a straight answer, but his attempt to unite with Peggy through an appreciation of her culture and language is well received. The remake removes this in its depiction of the same scene; indeed, there is no talk of marriage at all from Sergeant Odd.

Yet, the possibility of a critical reading of the 2016 film which attempts to understand its formal and narrative strategies, as well as their similarity to or difference from the 1949 film and their differing socio-political and historical environments of production, is fraught with difficulty. The timidity of the remake is reflected in its critical reception, where it is described variously as: 'twee, comfy-cardigan film-making' (Pulver 2016); 'an inoffensive piece of twaddle' (Catsoulis 2017); 'innocuous, unmemorable' (Lodge 2017); and 'stuck in a weird time warp' (Harkness 2016). Where the original seems daring in the islanders' defiance of authority and the mocking of officious representatives of the state (Captain Wagget), as well as topical with its references to contemporary events (such as Wallis Simpson, who caused the abdication of Edward VIII in 1936), the remake offers no room for a critical re-reading of the story of Scottish islanders mischievously trying to get the better of their English overlords – even when the context would seem ripe for precisely that. Indeed, some of the criticism of 2017's most successful Scottish 'reboot', *T2: Trainspotting* (2017), was precisely its lack of interest in contemporary Scottish politics (Bradshaw 2017). In calling for a move beyond thinking about fidelity, Stam (2005: 45) argues that one of the ways of thinking critically about adaptations and remakes is to analyse the ways in which they might 'reveal something about ambient discourses in the moment of reaccentuation'. What, then, of *Whisky Galore!* which is so bound by fidelity that it seems to offer no gestures to contemporary discourses of Scottish-British relations, beyond their notable absence?

FROM NATIONAL FILM INDUSTRY TO NEOLIBERAL CREATIVE INDUSTRIES

The differing production contexts for the films also serve to highlight the divergent practices and discourses of their respective eras. The first film served to further enhance the reputation of Ealing Studios, producer Monja Danischewsky and head of production, Michael Balcon. As McArthur (2003:

21–28) details, the film's existence hinged on the peculiarities of its moment of production. The British government had imposed a 75 percent customs tax on imported films after World War II in order to help pay back large deficits. This encouraged British filmmakers to take advantage of the need for films to fill cinema screens and, stimulated by support from the government, Balcon raised the necessary funding from another British film company, Rank Organisation, to produce *Whisky Galore!* With limited studio space, Balcon instructed Danischewksy to find a project suitable for filming on location, and Alexander Mackendrick was taken on as a first-time director, having been employed at Ealing for several years prior. The production of *Whisky Galore!* in 1948/9 shows how the original film fitted into a model of studio production not dissimilar to classic Hollywood. A studio with a reputation for a specific style bought the rights to a popular novel, used its in-house employees to bring it to fruition and, after several good reviews, cleverly marketed and promoted the film to ensure good box office returns.

The production of the 2016 version was markedly different. A passion project of director Gillies Mackinnon and writer Peter McDougall, the film took fourteen years to finance. In the contemporary period, most Scottish productions are likely to have been funded by some form of public support. *Filth* (2014), *Under the Skin* (2013), *Sunset Song* (2015), *The Legend of Barney Thompson* (2015) and *T2: Trainspotting* are examples of adaptations, remakes and sequels which have all received funding from the national arts body Creative Scotland, and most also have support from other UK-wide public organisations such as the BBC and BFI. *Whisky Galore!* (2016) was funded entirely through private sources, although the producers almost certainly applied to Creative Scotland for production funding, having previously received a small amount for location scouting (Ferguson 2016). Creative Scotland refused to release the application documents for the film, which they routinely do for those that have received funding, for reasons of commercial sensitivity.[2] Producer Iain Maclean (Ferguson 2016) was forthright about his surprise that the film was not funded:

> Obviously I'm not the only person that's after funding from Creative Scotland or the BBC. To what extent you get prioritised I'm not sure. For one reason or another we weren't picked out of the bunch. I was surprised, as I almost look upon Whisky Galore as Scotland's national movie. I thought it would definitely have a 'yes' behind it. I think it really says something about the state of the industry more than anything else.

The above description raises the spectre of the 'ambient discourses' to which Stam (2005) refers; it also raises the elusive idea of Scottishness in the contemporary period, an idea garnering debates in which Creative Scotland has frequently become embroiled. For example, Creative Scotland's refusal to support a proposed film, written by *Trainspotting* author Irvine Welsh, was relayed in the press as the agency turning down the film for not being 'Scottish enough' (Ferguson 2017). What we might surmise from this is that the production of *Whisky Galore!* in 1949 had no recourse to 'Scottishness', but rather portrayed a quaint ethnographic-realist depiction of Scotland as viewed from the centre (London). Furthermore, while privately financed, the film took advantage of public intervention in the film industry after World War II. Leaving aside the likelihood that the remade script itself may not have appealed to Creative Scotland, a film which reiterates – without updating for contemporary political sub-text – McArthur's sense of the Scottish discursive unconscious is unlikely to appeal to the 'ambient discourses' of post-indyref Scotland. In addition to the unfavourable reviews, the film was not successful at the UK Box Office. With an estimated production budget of £5.4 million (IMDB 2016), it brought in less than £50,000 in its first week of release (BFI 2017a), ultimately returning a total of £330,000 (BFI 2017b). The film fared little better overseas, making $21,551 in the United States, although it did recover $161,834 in New Zealand (Box Office Mojo 2018). This stands in great contrast to *Filth*, *Sunshine on Leith* and *T2: Trainspotting* which grossed £3.9 million (BFI 2014), £4.6 million (BFI 2014) and £17.1 million (BFI 2018), respectively. Furthermore, more than 30 percent of the UK-wide takings for *Filth* and *Sunshine on Leith* came from Scottish audiences, indicating their popularity north of the border.[3]

As Hill (1999) has noted, the British film industry has historically had two strategies: to compete with Hollywood in international markets, and to rely on domestic markets for commercial viability. In 1949 these strategies, and the corresponding levy, could make *Whisky Galore!* a viable production with little risk. As the British film industry has now largely accepted Hollywood's dominance, its primary strategy is to compete with other countries to be the site of their productions. The shift from the protectionist measures of 1949 to the current use of tax credits to incentivise film production, which largely exists as a subsidy for Hollywood productions to come to Britain, exemplify this. In this environment, the 2016 version of *Whisky Galore!* offers little cultural capital in art house cinema markets or commercial imperative for public funders, due to its lack of stars recognizable beyond Britain or Scotland and its period setting which relies on none of the historic signifiers with which Scotland is usually represented in the cinema.

FROM KNOWING REALISM TO POSTCARD BANALITY: REMAKING *WHISKY GALORE!*

The opening of *Whisky Galore!* (2016) shares with the 1949 film an unseen narrator. He is a narrator in that he both locates the action in its historical period – 'the fight with Hitler has hardly touched the island' – and also presents the island and its people as mythological and timeless and gendered in a familiar way: 'They say our little island is named after a love-sick princess who flung herself from the Skerry-dubh'. This narration is provided against images of coastline, glistening sea and ancient rock (the fateful, boat-sinking Skerry-dubh). This beginning sets a tone markedly different from the 1949 film in that we seem to be immediately immersed into a more romanticised version of Scottishness. But while the tone is different, the contrast is more complicated. The 1949 film assuredly romanticises an island people, but as Kemp (1991: 33) notes, in a manner more familiar to the British documentary tradition. In terms of genre or mode, we might suggest that, while the 1949 film owes much to the 1920s and 1930s British documentary tradition, the 2016 film belongs to heritage tourism. Indeed, Philip Kemp describes the opening of the earlier film as a 'parody' (1991: 33) of Grierson et al., and if we accept this description, then it is most obvious in two early visual gags which produce an ironic incongruity between on-screen image and off-screen voice over – that is, Finlay Currie's benign ethnographic descriptions of islanders as 'inhabitants scrap[ing] a frugal living from the sea and the sand and the low-lying hills of coarse grass and peat bog', accompanied by an image of The Biffer (Morland Graham) on his fishing boat with a big grin and even bigger lobster in his hand; and 'a happy people, with few and simple pleasures', accompanied by an image of husband (mending nets) and wife (spinning at a wheel) at their cottage door in the sun, cutting to nine children running out of the door toward the beach, happy and laughing (simple pleasures).

The 1949 film, then, seeks to produce ironic distance from the excesses of the Scottish discursive unconscious. How this distance is achieved is debatable – for example, if these gags are beautifully economic and visual, whether this should be attributed to the virtuosity of MacKendrick or the film's editor (Charles Crichton), or to the Ealing style and score, or indeed to Finlay Currie's uncredited voice-over is unclear. What is clear is that this ironic distance is absent from the opening of the 2016 film. What we have instead is more colour (obviously! – but a consistent use of colour which we will consider) and sunlight, longer shots and an opening sequence that invites immersion. The voice-over, indeed, takes us into the immediacy of the diegesis and live-action via character, and the narrator is shown to be the postmaster Joseph Macroon (Gregor Fisher), now on the beach with his daughters collecting seaweed. This relatively autonomous scene performs a number of functions.

Firstly, it establishes significant ways in which the 2016 film is told, which are markedly different from the 1949 version. *Whisky Galore!* (2016) is more strongly focused on Macroon and his daughters (especially Peggy, played by Naomi Battrick). Secondly, the sense of loss that Macroon feels as he watches his daughters grow up, gravitate toward the modern and get married is given greater emphasis in the 2016 film. In this respect, *Whisky Galore!* (2016) is arguably part of 'remake genealogies whose oedipal patterns are potentially analogous to cinematic (and to a certain extent social) history' (Braudy 1998: 329). In this regard, *Whisky Galore!* (2016) does little to complicate what Braudy indicates is a familiar masculine oedipal patterning, in that the film revolves around Macroon and the pain he feels for the loss of his daughters. Moreover, for all the greater emphasis and screen time given to Peggy and Catriona, *Whisky Galore!* (2016) does not amount to a 'female remake' (Braudy 1998: 332). What does distinguish the film's oedipal pattern is the almost complete absence of generational tension and the profound focus on melancholia and loss.

The third function performed by the relatively autonomous beach scene is that the specific types of utopia at the centre of the 2016 film are more closely aligned with the visual spectacles and aural design of heritage tourism. As Martin-Jones argues, film tourism is now more widely recognized as heritage tourism, which is 'a robust tradition with greater longevity' (2014: 164). This is particularly so with regard to Scotland. However, what film tourism gives to heritage tourism, so Martin-Jones notes, are images and ideas able to reach broader audiences more quickly. In this respect, films like *Whisky Galore!* (2016) are able to tap into a long history of Scotland as a heritage tourism destination and can also appeal to a diaspora, many of whom may never have visited Scotland, but who nevertheless 'know' it as a 'heritage landscape' and 'lost homeland' (Martin-Jones 2014: 163). This process, as Martin-Jones indicates, is about location marketing and branding, as well as the negotiation of transnational identities, which are 'at times complex constructions of memory, history, and heritage, be they understood individually or collectively' (2014: 159).

In this respect, the opening of the 2016 *Whisky Galore!* establishes a film in which fetishised postcard heritage tourism shots predominate. In the opening, it is difficult to pick out shots that are not staged and performed. For example, the seaweed gatherers make a model of family unity and sunny utopian work; work so utopian as to verge on fairy-tale, with George (Kevin Guthrie) leading eight red-haired school children along the small pier beside the seaweed gatherers; and a beautifully polished Victorian horseshoe bar, where a close-up of pouring whisky captures the light and colour of the room, the spirit and the crystal glass. The five-minute opening sequence finishes with an artfully arranged long overhead shot of children playing in a schoolyard, harbour and sea beyond.

This final shot is redolent of a highly staged postcard. Beyond the film on the screen, this postcard sensibility is furthermore conveyed by the inside cover of the DVD distributed in the UK by Arrow Films. On it is a map of Scotland imprinted on wood – the wooden crates of the whisky galore. At the foot and in the foreground are carefully coloured images of mooring rope, sea pebbles and a bottle of whisky. In columns on either side of the Scotland map are the 2016 film's locations – short descriptions of them, but also photo images, bright and colourful and recently produced, but akin nonetheless to relatively timeless postcards; postcards of, among others, the coastlines and beaches and harbours of Portsoy, Pennan and St Abb's Head, as well as the attractive horseshoe bar at Renton in Glasgow. On the back of the DVD cover is a still from the film's opening – George, waving, it now seems, to us rather than Catriona (Ellie Kendrick), as he leads the children along the small pier. Above the line of children is a quote from *Daily Business Magazine*: 'A love letter to Scotland'. The sense of postcards and love letters to or from Scotland is underlined at the end of the 2016 film when the closing credits are joined by affective vignettes (eighteen in total), mostly from the film, arranged indeed like postcards from a world on-going, but untouched by time.

The 2016 film's love for its settings and objects is unambiguous. One of the film's few moments of ambiguity, however, occurs in the opening scenes. When Macroon the narrator turns into Macroon the character on the beach with his daughters, he is given a short line of dialogue. George gives a hearty wave and shouts from the pier: 'Good morning, Catriona'. As Catriona looks up, smiles and replies, the camera plays on Macroon's reaction to the greeting. For many viewers, this reaction may be hard to understand. Head swivelling, he is disoriented and looks and sounds incredulous: 'God, is there no end to it?!' This is a strong reaction to what seems a friendly and innocuous greeting. Audiences might assume that there is a backstory of tension or animosity to which they are still to be introduced. In truth, there is no animosity between Macroon and George, and what we are really introduced to is Macroon's repeated lament for the loss of his daughters, as well as the character Macroon: grumpy and disbelieving, but essentially lovable and devoid of sharp edges.

More broadly, a particularly masculine and European sense of nationhood appears to weigh on Macroon. Following Anne McClintock's analysis of gender and nation, Macroon is the modern nation-state's 'repository of male hopes' (1993: 77). His rule over his socially immature children is benign, and this is one way, as McClintock suggests, in which nationhood is made to seem timeless and organic (1993: 64). This, certainly, as we noted above, is how narrator Macroon introduces Todday to viewers, with the island and its version of Scottishness seeming to spring from sea and ancient rock and 'masculinized memory' (McClintock 1993: 62). This timeless memorialising by Macroon quickly shifts to express loss (of pre-war peace and daughters) and focus on family. In doing so, it captures what McClintock describes as the inescapable contradictions of family time within modern nationhood. That is, family is both a key conduit for and symbol of progress within European narratives of nation, but it must also be protected from the violence of history by being mythologised as outside of history (1993: 63). Macroon, then, however much *Whisky Galore!* (2016) puts emphasis on the latter, is fearful of losing his daughters to both imperial time (the march of progress) and mythological time (the loss of purity).

In this respect, *Whisky Galore!* (2016) is – as Diffrient and Burgchardt (2017: 12) argue of *Le Voyage du Ballon Rouge* (2007) – 'both a homage and a memorialization'. However, while *Le Voyage*, as Diffrient and Burgchardt (2017: 12) argue, represents a 'critical intervention in the nostalgic framing' of the film it remakes (*The Red Balloon* [*Le Ballon Rouge*, 1956]), 'producing a new vision through reversioning' (Diffrient and Burgchardt 2017: 12), *Whisky Galore!* (2016) seems weighed down and paralysed by the memory of its 1949 progenitor. In this regard, *Whisky Galore!* (2016) fails to resist a number of 'magnetic pull(s)' (Craig 2009: 62). As Cairns Craig suggests, all film in one way or another is marked by nostalgia (2009: 69); yet, the nostalgia for a lost home, arguably, is particularly hard for Scottish film to avoid – and is expressed via 'despondency, melancholia (and) excessive emotion' (Craig 2009: 62). This characterises the 2016 version of Macroon, and – along with its love-letter and postcard-like qualities – is a key point of distinction from the earlier film. Critics, then, who show disdain for the contemporary version of *Whisky Galore!* are what Craig would call 'nostophobes' – hostile to the film's predictable nostalgia, which is also an expression of the Scottish discursive unconscious. As Craig argues, however, this type of phobia also has its own unconsciousness and may be no less nostalgic in its disposition. In place of the most suspect versions of nostalgia, so Craig suggests, nostophobia tends to imagine shared moments of publicness and authenticity no more real or separable from distinctive, modern popular cultures than the despised phobic object. Here, then, we want to argue that one of the homes or losses that bears most heavily on *Whisky Galore!* (2016) and its disappointed audiences and critics is the film that preceded it. Macroon's lost object and his narrated love letter are complicated and variously originated, but his lament for a beauty and simplicity and unity that never was, at one level, is a lament for an on-going and multiply-produced nostalgic fantasy – that is, the imagined simplicity, beauty and unity, and in some ways publicness, of *Whisky Galore!* (1949).

One particular scene which is perhaps most celebrated in the 'public' memory of *Whisky Galore!* (1949) and which is held up as a model of simple and profound unity (in reference to both the production values and the solidarity of ordinary folk) is the hiding-the-whisky scene. In the 2016 film, the scene lasts approximately six minutes, running from Mr Brown's (Michael Nardone) and then Hector's (Andrew Dallmeyer) phone call to the post office, to the departure of Farquharson (Kevin Mains) and his colleagues from the post office. It is strongly focused around Macroon and heritage tourism. One obvious difference in the 2016 treatment of this scene is that it occurs during the day; as for most of the film, the day is sunny. This serves to accentuate the beauty of Scotland, as well as to remove the dark, sinister and dramatic quality of the scene in the 1949 film. As Kemp (1991: 32) has noted, not only is the treatment of Farquharson (Henry Mollison) and his men's night-time visit in the earlier film distinctly noirish, but Farquharson's cool vindictiveness verges on Nazism; the exchange between Farquharson and Macroon in the 1949 film combines irony with some degree of venom. The 2016 scene sets a lighter tone by starting with a beautiful big shot of coastline and cloudless sky, as first Mr Brown and then Hector telephone the post office to warn of Farquharson's visit. As we move between the approaching boat and the post office, we are given repeated picture-perfect images of the harbour before moving into the dramatic hiding scene. A fast-cutting montage works to build an organic and unified resistance to the authorities, as in the 1949 film. It was inevitable that the 2016 film would have to struggle to match the 1949 version for brevity and heightened connectedness; however, it seems that the later film constructs its own obstacles in this respect. Firstly, there is an editorial decision to layer dialogue over the hiding sequence – the discussion of tactics between Farquharson and Wagget (Edie Izzard) – which has the effect, arguably and especially compared to the wordless 1949 montage, of decreasing rather than increasing momentum and urgency. The 2016 film also picks out characters in more expansive shots – for example, Biffer (Anthony Strachan) and Sammy (Iain Robertson) at a graveside in dappled sunlight, and Reverend Macalister (James Cosmo) in a beautifully presented dining room. The characters given most attention in the montage and in the hiding scene are Macroon and his daughters in the immaculate post office. Two consecutive shots are given the heaviest treatment. The first is of the two young women hiding whisky in a water tank in the attic. The second is Macroon at his kitchen sink, taking a glass of water and deeply appreciating the moment of drinking (it is whisky, of course) – holding it in close-up close to his face, lovingly, a shaft of sun backlighting Macroon and playing again on the amber of the spirit.

It is this shot that makes *Whisky Galore!* (2016) most unabashedly a heritage-style advertisement for whisky. Yet, it also serves to individuate Macroon, and in doing so removes from the 2016 film not only a measure of solidarity, but also one of the 1949 film's most memorable gags and moments of ironic punctuation. In the 1949 film, Macroon is in the kitchen with his daughters and waits until Farquharson and his men have departed before taking a glass of water (whisky) from the sink. He drinks it with relish and remarks on the dirtiness of Farquharson's job. The action is brief and gives us and Peggy (Joan Greenwood) – our delegate, as it were, in the medium-close shot – enough time to appreciate the moment and the joke. The 2016 film is wordier and slower and generally more focalised around Macroon, who gets this moment of appreciation all to himself and before he has successfully deceived Farquharson. The dirtiness of Farquharson's job is then turned into a more elaborate (and rather weak toilet) joke at the end of his visit – dependent on the minor dramatic tension of Farquharson washing his hands in the kitchen sink.

The ending of *Whisky Galore!* (2016) gives further support to the argument we have developed in this essay and is also usefully compared to the conclusion of the 1949 film. At the start of the 2016 ending sequence, Wagget's undoing is softened by whisky. Constable McPhee (Ciaron Kelly) consoles a defeated Wagget by pouring him and his wife (Fenella Woolgar) a dram from his hip flask. We then cut to the triumphant islanders, still at the truck that saved the whisky, celebrating their victory and toasting Wagget's departure with now abundant drink. As in the 1949 film, they remark ironically that Wagget will miss the wedding; however, unlike in the earlier film, we are then taken, with a cut, to the wedding of Peggy and Sgt Odd (Sean Biggerstaff), and Catriona and George. The wedding is given a heavy and uncomplicated treatment with traditional music, warm light and colours and sepia tones, as well as the timeless affectivity of island life. Its broad intention is to exclude no one in its celebration of Scottish culture. The scene puts Macroon firmly at its centre. He moves in the three-minute wedding scene from looking once again doleful, morose and bereft, to loving, proud and teary-eyed, as his daughters fuss over him once more, and finally to unrestrainedly joyful, as he shakes off his jacket and proclaims: 'There was never a wind blew that did not fill somebody's sail!' He launches himself into the middle of the dance as the crowd cheers, throwing his hat in the air with a yelp. This leads seamlessly into the postcard vignettes which accompany the beginning of the closing credits.

The brakes on immersion and romance now seem to be off entirely, and the contrast with the irony of the 1949 film's ending is marked. The very end of the 1949 film is beautiful, external and romantic, to be sure. In a long, expansive shot, Sgt Odd (Bruce Seton) and Peggy (now married, we assume) walk along the beach and sunlit coastline of Todday/Barra. The romance of this scene is not dispelled but somewhat undercut by a signature blast of Ealing-finale music as very brief credits roll. It is also destabilised by the sharp irony which has preceded it. Firstly, the Wagget and Farquharson dining room scene finishes with the uncontrollable and near-ghoulish laughter of Mrs Wagget (Catherine Lacey) and a close-up of the dishevelled and devastated face of Wagget (Basil Radford). The echoing, jarring laughter bleeds across cuts, first to Wagget and Farquharson's departing boat, and then to the islanders, joyous to a man and woman, and their réiteach. At this second cut, Mrs Wagget's laughter effectively becomes their laughter and the whole island's laughter. When on this latter cut we join the réiteach, the first face we see is that of Macroon. He is neither alone nor morose; moreover, this scene is focused on Peggy and Sgt Odd, not Macroon. The film's final shots recall its opening and are joined again by the ironic, tale-telling-cum-travelogue voice of Finlay Currie.

The differences in these conclusions are marked. In *Whisky Galore!* (2016), they typify what characterises a slower, more mournful and remarkably un-ironic film. The ending, and the more recent film generally, represents a kind of pathological, melancholic holding-on-to, the vignettes indeed insisting that this world, this moment, this thing will never end. While appearing, then, to invite immersion, it negates nonetheless all animation and dialogue. It is the furthest reaches of the remake as 'tribute' (Noordenbos and Souch 2021) and 'historical fetish' (Diffrient and Burgchardt 2017: 11). Heritage tourism threatens to be supplanted entirely by the distance of 'museum value' (ibid.). Any opportunity for revisioning and transnational negotiation, like the past that Macroon imagines, is lost.

CONCLUSION

In the preceding pages we have outlined the ways in which the 2016 remake of *Whisky Galore!* is so inebriated with both a sense of fidelity to its predecessor and an audio-visual faithfulness to a heritage tourist vision of Scotland that its indoctrination in the Scottish discursive unconscious is whole. A critical reading of the text, as well as its relationship to the critical thinking on Scottish cinema in which it moves, brings us to the conclusion that the film can primarily be thought of as animating the latent discourses of its period of production and reception primarily through its lack of ability (or desire) to animate them. If postmodernism is perceived as a mode of thought and action which uses parody and pastiche to highlight the instability of meaning, then *Whisky Galore!* (2016) provides an example of our post-postmodernist moment. Its cloying attempts to reanimate a sixty-year-old film in a very different socio-political era and context, its unashamedly sentimental postcard simulacra of Scottish island life and its lack of any underpinning irony or playful critique mark the film as something beyond pastiche and parody, but push it towards an affectless imitation. Its failure to engage critically with the prevailing discourses of its moment (the fracturing of the British state) which its narrative seems to invite is itself indicative of a general air of nostalgia that the film cannot avoid, not only in its reverence for the original film and a 'lost' way of life, but also a more general nostalgia among certain British publics, made apparent by the referendum on Brexit. As our analysis of the remake of *Whisky Galore!* shows, the film in its fetishised design makes everything sunnier in the shared, imagined memory of a lost homeland.

NOTES

1. Indeed, the ongoing controversy over the use of Prestwick airport on Scotland's west coast as a pit-stop for the American military provides contemporary relevance (McLaughlin 2019).
2. Robert Munro has previously been successful in obtaining documents from Creative Scotland through freedom of information, relating to the films listed in the preceding sentence.
3. Unfortunately, this measure was discarded by the BFI's 2018 statistical yearbook.

REFERENCES

BFI (2014), 'Statistical Yearbook 2014', *BFI* [online], available at: http://www.bfi.org.uk/sites/bfi.org.uk/files/downloads/bfi-statistical-yearbook-2014.pdf (last accessed 21 October 2016).

BFI (2018), 'Statistical Yearbook 2018', *BFI* [online], available at: https://www.bfi.org.uk/sites/bfi.org.uk/files/downloads/bfi-statistical-yearbook-2018.pdf (accessed 27 November 2019).

Bradshaw, P. (2017), 'T2 Trainspotting Review – Choose a Sequel That Doesn't Disappoint', *Guardian* [online], available at: https://www.theguardian.com/film/2017/jan/19/t2-trainspotting-review-ewan-mcgregor-danny-boyle-sequel (last accessed 26 November 2019).

Braudy, L. (1998), 'Afterword: Rethinking Remakes', in A. Horton and S. McDougal (eds), *Play it Again Sam: Retakes on Remakes*, Berkeley: University of California Press.

Brown, J. (1983), 'Land Beyond Brigadoon', *Sight & Sound*, 53: 1, 40–46.

Catsoulis, J. (2017). 'Review: Even Laughs Are Rationed in a 'Whisky Galore!' Reboot', *New York Times* [online], available at: https://www.nytimes.com/2017/05/11/movies/whisky-galore-review-eddie-izzard.html (last accessed 26 November 2019).

Craig, C. (2009), 'Nostophobia', in J. Murray, F. Farley and R. Stoneman (eds), *Scottish Cinema Now*, Newcastle upon Tyne: Cambridge Scholars Publishing.

Diffrient, D. and Burgchardt, C. (2017), 'A Tale of Two Balloons: Intercultural Cinema and Transnational Nostalgia in *Le Voyage du Ballon Rouge*', in I. Smith and C. Verevis (eds), *Transnational Film Remakes*, Edinburgh: Edinburgh University Press.

Ferguson, B. (2016), 'Gillies Mackinnon 'May Never' Make Another Film in Scotland', *Scotsman* [online], available at: https://www.scotsman.com/news-2-15012/gillies-mackinnon-may-never-make-another-film-in-scotland-1-4164519 (last accessed 13 August 2019).

Ferguson, B. (2017), 'Irvine Welsh Film Rejected for "Not Being Scottish Enough"', *Scotsman* [online], available at: https://www.scotsman.com/news/people/rvine-welsh-film-rejected-for-not-being-scottish-enough-1-4422798 (last accessed 26 November 2019).

Harkness, A. (2016), 'Film Review: Whisky Galore!', *Scotsman* [online], available at: https://www.scotsman.com/arts-and-culture/film-and-tv/film-review-whisky-galore-1-4163430 (last accessed 26 November 2019).

Hill, J. (1999). 'Cinema', in J. Stokes and A. Reading (eds), *The Media in Britain: Current Debates and Developments*, Basingstoke: Palgrave, pp.74–87.

IMDB. (2016), 'Whisky Galore', *IMDB* [online], available at: https://www.imdb.com/title/tt4769214/ (last accessed 20 February 2020).

Lodge, G. (2017), 'Film Review: "Whisky Galore!"', *Variety* [online], available at: https://variety.com/2017/film/reviews/whisky-galore-review-1202424743/ (last accessed 26 November 2019).

McArthur, C, ed. (1982), *Scotch Reels: Scotland in Cinema and Television*, London: BFI.

McArthur, C. (2003), *Whisky Galore! & The Maggie*, London: BFI, I. B. Tauris.

McClintock, A. (1993), 'Family Feuds: Gender, Nationalism and the Family', *Feminist Review*, 44: 3, 61–80.

McLaughlin, M. (2019), 'The Growing Scandal over Donald Trump and Prestwick Airport – Martyn McLaughlin', *Scotsman* [online], available at: https://www.scotsman.com/news/opinion/columnists/the-growing-scandal-over-donald-trump-and-prestwick-airport-martyn-mclaughlin-1-5001401 (last accessed 10 September 2019).

Martin-Jones, D. (2014), 'Film Tourism as Heritage Tourism: Scotland, Diaspora and *The Da Vinci Code* (2006)', *New Review of Film and Television Studies*, 12: 2, 156–77.

Murray, J. (2019), 'Trainspotter's Delight: Issues and Themes in Scottish Film Criticism', in J. Hill (ed.), *A Companion to British and Irish Cinema*, London: Wiley-Blackwell, pp. 490–509.

Newland, P. (2011), 'To the West There is Nothing . . . Except America: The Spatial Politics of *Local Hero*', *Visual Culture in Britain*, 12: 2, 171–83.

Noordenbos, B. and Souch, I. (2021), 'Nostalgic Mediations of the Soviet Past in Nikolai Lebedev's Remake *The Crew* (2016)', in E. Cuelenaere, G. Willems and S. Joye (eds), *European Film Remakes*, Edinburgh: Edinburgh University Press, pp. 149–62.

Petrie, D. (2000), *Screening Scotland*. London: BFI, I. B. Tauris.

Pulver, A. (2016), 'Whisky Galore! Review – Twee, Comfy-Cardigan Film-Making', *Guardian* [online], available at: https://www.theguardian.com/film/2016/jun/26/whisky-galore-review-remake-postwar-ealing-comedy-alexander-mackendrick-gillies-mackinnon (last accessed 26 November 2019).

Stam, R. (2005), 'Introduction: The Theory and Practice of Adaptation', in R. Stam and A. Raengo (eds), *Literature and Film: A Guide to the Theory and Practice of Film Adaptation*, Oxford: Blackwell, pp. 1–52.

Verevis, C. (2006), *Film Remakes*, Edinburgh: Edinburgh University Press.

CHAPTER 14

'Remakable' Directors: The Contemporary Spanish Media Industry and Popular Discourses on Remakes and National Authorship*

Núria Araüna Baró

Open Your Eyes (*Abre los ojos*, 1997), Chilean-Spanish director Alejandro Amenábar's sophomore feature, is one of the most renowned movies from the Spanish revival of genre films beginning in the mid-90s (Willis 2003). Although widely praised by audiences, the film divided critics between those who viewed the young director's work as an achievement in national cinema and those who considered it merely a skilful use of genre clichés and audiovisual language characteristic of the Hollywood style. The polarised debate considers Amenábar's second film across two critical lines: as that of a promising *auteur* of Spanish cinema capable of successfully contributing unique names to the market and as that of a '*metteur-en-scène*', as described by Alexandre Astruc (in D'Lugo and Smith 2013), skilfully emulating the American (genre) cinema to make work with mass appeal for international audiences. The subsequent international interest resulted in the remake *Vanilla Sky* (2001), produced by and starring Tom Cruise, with Cameron Crowe as director, which was criticised for tempering the original film (Kercher 2015). With the premiere date notably close to that of Amenábar's film and the remake faithfully following its storyline, comparisons were inevitable – unsurprisingly, to the detriment of the American version. The debate around the remake reinforced the dichotomies between 'European/original' and 'Hollywood/copy' signalled by Mazdon (2000). Underlying this discussion was a negotiation of the notion of authorship in relation to genre and mode of production that has continued to be reproduced and that informs current evaluations of Spanish cinema.

The difficulties in defining what a remake is, or should be, as well as its blurred boundaries regarding adaptations, parodies, sequels and plagiarism, are indicative of the flexibility of its uses by different agents in the industry and the interpretations of audiences. As Kelleter and Loock (2017: 125) suggest, 'what counts as a "remake" and what counts as a "sequel" changes throughout the medium's history'. In particular production contexts, remaking practices are linked to prestigious filmmaking and acquire a value-added status (Verevis 2017), revealing the reactions to the underlying power relations of a transnational industry, the distinction between fluctuating genres and the *auteur*'s ability to navigate them. While remakes can make 'peripheral auteurs' known in the transnational circuit, in contemporary Spain the remaking of popular films authored by national directors has been interpreted as a recognition of salient local talents by relevant (that is, foreign, preferably Hollywood or other Anglo-Saxon) film industries. This has been the case with some of the most popular Spanish films remade abroad, such as the previously mentioned *Open Your Eyes* by Alejandro Amenábar, *[REC]* (2007), which inaugurated the saga signed by Jaume Balagueró and Paco Plaza, remade in the United States as *Quarantine* (2008), or *The Unknown* (*El Desconocido*, 2015), remade in Germany as *Steig. Nicht. Aus!* (2018) and with a highly publicised announcement in Spain of an as-yet-unfilmed American remake in 2017, reported to star Liam Neeson. In these three cases, the 'remakability' of the films has been interpreted by critics and the media as a seal of approval of the original features. In many cases, 'being remade' is understood as proof of individual directing skills, often related to a specific thematic sensitivity, as it occurred in relation to childhood illness and disability with the TV series *Red Banners* (*Polseres Vermelles*, 2011–13). Produced by Catalan TV, it was remade for audiences in Italy, Germany, Peru, Chile, Russia, France and, with less success, in the US. All were celebrated by the Spanish and Catalan press.

The discourses found in some reviews and cinephile online platforms reveal the persistence of stereotypes about Spanish cinema. These stereotypes are based on assumptions regarding budgetary constraints and overall quality of national audiovisual fiction, which is further reified in discourses that contribute to the problematic idea of peripheral talent being 'discovered by Hollywood'. The ideal that local talent could be picked up by Hollywood resonates with the Spanish versions of American films produced in Hollywood in the late 1920s and early 1930s (Riambau 2019).

In contrast to this model of authorship within the commercial transnational industries, the external image of Spanish cinema has been shaped by a specific kind of *auteur* cinema (Borau 1999), one which has had more resonance in select international film festivals than on the domestic market (Palacio and Ibáñez 2015) and which is understood as opposed to commerce and convention. For Borau, at least from the 1950s and until the 1990s, 'auteurs [. . .] accepted responsibility for guiding and redefining the film industry to which they belonged' (Borau 1999: xviii). The financial crisis in 2008 brought severe budget cuts, which affected the circuit of art house venues and independent film festivals developed since the late 1990s, as well as funding for film production (Perriam and Whittaker 2019). In this context, directors such as Ion de Sosa have employed strategies such as intertextuality and, in the following case-study, remaking and genre practices. These confer prominence in their work, adding a 'noise factor' to their minority products (Verevis 2017). Thus, by evoking *Blade Runner* (1982) in his second feature, *Androids Dream* (2014), Ion de Sosa promoted the film to broader audiences than would normally be expected for an experimental film. At the same time, the remake becomes an exercise in intertextual readership, as viewers can contrast the well-known original script and the novel by Philip K. Dick (on which *Blade Runner* is also based) with the new material offered by Sosa. This procedure of ironically incorporating low-status popular culture (such as 'remaking' and 'sci-fi') into directing of good repute is not an uncommon device in experimental/art film.

The public discourses by the Spanish film industry, directors and critics regarding these remaking practices give evidence as to how iterative narratives are a key mechanism to assess emerging Spanish directors. Hence, the relocation processes of remakes involve alterations in the generic understanding of the products and the evaluation or judgment of their auteurist quality. This essay observes the public discourses surrounding two highly contrasted remake practices in the context of the quality assessment of 'Spanish cinema'. Transnational remakes are approached for their ability to contribute 'to the "problematisation" of "national cinema" paradigms' (Herbert 2017: 211) by de-essentialising cinematic borders.

REMAKABLE TALENT

The fact that Spanish feature films have been remade in the United States has led to unusual academic and media attention paid to these productions, as demonstrated by the high number of papers devoted to *Open Your Eyes* and its American remake *Vanilla Sky* (among others, White 2003; Smith 2004; Simerka and Weimer 2005; Herbert 2006; Berthier 2007 and Jordan 2012a), which mostly focused on the intertextual relationships between both films. There is a notable critical pattern that describes the hidden potential and personality of low-budget 'international' films being discovered by studios powerful enough to make them shine. This critical appraisal seems to apply more often to the remake, even in cases where the original film had a high profile among local audiences. For example, *Open Your Eyes* was eagerly anticipated by audiences in Spain after Amenábar's successful debut *Thesis* (*Tesis*, 1996), a film halfway between thriller and horror, which handles themes of voyeurism and snuff movies. Amenábar's *opera prima* won seven Goya Awards from the Spanish Film Academy, including Best New Director, which placed him in a visible position. *Open Your Eyes* had support in its production from José Luis Cuerda – a prominent figure in Spanish cinema, who knew Amenábar from his work on short films and had previously produced *Thesis* – paving the way for the European co-productions of Sogecable and its film production branch Sogecine, after the Cable Law of 1995. This transnational corporate model of production coincided with José Maria Aznar's conservative government's cut-backs on public subsidy (Stone 2002; Herbert 2006). The film is a co-production between Las Producciones del Escorpión, Les Films Alain Sarde and Lucky Red for Sogetel (part of Sogecable) and, as Herbert (2006) indicates in his accurate analysis, therefore constitutively transnational. The film has a more refined texture than *Thesis* and marked a period of appreciation of the possibilities of Spanish cinema to align more closely with the assumed image and sound quality of American commercial audiovisuals. The fact that a Hollywood film star, Tom Cruise, noticed the filmmaker's second film and insisted on producing a remake in which he would also star seemed to establish Amenábar's position as a global director (Kercher 2015).

Given that *Open Your Eyes* has already been thoroughly analysed – both on its own and alongside its remake – I will simply summarise that the film and its remake deal with the identity crisis of César/David (Eduardo Noriega/ Tom Cruise), a rich and handsome young man who, following an accident that disfigures his face, is plunged into an indescribable nightmare. In some scenes, his physique is restored to its original beauty, while in others his face appears deformed. In much the same way, the troubled woman who caused the accident (Najwa Nimri/Cameron Diaz) and the good, 'pure' other woman who is the object of his desire (Penelope Cruz in both titles) are also superimposed in his perception, and so he becomes unable to distinguish them. The tragic fate causes the confused protagonist, in an attack of bewilderment, to kill the one he loves. Finally, the unintelligible puzzle is explained by showing that, following an accident 150 years before the diegesis, the protagonist agreed to be cryogenised by a multinational company, which sold him a designed 'mental happy life'. Everything that the viewer and the protagonist have experienced throughout the film, therefore, is nothing more than a fabricated dream contracted from the global company, a dream that somehow became violently distorted. Here the meta-reflexivity that Amenábar had exhibited in previous works, together with his reference to transnational media corporations in interviews (Lázaro-Reboll 2012), have led to the film being interpreted as a metaphor for the identity crisis of the national cinema, at a time when corporate capitalism consolidated his presence in the cable industries in Spain.

This transnational anger also informs the wider critical discourses around the films. Both in the IMDb and FilmAffinity online databases, which contain production data and user evaluations of films, *Open Your Eyes* aggregates better overall scores and ratings than *Vanilla Sky*. The cliché that the American industry tends to simplify and reduce the complexity of adapted works (Mazdon 2000) is reproduced in user comments, particularly in FilmAffinity, the largest Spanish-speaking online film community (Gavilán,

Martínez-Navarro and Fernández-Lores 2018). One user titles their post 'Cruise, Open Your Eyes' (Jorgitoxx, FilmAffinity 2007), in reference to the producer and leading man in *Vanilla Sky*, critiquing the remake as less skilful than Amenábar's original, before concluding that both versions are 'more or less of the same sort but [in the American remake] with an ending for idiots' (MoRcI, Filmmaffinity 2007). Despite the negative ratings for the remake, the sole fact that its rights were optioned by an American star is a recurring argument about the top-quality storytelling of *Open Your Eyes*, emphasising that 'Tom Cruise was so impressed with this "work of art", that he bought the rights to remake it [. . .] although the deeply flawed *Vanilla Sky* has nothing to do with the good one by Amenábar'. In this storyline, the American industry plays the role of peripheral talent scout and, since 'Americans aren't stupid', it is understood that 'Tom Cruise bought the rights to this film from Amenábar for a reason, even if the Hollywood result was disastrous' (turistf, FilmAffinity 2006). Hollywood's lack of artistic talent is reiterated, while its cultural power is simultaneously recognized by considering that the selection of a work by the American industry is a certification of quality. In the majority of the critical comparisons between the two films, with regards to the American version, Tom Cruise is largely referred to as the authorial reference, rather than Cameron Crowe. This ultimately minimises the director's authorship, despite Crowe's effort to show his own style and cross-reference of Amenábar's text. This is symptomatic of the Spanish audiences' interpretation of the celebrity-oriented status of Hollywood remaking.

On these online platforms (IMDb and FilmAffinity), contributors define quality as standardisation with respect to an international film model, mainly represented by American and international directors who moved to Hollywood and hold an *auteur* status: '[I]t may be my favourite film in Spanish cinema, up there with those directed by D. Lynch, R. Polanski, Cronenberg and even Hitchcock' (stikma, FilmAffinity 2009), or, as another viewer points out with a scathing critique of the role of the remake: 'Until last night, I still thought we were well below the level of quality that had been set by directors such as Polanski, Hitchcock, Bergman or even Nolan [. . .]. It was until yesterday, when I still hadn't seen *Open Your Eyes* [. . .].' She adds: 'For those who are against the remakes, I'll say, that they sometimes have their function, and it is nothing other than to exalt the sublime in the original' (Andrea Ballesta Manzano, FilmAffinity 2012). Following this argumentation, the 'remakability' of films by a more powerful industry is identified as the 'remarkability' of local directors, who in this imaginary stand out as exceptions, not at all representative of the general perception of local cinema. At the same time, this exceptionality is highlighted by contrast to an extended distrust and lack of acceptance towards Spanish cinema (D'Lugo and Smith 2013). A comment from 2007, a decade after the release of *Open Your Eyes*, states: '[I]t's fucking brilliant. And it shows. It's commercial cinema made in Spain, so successful that Hollywood was forced to make its own version [. . .]. Fuck, more films like this and the national industry would be on the rise' (metabaron, FilmAffinity 2007).

It is significant that, although the last decade of the twentieth century marked a period of inexhaustible film production and reinvigoration of Spanish cinema, with on average a quarter of new-release films being directorial debuts (Heredero 1999), the online critiques of *Open Your Eyes* point to the continuation of certain stereotypes regarding Spanish film. These implications echo the well-known provocative (and propagandistic) diagnosis of the Congress of Salamanca, which deemed national cinema as 'politically futile, socially false, intellectually worthless, aesthetically valueless and industrially paralytic' (Bardem, in MacKenzie 2014). Thus, although the interest in directors such as Amenábar will once again breathe fresh air into Spanish theatres, public reviews suggest that dismissive notions regarding the inferiority of local productions, motivated by the unequal industrial relations in the transnational field, still persist.

Notwithstanding its popular recognition, the authorial status of Amenábar has been challenged on occasion by some film critics for the lack of national markers in his work. The similarity with *Vanilla Sky* and the idea that *Open Your Eyes* was so easily 'translatable to other cultural contexts' (D'Lugo and Smith 2013: 145) might have contributed to this resistance. In fact, Triana Toribio (2003) closes her book on the history of Spanish popular cinema by considering the challenges that the director's third film, *The Others* (2001), poses for the definition of national cinema. Amenábar is said to have resorted to an academic construction of authorship that emphasises the metadiscursive character of his work (Lázaro-Reboll 2012) and naturalises Hollywood shooting techniques and genres (D'Lugo and Smith 2013). In some ways, Amenábar aligns with the romantic pattern of the *auteur* in the terms established by Andrew Sarris (in Jordan 2012a): self-taught, outrageously young in his first films, creator and screenwriter of his own ideas, director and composer of the soundtrack in many works, and selective, with a career of only seven feature-length films in a quarter of a century. In addition, his cinematic oeuvre, at least in the first two films, exhibits elements of generic and casting reiteration. His work is partially responsible for the relative international success of Spanish cinema in the 1990s and the increase in the audience share of national cinema, especially among young people. Even so, the positive aspects most highlighted in reviews are the technical quality, particularly of the cinematography, and narrative skill – which again some critics consider deceptive. In line with the discourses that have defended genre cinema in Spain, Amenábar has been defined as an author of a 'fresh' and uninhibited cinema that connects with audiences and is capable of reconciling art and commerce (Smith 2004). Herbert (2006) also points to the connection between Amenábar's cinema and a repositioning of Spanish identity in the 1990s, in the context of full integration into the European Union, the desire to standardise democracy and a change in the policy concerning subsidies for cinema that would prioritise the commercial results of films. For this author, there exists a relationship between Amenábar's cinema and 'the nation's increasing conformity with the global trends' (Herbert 2006: 29). From this perspective, the film would have been conceived with few markers of Spanish culture (and thus already 'Americanised'), rendering it suitable to be modulated in any context (Triana Toribio 2003). Thus, the remake would be a natural consequence of making the most of the (economic) potentialities of the text. This position – taken by some local critics averse to Amenábar since *Thesis* – is epitomised in Jordi Costa's comic book titled *My Problems with Amenábar* (see Lázaro-Reboll 2012). Jordi Costa is a renowned film critic and Spanish counterculture scholar who insisted on the idea that 'Amenábar generates consensus [. . .]. He has become a role model for later filmmakers who believe that being somewhat neutral, inoffensive, is a good thing' (Costa, in López-Palacios 2009).

All these tensions emerge in the discourses surrounding *Open Your Eyes* and its remake within the Spanish circuits. The meanings mobilised by the practice of the remake undoubtedly contribute to Amenábar's image as a young and cosmopolitan *auteur* responsible for the reinvigoration of Spanish cinema. This model of the *auteur* seems capable of traversing commercial paths and achieving the transnational impact of a Hollywood remake from a Spanish industry that has 'historically failed to produce international hits' (Rodríguez Ortega 2013: 253). However, comparisons between original and remake have tended to highlight the similarities and, as such, the international approval of Amenábar.

ANDROIDS DREAM: AGAINST GLAMOUR, THE NATION

The box-office success of Amenábar's first two features has influenced subsequent productions (Jordan 2012b) such as *Darkness* (2002) and *Fragile* (2005), both films by Jaume Balagueró released before *[REC]*. Its resonance also appears in the sound debut of José Antonio Bayona, *The Orphanage* (2007), defined by Jordan as almost a remake of Amenábar's *The Others* (2001). In fact, Bayona's expansive movement from horror towards other genres epitomises one of the two cinematic traditions that, according to Palacio and Ibáñez (2015), embody the contemporary debate on Spanish cinema and, particularly, on whether the model should be defended (and subsidised) by the state. Opposing the model of 'industrial films aimed at box-office takings' (Amenábar's and Bayona's) is what some critics call, not without debate, the *Other Spanish Cinema*, 'conceived with greater creative license and less subordination to market conditions and the interests of the television industry' (Palacio and Ibáñez 2015). This term was coined by critic Carlos Losilla (2013) in the Spanish reference magazine

Caimán to define a heterogeneous movement which responds more faithfully to romanticised auteurist ambitions and, for some, reiterates the controversial model of 'low-cost' filmmaking (Engel 2015). For Perriam and Whittaker, the label embraces a current of 'exportable art cinema' (2019: 5).

In this vein, the critical dialogue around the remake *Androids Dream* (*Sueñan los Androides*, 2014) allows us to observe another semantic contour from the disputed label *Other Spanish Cinema* in relation to modes of authorship and nationality. The film title makes a clear allusion to Philip K. Dick's novel *Do Androids Dream of Electric Sheep?* which inspired Ridley Scott's *Blade Runner*. The film was shot in Spain and released in 2014; it has been described as a '*castizo*' (genuine Spanish) *Blade Runner*, an idea further reflected in the programmers' discourses and press reviews of the film. *Androids Dream* cost roughly 70,000 Euros. None of the crew were paid for their work (yet salaries were budgeted), a situation not uncommon in the work of emerging independent filmmakers in Spain. The film was shot over a period of three years, one week per year, and received a grant of 20,000 Euros from an experimental German fund (Berlin-Brandenburg Medienboard). This was the second feature film by director Ion de Sosa. His first feature, *True Love* (2011), was a self-fiction personal diary that, according to some critics, opened up the *Other Spanish Cinema* movement (Engel 2015). In *Androids Dream*, De Sosa was legally advised to ensure that the narrative structure remained loose so that the film would not be (legally) considered a remake or adaptation of Philip K. Dick's novel (De Sosa, in Salas and Granero 2015). However, the film is set in 2052, the year in which K. Dick's copyright expires, so that in case of legal issues the director may argue that the film 'came to him from the future' (De Sosa, interviewed by Pérez Guevara 2016). Despite not having the rights necessary for a remake of *Blade Runner* or an official adaptation of *Do Androids Dream of Electric Sheep?* the film is constructed through a combination of Philip K. Dick and Ridley Scott's narratives and visual motifs. Basically, we follow Rick Deckard's pursuit of the replicants. Thus, while maintaining Philip K. Dick's despairing subtext, *Androids Dream* takes the story to Benidorm. The coastal city is known particularly in northern Europe as a tourist resort for retirees, loaded with kitsch references thanks to productions such as the popular *Benidorm* TV series, and constitutes a cliché in Spanish development-era films (Martínez-Puche and Martínez Puche 2018). Benidorm embodies a kitsch sensibility and an economic model (based on construction and tourism) that led to the collapse of the Spanish economy in 2008. The director's statement elaborates on the importance of location: '[V]acation cities that experienced such growth in a very short period of time are enclaves designed in the late fifties, to sell an idyllic image of Spain as a society based on a serving staff economy and a place of leisure and fun [. . .] it is a slow-motion dying paradise' (De Sosa 2015). In the film, the androids are young blue-collar workers and practically the only characters who talk and demand the viewer's identification. Through time, camera focus and *mise-en-scène*, emphasis is placed on their work, in contrast to the leisure and folkloric non-activities of the rest of the (older) population. Like many other remakes, it adapts some of its storytelling and meaning devices to another context, time and space. Here, however, contemporary Spain is not merely the setting, but the main theme, highlighted by wide shots of landscapes, folk music ('*coplas*') that replaces Vangelis' soundtrack, the characters' modes of expression and its portrayal of the country as pessimistically attached to the past. De Sosa's strategy is to accentuate a particular kind of 'Spanishness' in *Androids Dream*, with Benidorm as a showcase for Franco's retro-progress. The remake renationalises the story, exoticising the décor and reminiscing about the *esperpento* genre – a Spanish genre developed by playwright Valle-Inclán to give expression to 'the tragic sense of Spanish life' (Valle-Inclán, in Dougherty 1980). The years during which Ion de Sosa shot *Androids Dream*, Spanish film production emphasised the effects of the crisis (Perriam and Whittaker 2019), by foregrounding crime and robbery movies (Álvarez 2018) and through the resurgence of a documentary that analyses the uncertain present (Araüna and Quílez 2018), in tension with the heterogeneous drawer of the *Other Cinema* (more depoliticised, according to Palacio and Ibáñez 2015). Between 2012 and 2013, when the film was shot, the unemployment rate in Spain had reached its highest level since General Franco's dictatorship (over 25 percent, according to the Spanish Statistical Office and the Organisation for Economic Cooperation and Development).

Androids Dream has circulated on the international film circuit but has not had major impact among Spanish mainstream audiences. It has only four user reviews on FilmAffinity and two on IMDb, one of which considers the film 'unintelligible' and 'huge crap' and recommends that viewers avoid it. This same reviewer seems unaware of the process of filmmaking and complains about the bad quality of the flashbacks and the lack of verisimilitude of the futuristic setting (Manuel, FilmAffinity 2014). None of the reviews explicitly mention the term 'remake' or 'adaptation'; yet, the reference to Scott's film is considered a 'tribute and/or cover [. . .] of] *the Spanish way*' (Turbolover 1984, FilmAffinity 2015). Also, the references to *Blade Runner* and Philip K. Dick's novel are framed as a 'metalinguistic film exercise' which mixes 'realist *costumbrism* [. . .] action thriller and surrealist dialogues which drift into a sci-fi fable' (Tomgut, FilmAffinity 2015). Overall, the Spanishness of the film devices and themes are recognized and highlighted as contrasting with the elegance of Ridley Scott's film. The D'A Festival brief of the film reads 'Halfway a minimalist remake of Blade Runner and a hilarious documentary on the future of Benidorm, *Androids* could be defined as *crappy* sci-fi [. . .]. Its aim is to counter the miserable essences of the most Spanish things to the sophistication of sci-fi'.

In his Berlinale report, film critic Gregorio Belinchón (2015) highlighted that films such as *Androids Dream* are difficult to find on regular Spanish screens on account of their radical character. It is important to remember that the preferred audience of *Androids Dream*, like most Spanish independent films, is in the international circuit of film festivals over local theatres (Arantzazu-Ruiz 2017). As Palacio and Ibáñez (2015) point out, Spanish cinema presents a unique case with a very high production ratio of films, which maintains an audience share that does not manage to reach the ceiling of 20 percent or to cement itself among the domestic audience, but which in turn has an area of legitimation at festivals. *Androids Dream* presents the formal references of an *auteur* within this circuit, one particularly connected to low-budget cinema. It is obviously uncomfortable to talk about *Androids Dream* as a remake. The story is only vaguely anchored in the 'original' and relies on the spectator's knowledge of the references to make sense of it. In fact, the selling point is not simply the idea of a remake, but this re-genrefication of *Blade Runner* (from sci-fi noir to bizarre Spanish quasi-documentary art film), which promises the pleasure of watching a *bad film*.

CONCLUSION: THE NATION UNDONE, THE NATION REDONE

This essay focused on how the interpretation and production practices of remakes function along a transnational axis of power relationships where national definitions are redrawn. The ability of films to move from one national context to another is read as a symptom of success in terms of quality, to some extent as a result of the 'engrained scepticism of Spanish audiences towards their own local cinema and its pretensions to quality' (D'Lugo and Smith 2013: 145). These meanings are reinforced by an apparent sense, expressed by Spanish reviewers online, of being a peripheral industry, in contrast to Hollywood's marketing machine (Kercher 2015). These interpretative frames still revolve around the idea of the author-director as primarily responsible for the overall meaning of films, overcoming contextual and production barriers. In the films analysed, the remaking practices are read as promoters of this authorship, precisely because of how they allow a group of directors to move between different fields of production and meaning. By selecting two contrasting cases in which the remaking practices intersect with the valorisation of 'national cinema', the remake becomes a practice of promotion of authorship, even when the result is considered bad – or, partially, *precisely* because of that. In this regard, we can agree with Cuelenaere, Willems and Joye (2019) that, in the practices of the remake as in the interpretation of other texts, the meanings always exist and emerge in relation to the similarities to and differences from others: *Androids Dream* constructs authorship in opposition to *Blade Runner*, and audiences reinforce Amenábar's authorship by contrasting it to its remake *Vanilla Sky*. Remakes as contrasting devices allow us to observe how Amenábar becomes 'transnationally viable' when seen through *Vanilla Sky*, while *Androids Dream* makes the most of national (ironic) specificity against *Blade Runner*, establishing a continuity with the Spanish *auteur* tradition of the 1960s and 1970s (D'Lugo and Smith 2013). This does not undermine the transnational appeal of *Androids Dream*, which also contains references to art film directors such as Antonioni, Godard, Clarke or Seidl (Engel 2015), when it is aimed at international film festivals. Yet, the appeal of *Androids Dream* with regard to *Blade Runner* is indeed to be 'very Spanish', while a look at the translateability of *Open Your Eyes* to *Vanilla Sky* 'suggests the inevitable dissolution of the nation as an operative category for classifying film productions' (D'Lugo 2013: 39).

Marsha Kinder (1993) points out that through 'the local/global interface' we can interpret how national meanings, which participate in a public redefinition of the nation, operate in cinema, warning of the risks of essentialising the national conditions of cinema. Both in Amenábar's virtual simulation and in De Sosa's domestic files implanted in the androids, identity fades and becomes a hallucination; something that has to be redone and yet easily loses any stable meaning. However, the evaluation around remakes shows that the recurring critiques against Amenábar's films, which have had much more audience than the *Other Spanish Cinema* works, are often justified by mobilising a tradition of authorship strongly anchored in the cultural context (for an account of the specificities of the *auteur* theory in Spain, see D'Lugo and Smith 2013).

The debate around the foundations of state nationalism is alive and well in Spain, forty years after a transition that aimed at standardising Spain among European democracies. Still wounded by an economic crisis that hit Spain in an especially traumatising way – in addition to the territorial crisis brought about by the Catalan referendum – the so-called 'Spanish Exceptionalism' might have come to an end (Turnbull-Dugarte 2019). Some consequences are the notable electoral results and the normalisation of a 'New Spanish Nationalism' far-right discourse (Minder 2019), which appeals to the catholic national values that have been so strongly satirised in the Spanish film *auteur* tradition. It is noteworthy that a screening of Amenábar's last film, *While at War* (*Mientras dure la guerra*, 2019), was interrupted by far-right protesters who entered the venue and shouted nationalist slogans such as 'Long live Spain'. In this context, it is pertinent to reflect on how different versions of Spanishness are redefined in cinema and played in its transnational circuits and, moreover, to observe which directors will be its ambassadors.

NOTES

* The author wishes to acknowledge the enormous work undertaken by the editors of this volume. Also, Ruth Gilbert has to be credited for her essential review of the English version of this essay. Finally, Toni L. Querol has provided insightful comments about Benidorm in Spanish cinema.

REFERENCES

Álvarez, Marta (2018), 'De la reivindicación a la ira: Espacios de crisis en el cine español contemporáneo', *Iberoamericana*, XVIII: 69, 81–102.
Arantzazu Ruiz, Paula (2017), 'Cine español, aclamado en festivales, poco visto en salas', *Cinemanía*, 1 July, available at: https://cinemania.20minutos.es/noticias/cine-espanol-aclamado-festivales-poco-visto-salas (last accessed 20 January 2020).
Araüna, Núria and Laia Quílez (2018), 'Crisis económica, transformación política y expresión documental: Crónica del anhelo (más que del cambio)', *Journal of Spanish Cultural Studies*, 19: 4, 427–43.
Bardem, José Luis [1955] (2014), 'Salamanca Manifesto and Conclusions of the Congress of Salamanca', in S. MacKenzie (ed.), *Film Manifestos and Global Cinema Cultures: A Critical Anthology*, California: California University Press, pp. 144–48.
Belinchón, Gregorio (2015), El triunfo del Otro Cine Español, *El País*, 12 February 12, available at: https://elpais.com/cultura/2015/02/12/actualidad/1423752953_582446.html (last accessed 22 December 2019).
Berthier, Nancy (2007), 'Cine y nacionalidad: El caso del remake' in P. Burkhard and J. Türschmann (eds), *Miradas glocales: Cine español en el cambio de milenio*, Iberoamericana Editorial, Madrid, pp. 337–50.
Borau, José Luis (1999), 'Prologue: The Long March of the Spanish Cinema towards Itself', in P. Williams Evans (ed.), *Spanish Cinema: The Auteurist Tradition*, Oxford: Oxford University Press, pp. i–xix.
Cami-Vela, M. (2014), 'Directoras de cine en Cataluña: Un recorrido histórico', *Revista d'Estudis Catalans*, 27, 27–45
Costa, Jordi, 'La bestia negra de Amenábar', *El País*, 9 October, available at: https://elpais.com/diario/2009/10/09/tentaciones/1255112574_850215.html (last accessed 12 January 2020).
Cuelenaere, Eduard, Gertjan Willems and Stijn Joye (2019), 'Remaking Identities and Stereotypes: How Film Remakes Transform and Reinforce Nationality, Disability, and Gender', *European Journal of Cultural Studies*, 22: 5–6, 613–29.
De Sosa, Ion (2015), 'Director's notes', available at: https://www.dropbox.com/sh/qvmwtr5yhbp6d45/AADbG3_fShHBcXPkvgI8tD46a?dl=0 (last accessed 17 January 2020).
D'Lugo, Marvin (2013), 'The Producer-Author as Transnational Enterpriser', in J. Labanyi and T. Pavlovic (eds), *A Companion to Spanish Cinema*, Oxford: Wiley-Blackwell, pp. 30–40.
D'Lugo, Marvin and Paul Julian Smith (2013), 'Auteurism and the Construction of the Canon', in J. Labanyi and T. Pavlovic (eds), *A Companion to Spanish Cinema*, Oxford: Wiley-Blackwell, pp. 113–19.
Dougherty, Dru (1980), 'The Tragicomic Don Juan: Valle-Inclán's Esperpento de las galas del difunto (The Dead Man's Duds)', *Modern Drama*, 23: 1, 44–57.
Engel, Philip (2014), '"Sueñan los Androides", o Blade Runner en Benidorm', *Fotogramas*, 11 November, available at: https://www.fotogramas.es/festival-de-cine-europeo-de-sevilla/a3539888/suenan-los-androides-o-blade-runner-en-benidorm/ (last accessed 12 January 2020).
Gavilán, Diana, Gema Martínez-Navarro and Susana Fernández-Lores (2018), 'Social Influence in Online Film Communities: Filmaffinity as Case Study', *Estudios del mensaje periodístico*, 24: 1, 551–65.
Heredero, Carlos F. (1999), *20 nuevos directores del cine español*, Madrid: Alianza Editorial.

Herbert, Daniel (2017), 'The Transnational Film Remake in the American Press', in I. Robert Smith and C. Verevis (eds), *Transnational Film Remakes*, Edinburgh: Edinburgh University Press, pp. 210–23.

Herbert, Daniel (2006), 'Sky's the limit: Transnationality and Identity in *Abre los Ojos* and *Vanilla Sky*', *Film Quaterly*, 60: 1, 28–38.

Jordan, Barry (2012a), *Alejandro Amenábar*, Manchester: Manchester University Press.

Jordan, Barry (2012b), 'Alejandro Amenábar and Contemporary Spanish Horror', in P. Allmer, E. Brick and D. Huxley (eds), *European Nightmares: Horror Cinema in Europe Since 1945*, London and New York: Wallflower Press, pp. 141–52.

Kelleter, Frank and Kathleen Loock (2017), 'Hollywood Remaking as Second-Order Serialization', in F. Kelleter (ed.), *Media of Serial Narrative*, Columbus: Ohio State University Press, pp. 125–47.

Kercher, Dona (2015), *Latin Hitchcock: How Almodóvar, Amenábar, De la Iglesia, Del Toro and Campanella Became Notorious*, New York: Columbia University Press.

Kinder, Marsha (1993), *Blood Cinema: The Reconstruction of National Identity in Spain*, California: University of California Press.

Lázaro-Reboll, Antonio (2012), *Spanish Horror Films*, Edinburg: Edinburgh University Press.

López Palacios, Íñigo (2009), 'La bestia negra de Amenábar', *El País*, 9 October, available at: https://elpais.com/diario/2009/10/09/tentaciones/1255112574_850215.html (last accessed 15 January 2020).

Losilla, Carlos (2013), 'Emerge "otro" cine español: Un impulso colectivo'. *Caimán Cuadernos de Cine*, 19, 6–8.

Martínez Puche, Salvador and Antonio Martínez Puche (2018), 'How Tourism Imaginary has been Updated in the New Spanish Sun-and-Beach Comedy: *Fin de curso*, *Atasco en la nacional* and *Benidorm, mon amour*', *Via*, 14, available at: https://journals.openedition.org/viatourism/2971?lang=es (last accessed 9 August 2020).

Mazdon, Lucy (2000), *Encore Hollywood: Remaking French Cinema*, London: British Film Institute.

Minder, Raphael (2019), 'Spain's Far Right Emerges as a Force by Tapping a New Nationalism', *The New York Times*, 11 November, available at: https://www.nytimes.com/2019/11/11/world/europe/spain-election-vox-abascal.html (last accessed 23 December 2019).

Palacio, Manuel and Juan Carlos Ibáñez (2015), 'A New Model for Spanish Cinema: Authorship and Globalization: The Films of Javier Rebollo', *Journal of Spanish Cultural Studies*, 16:1, 29–43.

Pérez Guevara, José Antonio (2016), 'Interview to Ion de Sosa', available at: https://www.youtube.com/watch?v=ZEHPwLnxZDw (last accessed 17 January 2020).

Perriam, Chris and Tom Whittaker (2019), 'Introduction: Contemporary Spanish Screen Media and Responses to Crisis and Aftermath', *Hispanic Research Journal*, 20: 1, 2–9.

Riambau, Esteve (2019), 'The Rise and Fall of Spanish Versions (1929–1931), According to Cinelandia Magazine', in M. E. De Las Carreras and J. C. Horak (eds), *Hollywood Goes Latin: Spanish-Language Cinema in Los Angeles*, Bloomington: Indiana University Press, pp. 43–50.

Rodríguez Ortega, Vicente (2013), 'Between the National and the Global: The Historical Film from the 1960s to the Present', in J. Labanyi and T. Pavlovic (eds), *A Companion to Spanish Cinema*, Oxford: Wiley-Blackwell, pp. 249–57.

Salas, Lucía and Lucas Granero (2015), 'Sueñan los Androides, entrevista a Ion de Sosa y Chema García Ibarra', *Las Pistas Cine*, 6 October, available at: https://laspistascine.wordpress.com/2015/10/06/suenan-los-androides-entrevista-a-ion-de-sosa-y-chema-garcia-ibarra/ (last accessed 18 August 2019)

Simerka, Barbara and Christopher Weimer (2005), 'Tom Cruise and the Seven Dwarves: Cinematic Postmodernisms in *Abre los ojos* and *Vanilla Sky*', *American Drama*, 14: 2, 1–15.

Smith, Paul Julian (2004), 'High Anxiety: *Abre los Ojos/Vanilla Sky*', *Journal of Romance Studies*, 4: 1, 91–102.

Triana Toribio, Núria (2003), *Spanish National Cinema*, London: Routledge.

Turnbull-Dugarte, Stuart J. (2019), 'Explaining the End of Spanish Exceptionalism and Electoral Support for Vox', *Research & Politics*, online first.

Verevis, Constantine (2017), 'New Millenial Remakes', in F. Kelleter (ed.), *Media of Serial Narrative*, Columbus: Ohio State University Press, pp. 148–66.

Vivar, Rosana (2016), 'A Film Bacchanal: Playfulness and Audience Sovereignty in San Sebastian Horror and Fantasy Film Festival', *Participations: Journal of Audience and Reception Studies*, 13: 1, 234–51.

White, Anne M. (2003), 'Seeing Double? The Remaking of Amenábar's *Abre Los Ojos* as Cameron Crowe's *Vanilla Sky*', *International Journal of Iberian Studies*, 15: 3, 187–96.

Willis, Andy (2003), 'Spanish Horror and the Flight from Art Cinema', in M. Jancovich et al. (eds), *Defining Cult Movies: The Cultural Politics of Oppositional Taste*, Manchester: Manchester University Press, pp. 71–83.

CHAPTER 15

Remakes and Globally-Oriented European Cinema: Contemporary Industrial Practices and Shifting Hierarchies

Christopher Meir

INTRODUCTION: THE CULTURAL IMPERIALISM
DEBATE REVISITED

Debates about the political economy of remakes of European films have always assumed the American industry as the sole hegemonic force and seen the practice as to varying degrees symptomatic of the macro-level relationships between Hollywood and the European film industry.[1] To put it crudely, Hollywood is seen as the stronger industry that exploits smaller industries such as those of Europe, virtually mining it for raw materials to turn into English-language remakes for international release, including in the home countries of the original films in question. Such assumptions are pervasive in popular culture and journalistic film reception up the present day, and they have also been omnipresent in academic discussions of the practice. Such can be seen in recent writing on European remakes, including articles by Mazdon (2015; 2017) and Leitch (2019), to name just a few, which posit remaking as something that the American screen industries 'do' to the European film industry.

These recent writings from eminent figures in remake studies are in various ways reactions to a long-standing academic concern with American remakes of European films, a concern which has profoundly shaped our understanding of remaking generally, as well as the collective understanding of the European film industry. To appreciate the fundamental role that debates around this specific practice have played in the field, we can look back to the academic discussions surrounding the wave of American remakes of French films in the 1980s and 1990s. As has been widely discussed, this wave of remaking produced a string of high-profile commercial successes in Hollywood, including

3 Men and a Baby (1987), *Sommersby* (1993), *True Lies* (1994) and many others. As the critical literature that examines this wave has shown, despite – or perhaps because of – the popularity of these remakes, journalistic discourses at the time took issue with the practice of remaking and routinely portrayed the European originals as the inherently superior object. Mazdon's book on the cycle (2000), as well as Forrest and Koos's collection *Dead Ringers* (2002a), sought to problematise the reductive and misleading logic of this reception and to push remake studies beyond its obsession with actual industrial hierarchies and supposed cultural ones. In doing so, these critical texts were formative for 'remaking' the field of remake studies, opening up new avenues of research that continue to produce stimulating work on remakes up to the present day.

Despite the seminal importance of these works, this chapter will argue that the time has come to revisit the issues that helped to draw critical attention to European remakes all those years ago. Thus, it will argue that the European film industry has undergone fundamental changes in the last two decades, changes that can be uniquely illustrated by remaking practices. In order to explore these changes, this chapter will first detail the corporate landscape of contemporary European cinema and then examine the remaking practices that have developed alongside those corporate shifts, showing that European enterprises are very much capable of the sorts of remaking that were long thought to be the exclusive domain of the Hollywood majors. It will then examine several as-of-yet unrealised film projects that perhaps speak to the limits of European studios' ambitions at the present moment. Uniting all the case-studies will be the overarching argument that remaking can tell us about larger industrial dynamics and *vice versa*. As will be seen, the exact permutations of this practice *vis-à-vis* European, American and other national producers and distributors help to throw evolving industrial power dynamics into relief, further problematising what Smith and Verevis have called the 'simplistic binaries' of Hollywood/Commerce versus Europe/Art that underpin discourses around remakes (2017: 3) and which I would argue implicitly structure the way in which the global film industry is understood generally.

THE EMERGENCE OF EUROPEAN MULTI-NATIONALS

Since the re-emergence of French multimedia conglomerate Vivendi following its near miss with bankruptcy in 2003, the industrial underpinning of European cinema has undergone fundamental changes. The most important of these changes has been the consolidation of a number of large-scale enterprises that have in various ways vertically and horizontally integrated – effectively combining distribution and production activities with expansion into television drama – while in several cases also expanding their operations to include multiple national markets. In a series of recent publications, I have attempted to chronicle and analyse these changes and their impact on the works produced in Europe, as well as the very idea of European cinema itself (for example, Meir 2016; 2018; 2019a; 2019b).

While these developments have thus been documented and analysed elsewhere, a brief recap of the major players involved will help to set the stage for the discussion that follows regarding the roles that these companies are playing in the arena of remaking European cinema. The single most influential company in this regard has been Studiocanal, the production and distribution arm of France's Canal Plus, itself part of the above-mentioned Vivendi conglomerate. Rising from the ashes of Vivendi Universal, the company has since 2006 built up a film distribution network that spans five countries and has also developed an extensive network of television drama producers (Meir 2016). Studiocanal's emergence as a global player in film and television has been highlighted by the *Paddington* film franchise – which will soon be expanded into a television series – as well as numerous popular and critically acclaimed drama series such as the British shows *Happy Valley* and *Years and Years*, among others.

Another major player has been Entertainment One, a London-based studio which at its peak had direct distribution operations in seven countries – the UK, the US, Canada, Belgium, the Netherlands, Spain and Germany, even though this was recently scaled back as the company ended its operations in Australia and New Zealand in January 2019 – as well as a prolific television production operation that generates hundreds of hours of content annually. While Entertainment One is by European standards a very big company indeed – in terms of overall revenue, the company brings in more than Studiocanal, for example – Entertainment One is not as invested in film production as its peers in the European sector, since much of its television production is based in Canada and its products are typically made for Canadian and American broadcasters. For this reason, it does not feature very prominently in my scholarship on European cinema, including this chapter. That said, among the many important films and series that the company has had a hand in are the Oscar-winning film *Spotlight* (2015) and series such as *Designated Survivor* and *Peppa Pig*, its single most iconic property.

Three additional players worth highlighting here are all based in France. These are Wild Bunch, which has distribution operations in five countries (Germany, France, Italy, Spain and Austria), as well as a portfolio of film sales operations (including the eponymous Wild Bunch label, as well as Insiders/ IMR and Elle Driver, among others). The company also has a television distribution business that has been involved in series such as *Medici* and *Four Seasons in Havana*, among others. Pathé is, of course, one of the oldest names in the film business and currently runs distribution operations in three European countries (France, the UK and Switzerland), while also running exhibition chains in three states (France, Switzerland and the Netherlands). Pathé is unique among this cadre of companies for not having expanded into television production or distribution, remaining instead a company focused exclusively on film.

Finally, EuropaCorp has been an important player during this period, even if only as a cautionary tale. The company sought to capitalise on the international success of its blockbuster films *Lucy* and the *Taken* franchise by starting its own American distribution operation in the form of RED, which was a joint venture with the American company Relativity Media. This subsidiary started operating in September of 2015, but was effectively shut down in January of 2017 – in a span of only fifteen months – after a string of box office failures on the US market and overspending on the production of Luc Besson's *Valerian and the City of a Thousand Planets* (2017). While EuropaCorp is thus no longer a major player in the European film industry –indeed, the company's fortunes have gone from bad to worse with a series of accusations of sexual misconduct lodged against founder and CEO Luc Besson – it was nevertheless an important player in this moment in the history of the European industry, even if it reminds us of the underlying fragility of that same industry.

Besides these multi-national players, there are also two other groups of relatively large, well-capitalised European films that are worth discussing here. The first of these is also made up of multi-nationals, but unlike those previously discussed, these companies tend to operate only as producers and distributors within specific regional and linguistic zones. Prominent examples of this kind of company include Scandinavia's two largest integrated players: TrustNordisk and SF Studios. Besides producing and distributing films and series in Scandinavian languages, the two have collectively made English-language titles such as *Borg/ McEnroe* (2017) and all of Lars von Trier's Anglophone works. German-based Constantin is also multi-national in that it distributes films in its home country, as well as in Austria and German-speaking Switzerland. This scale has allowed the company to produce Anglophone blockbusters such as the *Resident Evil* franchise and more modestly budgeted films, such as *Polar* (2019) and others, in addition to its consistent output of German-language films.

Besides these multi-nationals, the contemporary period has seen the emergence of several single-country studios with the capacity to produce and distribute films and series internationally, albeit on a more sporadic basis than their larger counterparts. The most pertinent example for this chapter's concerns is Gaumont, one of the world's oldest continuously operating film studios. Unsurprisingly, Gaumont has had many French-language hits in France; some of these have also been distributed abroad, most notably in recent years *Intouchables* (*Les Intouchables*, 2011), which grossed over $400 million internationally, previously unheard-of for Francophone cinema. Gaumont has also been active in Anglophone film and television production, having made films such as *The Death of Stalin* (2017), as well as television series such as *Hannibal* (NBC,

2013–15) and the *Narcos* franchise, among others. While Gaumont is not the only single-country studio with such international ambition – see, for example, the Italian public service broadcaster RAI – it has been the most active and influential among its peers.

Whatever their specific scale or regional coverage, the collective emergence of these companies has had and continues to have profound effects on European cinema. I have elsewhere attempted to catalogue and analyse many of these, but in what follows I will focus on how these companies have brought two particular brands of remaking to the European film industries. As Forrest and Koos have argued (2002: 26), virtually every national industry in the world remakes films, and in recent years numerous scholars have demonstrated that European industries are no different when it comes to remaking films in local languages (see, for example, Cuelenaere et al. 2019; Fernández Labayen and Martín Morán 2019). What appears remarkable about the contemporary period in European industrial history, however, and what has gone without significant commentary is that for the first time European companies are making concerted efforts to remake films in English, effectively usurping the business model long deployed by the Hollywood studios. Even if these studios do not have the global distribution network that their Hollywood counterparts do, European studios are currently capable of taking existing non-Anglophone films and remaking them for international audiences, including their respective distribution territories (in the cases of films being remade as films), but also elsewhere in the world via their international sales operations. In the following two sections, this essay will examine two variations on this practice, each of which tells us slightly different things about the relative position of each company in the economic hierarchy of the global film industry.

NEW REMAKING PRACTICES IN EUROPEAN CINEMA I: LIBRARY-BASED REMAKES

The first practice that I will examine involves studios taking their own libraries of films and television programmes and in many cases remaking them into English, or in the case of already Anglophone films at least updating the films by remaking them. The ability of the studios to carry out such a strategy can be traced back to an important corporate development that happened gradually over time but accelerated especially from the 1990s onwards. This was the establishment and development by European studios of large libraries of rights to existing films and television series. As numerous historians have demonstrated, the ownership of such libraries of content has been vital to the financial strength of the Hollywood studios, who have leveraged these assets to create ancillary lines of revenue beyond theatrical distribution while also re-releasing and remaking library titles as 'new' films or series (for example, Hoyt 2014; Puttnam 1997). Until the 1990s, the lack of such a resource was considered a major impediment to the industrial development of European companies, depriving them of the relatively stable cash flow afforded by such an asset (Puttnam 1997: 184).

At the very same time as David Puttnam was pointing out this shortcoming in his book-length polemic against Hollywood's dominance over European screens (Puttnam 1997), two European studios with global ambitions were actively engaged in buying up back catalogues of content: the Dutch-based Polygram Filmed Entertainment (PFE) and Le Studio Canal+ (LSC) (along with its corporate siblings Canal+ and Canal Image), the forerunner of today's Studiocanal. Both pursued libraries very aggressively during this decade and often bid against one another in library auctions. PFE, for example, was said to have paid over $100 million more than the lowest bidder in an auction for the Epic catalogue in 1997 (Peers and Weiner 1997). Such spending, along with aggressive spending on distribution subsidiaries, would contribute to deficits at the company that ultimately helped convince corporate parents Philips to sell its entire Polygram Music division to Seagram's, which promptly shut down PFE and sold off its assets (Meir 2019a: 43). In LSC's case, it was a mix of opportunism *vis-à-vis* faltering independent studios in Hollywood (for instance, DEG and Carolco), on one hand, and the parent company Canal+'s ambition to expand into the rest of the Western European market, on the other, that helped to underpin the library-buying spree at the company, as it had formed a partnership with Germany's Bertelsman and was set on acquiring content for a pan-European pay-television network (Meir 2019a: 67–71). While PFE did not survive the 1990s, LSC/Studiocanal did and, following the Vivendi Universal debacle of the early 2000s, was able to emerge with a library that, according to different estimates, varies in size between 6,000 and 9,000 titles. In either case, this would make it one of the largest libraries in the western world.

This library has played a major role in Studiocanal's re-emergence as a global player since its acquisition of the British distribution outfit Optimum Releasing in 2006. Speaking to the multi-faceted importance of the library, the groundwork for this acquisition was laid by discussions between Optimum and Studiocanal regarding the rights to re-release Carol Reed's *The Third Man* (1948) (Meir 2019a: 105). Most of its works since this point as an integrated production-distributor fall into this category of library-based remakes (and as we will see, many others fall into the other category that I will outline below), including the second Anglophone film it made during this period, *Chloe* (2009), a remake of the French film *Nathalie* . . . (2003). Subsequent library remakes include *The Tourist* (2010), based on the French film *Anthony Zimmer* (2005), *A Bigger Splash* (2015), based on *La Piscine* (1969), and remakes of the British films *Brighton Rock* (1948) and *And Soon the Darkness*... (1970), both remade in 2010. In addition to these remakes which have made it to the screen, numerous others have been reported to be in development, including projects based on the Nicholas Roeg film *Don't Look Now* (1973) and the Graham Greene adaptation *The Fallen Idol* (1948).

The company has also been very active in attempting to get its films remade as TV series, although with limited success. Following the company's entry into the television production business in 2012–13 with the acquisition of Germany-based Tandem Communications and the UK's Red Productions, Studiocanal set a number of films for development into series, seeking to imitate the success that the Hollywood studios have had in recent years with such film spin-offs as *Twelve Monkeys*, *Fargo* and others. Red Productions, for example, developed projects in this vein based on a range of British films to which Studiocanal had acquired the library rights, including *Billy Liar* (1963), *The Wicker Man* (1973) and numerous others, with at the time of writing no actual commissions to show for this work and only one instance of a network coming on board to co-finance development, this being BBC America's collaboration with the producer on a remake of *The Quatermass Xperiment* (1955) (Meir 2019c: 310–11). Less has been publicly disclosed about Tandem's remake activities, but the company recently announced its receipt of a commission from US streaming platform CBS All-Access to produce a series based on the Studiocanal library title *The Man Who Fell to Earth* (1976) (Andreeva 2019a).

Whereas Studiocanal's development of a major library was achieved largely through acquisition, long-standing companies such as Gaumont and Pathé steadily continued accumulating their own through decades of ongoing production. It would be some time before either moved into fully-fledged remaking, but by the late 1990s Gaumont was at least openly offering its library to foreign producers for remake rights, hoping to share in the profits of the Anglo-Franco remake boom (Mazdon 2000: 25). Pathé has yet to be active in remaking based on its library, but Gaumont has tried its hand at the practice. In 2017, the company set up a US-based production subsidiary whose *raison d'être* the trade press described as partly consisting of finding opportunities to produce Anglophone projects based on its library of intellectual property, purportedly made up of 1,100 titles (Wyche 2017). The specific projects described in this initial launch included the remake of the 2010 film *Point Blank* (*À bout portant*), which to date is the only project to have been realised. This took the form of the film *Point Blank* (2019), which was financed and distributed by Netflix. While on one level this deal resembles the older, more passive acts of licensing titles to American companies, Gaumont retained creative input on the project through Johanna Byer, who served as the head of Gaumont USA and who received a producer credit for the American remake; significantly, her name is listed in the film's credits with a PGA designation, a form of credit that according to the

Producer's Guild standards denotes significant creative involvement in a project ('The Producer's Mark').

The extent of Gaumont's ongoing commitment to this strategy is unclear, however. Other projects described in the initial announcement have yet to come to fruition, a point to which I will return below. More significantly for the schema I am outlining in this chapter, they were not based on Gaumont library titles: these included the South Korean horror film *Train to Busan* (2016) and *Barbarella* (1968) which was originally financed and distributed by Paramount. The exact significance of Gaumont's remake of *Point Blank* in the context of European film history thus remains to be seen. If it is followed by further library remaking by Gaumont, it could become part of the larger trend I am documenting in this section of the chapter. If, on the other hand, it proves to be a one-off followed by Gaumont's retreat to more passive licensing of its rights, it could help to highlight the fragility of European ambitions to emulate Hollywood practices. This is a possibility that I will consider below.

Luc Besson's EuropaCorp took a different route than almost all of its European peers when it came to remaking. As Mazdon points out, Besson was at one point a staunch critic of Anglophone remaking, having withdrawn from the television remake of his film *La femme Nikita* (1990), on the grounds that it was 'a purely financial procedure' (2000: 4). But perhaps as the result of his own company's oscillating fortunes (*La femme Nikita* was financed by Gaumont), he changed his tune. Besson launched EuropaCorp as a stand-alone entity in 2000; it has never made a major library acquisition, nor has it had time to organically accumulate a large corpus of films. Instead, the company has depended exclusively on relatively recently made films for its intellectual property. As mentioned above, the company kicked off its American distribution operation with a reboot of *The Transporter*. This film did not do particularly well on the US market (it grossed $16 million), and despite performing better abroad (grossing $72 million in total), the franchise went on the backburner. Before and after this film, the company remade its library titles for TV series for global markets. This resulted in two drama series, one based on the *Taxi* franchise and another on the *Taken* films. Both were commissioned by American networks – TNT and NBC, respectively – with *Taxi Brooklyn* running for a single season in 2014 and *Taken* for two, from 2017 to 2018. EuropaCorp's stunning fall from grace after the collapse of RED, the failure of *Valerian* and the accusations levelled at Besson mean that the company is in full-scale retreat. At the present time, it is difficult to imagine that it will be able to continue playing an active role in reworking its library for international audiences.

Other cases of European library-based remaking that are difficult to assess fully include SF Studio's development of an Anglophone remake of its 2016 Oscar-nominated film *A Man Called Ove* (*En man som heter Ove*, 2015), which is said to have Tom Hanks attached to star in the title role (Fleming 2017). Constantin has also announced plans to reboot its *Resident Evil* franchise as both a TV series and a new series of feature films (Andreeva 2019). Even if these projects are never realised, their very existence as development projects speaks to the larger trend documented in this chapter, a trend that is an indication of a maturity and strategic sophistication in the European film and television industries and that stands without historical precedent.

NEW REMAKING PRACTICES II: ANGLOPHONE REMAKES OF SMALLER COMPANIES' WORKS

Whereas library-remaking is indicative of important developments in the corporate make-up of the European studios, the other trend which this chapter examines is more of an expression of brute economic strength of European studios relative to other players. This trend consists of European companies acquiring films or series which they have not made or to which they previously acquired the rights and then remaking or attempting to remake those works in English for international distribution. If we see library-building and developing synergies around libraries as indications of growing corporate sophistication on the part of the studios, we can also see the purchase of other films specifically for remaking as expressions of industrial power relative to smaller players. As we have seen, such has long been the perception of Hollywood's use of this precise economic and creative strategy, but now it is the European studios who find themselves taking from others.

Perhaps unsurprisingly, it is Studiocanal that is the foremost practitioner of this form of European remaking. As seen in the case of *Chloe*, library-based remaking was key to the company's relaunch as a global player, but an even more important film was 2011's *Tinker Tailor Soldier Spy*. While, legally speaking, this film was not a remake of the highly regarded 1979 BBC miniseries,[2] it nevertheless functioned exactly like one, with promotion and reception focusing in part on a comparison between the two works (Meir 2019a: 144). As I have shown elsewhere, within the context of Studiocanal's growth during this period, this was a pivotal film that established the studio as a legitimate player capable of making prestige fare (the film was nominated for several Oscars) that was also commercially viable, grossing $82 million worldwide on a reported budget of $21 million (Meir 2019a: 98). The economic power to acquire the rights to a famous property was thus crucial to that emergence.

As the company has grown during the period, so too has remaking of acquired properties remained a fixture of its strategies. Subsequent to *Tinker Tailor Soldier Spy*, Studiocanal has turned the television series *Shaun the Sheep* into a would-be franchise that so far includes two films; furthermore, it has remade the Norwegian film *In Order of Disappearance* (*Kraftidioten*, 2014) into the Liam Neeson action vehicle *Cold Pursuit* (2019). In the realm of its television series production, the company has remade the British series *Fleabag* and the French film *Hippocrate* (2014) as French-language series for Canal+. Besides these normative remakes, the company has also deployed a similar strategy of re-adapting famously and widely adapted literary works such as *Macbeth* (2015), Daniel Defoe's novel *Robinson Crusoe* (2016) and *The Secret Garden*, which was released in 2020 following numerous filmic treatments. Finally, in addition to these already completed remakes and re-adaptations, the company has developed numerous other projects in this vein, including film remakes of the Spanish film *Retribution* (*El Desconocido*, 2015), the Chinese action film *Drug War* (2012), the Swedish film *Easy Money* (*Snabba Cash*, 2010) and a television series re-adaptation that was the source of the 1987 film *Pelle the Conqueror*, among others.

Studiocanal has thus been prolific when it comes to this particular practice, and while its counterparts have also developed such projects, at the time of writing only Wild Bunch – due to its involvement in the drama series *The Name of the Rose*, based as it was on the 1986 film by the same name – has had a project come to fruition. The company is also involved in a television re-adaptation of *Dr Zhivago*. Besides these remakes, Entertainment One produced and distributed an extension of the BBC series *The Office* with its *David Brent: Life on the Road* (2016), but this is more of a sequel than a remake *per se*. This paucity of actual completed projects notwithstanding, the range of development of third-party remaking among the European companies is nevertheless important. Entertainment One, via its production affiliate The Mark Gordon Company, has been leading the development of a reboot of the *Narnia* franchise based on the books of C. S. Lewis, financed by Netflix (Otterson 2018). Pathé has acquired from the smaller French company Mars Distribution the rights to remake in English the French hit film *La famille Bélier* (2014) (Wiseman 2019). Wild Bunch has also underwritten the development of remakes of the *Maniac Cop* franchise which was created by Larry Cohen (Tartaglione 2016).

THE LIMITS OF EUROPEAN REMAKING

These projects collectively speak to a shifting hierarchy that sees some European companies wielding economic power over others in Europe as well as elsewhere, including in some cases Anglophone countries. But exactly how we should understand the significance of these attempts ultimately hinges on their outcomes. To appreciate this, we can return to the case of Gaumont. As mentioned above, the company has been engaged in remaking *Train to Busan* and

Barbarella. To begin with, we should note that these must be very ambitious projects in financial terms, given the extent of special effects that would be required to realise the same level of action found in the original films, *Train to Busan* being an apocalyptic zombie film that culminates in a spectacular train wreck and *Barbarella* being set in outer space. While no definitive statement has been made about the fate of these two projects, a curious thing happened when it was announced in 2018 that New Line, a division of Warner Bros, had acquired *Train to Busan* for remaking, with the New Line-affiliated genre producer James Wan taking creative charge of the project (Kit 2018). This came approximately two years after Gaumont had been announced as having won an auction for those same rights (Kil and Keslassy 2016). While the trade press reported that Gaumont would still be producing the film, the fact that Wan came aboard after New Line had won 'an auction' and that he brought with him Gary Dauberman, a collaborator of his on previous films, to direct the film seems to indicate that New Line had effectively taken the project away from Gaumont.

The European studio was thus side-lined by the bigger and stronger Hollywood studio, an all-too-familiar scenario for observers of European cinema. This is perhaps an opportune moment to remember that remakes can indeed illustrate industrial hierarchies and that such windows into the political economy of the film industry can also show us the limits of the power of European companies. For whatever specific reason, Gaumont did not have the economic and/or creative wherewithal to make this particular remake and had to leave it to a Hollywood major whose abilities are still at the top of the global food chain when it comes to filmmaking.

Gaumont is not alone in finding itself in this subordinate position. In 2014, Studiocanal sold its remake rights for *Escape from New York* (John Carpenter, 1981) to Fox, even though it had been developing the project for several years, at times with studio partners and at times without (Fleming 2015). Similarly, the company also recently gave up on its efforts to remake the 1993 action film *Cliffhanger*, a project that was once touted as a potential franchise for the company (Meir 2019a: 57–58). In this case, the company agreed to let Neal Moritz seek an alternative financier for the project (Vlessing 2019). Both of these original films heavily relied on action and special effects, and it is not implausible to assume that they would have required large budgets to produce. While the European studios have grown in their production capacity over the past decade, they are still largely averse to going beyond what would be considered middle-budget filmmaking by international standards (Meir 2016: 56); exceptions such as EuropaCorp's *Valerian* with its reported budget of $180 million prove the rule in this case, as the budget of that film will ultimately be remembered as one of the greatest mistakes in the history of European film production.

Going hand in hand with these probable indications of financial limitations is the fact that the old-fashioned practice of American companies buying European film remake rights is very much alive and well in contemporary European cinema. Recent titles in this vein include the high-profile remake of *The Girl with the Dragon Tattoo* (2009; 2011), a remake of TrustNordisk's *After the Wedding* (2006; 2019), *auteur* Steve McQueen's remake of a British miniseries in the form of *Widows* (2018) made for Fox, Luca Guadagnino's Amazon-financed remake of Dario Argento's *Suspiria* (2018 for the new version; Argento's was released in 1977), Universal's remakes *Contraband* (2012; based on the Icelandic thriller *Reykjavík-Rotterdam* [Óskar Jónasson 2008]) and *State of Play* (2009) based on a British miniseries of the same name, as well as numerous others.

The European studios have also been involved in these more traditional transactions, with Gaumont selling the remake rights to *Intouchables* to the Weinstein Company which turned the film into *The Upside* (2019), a film that grossed over $100 million in the US once it was untangled from TWC's recent financial meltdown. Gaumont also dealt the remake rights to the thriller *Anything for Her* (*Pour elle*, 2008), which Lionsgate turned into *The Next Three Days* (2012). Studiocanal has likewise continued optioning rights to American producers for remaking, including *The Bell Jar* (1979), *Le convoyeur* (2004) and several others. While the European studios may thus have been emboldened by their recent growth, we should be careful not to overstate the significance of the works in which they have exerted more control over their remakes. While their relative position in the hierarchy *vis-à-vis* Hollywood and the American film industry generally has shifted, there has been a radical break from the past.

CONCLUSIONS: REMAKING AS A WAY INTO INDUSTRY STUDIES, AND *VICE VERSA*

This chapter has argued that much has changed in the European film industry when it comes to remaking, marking a stark contrast with the landscape that was encountered by remake scholars of the mid-1990s and early 2000s. At that point in time, Gaumont, LSC/Studiocanal and EuropaCorp were largely passive players making their first halting steps into the global version of the practice. Twenty years later, many strides have been made, and European companies are now responsible for films that critics and audiences might initially think are yet more examples of Hollywood raiding the vaults of European cinema. Even if Hollywood is still the dominant global player, this is laudable progress in the sense that European companies are exerting more control over the remakes that are derived from their films and presumably retaining more of the earnings that come from those films. In deploying such strategies, European firms are taking advantage of their own growing scale when it comes to production and distribution, as well as their development and/or acquisition of libraries of content. The remakes themselves span a variety of genres – from the art cinema of films like *La Piscine*, to the high-concept genre fare of films such as *Anthony Zimmer* or *Point Blank* – while the only genres that seem to be off-limits are action or science fiction spectacles such as *Cliffhanger* or *Train to Busan*, which perhaps remain prohibitively expensive and therefore too risky for the still fragile European industries.

On a less positive note, however, it warrants emphasising that the remaking strategy is yet another sign of the growing artistic and industrial conservatism so characteristic of the contemporary European film industry. With growth in scale, more and more European studios are imitating the working methods of their Hollywood counterparts, including favouring remakes and other forms of well-known intellectual property, but also a range of other practices that have long been held to be antithetical to artistic risk-taking (see, for instance, Meir 2019b). While there is thus some encouragement to be taken from the fact that the studios are consolidating and making strategic use of their holdings, the direction in which they are heading cannot be overlooked.

One final point to make about the issues discussed in this chapter is that all of these aspects of the European film industry could be seen through the lens of the remake. I hope that this demonstrates that media industry studies approaches can help to illuminate remaking as a practice, while remaking itself can also provide us with a more detailed understanding of the larger industrial shifts of which they are a part. It is thus with the desire of generating further insights into industries and remakes that I hope this work will inspire others to return to the issues of political economy, which helped to found remake studies as a subfield. As we have seen in this chapter, this is still an extremely rewarding line of research with which to investigate this ongoing and ever-fascinating creative and industrial practice.

NOTES

1. This chapter has grown out of a larger research project which has received funding from the Universidad Carlos III de Madrid, the European Union's Seventh Framework Programme for Research, Technological Development and Demonstration under grant agreement n° 600371, el Ministerio de Economía, Industria y Competitividad (COFUND2014-51509) el Ministerio de Educación, Cultura y Deporte (CEI-15-17) and Banco Santander.
2. Producer Tim Bevan from Working Title Films has said that, while the BBC bought the television rights to the John Le Carré source novel, the rights to adapt the novel into a feature film were still available (Meir 2019a: 225–26).

REFERENCES

Andreeva, Nellie. (2019a), '*The Man Who Fell to Earth* TV Series from Alex Kurtzman Ordered by CBS All Access', *Deadline Hollywood*, 1 August, available at: https://deadline.com/2019/08/the-man-who-fell-to-earth-tv-series-alex-kurtzman-ordered-cbs-all-access-1202657384/ (last accessed 9 August 2020).

Andreeva, Nellie (2019b), '*Resident Evil* TV Series in the Works at Netflix', *Deadline Hollywood*, 24 January, available at: https://deadline.com/2019/01/resident-evil-tv-series-in-works-netflix-1202541277/ (last accessed 9 August 2020).

Cuelenaere, Eduard, Stijn Joye and Gertjan Willems (2019), 'Local Flavors and Regional Markers: The Low Countries and their Commercially Driven and Proximity-Focused Film Remake Practice', *Communications* 44: 3, 262–81.

Fleming, Mike (2015), '*Escape from New York* Remake Rights Deal Won by Fox,' *Deadline Hollywood*, 13 January, available at: http://deadline.com/2015/01/escape-from-new-york-remake-fox-john-carpenter-1201349382 (last accessed 9 August 2020).

Fleming, Mike (2017), 'Tom Hanks to Star in Remake of Swedish comedy *A Man Called Ove*', *Deadline Hollywood*, 21 September, available at: https://deadline.com/2017/09/tom-hanks-a-man-called-ove-remake-swedish-film-1202174361/ (last accessed 9 August 2020).

Forrest, Jennifer and Leonard Koos, eds (2002a), *Dead Ringers: The Remake in Theory and Practice*, Albany: SUNY Press.

Forrest, Jennifer and Leonard Koos (2002b), 'Reviewing Remakes: An Introduction', in Jennifer Forrest and Leonard Koos (eds) (2002), *Dead Ringers: The Remake in Theory and Practice*, Albany: SUNY Press, pp. 1–36.

Hoyt, Eric (2014), *Hollywood Vault: Film Libraries before Home Video*, Berkeley: University of California Press.

Kil, Sonia and Elsa Keslassy (2016), 'Korea's *Train to Busan* English-Language Remake Rights go to Gaumont', *Variety*, 7 December, available at: https://variety.com/2016/film/asia/train-to-busan-english-remake-gaumont-1201933494/ (last accessed 9 August 2020).

Kit, Borys (2018), 'New Line Wins Bidding War for *Train to Busan* Remake from James Wan and Gary Dauberman', *The Hollywood Reporter*, 25 September, available at: https://www.hollywoodreporter.com/heat-vision/new-line-wins-bidding-war-train-busan-remake-james-wan-1146253 (last accessed 9 August 2020).

Labayen, Miguel Fernández and Ana Martín Morán (2019), 'Manufacturing Proximity through Film Remakes: Remake Rights Representatives and the Case of Local-Language Comedy Remakes', *Communications* 44: 3, 282–303.

Leitch, Thomas (2019), 'Instead of the Real Thing: Six Ways to Talk About What Hollywood Does to European Films', *Communications* 44: 3, 342–51.

Mazdon, Lucy (2000), *Encore Hollywood: Remaking French Cinema*, London: BFI.

Mazdon, Lucy (2015), 'Hollywood and Europe: Remaking *The Girl with the Dragon Tattoo*', in Mary Harrod, Mariana Liz and Alyssa Timoshkina (eds), *The Europeanness of European Cinema: Identity, Meaning and Globalization*, London: I. B. Tauris, pp. 199–212.

Mazdon, Lucy (2017), 'Disrupting the Remake: *The Girl with the Dragon Tattoo*', in Iain Robert Smith and Constantine Verevis (eds), *Transnational Film Remakes*, Edinburgh: Edinburgh University Press, pp. 21–35.

Meir, Christopher (2016), 'Studiocanal and the Changing Industrial Landscape of European Film and Television' *Media Industries* 3:1, 49–63.

Meir, Christopher (2019a), *Mass Producing European Cinema: Studiocanal and its Works*, New York: Bloomsbury.

Meir, Christopher (2019b), 'European Cinema in an Era of Studio-Building: Some Artistic and Industrial Tendencies in Studiocanal's Output, 2006-Present', *Studies in European Cinema*, 16: 1, 5–21.

Meir, Christopher (2019c), 'Becoming a Global Producer: Creative and Industrial Change at Post-Studiocanal RED', *Journal of British Cinema and Television*, 16: 3, 305–26.

Otterson, Joe (2018), '*Chronicles of Narnia* Series, Films in the Works at Netflix', *Variety*, 3 October, available at: https://variety.com/2018/tv/news/chronicles-of-narnia-series-films-netflix-1202966920/ (last accessed 9 August 2020).

Peers, Martin and Rex Weiner (1997), 'PolyGram's Epic Win', *Variety*, 3 December, available at: http://variety.com/1997/film/news/polygram-s-epic-win-111728574/ (last accessed 9 August 2020).

'The Producers' Mark', Producers Guild of America website, available at: https://www.producersguild.org/page/producer_mark (last accessed 9 August 2020).

Puttnam, David (1997), with Neil Watson, *The Undeclared War: The Struggle for Control of the World's Film Industry*, London: HarperCollins.

Smith, Iain Robert and Constantine Verevis (2017), 'Introduction: Transnational Film Remakes', in Iain Robert Smith and Constantine Verevis (eds), *Transnational Film Remakes*, Edinburgh: Edinburgh University Press, pp. 1–18.

Tartaglione, Nancy (2016), 'Nic Winding Refn's Space Rocket in First-Look with Wild Bunch & Vendian', *Deadline Hollywood*, 16 May, available at: https://deadline.com/2016/05/nicolas-winding-refn-wild-bunch-vendian-first-look-deal-maniac-top-cannes-1201757165/ (last accessed 9 August 2020).

Vlessing, Etan (2019), 'Ana Lily Amirpour to Direct Female-Led *Cliffhanger* Reboot', *The Hollywood Reporter*, 8 May, available at: https://www.hollywoodreporter.com/news/ana-lily-amirpour-direct-cliffhanger-reboot-jason-momoa-cameo-1209001 (last accessed 9 August 2020).

Wiseman, Andreas (2019), 'Pathé and Vendôme Sign Pact', *Deadline Hollywood*, 13 May, available at: https://deadline.com/2019/05/pathe-vendome-sign-pact-first-pic-coda-will-be-sold-by-pathe-philippe-rousselet-patrick-wachsberger-on-croisette-cannes-1202613433/ (last accessed 9 August 2020).

Wyche, Elbert (2017), 'Gaumont Launches US Film Division', *Screen International*, 1 February, available at: http://www.screendaily.com/news/gaumont-launches-us-film-division/5114452.article?blocktitle=Latest-news&contentID=276 (last accessed 9 August 2020).

Index

3 Men and a Baby, 226
20th Century Fox, 136, 235–6
2019: After the Fall of New York, 79

AB Artistfilm, 119
AB Sandrews (Sandrews), 117, 119, 122, 125
AB Svensk Filmindustri (SF), 117, 119–20, 122–3, 125, 228, 232
AB Wivefilm, 120
Adamczyk, P., 139
After the Wedding, 236
Agascope, 120
Âge d'or, L', 37
Aleinikov, G., 149
Aleinikov, I., 149
Alexander, P., 110–12
Alien, 77
Alien III, 40
Aliens, 77
Ali: Fear Eats the Soul, 50, 52–3
All Is Love, 141
All that Heaven Allows, 50–3
All the Colors of the Dark, 79
Always, 48–9
Amarcord, 152
Amazon, 236
Amenábar, A., 211–17, 220–1
Androids Dream, 213, 217–21
And Soon the Darkness . . . , 231
Ange du foyer, L', 95

Anthony Zimmer, 230, 237
Antonioni, M., 34, 38, 43, 49, 179, 221
Anything for Her, 236
Are you lonesome tonight, 111
Argento, D., 34, 177, 236
Arrival of a Train, The, 1
Arrow Films, 202
Ascenseur pour l'échafaud, 179
Aslan, M., 82
Assistance publique, L', 97, 99
Avare, 76
Aviator's Wife, The, 34

Bachelors' Paradise, 111
Bajor, I., 170
Balagueró, J., 212, 217
Balcon, M., 198–9
Barbarella, 232, 235
Barbershop, The, 1
Bardelli, M., 183
Barry, J., 83
Barry Lyndon, 48
Bass, S., 35
Batman, 76
Batwoman, The, 76
Bayona, J. A., 217
BBC, 196, 199, 233–4
BBC America, 231
Before Sunrise, 113
Bell Jar, The, 236
Benoit-Lévy, J., 90, 93, 95–7

Bergman, H., 117, 119, 122, 124
Bergman, I., 38, 42
Berlin Alexanderplatz (film), 10, 59, 69
Berlin Alexanderplatz (novel), 59, 68
Berlin Alexanderplatz: The Story of Franz Biberkopf, 59
Bertelsman, 230
Besson, L., 228, 232
BFI, 196, 199
Bigger Splash, A, 12, 177–8, 181–4, 187, 189–90, 230
Bigger Splash, A (documentary), 178, 180–1
Bigger Splash, A (painting), 178, 180–1
Billy Liar, 231
Birkin, J., 177, 179
Birtwell, C., 181
Bjørnson, B., 119
Blade Runner, 213, 218–21
Blow Out, 34
Blow Up, 34, 79
Blow Upon Blow, 111
Blue Eyes of the Broken Doll, The, 84
Body Heat, 45
Bogdanovich, P., 48–9, 56
Borg/McEnroe, 228
Bowie, D., 182
Breaking the Waves, 40
Bresson, R., 49, 56
Briefträger Müller, 108
Brighton Rock, 231
Bringing Up Baby, 49
Buñuel, L., 37
Burglars, The, 83
Byer, J., 231

Cahiers du cinéma, 41, 49
Cain, J. M., 79
Call Me by Your Name, 177
CANAL+, 227
Cannarozzi, A., 182
Capra, F., 167
Capron, M., 97
Career of Nikodem Dyzma, The, 135
Car of Dreams, 164, 167–71
Carpenter, J., 38, 84
Cassavetes, J., 38
Catalan TV, 212
Catch-22, 50
CBS All-Access, 231

Champo, Le, 41
Charvet, 183
Chien Andalou, Un, 37
Chinatown, 48
Chloe, 230, 233
Christie, A., 79
Christine, 178
Cinema Republic, 6
Clarke, A., 221
Clark, O., 181
Clement, R., 53
Cliffhanger, 235, 237
Coca-Cola, 110–11
Cohen, L., 234
Cold Pursuit, 234
Constantin, 228, 232
Contamination, 77
Contraband, 236
Conversation, The, 46, 50, 54, 57
Convoyeur, Le, 236
Coppola, F. F., 46–7, 54, 57
Corman, R., 48
Costa, J., 217
Courrèges, A., 177, 179–80, 182
Cozzi, L., 77
Crainquebille, 93
Craven, W., 38
Crazy Cow, 6, 142
Creative Scotland, 196, 199–200
Crew, The 12, 149, 151–9
Criminal Code, The, 48
Crowe, C., 211, 215
Cruise, T., 211, 214–15
Cuerda, J. L., 213
Currie, F., 201, 206
Curtis, R., 141

Daban, A., 97
Daemen, M., 142
D'A Festival, 219
Dahlqvist, Å., 120, 123–4
Danischewsky, M., 198–9
Darkness, 217
Das kann doch einen Seemann nicht erschüttern, 112
Dauberman, G., 235
David Brent: Life on the Road, 234
Dawn of the Dead, 77
Death of Stalin, The, 228
Death Proof, 43

de Balzac, H., 90
Deep Red, 34
Dekalog: Three, 42
Delon, A., 34, 177–80
de Mendoza, 80
Deodato, R., 77
De Palma, B., 34, 46–7, 54, 84
Desert, 76
De Sica, V., 179
Designated Survivor, 227
de Sosa, I., 212–13, 218–19, 221
Diaboliques, Les, 79
Diamant-Berger, H., 90, 96–8
Diamonds are Forever, 83
Dick, P. K., 213, 218–19
Dior, 177, 180, 182, 188
Do Androids Dream of Electric Sheep?, 218
Döblin, A., 59–61, 63, 65–9
Dolega-Mostowicz, T., 135
Don't Look Now, 231
Double Indemnity, 45
Doyle, A. C., 79
Dracula, 45
Dragonfly for Each Corpse, A, 84
Draughtsman's Contract, The, 34
Dressed to Kill, 46, 57
Drug War, 234
Dr Zhivago, 234
Duvivier, J., 93

Ealing Studios, 195, 198
Eastmancolor, 120
Easy Money, 234
Edinburgh International Film Festival, 195
Edison Manufacturing Company, 1
Edward II, 182
Eichhorn, B., 108
Eisenstein, S., 63
Ekipazh, 151
Endemol, 7
Entertainment One, 227, 234
Epstein, J., 95
Epstein, M., 90, 93, 95–7
Emotional Rescue (album), 185
Emotional Rescue (song), 185
Escape from New York, 79, 235
Eternal Sunshine of the Spotless Mind, 37
E. T. the Extra-Terrestrial, 73–4
EuropaCorp, 228, 232, 235–6

Exiting the Factory, 1
Exorcist, The, 73, 78
Eyes Wide Shut, 41–2

Fallen Idol, The, 231
famille Bélier, La, 234
Fassbinder, R. W., 10, 49–54, 56, 59–69
Feast of Satan, The, 79
Fellini, F., 152
Feltz, K., 111
femme Nikita, La, 232
Fenech, E., 80, 82
Ferien vom Ich, 113
Ferragamo, 184
Fight Club, 42
FilmAffinity, 214–16, 219
Films Alain Sarde, Les, 214
Film Technique, 63
Filth, 199–200
Fincher, D., 40, 42
Five Chicks One Rooster, 78
Flaubert, G., 90
Fleabag, 234
Fleming, V., 48
Flickan i Frack, 119, 120
Florman, E., 1
Ford, A., 135
Ford, J., 39, 48–9, 56
Four Seasons in Havana, 227
Fragile, 217
Francis, F., 84
Frapié, L., 89–94, 97
Frears, S., 36–7
FremantleMedia, 7
Frenesy, 184
Freud, S., 41
Friedman, D. F., 75
Fritsch, W., 108
Fulci, L., 77
Fuller, S., 49
Future maman, La, 95

Gaál, B., 167
Gainsbourgh, S., 179
Gance, A., 35, 41
Ganghofer, L., 108
Garden, The, 182
Gaumont, 228–9, 231, 234–6
Gaumont USA, 231
Gdynia Film Festival, 136

Gevacolor, 120, 123
Gietz, H., 111
Gil, M., 80
Girl in Tails, 119, 122, 124–5
Girl of Solbakken, A, 119–22
Girl with the Dragon Tattoo, The, 236
Godard, J., 221
God Forgives . . . I Don't!, 76
Golem, The 5
Golem: A Legend of Prague, The 5
Gondry, M., 37
Greenaway, P., 34, 37
Greene, G., 231
Green Room, The, 35, 41
Grifters, The, 36–7
Grisebach, V., 54–7
Grizzly, 76
Guadagnino, L., 12, 177, 180–4, 187–8, 190, 236
Guy Named Joe, A, 48–9
Gyöngyössy, B., 166

Halbstarken, Die, 112
Haley, B., 110, 112
Hammett, D., 79
Hanks, T., 233
Hannıbal, 228
Happiness, 53–7
Happy Valley, 227
Hawks, H., 38, 41, 49, 56
Hazan, J., 178, 180–1, 188
Heaven, 188
Heesters, J., 112
Herr Arnes, 121, 123–4
Herzog, W., 45
Hess, D., 77
Highsmith, P., 53
Hilton, G., 80, 82
Hippocrate, 234
Hippolyt, 164–5, 169–70
Hitchcock, A., 34–7, 41, 46–7, 49, 54, 215
Hockney, D., 178, 180–1
Homo Eroticus, 78
House on the Edge of the Park, The, 77
Howard, R., 39
Hryniak, J., 134, 136–9, 144
Hungarian Film Newsreel, 168
Huston, J., 39
Hyppolit, the Butler, 167–70

Iakovleva, A., 158
I Am Love, 177, 182, 188
Inanç, Ç., 78
Inanir, K., 82
In Order of Disappearance, 234
Intouchables, 211, 236

James, H., 41
Jarman, D., 177, 181–2
Jarmusch, J., 182
Jaws, 76
Je t'aime je t'aime, 37
Je t'aime . . . moi non plus, 179
Jetée, La, 37
Jia, Z., 38
Journey to Italy, 184
Joy of Fatherhood, 2
Jump into the Fire, 189
Jutzi, P., 59–69

Kabay, B., 165–6
Kabos, G., 170
Kajganich, D., 182–3
Karloff, B., 48
Kasdan, L., 45
Kieslowksi, K., 42
Kiler, 136
Killing in Istanbul, 78
Kind Hearts and Coronets, 196
Kleiner Mann, ganz groß, 107
Klimovsky, L., 84
Klockorna i Gamla Sta'n, 119
Klosterjäger, Der, 108–9
Knife in the Water, 136–7
Koltai, R., 170
Kubrick, S., 41–2, 48
Kurosawa, A., 74
Kwieciński, M., 134, 141–3, 145

Ladykillers, The, 196
Lagerlöf, S., 117, 123–4
Lang, F., 108
Langlois, H., 41
Larsson, L., 123
Last House on the Left, 38, 77
Last of England, The, 182
Last Picture Show, The, 48–9
Last Shark, The, 76
Latabár, K., 171
Lavender Hill Mob, The, 196

Lebedev, N., 151–3, 155, 157–8
Lee, B., 74
Legend of Barney Thompson, The, 199
Legrand, M., 180
Lepkowska, I., 137–8
Letters to Santa, 141–2
letzte Walzer, Der, 107
Lewis, C. S., 234
Lionsgate, 236
Local Hero, 196–7
Logan, A., 181
Long Goodbye, The, 50
Longing, 54–7
Losey, J., 34–5, 37
Love Actually, 141
Love Is All, 134, 141–3, 145
Lucky Red, 214
Lucy, 228
Lumière, L., 1
Lynch, D., 38, 43

Macbeth, 234
McDougall, P., 199
Machulski, J., 136
MacKendrick, A., 199, 201
Mackenzie, C., 195
Mackinnon, G., 196, 199
Maclean, I., 196, 199
McQueen, S., 236
Made for each other, 2
Mad Max, 79
Maggie, The, 196
Man Called Ove, A, 232
Maniac Cop, 234
Mann, A., 49
Man One Talks About, The, 110
Man Who Fell to Earth, The, 231
Man Who Saves the World, The 73, 78
Man with a Movie Camera, 63
Marker, C., 37
Mark Gordon Company, 234
Mars Distribution, 234
Martini, 108
Martino, S., 79, 80, 82
Maternelle, La 11, 87, 89–91, 93–8
Maternité, 93
Mattei, B., 77
Mattsson, A., 124
Medici, 227

Meeting Place Cannot Be Changed, The, 149
Méliès, G., 1
Melville, J., 179
Memory of the Camps, 35
Metropole, 186
Minghella, A., 53
Misfit, 2
Missing, The, 39
Miss Manhattan, 186
Mitta, A., 151–3, 157–8
Molander, G., 119, 123–5
Mondadori, 79
Mondo Sex, 79
Monsieur Klein, 34–5
Moon Is Up, 185
More Than Death at Stake, 141
Moritz, N., 235
Morricone, E., 83
Moser, H., 111–12
Mother, 63
Mulholland Drive, 38, 43
Murnau, F. W., 45
Muss man sich gleich schneiden lassen?, 108
My Problems with Amenábar, 217

Naked and Violent, 79
Name of the Rose, The, 234
Narcos, 229
Narnia, 234
Nathalie . . . , 230
NBC, 232
Neeson, L., 212, 234
Netflix, 231, 234
New Hollywood, 37, 48–50
New Line, 235
Next Three Days, The, 236
Nibelungen, Die, 108
Nid, Le, 95
Nilsson, 189
North by Northwest, 34–5
Nosferatu: A Symphony of Horror, 45
Nosferatu, the Vampyre, 45
Nouvelle Vague, 40, 47, 49, 56

O'Brien, G., 183
October, 63
Office, The, 234
Oh, Charles, 137, 139, 141–2
Oh, Charles 2, 134, 138–41, 143–4

One Fool Makes a Hundred, 164, 167, 172
One Skirt and a Pair of Trousers, 164, 167, 171–2
Open Your Eyes, 211–17, 221
Optimum Releasing, 230
Orphanage, The, 217
Other Spanish Cinema, 217–18, 221
Others, The, 216–17

Pabst, G. W., 37
Paddington, 227
Palahniuk, C., 42
Paper Moon, 49
Paradise Lost, 35, 41
Pasikowski, W., 141
Passport to Pimlico, 196
Pathé, 1, 96, 227–8, 231, 234
Pathétique, 123
Paul, R. W., 1
Pelle the Conqueror, 234
People of Hemsö, The 124
Peppa Pig, 227
Perfect Strangers, 2, 142–4
Persona, 42
Philips, 230
Piechociński, J., 139–40
Piersanti, G., 177, 182
Piranha, 76
Piscine, La, 177, 230, 237
Piwowski, M., 137
Plaza, P., 212
Plein soleil, 179
Poil de carotte, 93
Point Blank, 231–2, 237
Polanski, R., 48, 136–7
Polar, 228
Polygram Filmed Entertainment, 230
Polygram Music, 230
Portrait of An Artist (Pool with Two Figures), 180
Potter, S., 177, 182
Poulbot, F., 95–6
Preminger, O., 179
Presley, E., 111
Producciones del Escorpión, Les, 214
Psycho (Hitchcock), 36–7, 46–7, 57, 170
Psycho (Van Sant), 46
Pudovkin, V., 63
Purple Noon, 53

Quarantine, 212
Quatermass Xperiment, The, 231

RAI, 229
Raiders of the Lost Ark, 50
Rambo: First Blood Part II, 78
Rank Organisation, 199
Rassimov, I., 80
Ray, N., 49
Rebel Without a Cause, 112
Reblaus, 111–12
RED, 232
Red Banners, 212
Red Productions, 231
Reed, C., 230
Rejs, 137
Relativity Media, 228
Resident Evil, 228, 232
Resnais, A., 37
Retribution, 234
Revenge of the South Seas Queen, 76
Reykjavík-Rotterdam, 236
Richter, P., 108
Rio Bravo, 38
Robinson Crusoe, 234
Rockets Galore!, 197
Roeg, N., 84, 231
Rohmer, É., 34, 37, 41
Roland, M., 108
Rolling Stones, 184–9
Romero, G. A., 77
Ronet, M., 177, 179
Rossellini, R., 38, 184
Roudès, G., 90, 93–7
RTL Klub, 165
Rühmann, H., 108, 110–12
Russo, F., 183
Rybkowski, J., 135

Sag die Wahrheit, 106
Sander, J., 182
Sången om, 120, 122–5
Sarafian, R. C., 43
Sarnowska, K., 142–5
Schlesinger, P., 181
Schloss Hubertus, 108, 113
Schneider, R., 177–80
Schnitzler, A., 41
Schrader, P., 49
Schweigen im Walde, Das, 108

Scorsese, M., 49, 56
Scott, R., 218–19
Seagram, 230
Searchers, The, 39, 49
Secret Garden, The, 234
Secrets of a Soul, 37
See you later alligator, 112
Seidl, U. M., 221
Sergio Rossi, 184
Seven Samurai, 74
Shaun the Sheep, 233
Shocking Dark, 77
Sieben Jahre Pech, 112
Sienkiewicz, H., 134–5
Simons, R., 177, 182
Sir Arne's Money, 119, 122
Sir Arne's Treasure, 119–20, 122
Sirk, D., 50, 52–4, 56, 69
Sjöström, V., 122
Śliwa, T., 134, 142
Slogan, 179
Smutniak, K., 144
Snakes on a Train, 76
Sogecable, 214
Sogecine, 214
Some Like it Hot, 78
Sommersby, 226
Song of the Red Flower, 119–20, 122
Sonnenfeld, B., 136
Spanish Film Academy, 213
Spatzen in Gottes Hand, 107, 113
Spielberg, S., 48–50
Spotlight, 227
Sprinkler Sprinkled, The 1
Star Crash, 77
Star Trek, 78
Star Wars, 73–4, 77–8
State of Play, 236
Stawka więcej niż życie, 141
Steel Wrist, 78
Steig. Nicht. Aus!, 212
Steinlen, T., 95–6
Stern von Rio, 107
Stiller, M., 119–20, 122–5
Still Life, 38
Stoker, B., 45
Story of a Sin, The, 135

Strange Vice of Mrs. Wardh, The, 74, 78–83
Stromboli, 184
Studiocanal, 7, 15, 177, 183, 227, 230–1, 233–6
Sunset Boulevard, 43
Sunset Song, 199
Sunshine on Leith, 200
Suspiria, 177, 236
Swedish Film Institute, 122
Swimming Pool, The, 177–82, 184, 187, 189–90
Swinton, T., 177, 182–3, 188, 190
Székely, I., 167

T2: Trainspotting, 198–200
Taken, 228, 232
Talented Mr. Ripley, The, 53
Tandem Communications, 231
Tarantino, Q., 43
Targets, 48–50
Tattoo You, 186
Taxi, 232
Taxi Brooklyn, 232
Taxi Driver, 49–50
Tchaikovsky, P. I., 123
Terminator 2, 77
Terminator, The, 76–7
Terror, The, 48
Teutonic Knights, The, 134–5, 137, 141
That Will Work, 110–12
Thesis, 213–14, 217
Third Man, The, 230
Third, The, 134, 136–7, 144
Thirsty for Love: Sex and Murder, 74, 78, 81–4
Tinker Tailer Soldier Spy, 233
TNT, 232
Torriani, V., 112
Torso, 79
Tourist, The, 230
Tractor Drivers, 149
Tractor Drivers 2, 149
Trainspotting, 199
Train to Busan, 232, 234–5, 237
Transmorphers, 76
Transporter, The, 232
Traumnovelle, The, 41

Tropical Malady, 38
True Lies, 226
True Love, 218
Truffaut, F., 35, 37, 41, 49
TrustNordisk, 228, 236
TV2, 165
Two Girls, The, 93
Two Kilers, 136

UFI, 107
Ulrich, K., 111
Under the Skin, 199
unentschuldigte Stunde, Die, 110
(Un)familiar People, 134, 143–5
Unforgiven, The, 39
Universal, 236
Unknown, The, 212
Upside, The, 236

Vagabond, 76
Valerian, 228, 232, 235
Valle-Inclán, R., 219
Vangelis, 219
Vanilla Sky, 211, 213–16, 220–1
Vanishing Point, 43
Van Sant, G., 45–7
Varda, A., 53–7
Vega, P., 141
Vertigo, 37
Vertov, D., 63
Vigo, J., 93
Virgin Spring, The, 38
Visconti, L., 179
Vivendi, 226–7, 230
von Cziffra, G., 111
Von Trier, 40, 228
Voodoo Lounge, 184
Voyage du Ballon Rouge, Le, 204

Wan, J., 235
Wanted: Dead or Alive, 76
Warner Bros, 235
War Requiem, 182
Watering the Flowers, 1
Wedding in Malinovka, 149
Weerasethakul, A., 38
Weinstein Company, 236
Weiser, G., 111
Weiß, W., 106
Welles, O., 38, 49, 56, 179
Welsh, I., 199
Wereśniak, P., 134, 138–40, 143
What's Up, Doc?, 49
When the Village Music Plays on Sunday Evening, 109–10
While at War, 221
Whisky Galore!, 12, 195–207
White Horse Inn, The, 104
Wicker Man, The, 231
Widows, 236
Wild Bunch, 227, 234
Wilder, B., 43, 45
Wild Grass, 37
Winnetou, 163
Wonderwall, 179
Worried about You, 186, 189

Years and Years, 227
Your Vice Is a Locked Room and Only I Have the Key, 79

Zabriskie Point, 43
Zaluski, R., 137, 140
Zeren, M., 82
Zero for Conduct, 93
Zola, É., 90
Zombi 2, 77
Żeromski, S., 135

EU representative:
Easy Access System Europe
Mustamäe tee 50, 10621 Tallinn, Estonia
Gpsr.requests@easproject.com

www.ingramcontent.com/pod-product-compliance
Lightning Source LLC
Chambersburg PA
CBHW051608230426
43668CB00013B/2031